International Financial Reporting

Companion Website

For open-access **student resources** specifically written to complement this textbook and support your learning, please visit **www.pearsoned.co.uk/melville**

Lecturer Resources

For password-protected online resources tailored to support the use of this textbook in teaching, please visit **www.pearsoned.co.uk/melville**

International Financial Reporting

A Practical Guide

Fourth Edition

Alan Melville
FCA, BSc, Cert. Ed.

Harlow, England • London • New York • Boston • San Francisco • Toronto • Sydney • Auckland • Singapore • Hong Kong
Tokyo • Seoul • Taipei • New Delhi • Cape Town • São Paulo • Mexico City • Madrid • Amsterdam • Munich • Paris • Milan

PEARSON EDUCATION LIMITED
Edinburgh Gate
Harlow CM20 2JE
United Kingdom
Tel: +44 (0) 1279 623623
Web: www.pearson.com/uk

First published 2008 (print)
Second edition published 2009 (print)
Third edition published 2011 (print)
Fourth edition published 2014 (print and electronic)

ISBN: 978-0-273-78597-2 (print)
       978-0-273-78602-3 (PDF)
       978-0-273-78598-9 (eText)

British Library Cataloguing-in-Publication Data
A catalogue record for this book is available from the British Library

Library of Congress Cataloging-in-Publication Data
A catalog record for the print edition is available from the Library of Congress

ARP Impression 98
Printed in Great Britain by Clays Ltd, St Ives plc

Front cover image: © Getty Images

NOTE THAT ANY PAGE CROSS REFERENCES REFER TO THE PRINT EDITION

Contents

25 The IFRS for SMEs (cont.)

Part 6 ANSWERS

Preface

The aim of this book is to explain International Financial Reporting Standards (IFRSs) and International Accounting Standards (IASs) at a level which is appropriate for students who are undertaking an intermediate course of study in financial reporting. It is assumed that the reader has already completed an introductory accounting course and is familiar with the basics of financial accounting. The book has not been written with any particular syllabus in mind but should be useful to second-year undergraduates studying for a degree in accounting and finance and to those who are preparing for the examinations of the professional accounting bodies.

IFRSs and IASs (referred to in this book as "international standards") have gained widespread acceptance around the world and most accounting students are now required to become familiar with them. The problem is that the standards and their accompanying documents comprise over 3,000 pages of fine print and much of this content is highly technical and difficult to understand. What is needed is a textbook which explains the main features of each standard as clearly and concisely as possible and provides students with plenty of worked examples and exercises. This book tries to satisfy that need.

The standards are of international application but, for the sake of convenience, most of the monetary amounts referred to in the worked examples and exercises in this book are denominated in £s. Other than this, the book contains very few UK-specific references and should be relevant in any country which has adopted international standards.

Each chapter of the book concludes with a set of exercises which test the reader's grasp of the topics introduced in that chapter. Some of these exercises are drawn from the past examination papers of professional accounting bodies. Solutions to most of the exercises are located at the back of the book but solutions to those exercises which are marked with an asterisk (*) are intended for lecturers' use and are provided on a supporting website.

This fourth edition is in accordance with all international standards or amendments to standards issued as at 1 January 2013.

Alan Melville
April 2013

Acknowledgements

I would like to thank the International Financial Reporting Standards Foundation for permission to use extracts from various IASB standards (Copyright © IFRS Foundation. All rights reserved. Reproduced by Pearson Education Limited with the permission of the IFRS Foundation ®. No permission granted to third parties to reproduce or distribute). The IASB, the IFRS Foundation, the authors and the publishers do not accept responsibility for any loss caused by acting or refraining from acting in reliance on the material in this publication, whether such loss is caused by negligence or otherwise.

I would also like to thank the following accounting bodies for granting me permission to use their past examination questions:

- ▸ Association of Chartered Certified Accountants (ACCA)
- ▸ Chartered Institute of Public Finance and Accountancy (CIPFA)
- ▸ Association of Accounting Technicians (AAT).

I must emphasise that the answers provided to these questions are entirely my own and are not the responsibility of the accounting body concerned. I would also like to point out that the questions which are printed in this textbook have been amended in some cases so as to reflect changes in accounting standards which have occurred since those questions were originally published by the accounting body concerned.

Please note that, unless material is specifically cited with a source, any company names used within this text have been created by me and are intended to be fictitious.

Alan Melville
April 2013

List of international standards

A full list of the International Financial Reporting Standards (IFRSs) and International Accounting Standards (IASs) which are in force at the time of writing this book is given below. Standards missing from the list have been withdrawn. Alongside each standard is a cross-reference to the chapter of the book in which that standard is explained.

It is important to realise that new or modified standards are issued fairly often. The reader who wishes to keep up-to-date is advised to consult the website of the International Accounting Standards Board (IASB) at www.ifrs.org.

International Financial Reporting Standards (IFRSs)		*Chapter*
IFRS 1	First-time Adoption of International Financial Reporting Standards	1
IFRS 2	Share-based Payment	–
IFRS 3	Business Combinations	6
IFRS 4	Insurance Contracts	–
IFRS 5	Non-current Assets Held for Sale and Discontinued Operations	8
IFRS 6	Exploration for and Evaluation of Mineral Resources	–
IFRS 7	Financial Instruments: Disclosures	11
IFRS 8	Operating Segments	24
IFRS 9	Financial Instruments	11
IFRS 10	Consolidated Financial Statements	18
IFRS 11	Joint Arrangements	20
IFRS 12	Disclosure of Interests in Other Entities	18, 20
IFRS 13	Fair Value Measurement	5
IFRS for SMEs	Small and Medium-sized Entities	25
International Accounting Standards (IASs)		
IAS 1	Presentation of Financial Statements	3
IAS 2	Inventories	10
IAS 7	Statement of Cash Flows	16
IAS 8	Accounting Policies, Changes in Accounting Estimates and Errors	4
IAS 10	Events after the Reporting Period	12
IAS 11	Construction Contracts	10

It should be noted that some of these standards are beyond the scope of this book and are considered no further here. These are IFRS2, IFRS4, IFRS6, IAS26 and IAS41.

As well as the international standards, two further IASB documents (neither of which is a standard) are dealt with in this book. These are:

(a) the *Conceptual Framework for Financial Reporting* (see Chapter 2) which sets out a number of concepts that underlie financial reporting and which is referred to by the IASB during the development of new and amended standards

(b) an IFRS Practice Statement entitled *Management Commentary* (see Chapter 3) which provides a non-binding framework for the presentation of a management commentary to accompany a set of financial statements.

Part 1

INTRODUCTION TO FINANCIAL REPORTING

Chapter 1

The regulatory framework

Introduction

Financial reporting is the branch of accounting that deals with the preparation of financial statements. These statements provide information about the financial performance and financial position of the business to which they relate and may be of value to a wide range of user groups. More specifically, the term "financial reporting" is most often used to refer to the preparation of financial statements for a limited company. In this case, the main users of the statements are the company's shareholders. However, the information which is contained in financial statements may also be of use to other user groups such as lenders, employees and the tax authorities (see Chapter 2).

The purpose of this book is to explain the rules which govern the preparation of financial statements for organisations which comply with international standards. This first chapter introduces the *regulatory framework* within which financial statements are prepared. The next chapter outlines the main features of a *conceptual framework* setting out the main concepts which underlie financial reporting.

Objectives

By the end of this chapter, the reader should be able to:

- list the main sources of accounting regulations and explain the need for regulation
- explain the term "generally accepted accounting practice" (GAAP)
- outline the structure and functions of the International Accounting Standards Board (IASB) and its associated bodies
- explain the purpose of an accounting standard and list the main steps in the standard-setting process adopted by the IASB
- outline the structure of an international financial reporting standard or international accounting standard
- explain the main features of IFRS1 *First-time Adoption of International Financial Reporting Standards*.

The need for regulation

Small business organisations are usually managed by their owners. This is generally the case for a sole trader, where the business is run by a single owner-manager, and for partnerships, where the business is owned and managed by its partners. Similarly, small private limited companies are often managed by their shareholders, who might all be members of the same family. In these circumstances, the owner or owners of the business can glean considerable amounts of financial information from their day-to-day involvement in managing its affairs and so do not depend solely upon formal financial statements to provide them with this information.

In contrast, large businesses (which are usually limited companies) are generally owned by one group of people but are managed by a different group. A large public company is owned by its shareholders, of whom there may be many thousands, but is managed by a small group of directors. Although some of the shareholders may also act as directors, it is likely that the large majority of the shareholders have no direct involvement in managing the company which they own. Such shareholders are almost entirely reliant upon the company's financial statements for information regarding the company's financial performance and position and to help them to determine whether or not the company is being properly managed. Other external user groups (such as the company's creditors) are also dependent to a large extent upon the information contained in financial statements when trying to make economic decisions relating to the company.

If the form and content of financial statements were not regulated, it would be possible for incompetent or unscrupulous directors to provide shareholders and other users with financial statements which gave a false or misleading impression of the company's financial situation. This would inevitably cause users to make poor economic decisions and so undermine the whole purpose of preparing financial statements. Therefore it is vital, especially in the case of larger companies, that financial reporting should be subject to a body of rules and regulations.

Sources of regulation

The rules and regulations which apply to financial reporting may be collectively referred to as the "regulatory framework". In practice, most of this framework applies only to companies, but it is important to realise that financial reporting regulations could be made in relation to any class of business entity. Indeed, the international standards which are the subject of this book generally refer to "entities" rather than companies. However, it may be assumed for the remainder of the book that we are dealing primarily with financial reporting by companies. The regulatory framework which applies to financial reporting by companies consists of the following main components:

(a) legislation

(b) accounting standards

(c)   stock exchange regulations.

Each of these is explained below.

Legislation

Most of the developed countries of the world have enacted legislation which governs financial reporting by limited companies. This legislation does of course differ from one country to another. In the UK, for example, the Companies Act 2006 contains rules relating to matters such as:

- the accounting records which companies must keep
- the requirement to prepare annual accounts (i.e. financial statements)
- the requirement that these accounts must give a "true and fair view"
- the requirement that the accounts must be prepared in accordance with either international standards or national standards
- the circumstances in which group accounts must be prepared (see Chapter 18)
- the circumstances in which an audit is required
- the company's duty to circulate its accounts to shareholders and to make the accounts available for public inspection.

Some of these rules have arisen as a result of European Union (EU) Directives and this is also true of the legislation in other member states of the EU.

Accounting standards

Whilst legislation generally sets out the broad rules with which companies must comply when preparing financial statements, detailed rules governing the accounting treatment of transactions and other items shown in those statements are laid down in *accounting standards*. Many of the developed countries of the world have their own standard-setting bodies, each of which is responsible for devising and publishing accounting standards for use in the country concerned. In the UK this is the Accounting Standards Board (ASB). The USA has a Financial Accounting Standards Board (FASB) and there are standards boards in other countries such as Germany, Japan, Australia etc.

In recent years, the increasing globalisation of business has fuelled the search for a single set of accounting standards. These standards would apply throughout the world and would greatly improve the consistency of financial reporting. To this end, the International Accounting Standards Board (IASB) has developed and is continuing to develop a set of international standards which it hopes will attain global acceptance. These standards are already used in a great many countries of the world (see later in this chapter) and a major step forward in this process was taken when the EU issued a regulation requiring all listed companies in the EU to prepare their group accounts (see Chapter 18) in accordance with international standards as from 1 January 2005.

Most of the remainder of this book is concerned with the international standards and an introduction to the work of the IASB is given later in this chapter.

Stock exchange regulations

A company whose shares are listed (or "quoted") on a recognised stock exchange must comply with the regulations of that stock exchange, some of which may relate to the company's financial statements. A stock exchange may, for example, require its member companies to produce financial statements more frequently than required by law (e.g. to publish interim financial reports at quarterly or half-yearly intervals) or to provide a more detailed analysis of some of the items in its financial statements than is required by law or by accounting standards.

Generally accepted accounting practice

The term "generally accepted accounting practice" (GAAP) refers to the complete set of regulations from all sources which apply within a certain jurisdiction, together with any general accounting principles or conventions which are usually applied in that jurisdiction even though they may not be enshrined in regulations. Since accounting rules and regulations currently differ from one country to another, it is correct to use terms such as "UK GAAP", "US GAAP" and so forth. At present, there is no internationally accepted set of accounting regulations and principles but the IASB is working towards that end and is trying to achieve convergence between the various regulations which are in force through-out the world (see later in this chapter). A distinction is sometimes drawn between big GAAP and little GAAP, as follows:

(a) The term "big GAAP" refers to the accounting regulations which apply to large companies (generally listed companies). The financial affairs of these companies can be very complex and therefore the regulations which comprise big GAAP need to be correspondingly complex. Some of the international standards described in this book appear to have been written mainly with large companies in mind.

(b) The term "little GAAP" refers to the simpler accounting regulations which apply to smaller companies. In the UK, for example, small companies may choose to adopt the *Financial Reporting Standard for Smaller Entities* issued by the UK Accounting Standards Board, rather than complying with UK accounting standards in full.

　At the international level, the International Accounting Standards Board has issued the *International Financial Reporting Standard for Small and Medium-sized Entities* (*IFRS for SMEs*). This is essentially a simplified version of the full international standards and is intended for use mainly by unlisted companies (see Chapter 25).

The International Accounting Standards Board

International standards are developed and published by the International Accounting Standards Board (IASB) which was formed in 2001 as a replacement for the International Accounting Standards Committee (IASC). Standards published by the IASB are known as International Financial Reporting Standards (IFRSs). Standards which were originally published by the IASC are known as International Accounting Standards (IASs). Many of these IASs are still in force, since they were adopted by the IASB on its inception. At present, the list of extant standards comprises thirteen IFRSs and twenty-eight IASs. A full list of these standards is given at the front of this book.

The IASB consists of sixteen members, of whom up to three may be part-time. The members of the IASB are chosen for their professional competence and their practical experience and are selected in such a way that a broad geographical balance is maintained on the Board. The current IASB Chairman is Hans Hoogervorst. The previous Chairman was Sir David Tweedie, who occupied the position for ten years and was formerly Chairman of the UK Accounting Standards Board.

The IASB is responsible to the trustees of the International Financial Reporting Standards Foundation (IFRS Foundation) as shown in the following diagram:

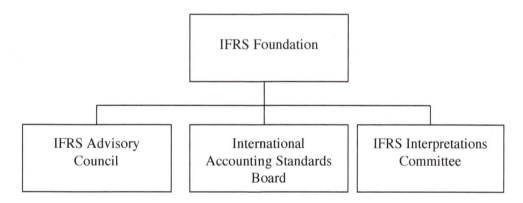

The IFRS Foundation

The constitution of the IFRS Foundation states that its objectives are as follows:

(a) to develop, in the public interest, a single set of high-quality, understandable, enforceable and globally accepted financial reporting standards based upon clearly articulated principles. These standards should require high quality, transparent and comparable information in financial statements and other financial reporting to help investors, participants in the world's capital markets and other users of financial information to make economic decisions;

(b) to promote the use and rigorous application of those standards;

(c) in fulfilling the objectives associated with (a) and (b), to take account of, as appropriate, the needs of a range of sizes and types of entities in diverse economic settings;

(d) to promote and facilitate adoption of International Financial Reporting Standards (IFRSs), being the standards and interpretations issued by the IASB, through the convergence of national accounting standards and IFRSs.

The IASB's *Preface to International Financial Reporting Standards* states that these are also the objectives of the IASB.

The activities of the IFRS Foundation are directed by twenty-two Trustees who are appointed subject to approval by a Monitoring Board (see below) and who are drawn from a diversity of geographical and professional backgrounds. The Trustees are responsible for appointing the members of the IASB and the other bodies shown in the above diagram and for establishing and maintaining the necessary funding for their work. The Trustees are also responsible for reviewing the effectiveness of the IASB. Financial support for the IFRS Foundation's activities is received from a variety of sources, including:

(a) national financing regimes based upon a country's Gross Domestic Product (GDP)

(b) income from publications and related activities

(c) major international accounting firms.

The Monitoring Board comprises high-level representatives of public authorities such as the European Commission and the US Securities and Exchange Commission. The Trustees are required to make an annual written report to the Monitoring Board.

The IFRS Advisory Council

The IFRS Advisory Council provides a forum for participation by organisations and individuals with an interest in international financial reporting. The Advisory Council comprises thirty or more members drawn from diverse geographical and functional backgrounds and has the following objectives:

(a) to offer advice to the IASB with regard to its agenda and priorities

(b) to inform the IASB of Council members' views on standard-setting projects

(c) to offer other advice to the IASB or to the Trustees.

The Chairman of the Advisory Council cannot be a member of the IASB or its staff.

The IFRS Interpretations Committee

The main role of the IFRS Interpretations Committee is to interpret the application of international standards and to provide timely guidance on financial reporting matters which are not specifically addressed in the standards. The Interpretations Committee has fourteen voting members and a non-voting Chair.

The standard-setting process

The IASB develops standards by means of a "due process" which involves accountants, users of financial statements, the business community, stock exchanges, regulatory authorities, academics and other interested individuals and organisations throughout the world. The main steps in this process (which are listed in the *Preface to International Financial Reporting Standards*) are as follows:

- identification and review of all the issues associated with the topic concerned
- consideration of the way in which the IASB's conceptual framework (see Chapter 2) applies to these issues
- a study of national accounting requirements in relation to the topic and an exchange of views with national standard-setters
- consultation with the Trustees and the Advisory Council about the advisability of adding this topic to the IASB's agenda
- publication of a discussion document for public comment
- consideration of comments received within the stated comment period
- publication of an exposure draft for public comment
- consideration of comments received within the stated comment period
- publication of the standard.

Publication of an international standard requires the approval of at least ten of the sixteen members of the IASB.

The *Preface* states that IFRSs and IASs are designed to apply to the general purpose financial statements and other financial reporting of profit-oriented entities, whether these are organised in corporate form or in other forms. For this reason, the standards refer to "entities" rather than companies. The word "entity" is also used in this book, although in practice the international standards apply principally to companies.

The structure of an international standard

An IFRS or IAS consists of a set of numbered paragraphs and is typically made up of some or all of the following sections:

- introduction
- objectives and scope of the standard
- definitions of terms used in the standard (these may be in an Appendix)
- the body of the standard
- effective date and transitional provisions
- approval by the IASB and any dissenting opinions by IASB members.

A standard may be accompanied by a Basis for Conclusions, which is not part of the standard itself but which sets out the considerations which were taken into account when the standard was devised. There may also be application or implementation guidance and illustrative examples.

The purpose of accounting standards

The main purpose of accounting standards (whether national or international) is to reduce or eliminate variations in accounting practice and to introduce a degree of uniformity into financial reporting. In particular, accounting standards usually set out requirements with regard to the recognition, measurement, presentation and disclosure of transactions and other items in financial statements. The main advantages of this standardisation are as follows:

(a) **Faithful representation**. If the preparers of financial statements are obliged to comply with a set of accounting standards, then it is more likely that the information given in the statements will provide a faithful representation of the financial performance and financial position of the organisation concerned. Accounting standards help to ensure that financial reporting is free from bias and that "creative accounting" practices are outlawed.

(b) **Comparability**. It is important that users should be able to compare the financial statements of an organisation over time so as to identify trends in its financial performance and position. It is also important that users should be able to compare the financial statements of different organisations and assess their relative strengths and weaknesses. Such comparisons will not be meaningful unless all of the financial statements concerned have been drawn up on a consistent basis. This is much more likely to be the case if accounting standards have been observed.

A more detailed explanation of these and certain other desirable characteristics of the information provided in financial statements is given in the IASB's conceptual framework (see Chapter 2).

It is the view of the IASB that standards should ensure that like items are accounted for in a like way and that unlike items are accounted for in different ways. Therefore the standards issued by the IASB do not generally permit any choice of accounting treatment. Some of the IASs which were adopted by the IASB on its inception do allow a choice of accounting treatment but the IASB has reconsidered (and will continue to reconsider) the items for which a choice of treatment is permitted, with a view to reducing the number of choices available or eliminating choice altogether.

It could, of course, be argued that accounting standards should allow some degree of flexibility and that compliance with the single accounting treatment permitted by a standard might sometimes be inappropriate. The IASB takes the view that this situation is very unlikely to occur. However, international standard IAS1 (see Chapter 3) allows an entity to depart from the requirements of a standard in the "extremely rare circumstances" in which compliance would prevent the financial statements from faithfully representing transactions and other items.

Worldwide use of international standards

As stated above, the goal of the IFRS Foundation is to develop a set of global accounting standards, promote their use and bring about convergence between national standards and international standards. This goal has not yet been achieved in full but the worldwide influence of international standards has increased significantly since the IASB was formed and seems likely to continue to increase.

At present, over ninety countries require listed companies to comply with international standards when preparing their group accounts. These countries include all EU members together with countries such as Australia, Brazil, Canada, Russia and South Africa. More than twenty other countries permit (but do not require) the use of international standards when preparing the group accounts of listed companies. Furthermore:

(a) India plans to converge with international standards at a date yet to be determined.

(b) Japan permits certain international companies to use international standards and may mandatorily adopt these standards by 2016.

(c) China has substantially converged its national standards with international standards.

(d) The USA has stated its commitment to global financial reporting standards. Foreign companies listed on US stock exchanges are already permitted to use IFRS. The US Financial Accounting Standards Board (FASB) has been working with the IASB on convergence between US GAAP and international standards, envisaging the eventual adoption of international standards for US domestic companies.

Perhaps understandably, international standards have made rather less impact in relation to unlisted companies, which tend to have straightforward financial affairs and to operate in one country only. Nonetheless, the use of international standards for such companies is mandatory in some countries and is permitted in others (e.g. the UK). The development by the IASB of an IFRS for SMEs (see Chapter 25) may encourage more countries to require compliance with international standards for all companies, whether listed or unlisted.

First-time adoption of international standards

In 2003, the IASB issued IFRS1 *First-time Adoption of International Financial Reporting Standards*. A revised version was issued in 2008. The objective of IFRS1 is to ensure that an entity's first financial statements which comply with international standards should contain high-quality information that:

• is transparent for users and comparable for all periods presented
• provides a suitable starting point for accounting under international standards
• can be generated at a cost that does not exceed the benefits to users.

This standard uses the term "IFRS" to refer to international standards in general (including the IASs) together with interpretations developed by the IFRS Interpretations Committee. The main features of IFRS1 are as follows:

(a) An entity's "first IFRS financial statements" are defined as the first financial statements in which the entity adopts international standards and makes an explicit and unreserved statement of compliance with those standards.

(b) The "first IFRS reporting period" is defined as the reporting period covered by the first IFRS financial statements.

(c) The "date of transition to IFRS" is defined as the beginning of the earliest period for which an entity presents comparative information in its first IFRS financial statements. Most sets of financial statements cover a period of one year and give comparative information for the previous year. So the date of transition to IFRS is normally the date which falls two years before the end of the first IFRS reporting period.

(d) When first adopting international standards, an entity must prepare an "opening IFRS statement of financial position" as at the date of transition to IFRS. This is the starting point for accounting in accordance with international standards. The opening IFRS statement of financial position must:

   (i) recognise all assets and liabilities whose recognition is required by international standards, but not recognise items as assets or liabilities if this is not permitted by international standards

   (ii) reclassify items which were recognised as one type of asset or liability under previous GAAP but which are classified as a different type of asset or liability under international standards

   (iii) apply international standards in measuring all recognised assets and liabilities.

   Note that the term "statement of financial position" has now replaced the term "balance sheet" throughout the international standards (see Chapter 3).

(e) The same accounting policies must be used in the entity's opening IFRS statement of financial position and in all periods presented in the first IFRS financial statements (i.e. the first IFRS reporting period and the comparative period(s)). In general, these accounting policies must comply with all international standards in effect *at the end of the first IFRS reporting period*, even if some of those standards were not in effect at the date of transition to IFRS or during some or all of the periods for which information is being presented.

(f) The first IFRS financial statements must include the following reconciliations:

   (i) a reconciliation of equity (share capital and reserves for a company) as reported under previous GAAP with equity re-calculated under international standards, for the date of transition to IFRS and for the end of the last period in which the entity reported under previous GAAP

(ii) a reconciliation of total comprehensive income for the last period in which the entity reported under previous GAAP with total comprehensive income as it would have been calculated under international standards.

Note that the term "total comprehensive income" refers to an entity's profit or loss together with certain other gains or losses such as revaluation gains (see Chapter 3).

(g) IFRS1 grants limited exemptions from some of its requirements in certain areas where it is considered that the cost of compliance would be likely to exceed the benefits to users of the financial statements.

EXAMPLE

A company which has always prepared financial statements to 31 December each year prepares its first IFRS financial statements for the year to 31 December 2013. These statements show comparative figures for the year to 31 December 2012.

(a) Identify the first IFRS reporting period and state the date of transition to IFRS.

(b) Explain the procedure which must be followed in order to prepare the financial statements for the year to 31 December 2013.

(c) Identify the reconciliations which the company must include in its financial statements for the year to 31 December 2013.

Solution

(a) The first IFRS reporting period is the year to 31 December 2013. The date of the transition to IFRS is the beginning of business on 1 January 2012, which is equivalent to the close of business on 31 December 2011.

(b) The procedure is as follows:

(i) An opening IFRS statement of financial position as at 31 December 2011 must be prepared in accordance with all international standards effective for accounting periods ending on 31 December 2013.

(ii) The company must then prepare a revised version of the financial statements for the year to 31 December 2012, again applying all international standards effective for periods ending on 31 December 2013. This provides comparative figures for the 2013 financial statements.

(iii) The financial statements for the year to 31 December 2013 are then prepared.

(c) The required reconciliations are:

(i) a reconciliation of the company's equity (i.e. share capital and reserves) as reported under previous GAAP with equity as calculated under international standards, at both 31 December 2011 and 31 December 2012.

(ii) a reconciliation of the company's total comprehensive income as reported under previous GAAP for the year to 31 December 2012 with total comprehensive income for that year as calculated under international standards.

Summary

‣ The regulatory framework within which the financial statements of companies are prepared consists of a mixture of legislation, accounting standards and (where applicable) stock exchange regulations.

‣ Legislation generally sets out the broad rules with which companies must comply when preparing their financial statements. Accounting standards provide detailed rules regarding the accounting treatment of transactions and other items.

‣ The increasing globalisation of business has led to the establishment of the IASB and the development of international standards. These standards have not yet achieved worldwide acceptance but their influence has increased greatly in recent years.

‣ The term "generally accepted accounting practice" (GAAP) refers to the complete set of accounting regulations and principles which are usually applied within a certain jurisdiction.

‣ The IASB is the standard-setting body of the IFRS Foundation. The IFRS Advisory Council offers advice to the IASB with regard to its agenda and priorities. The IFRS Interpretations Committee is responsible for the interpretation of international standards and for providing timely guidance on matters not specifically addressed in the standards.

‣ The standard-setting process adopted by the IASB involves the publication of a discussion document and an exposure draft (with consideration of comments received at each stage) before the final standard is published.

‣ The main purpose of accounting standards is to reduce or eliminate variations in accounting practice and to introduce a degree of uniformity into financial reporting.

‣ IFRS1 *First-time Adoption of International Financial Reporting Standards* sets out the procedure which must be followed when an entity adopts international standards for the first time.

Exercises

1.1 Explain the term "regulatory framework" as it applies to financial reporting. Why is this framework needed?

1.2 Explain the term "generally accepted accounting practice" (GAAP). Is there just one GAAP which is accepted worldwide? If not, why not?

1.3 Outline the structure and functions of:

(a) the IFRS Foundation

(b) the International Accounting Standards Board (IASB)

(c) the IFRS Advisory Council

(d) the IFRS Interpretations Committee.

1.4 Outline the structure of an international standard (IFRS or IAS).

1.5 Explain the purpose of accounting standards (whether national or international) and identify the advantages that stem from the standardisation of accounting practice. Are there any disadvantages?

1.6 A company adopts international standards for the first time when preparing its financial statements for the year to 30 June 2014. These financial statements show comparative figures for the previous two years.

Explain the main requirements of IFRS1 *First-time Adoption of International Financial Reporting Standards* which must be satisfied when preparing the company's financial statements for the year to 30 June 2014.

1.7 The term "regulatory framework" refers to the body of rules and regulations which apply to the financial statements of limited companies. This framework includes company law, accounting standards and (for listed companies) stock exchange regulations.

(a) State the objectives of the International Accounting Standards Board. Also explain the role of the IFRS Advisory Council and the IFRS Interpretations Committee.

(b) Explain the term "Generally Accepted Accounting Practice" (GAAP). *(CIPFA)*

*1.8 The International Accounting Standards Board (IASB) develops international standards by means of a "due process". The main stages of this process are listed in the *Preface to International Financial Reporting Standards*. The *Preface* also states the objectives of the IASB and explains the scope of international standards.

(a) State the objectives of the IASB.

(b) Explain the scope of international financial reporting standards and international accounting standards.

(c) List the main stages of the IASB due process.

*1.9   IFRS1 *First-time Adoption of International Financial Reporting Standards* lays down the procedure which must be followed when an entity prepares its first financial statements that comply with international standards (IFRSs and IASs).

(a)   State the objective of IFRS1.

(b)   Explain the terms "first IFRS reporting period" and "date of transition to IFRS" as defined by IFRS1.

(c)   A company adopts international standards for the first time in its financial statements for the year to 31 October 2014. These financial statements provide comparative figures for the previous five years. Explain the requirements of IFRS1 which must be satisfied when preparing these financial statements.

Chapter 2

The IASB conceptual framework

Introduction

A "conceptual framework" for financial reporting consists of a set of agreed fundamental principles which underpin financial accounting and so provide a sound theoretical basis for the development of accounting standards. A conceptual framework is defined by the US Financial Accounting Standards Board (FASB) as:

> "*a coherent system of inter-related objectives and fundamentals that can lead to consistent standards and that prescribes the nature, function and limits of financial accounting and financial statements*".

In the absence of a conceptual framework, standards are more difficult to develop since each standard must begin from scratch. It is also more likely that there will be inconsistencies and contradictions between one standard and another.

The IASB contribution to the development of a conceptual framework is its *Conceptual Framework for Financial Reporting*. Although devised by a standard-setting body, the IASB *Conceptual Framework* is not itself an accounting standard and does not override any standards. If there is a conflict between the *Conceptual Framework* and an IFRS or IAS, then the standard prevails. But the *Conceptual Framework* identifies certain concepts which, in the view of the IASB, underlie the preparation and presentation of financial statements for external users. The purpose of this chapter is to explain these concepts.

Development of the Conceptual Framework

The IASB *Conceptual Framework* is being developed in a series of phases and replaces the *Framework for the Preparation and Presentation of Financial Statements* which was published in 1989. The first version of the new *Conceptual Framework* was published in 2010 and contains revised material, agreed with the US FASB, on the objective of financial reporting and the qualitative characteristics of useful financial information.

The remainder of the 2010 *Conceptual Framework* consists of text transferred from the original 1989 *Framework* but the IASB's intention is to replace this text gradually with updated material as each phase of the development project is completed. Several further sections are expected to be published by September 2015.

The progress of this project may be followed on website www.ifrs.org.

Objectives

By the end of this chapter, the reader should be able to:

- state the main purposes of the IASB *Conceptual Framework*
- state the objective of general purpose financial reporting and identify the primary users of financial reports
- state and explain the qualitative characteristics of useful financial information
- state and explain an important assumption which underlies the preparation of financial statements
- define each of the main elements of financial statements
- explain the criteria which determine whether or not an element should be recognised in the financial statements
- explain the measurement bases which are identified in the *Conceptual Framework*
- distinguish between financial capital maintenance and physical capital maintenance.

Purposes and scope of the IASB *Conceptual Framework*

As stated above, the IASB *Conceptual Framework* sets out the concepts that underlie the preparation and presentation of general purpose financial statements prepared for the benefit of external users. The main purposes of the *Conceptual Framework* are:

(a) to assist in the development of future international standards and in the review of existing standards

(b) to provide a basis for reducing the number of alternative accounting treatments permitted by international standards

(c) to assist national standard-setters in developing national standards

(d) to assist preparers of financial statements in applying international standards and in dealing with topics which are not yet covered by international standards

(e) to assist auditors in forming an opinion as to whether financial statements conform with international standards

(f) to assist users of financial statements in interpreting the information contained in financial statements prepared in accordance with international standards

(g) to provide those who are interested in the work of the IASB with information about its approach to the formulation of international standards.

Scope

The *Conceptual Framework* deals with the following matters:

(a)   the objective of general purpose financial reporting

(b)   the qualitative characteristics of useful financial information

(c)   the going concern assumption

(d)   the elements of financial statements

(e)   recognition of the elements of financial statements

(f)   measurement of the elements of financial statements

(g)   concepts of capital and capital maintenance.

Each of these is explained below. As mentioned earlier, the first two items on this list refer to matters agreed in 2010 between the IASB and the US FASB. The remaining five items are dealt with in text transferred from the original 1989 *Framework*.

Objective of general purpose financial reporting

The *Conceptual Framework* states that the objective of general purpose financial reporting is "*to provide financial information about the reporting entity that is useful to existing and potential investors, lenders and other creditors in making decisions about providing resources to the entity*". Such decisions may be concerned with buying, selling or holding equity in the entity (e.g. shares) or with providing credit to the entity (e.g. loans). Existing and potential investors, lenders and other creditors are referred to collectively as "primary users". In more detail, the *Conceptual Framework* states that:

(a)   Decisions by existing and potential investors depend upon the returns they expect to receive from an investment in the entity concerned (e.g. dividends or increases in the market value of the entity's shares). Decisions by lenders and other creditors also depend upon expected returns (e.g. loan interest and debt repayments). Therefore these "primary users" need information that will help them to assess the prospects for future cash inflows to an entity.

   Such information will include information about the entity's resources and the claims against the entity. It will also include information about the efficiency and effectiveness with which the entity's management uses the entity's resources.

(b)   The primary users cannot require an entity to provide information directly to them and so they rely on general purpose financial reports for much of the information which they need. However, these financial reports cannot provide all of the required information and primary users will also need to consider information from other sources (e.g. general economic forecasts, industry outlooks etc.).

(c)   General purpose financial reports are not designed to show the value of the reporting entity but may help primary users to estimate the entity's value.

(d) Individual primary users may have differing information needs. When developing international standards, the IASB seeks to ensure that financial reports prepared in accordance with those standards will provide information that meets the needs of the maximum number of primary users. However, there is nothing to prevent an entity from disclosing additional information that might be useful to a particular subset of primary users.

(e) Financial reports are based to some extent upon estimates, judgements and models and so cannot be exact. The *Conceptual Framework* establishes the concepts that underlie those estimates, judgements and models.

(f) In addition to the primary users, other parties might find general purpose financial reports useful, although these reports are not primarily intended for their benefit. The new *Conceptual Framework* does not list these other parties but the 1989 *Framework* indicated that the users of financial reports might also include:

(i) employees and their representatives, who may use financial reports to help them assess the profitability and stability of an entity and so determine the entity's ability to provide employment opportunities, fair pay and retirement pensions

(ii) customers, who may use financial reports to help them assess whether the entity is likely to continue in business and so act as a reliable source of supply

(iii) governments and their agencies, who may use the information provided in financial reports to help determine taxation policies, regulate business and compile national statistics

(iv) the public, who may wish to assess an entity's prosperity and developments in its range of activities, especially if that entity makes a substantial contribution to the local economy (e.g. by providing local employment or by its patronage of local suppliers).

The management of an entity is obviously interested in financial information about that entity. However, management is able to obtain financial information internally and so does not rely upon general purpose financial reports.

Information about an entity's resources and claims

General purpose financial reports should provide information about the *financial position* of the reporting entity (i.e. information about the entity's economic resources and claims against the entity). Financial reports should also provide information about transactions and other events that change the entity's financial position. Changes in financial position may result from the entity's *financial performance* (e.g. the making of a profit) or from other events such as share issues. Both of these types of information are useful when making decisions about providing resources to the entity. Note that:

(a) Information about an entity's financial position helps primary users to identify that entity's financial strengths and weaknesses and to assess its liquidity and solvency.

(b) Information about an entity's financial performance helps primary users to understand the return that the entity has made on the resources at its disposal. Financial performance information also indicates whether those resources have been managed efficiently and effectively. In other words, financial performance information helps users to assess the "stewardship" of management. Information about past financial performance may also be of assistance when predicting future returns on an entity's economic resources.

(c) Financial performance information is prepared on an "accrual accounting" basis. This means that transactions and other events are recognised in the periods in which they occur (not necessarily the periods in which cash is received or paid). This approach provides better financial performance information than information based solely on cash receipts and payments occurring during a reporting period.

However, information about cash flows during a period is also important, since it indicates how an entity generates and spends cash and helps users to assess the entity's ability to generate future net cash inflows.

(d) Finally, information about changes in an entity's financial position which have not resulted from its financial performance (e.g. changes caused by share issues) is also necessary since it gives users a complete understanding of how and why the entity's financial position has changed.

The *Conceptual Framework* does not specify or name the financial statements in which each of the four classes of information listed above should be presented. However, these financial statements are identified in international standard IAS1 (see Chapter 3).

Qualitative characteristics of financial information

The *Conceptual Framework* identifies six "qualitative characteristics" of useful financial information. These characteristics indicate the types of information that are likely to be most useful to the primary users of financial reports. Two of the qualitative characteristics are stated to be "fundamental". These are:

• relevance
• faithful representation.

The remaining four qualitative characteristics are described as "enhancing" since they further enhance the usefulness of financial information that is already relevant and faithfully represented. The enhancing characteristics are:

• comparability
• verifiability
• timeliness
• understandability.

Each of these characteristics is explained below.

Relevance

The first fundamental qualitative characteristic of useful financial information is that it must be relevant to users' decision-making needs. Irrelevant information is obviously not useful. In particular, information is relevant if it has predictive value or confirmatory value, as follows:

(a) Information has "predictive value" if can help users to predict future outcomes (e.g. future financial performance). In order to have predictive value, information does not have to take the form of an explicit forecast, since information on past transactions or events may be used as a basis for predictions about the future.

(b) Information has "confirmatory value" if it provides feedback which helps to confirm or refute previous predictions.

The relevance of information is affected not only by its nature but also by its level of materiality. Materiality is mainly concerned with the size or monetary amount of an item and information is said to be "material" if its omission or mis-statement could influence users' decisions. Information about an item which is so small as to be immaterial will not be relevant to users' needs. The IASB cannot specify a generally applicable materiality threshold, since materiality is an entity-specific matter.

Faithful representation

The second fundamental qualitative characteristic of useful financial information is that it must faithfully represent the transactions and other events that it purports to represent. A perfectly faithful representation would be *complete*, *neutral* and *free from error*. The objective of the IASB is to maximise these qualities to as great an extent as possible.

(a) **Completeness**. Financial information is complete if it includes all of the information required in order that a user should understand the transactions and other events being represented, including all necessary descriptions and explanations.

(b) **Neutrality**. A neutral representation is one that is unbiased. Financial information is not neutral if it is manipulated in some way to achieve a predetermined result, with the aim of increasing the probability that the information will be received favourably (or unfavourably) by users.

(c) **Freedom from error**. Financial information does not have to be 100% accurate but it must be free from material error. Freedom from error implies that there are no errors or omissions in the description of the items being represented and that no errors have been made when selecting and applying the process used to produce the reported information. For instance, an estimate of an item's value cannot be 100% accurate, but that estimate may be regarded as being free from error as long as the amount is clearly described as being an estimate, the estimating process is fully explained and no errors are made when selecting or applying that process.

It is worth noting that the *Basis for Conclusions* which accompanies the IASB *Conceptual Framework* states that financial information which faithfully represents transactions and other events will represent their economic substance rather than merely representing their legal form. However, the inclusion of "substance over form" in the list of qualities that contribute to a faithful representation was thought to be unnecessary.

Another item which is omitted from this list of qualities (but was included in the original 1989 *Framework*) is the notion of "prudence". Prudence involves exercising a degree of caution when making estimates, to ensure that assets and income are not overstated and that liabilities and expenses are not understated. However, the IASB now takes the view that prudence is inconsistent with neutrality and that "an admonition to be prudent is likely to lead to a bias". Despite this view, many of the existing international standards adopt a prudent approach and it remains to be seen whether any of these standards will eventually be amended to reflect the absence of a prudence principle in the *Conceptual Framework*.

Enhancing qualitative characteristics

As stated above, the enhancing qualitative characteristics are comparability, verifiability, timeliness and understandability.

(a) **Comparability**. This characteristic enables users to compare financial information about an entity for a reporting period with similar information about other entities for the same period and with similar information about the same entity for other periods. Such comparisons will help users to make economic decisions.

   Comparability is improved through consistency. Consistency refers to the use of the same accounting treatments for the same types of item, either from period to period by one reporting entity or in a single period across entities. The IASB takes the view that permitting alternative accounting treatments for an item diminishes consistency and so diminishes comparability. This is an argument in favour of the IASB's stated intention of reducing the number of choices of accounting treatment allowed by international standards or possibly eliminating choice altogether (see Chapter 1).

(b) **Verifiability**. Financial information is said to be verifiable if different independent, knowledgeable observers are able to agree that the information concerned provides a faithful representation. Verification may be direct or indirect.

   Direct verification involves verifying information by means of direct observation (e.g. by counting cash). Indirect verification means that the inputs to a model or formula are checked and then the outputs of that model or formula are recalculated. For example, closing inventory measured by means of the FIFO cost formula (see Chapter 10) may be verified by checking inventory movements and costs during the period and by then using the FIFO formula to recalculate closing inventory.

(c) **Timeliness**. Financial information is timely if it is made available to users in time for it to be capable of influencing their economic decisions.

(d) **Understandability**. It is clearly desirable that the information provided in financial reports should be understandable by users. Incomprehensible information would have no value. The understandability of financial information is improved if it is classified and presented clearly and concisely. But omitting unavoidably complex information from financial reports on the grounds that it would be difficult to understand is not acceptable since this would make those reports incomplete.

The *Conceptual Framework* states that financial reports are prepared for users who "have a reasonable knowledge of business and economic activities and who review and analyse the information diligently". These are the users who should generally be able to understand financial reports. However, it is accepted that even well-informed users may sometimes need the help of an advisor to understand information about complex transactions and other events.

The cost constraint on useful financial reporting

The *Conceptual Framework* recognises that there are cost constraints on the information that can be provided in financial reports. Reporting financial information imposes costs and obviously these costs should be justified by the benefits of reporting that information. Although the costs of financial reporting are borne initially by the providers of financial reports, these costs are borne ultimately by users (e.g. shareholders) in the form of reduced returns (e.g. lower profits). Users may also bear the additional costs of analysing and interpreting the information provided in financial reports.

When developing an international standard, the IASB assesses whether the benefits of reporting the information required by that standard are likely to justify the costs incurred to provide and use it. This assessment is conducted in the light of information obtained from providers, users, auditors and others about the expected costs and benefits.

As stated at the start of this chapter, the remainder of the 2010 *Conceptual Framework* consists of text transferred from the *Framework for the Preparation and Presentation of Financial Statements* issued in 1989. It should be noted that the IASB has not amended this text to reflect terminological changes made by international standard IAS1 in 2007 (see Chapter 3). For instance, the transferred text still uses the term "balance sheet" rather than "statement of financial position".

Underlying assumption

The *Conceptual Framework* states that financial statements are normally prepared on the assumption that the reporting entity is a "going concern" and will continue in operation for the foreseeable future. It is assumed that the entity has neither the intention nor the need to close down or materially reduce the scale of its operations. This allows (for example) the net realisable value of inventories to be based upon their normal sale price and items such as property, plant and equipment to be depreciated over their normal useful lives.

However, if an entity is not a going concern, the financial statements will have to be prepared on a different basis and that basis should be disclosed.

Elements of financial statements

This section of the *Conceptual Framework* identifies the main elements of financial statements and offers a definition of each element. The most important definitions are those of "asset" and "liability" since each of the other elements is defined in terms of its relationship to an entity's assets or liabilities.

Elements relating to financial position

The elements directly related to the measurement of financial position are assets, liabilities and equity. These are defined as follows:

(a) **Assets**. An asset is "*a resource controlled by the entity as a result of past events and from which future economic benefits are expected to flow to the entity*". Note the following points with regard to this definition:

  – There is no requirement for an item to be legally owned by an entity in order that it should be an asset, merely that the item should be controlled by the entity. This means that certain leased items may be classed as assets (see Chapter 9). This is an application of the principle of substance over form.

  – An asset can arise only as the result of a past event. This is usually the purchase or manufacture of the item concerned. Expected future transactions (e.g. the mere intention to buy an item) do not give rise to assets at the present time.

  – An item cannot be classed as an asset unless it is expected to generate future economic benefits for the entity.

(b) **Liabilities**. A liability is "*a present obligation of the entity arising from past events, the settlement of which is expected to result in an outflow from the entity of resources embodying economic benefits*". Note that:

  – An essential characteristic of a liability is that the entity must be under an obligation. This means that the entity must have a duty or responsibility to transfer resources embodying economic benefits. However, there is no requirement that the obligation should be legally enforceable, even though this would normally be the case. For instance, if it is an entity's policy to rectify faults in its products even after the warranty period has expired, the amounts expected to be expended in relation to goods already sold are obligations of the entity, even though they are not legally enforceable. Such obligations are known as "constructive obligations" (see Chapter 12).

- A further characteristic of a liability is that the obligation must be a *present obligation*, not a future commitment. For instance, a decision by management to buy an asset in the future does not give rise to a present obligation to pay for the asset, since the decision could be reversed.

- A liability can arise only as the result of a past event, such as the acquisition of goods or services or the receipt of a bank loan.

- Liabilities which can be measured only by using a substantial degree of estimation are referred to as "provisions" (see Chapter 12).

(c) **Equity**. Equity is "*the residual interest in the assets of the entity after deducting all its liabilities*". This is of course an expression of the well-known accounting equation (assets = liabilities + capital). However, the IASB favours the term "equity" rather than "capital". In the case of a company, equity will usually consist of share capital, retained earnings and other reserves.

It is important to note that an item might satisfy one of these definitions and yet still be excluded from the entity's financial statements because it fails to meet certain recognition criteria which are specified in the *Conceptual Framework* (see below).

On the other hand, the *Conceptual Framework* states that balance sheets (or statements of financial position) that are drawn up in accordance with current international standards may include items that do not satisfy the definitions of an asset or liability and are not part of equity. However, the definitions set out above will underlie future reviews of existing standards and the development of new standards.

Elements relating to financial performance

The *Conceptual Framework* states that profit is frequently used as a measure of performance and that the elements directly related to the measurement of profit are income and expenses. These are defined as follows:

(a) **Income**. Income is "*increases in economic benefits during the accounting period in the form of inflows or enhancements of assets or decreases of liabilities that result in increases in equity, other than those relating to contributions from equity participants*". Note that:

- The term "income" encompasses both revenue which arises in the course of an entity's ordinary activities and also gains (e.g. gains arising on the disposal or revaluation of long-term assets).

- Income is defined in terms of an increase in net assets.

(b) **Expenses**. Expenses are "*decreases in economic benefits during the accounting period in the form of outflows or depletions of assets or incurrences of liabilities that result in decreases in equity, other than those relating to distributions to equity participants*". Note that:

- The term "expenses" encompasses both expenses which arise in the course of an entity's ordinary activities and also losses (e.g. losses arising on the disposal or revaluation of long-term assets).
- Expenses are defined in terms of a decrease in net assets.

The fact that income and expenses are defined in terms of increases or decreases in net assets means that profits (or losses) are also defined in these terms.

Recognition of the elements of financial statements

Recognition is defined as "*the process of incorporating in the balance sheet or income statement an item that meets the definition of an element and satisfies the criteria for recognition*". Recognition involves the depiction of the item in words and by a monetary amount and "*the inclusion of that amount in the balance sheet totals or income statement totals*". Items which are merely disclosed in the notes that accompany the financial statements have not been recognised. This definition of "recognition" has not yet been amended to reflect the terminological changes made by IAS1 in 2007 (see Chapter 3).

The *Conceptual Framework* states that an item which satisfies the definition of an element should be recognised in the financial statements so long as:

(a) it is probable that any future economic benefit associated with the item will flow to or from the entity, and

(b) the item has a cost or value that can be measured with reliability.

These criteria apply principally to the recognition of assets and liabilities, since equity is defined as the difference between an entity's total assets and total liabilities and the other elements of the financial statements (income and expenses) are defined in terms of changes in the entity's assets and liabilities. Note that:

(a) The use of the word "probable" in these recognition criteria is an acceptance of the fact that the future is uncertain. If recognition required certainty, it would be impossible to draw up meaningful financial statements at all. For example, it may be uncertain whether an amount owed to an entity will ever be received. However, if it is probable (on the basis of the evidence available) that the amount will be received in due course, then recognition of this amount as an asset is justifiable.

(b) The use of the word "reliability" in the recognition criteria does not mean that costs or values must be capable of precise measurement before they can be recognised. The *Conceptual Framework* acknowledges that the use of estimates is an essential part of the preparation of financial statements and this does not undermine their reliability. However, an item for which a reasonable estimate cannot be made should not be recognised in the financial statements.

(c) An item which qualifies as an element but fails to satisfy the recognition criteria may instead warrant disclosure in the notes that accompany the financial statements.

Measurement of the elements of financial statements

Measurement is the process of determining the monetary amount at which an element is to be shown in the financial statements. The *Conceptual Framework* identifies four different measurement bases which could be used in principle. These are:

(a) **Historical cost**. Assets are recorded at the amount paid to acquire them. Liabilities are recorded at the amount of proceeds received in exchange for the obligation, or in some circumstances (e.g. tax liabilities) at the amount expected to be paid to satisfy the obligation in the normal course of business.

(b) **Current cost**. Assets are shown at the amount that would have to be paid to acquire an equivalent asset currently (i.e. replacement cost). Liabilities are shown at the undiscounted amount which would be required to settle the obligation currently.

(c) **Realisable value**. Assets are shown at the amount which could be obtained by selling the asset in an orderly disposal. Liabilities are shown at the undiscounted amount expected to be paid to satisfy the obligation in the normal course of business.

(d) **Present value**. Assets are shown at the present discounted value of the future net cash inflows that the asset is expected to generate in the normal course of business. Liabilities are shown at the present discounted value of the future net cash outflows that are expected to be required to settle the liability in the normal course of business.

Readers who are not familiar with the concepts of discounting and present value are referred to the appendix at the end of this chapter in which these concepts are explained.

Selection of measurement basis

The *Conceptual Framework* states that the basis most commonly used is historical cost but adds that this is sometimes combined with other bases (e.g. when valuing inventory at the lower of cost and net realisable value). Furthermore, some entities use current cost to deal with the effects of changing prices in assets such as property. However, the *Conceptual Framework* does not prescribe the use of any particular basis and provides no guidance (at present) as to the selection of an appropriate basis.

Concepts of capital and capital maintenance

The final section of the *Conceptual Framework* is concerned with different concepts of the term "capital" and its relationship to the calculation of profit. We have already seen that an entity's capital or equity is equal to its net assets and that income and expenses are defined in terms of changes to those net assets. Therefore another way of looking at profit is to say that an entity's profit (or loss) for an accounting period is equal to the increase (or decrease) in the entity's capital during that period. Hence the calculation of profit is closely linked to the measurement of capital.

In general, it could be said that an entity has "maintained" its capital if it has as much capital at the end of an accounting period as it had at the start of that period. Any amount by which capital at the end of a period exceeds the amount required to maintain opening capital is profit. The *Conceptual Framework* distinguishes between two main ways of comparing an entity's capital at the beginning and end of an accounting period and so determining the profit for that period. These are as follows:

(a) **Financial capital maintenance**. Under this concept, a profit is earned only if the financial or money amount of the net assets at the end of an accounting period is greater than the financial or money amount of the net assets at the beginning of that period, after adjusting for any amounts contributed by or distributed to owners during the period. Financial capital can be measured either in nominal monetary units or in units of purchasing power, where purchasing power is determined in accordance with changes in an index of general prices.

(b) **Physical capital maintenance**. Under this concept, a profit is earned only if the physical operating capability of the entity at the end of the accounting period is greater than its physical operating capability at the start of the period, after adjusting for any amounts contributed by or distributed to owners during the period.

In practice, most entities use the concept of nominal financial capital maintenance, if only because this avoids the accounting complexities associated with the alternatives.

The *Conceptual Framework* states that an entity's choices of measurement bases and capital maintenance concept determine the accounting model used in the preparation of the financial statements. However, the IASB does not prescribe the use of any particular model, except in the special case of those entities which are reporting in the currency of a hyperinflationary economy (see Chapter 17). Instead, the *Conceptual Framework* merely points out that each model exhibits different levels of relevance and reliability and states that an entity's management should seek a balance between these characteristics when choosing an appropriate model.

EXAMPLE

At the beginning of an accounting period, a business had cash of £1m and capital of £1m. The cash was spent on acquiring inventory which was all sold during the accounting period for £1.25m. There were no other transactions.

(a) Calculate the profit for the period in nominal money terms.

(b) If the general prices index stood at 100 on the first day of the accounting period and at 110 on the last day of the period, calculate the profit for the period in terms of the general purchasing power of the business.

(c) If it would cost £1.13m at the end of the accounting period to replace the sold inventory, calculate the profit for the period in terms of the power of the business to maintain its physical operating capability.

Solution

	Financial capital maintenance (nominal)	Financial capital maintenance (purchasing power)	Physical capital maintenance
	£m	£m	£m
Assets at the end of the period	1.25	1.25	1.25
Assets required at the end of the period to be as well off as at the beginning of the period:			
(a) nominal monetary units	1.00		
(b) general purchasing power units (£1m x 110/100)		1.10	
(c) physical operating capability			1.13
Net profit for the period	0.25	0.15	0.12

Notes:

(a) In nominal monetary terms, the business is £0.25m better off at the end of the period than it was at the beginning of the period. This is the profit figure which would be shown by a conventional set of financial statements.

(b) £1.1m is needed at the end of the period to give the same general purchasing power as was given by £1m at the beginning of the period. Since the business has capital of £1.25m at the end of the period, its profit is calculated as £1.25m – £1.1m = £0.15m.

(c) £1.13m is needed at the end of the period to buy the same inventory as could be bought for £1m at the start of the period. Since the business has capital of £1.25m at the end of the period, its profit is calculated as £1.25m – £1.13m = £0.12m.

It could be argued that the conventional approach to profit measurement (maintenance of nominal financial capital) has overstated the profit figure. Even though profits are stated to be £0.25m, no more than £0.15m could be withdrawn from the business without reducing its general purchasing power and no more than £0.12m could be withdrawn without reducing the power of the business to replace its inventory and maintain its physical operating capability. If conventionally-calculated profits were withdrawn in full each year, the business would suffer depletion of its capital. This would lead to a reduction in the operating capability of the business and, in the long run, to its eventual closure.

Summary

▸ The IASB *Conceptual Framework* consists of a set of fundamental principles and definitions which underlie financial accounting. The *Conceptual Framework* is being redeveloped in a series of phases and this work is not expected to be completed until 2015 at the earliest. One of the main purposes of the *Conceptual Framework* is to assist in the development and review of international standards.

▸ The *Conceptual Framework* states that the objective of general purpose financial reporting is to provide financial information about the reporting entity that is useful to existing and potential investors, lenders and other creditors in making decisions about providing resources to the entity.

▸ The primary users of general purpose financial reports are investors, lenders and other creditors. However, other parties such as employees, customers, governments and the public might also find these reports useful.

▸ General purpose financial reports provide information about the financial position and financial performance of the reporting entity. Financial performance information should be prepared on the accruals basis but information about cash flows is also important. In addition, information should be provided about changes in an entity's financial position not resulting from its financial performance (e.g. changes caused by share issues or dividend payments).

▸ Financial information is useful if it possesses certain qualitative characteristics. The fundamental characteristics are relevance and faithful representation. The enhancing characteristics are comparability, verifiability, timeliness and understandability.

▸ Financial statements are normally prepared on the going concern basis. But if the reporting entity is not a going concern, the financial statements should be prepared on a different basis and that basis should be disclosed.

▸ The main elements of financial statements are assets, liabilities, equity, income and expenses. Each of these elements is defined in the *Conceptual Framework*.

▸ An element is recognised in the financial statements if it is probable that any economic benefits associated with the element will flow to or from the entity and if the element has a cost or value which can be reliably measured.

▸ Elements may be measured at their historical cost, current cost, realisable value or present value. The *Conceptual Framework* does not prescribe a measurement basis.

▸ Profits and losses may be measured in terms of changes in the financial amount of an entity's net assets (financial capital maintenance) or in terms of changes in the entity's physical operating capability (physical capital maintenance). Financial capital may be measured either in nominal monetary units or in units of purchasing power.

Appendix

Discounting and present value

The IASB *Conceptual Framework* states that an asset might be measured at the "present discounted value" of the future cash inflows that the asset is expected to generate. Similarly, a liability might be measured at the present discounted value of the future cash outflows that are expected to be required to settle the liability. Various international standards also refer to the concepts of discounting and present value, including:

	Chapter
IAS17 *Leases*	9
IAS18 *Revenue*	13
IAS19 *Employee Benefits*	14
IAS36 *Impairment of Assets*	7
IAS37 *Provisions, Contingent Liabilities and Contingent Assets*	12
IAS39 *Financial Instruments: Recognition and Measurement*	11
IFRS9 *Financial instruments*	11

Therefore, an understanding of present value calculations is a necessary prerequisite to a grasp of these international standards.

The concept of present value is fairly simple and is concerned with the fact that money has a "time value". For instance, if money can be invested at an interest rate of 10% per annum, each £1 invested now will grow to become £1.10 after one year, £1.21 after two years and so forth. So the current equivalent (or "present value") of £1.10 to be received in a year's time is £1. Similarly, the present value of £1.21 to be received in two years' time is also £1 (assuming interest at 10% per annum).

The process of determining the present value of an amount to be received (or paid) in the future is known as "discounting" and involves multiplying the amount concerned by a discounting factor. Discounting factors can either be calculated or looked up in a set of present value tables. In this book, discounting factors are calculated.

EXAMPLE

Determine the present values of the amounts listed below. The applicable "discounting rate" is 8% (i.e. money can be invested at an interest rate of 8% per annum).

(a) £1,000 to be received in one year's time

(b) £5,000 to be received in two years' time

(c) £20,000 to be received in three years' time.

Calculate discounting factors to three decimal places only.

Solution

(a) Since money can be invested at 8%, £1 invested now will become £1.08 after one year. So the present value of an amount to be received in one year's time is equal to that amount divided by 1.08. Dividing by 1.08 is the same as multiplying by a discounting factor of 0.926 (1/1.08). Therefore the present value of £1,000 to be received in one year's time is £926 (£1,000 x 0.926).

Check: interest at 8% on £926 is £74 and £926 + £74 = £1,000.

(b) £1 invested at 8% will become £1 x 1.08 x 1.08 after two years. So the present value of an amount to be received in two years' time is equal to that amount divided by $(1.08)^2$. This is the same as multiplying by a discounting factor of 0.857 (1/1.08^2). The present value of £5,000 to be received in two years' time is £4,285 (£5,000 x 0.857).

Check: interest at 8% on £4,285 for one year is £343, giving a total of £4,628. Interest on £4,628 for the second year is £370, giving a total of £4,998. This is not quite £5,000 because the discounting factor was rounded to three decimal places.

(c) £1 invested at 8% will become £1 x 1.08 x 1.08 x 1.08 after three years. So the present value of an amount to be received in three years' time is equal to that amount divided by $(1.08)^3$. This is the same as multiplying by a discounting factor of 0.794 (1/1.08^3). The present value of £20,000 to be received in three years' time is £15,880 (£20,000 x 0.794).

Check: interest at 8% on £15,880 for one year is £1,270, giving a total of £17,150. Interest on £17,150 for the second year is £1,372, giving a total of £18,522. Interest on £18,522 for the third year is £1,482, giving a total of £20,004. There is a rounding difference of £4.

Exercises

2.1   Explain what is meant by a "conceptual framework" for financial reporting and list the main purposes of the IASB *Conceptual Framework for Financial Reporting*.

2.2   (a)   State the objective of general purpose financial reporting.

           (b)   Identify the primary users of general purpose financial reports and any other parties who might find these reports useful. Explain why each user group might be interested in the information provided in general purpose financial reports.

2.3   Identify the main classes of information that should be presented in general purpose financial reports.

2.4   Identify and explain the qualitative characteristics of useful financial information, distinguishing between fundamental characteristics and enhancing characteristics.

2.5   Define each of the five elements of financial statements. Also explain the circumstances in which an element should be recognised in the financial statements.

2.6   The *Conceptual Framework* states that an entity's choices of measurement bases and capital maintenance concept determine the accounting model used in the preparation of the financial statements.

           (a)   Explain the measurement bases identified in the *Conceptual Framework*.

           (b)   Explain the capital maintenance concepts identified in the *Conceptual Framework*.

2.7   The qualitative characteristics of relevance, faithful representation and comparability which are identified in the IASB *Conceptual Framework* are some of the attributes that make financial information useful to the various users of financial statements.

           Explain what is meant by relevance, faithful representation and comparability and how they make financial information useful.   *(ACCA)*

*2.8   Assuming that today's date is 1 January 2014, calculate the present value of each of the following:

           (a)   £50,000 to be received on 1 January 2017

           (b)   £100,000 to be received on 1 January 2019

           (c)   £10,000 to be received on I January each year from 2015 to 2018 inclusive.

           Use a discount rate of 7% in each case.

*2.9   The main role of the International Accounting Standards Board (IASB) is to devise and publish International Financial Reporting Standards (IFRSs) and revised versions of International Accounting Standards (IASs). IASs were originally published by the IASB's predecessor body, the International Accounting Standards Committee (IASC).

The IASB has also published a *Conceptual Framework for Financial Reporting*. Some of the text of this document has been transferred from the *Framework for the Preparation and Presentation of Financial Statements* published by the IASC in 1989 and adopted by the IASB in 2001. This document is not an accounting standard.

Required:

(a)   Explain the main purposes of the *Conceptual Framework* document.

(b)   Identify the objective of general purpose financial reporting, as stated in the *Conceptual Framework*.

(c)   Identify the primary users of general purpose financial reports and four further user groups. In each case, explain what information each user group would be seeking from the financial reports.

(d)   Identify and explain the assumption which (according to the *Conceptual Framework*) underlies the preparation of financial statements.

(e)   Identify and explain the qualitative characteristics that make financial information useful.

(f)   Explain why it is not always possible to produce financial statements which possess all of the qualitative characteristics discussed in (e) above.

(CIPFA)

Chapter 3

Presentation of financial statements

Introduction

The main purpose of this chapter is to explain the requirements of international standard IAS1 *Presentation of Financial Statements*. The objective of IAS1 is to specify the overall structure and content of general purpose financial statements and so ensure that an entity's financial statements for a reporting period are comparable with those of other periods and with those of other entities. The standard sets out:

(a) the general features of financial statements

(b) guidelines with regard to their structure, and

(c) minimum requirements for their content.

This chapter also outlines the main requirements of international standard IAS34 *Interim Financial Reporting* and summarises the guidance provided by the IASB to entities that include a "management commentary" in their annual report.

Objectives

By the end of this chapter, the reader should be able to:

* identify the components of a complete set of financial statements

* explain the general features of a set of financial statements

* explain the structure and content of each component of a set of financial statements

* distinguish between current and non-current assets and between current and non-current liabilities

* prepare a statement of financial position, a statement of comprehensive income and a statement of changes in equity, in accordance with the requirements of IAS1

* outline the main requirements of international standard IAS34

* summarise the guidance provided by IFRS Practice Statement *Management Commentary*.

Purpose of financial statements

The requirements of IAS1 apply to all general purpose financial statements prepared and presented in accordance with international standards. General purpose financial statements are those intended for users who are not in a position to demand reports that are tailored for their own particular information needs.

According to IAS1, the objective of such financial statements is "*to provide information about the financial position, financial performance and cash flows of an entity that is useful to a wide range of users in making economic decisions*". To meet this objective, general purpose financial statements should provide information about an entity's:

(a)   assets, liabilities and equity

(b)   income and expenses, including gains and losses

(c)   contributions by and distributions to owners in their capacity as owners

(d)   cash flows.

This information is given in four primary financial statements. Further information is given in the notes which accompany these statements.

Components of financial statements

IAS1 states that a complete set of financial statements comprises:

(a)   a statement of financial position as at the end of the accounting period

(b)   a statement of profit or loss and other comprehensive income for the period

(c)   a statement of changes in equity for the period

(d)   a statement of cash flows for the period

(e)   a set of notes, which provide a summary of the entity's significant accounting policies together with other explanatory information

(f)   comparative information in respect of the previous period (see later in this chapter)

(g)   a statement of financial position as at the *beginning* of the previous period, in the case that the entity has applied an accounting policy retrospectively or has made a retrospective restatement of items in its financial statements (see Chapter 4).

These titles have replaced the more traditional titles used in previous versions of IAS1 (e.g. "balance sheet") and are thought by the IASB to reflect more closely the function of each statement. However, entities are allowed to use titles for the financial statements other than those used in the standard if they so wish. In particular, IAS1 states that an entity may use the title "statement of comprehensive income" rather than "statement of profit or loss and other comprehensive income". For the sake of brevity, this is the practice adopted throughout this textbook.

The structure and content of most of these statements is specified in IAS1. But the statement of cash flows is dealt with by IAS7 *Statement of Cash Flows* (see Chapter 16). The notes which accompany the four primary statements are an integral part of the financial statements and so fall within the scope of IAS1 and all other international standards.

In addition to the financial statements, IAS1 recognises that an entity's annual report may contain a management review which explains the main features of the entity's financial position and performance. Such a review is outside the scope of international standards but the IASB has issued a non-binding Practice Statement to assist entities that wish to include a "management commentary" in their annual reports (see later in this chapter).

General features

Under the heading "general features", IAS1 sets out a number of general rules which relate to the presentation of financial statements. Many of these are clearly based upon principles established in the *Conceptual Framework* (see Chapter 2). The main areas dealt with in this part of IAS1 are:

(a) fair presentation and compliance with international standards

(b) going concern basis and accrual basis

(c) materiality and aggregation

(d) offsetting

(e) frequency of reporting

(f) comparative information

(g) consistency of presentation.

Each of these is considered below.

Fair presentation and compliance with international standards

Financial statements must present fairly the financial position, financial performance and cash flows of the entity concerned. This requires that the effects of transactions and other events should be faithfully represented in accordance with the definitions and recognition criteria for assets, liabilities, income and expenses set out in the *Conceptual Framework*. It is assumed that the application of international standards will result in financial statements that achieve a fair presentation. An entity which produces financial statements that comply with international standards must make an explicit and unreserved statement to that effect in the notes. A fair presentation also requires the entity to:

(a) select and apply appropriate accounting policies in accordance with the requirements of international standard IAS8 (see Chapter 4)

(b) provide information that is relevant, reliable, comparable and understandable

(c) provide further disclosures if compliance with international standards is insufficient to enable users to understand the impact of transactions and other events.

On very rare occasions, compliance with a requirement in an international standard may produce misleading information and so conflict with the objective of financial statements. In these circumstances, the entity should depart from that requirement and the notes should disclose that the entity has complied with international standards except that it has departed from a particular requirement in order to achieve a fair presentation. The notes should identify the title of the standard concerned, the nature of the departure, the reason for the departure, the accounting treatment that the standard would have required, the accounting treatment actually adopted and the financial impact of the departure.

Going concern basis and accrual basis

Financial statements should be prepared on the going concern basis (see Chapter 2) unless the entity intends to cease trading or has no realistic alternative but to do so. If there are significant doubts concerning the entity's ability to continue as a going concern, the uncertainties which give rise to these doubts should be disclosed. If financial statements are *not* prepared on a going concern basis, that fact should be disclosed, together with the basis on which the financial statements are prepared and the reasons for which the entity is not regarded as a going concern.

Financial statements other than the statement of cash flows should also be prepared using the accrual basis of accounting (see Chapter 2). The statement of cash flows is an obvious exception to this rule since, by definition, it is prepared on a cash basis (see Chapter 16).

Materiality and aggregation

IAS1 defines materiality by stating that "*omissions or mis-statements of items are material if they could, individually or collectively, influence the economic decisions that users make on the basis of the financial statements*". IAS1 further states that materiality should be judged in context and that either the size or nature of an item, or a combination of both, could determine whether or not the item is material.

In general, financial statements are prepared by analysing transactions and other events into classes and then aggregating (i.e. totalling) each of these classes to produce line items which appear in the statements. For instance, all sales transactions are aggregated into a single revenue figure shown in the statement of comprehensive income. IAS1 requires that each material class of similar items should be presented separately in the financial statements. If an item is not individually material, it may be aggregated with other line items.

IAS1 explicitly states that there is no need to satisfy the disclosure requirements of an international standard if the information disclosed would not be material. This means that compliance with the standards can be achieved without having to disclose immaterial items, whether in the primary financial statements or in the accompanying notes.

Offsetting

In general, assets and liabilities should be reported separately in the statement of financial position and should not be offset against one another. Similarly, income and expenses should be reported separately in the statement of comprehensive income. IAS1 takes the view that offsetting should not be allowed, since this would normally detract from users' ability to understand transactions and other events.

However, this general rule does not apply in a specific instance if another international standard permits or requires offsetting in that instance.

Frequency of reporting

Financial statements should normally be presented at least annually. If an entity changes its accounting date and so presents a set of financial statements for a period which is longer or shorter than one year, the entity should disclose:

(a) the reason for using a period that is longer or shorter than one year

(b) the fact that the comparative amounts given for the previous period are not directly comparable with those given for the current period.

Comparative information

Unless another international standard permits or requires otherwise, IAS1 requires that entities should present (as a minimum) comparative information in respect of the previous period for all amounts reported in the financial statements. Comparatives should also be given for narrative information if this would be relevant to an understanding of the current period's financial statements.

Consistency of presentation

In order to maintain comparability, the way in which items are presented and classified in the financial statements should generally be consistent from one accounting period to the next. However, this rule does not apply if:

(a) it is apparent that a different presentation or classification would be more appropriate, following either a significant change in the nature of the entity's operations or a review of its financial statements

(b) a different presentation or classification is required by an international standard.

Structure and content of financial statements

The majority of IAS1 is concerned with the structure and content of an entity's financial statements. The standard requires that certain items should be shown in the statement of financial position, the statement of comprehensive income and the statement of changes in equity. Other items should be shown either in these statements or in the notes. IAS1 does not deal with the statement of cash flows, since this is the subject of IAS7 *Statement of Cash Flows* (see Chapter 16). The main headings in this part of IAS1 are:

(a) identification of the financial statements

(b) the statement of financial position

(c)   the statement of profit or loss and other comprehensive income

(d)   the statement of changes in equity

(e)   the notes.

Each of these is considered below.

Identification of the financial statements

The first point made in this part of IAS1 is that the financial statements should be clearly identified as such and distinguished from any other information which may be given in the same published document (e.g. a management review). Since international standards apply only to the financial statements, it is important that users can distinguish information that has been prepared in accordance with standards from information that has not.

Furthermore, each component of the financial statements should be clearly identified and the following information should be displayed prominently and repeated where necessary for a proper understanding of the information presented:

(a)   the name of the reporting entity

(b)   whether the financial statements are for a single entity or a group (see Chapter 18)

(c)   the date of the end of the reporting period or the period covered by the set of financial statements or notes

(d)   the presentation currency used

(e)   the level of rounding used (e.g. £000 or £m).

The statement of financial position

A statement of financial position (formerly referred to as a balance sheet) shows an entity's assets, liabilities and equity.

An important requirement of IAS1 with regard to the statement of financial position is that current and non-current assets should be presented separately and that current and non-current liabilities should also be presented separately. For an entity which supplies goods or services within a clearly identifiable operating cycle, this separation provides useful information by:

(a)   distinguishing the net assets that are continuously circulating as working capital from those used in the long-term, and

(b)   highlighting the assets that are expected to be realised within the current operating cycle and the liabilities that are due for settlement within the same period.

IAS1 establishes a set of criteria which should be used to distinguish between current and non-current assets and another set of criteria which should be used to distinguish between current and non-current liabilities.

Current and non-current assets

An asset is classified as a current asset if it satisfies *any* of the following criteria:

(a) it is expected to be realised, or is intended for sale or consumption, within the entity's normal operating cycle

(b) it is held primarily for the purpose of being traded

(c) it is expected to be realised within twelve months after the reporting period

(d) it is cash or a cash equivalent as defined by standard IAS7 (see Chapter 16) unless it is restricted from being exchanged or from being used to settle a liability for at least twelve months after the reporting period.

An asset that satisfies none of these criteria is a non-current asset. The operating cycle of an entity is defined as "*the time between the acquisition of assets for processing and their realisation in cash or cash equivalents*". If an entity's normal operating cycle cannot be clearly identified, it is assumed to be twelve months. Note that current assets include items such as inventories and trade receivables that are expected to be realised during the normal operating cycle, even if they are not expected to be realised within twelve months.

  IAS1 does not require the use of the terms "current" and "non-current" and other descriptions could be used so long as their meaning is clear. However, these terms are used extensively in practice.

Current and non-current liabilities

A liability is classified as a current liability if it satisfies *any* of the following criteria:

(a) it is expected to be settled in the entity's normal operating cycle

(b) it is held primarily for the purpose of being traded

(c) it is due to be settled within twelve months after the reporting period

(d) the entity does not have an unconditional right to defer settlement of the liability for at least twelve months after the reporting period.

A liability that satisfies none of these criteria is a non-current liability. Current liabilities include items such as trade payables and accrued expenses that are expected to be settled during the normal operating cycle, even if they are not expected to be settled within twelve months. Current liabilities also include items such as bank overdrafts, dividends payable and taxes which are not settled as part of the normal operating cycle but which are due to be settled within twelve months.

Information to be presented in the statement of financial position

IAS1 does not specify any particular format for the statement of financial position. Nor does it prescribe the order in which items should be shown. But the standard does provide a minimum list of line items that should be presented separately in the statement if their size or nature is such that separate presentation is relevant to an understanding of the entity's financial position. Additional line items, headings and subtotals should also be presented where relevant. The main line items listed by IAS1 are as follows:

		Chapter of this book
(a)	property, plant and equipment	5
(b)	investment property	5
(c)	intangible assets	6
(d)	financial assets	11
(e)	investments accounted for by the equity method	20
(f)	inventories	10
(g)	trade and other receivables	11
(h)	cash and cash equivalents	16
(i)	assets classified as "held for sale"	8
(j)	trade and other payables	11
(k)	provisions	12
(l)	financial liabilities	11
(m)	current tax assets and liabilities	15
(n)	deferred tax assets and liabilities	15
(o)	liabilities included in disposal groups held for sale	8
(p)	non-controlling interests	18
(q)	issued equity capital and reserves	11

The order of the items and the descriptions used may be amended in accordance with the nature of the entity and its transactions, so as to provide relevant information. As indicated above, each of these items is addressed in later chapters of this book. Item (p) will arise only if the entity is a member of a group.

Format of the statement of financial position

Although IAS1 does not prescribe a format for the statement of financial position, the implementation guidance that accompanies the standard includes an illustration which shows one way in which the statement may be presented. A slightly simplified version of this illustration is shown in Figure 3.1 below. This illustrative format is not prescriptive and other formats may be used if appropriate.

XYZ plc - Statement of financial position as at 31 December 2013

	2013 £000	2012 £000
ASSETS		
Non-current assets		
Property, plant and equipment	xxx	xxx
Intangible assets	xxx	xxx
Investments	xxx	xxx
	xxx	xxx
Current assets		
Inventories	xxx	xxx
Trade receivables	xxx	xxx
Cash and cash equivalents	xxx	xxx
	xxx	xxx
Total assets	xxx	xxx
EQUITY AND LIABILITIES		
Equity		
Share capital	xxx	xxx
Retained earnings	xxx	xxx
Other reserves	xxx	xxx
Total equity	xxx	xxx
Non-current liabilities		
Long-term borrowings	xxx	xxx
Deferred tax	xxx	xxx
Long-term provisions	xxx	xxx
Total non-current liabilities	xxx	xxx
Current liabilities		
Trade and other payables	xxx	xxx
Short-term borrowings	xxx	xxx
Current tax payable	xxx	xxx
Short-term provisions	xxx	xxx
Total current liabilities	xxx	xxx
Total liabilities	xxx	xxx
Total equity and liabilities	xxx	xxx

Figure 3.1 Illustrative format of the statement of financial position

Information in the statement of financial position or in the notes

IAS1 requires that the line items presented in the statement of financial position should be analysed into sub-classifications, either in the statement itself or in the notes. These sub-classifications should be appropriate to the entity but also depend to some extent on the requirements of other international standards. For instance, property, plant and equipment is analysed in accordance with IAS16 *Property, Plant and Equipment* (see Chapter 5) and inventories are analysed in accordance with IAS2 *Inventories* (see Chapter 10).

IAS1 also requires further disclosures with regard to share capital and reserves. These disclosures may be given in the statement of financial position or the statement of changes in equity, or in the notes. The disclosures include:

(a) for each class of share capital:

 (i)   the number of shares authorised and the par value per share

 (ii) the number of shares issued and fully paid, and issued but not fully paid

 (iii) a reconciliation of the number of shares outstanding at the beginning and end of the accounting period

 (iv) the rights, preferences and restrictions attaching to that class of shares

(b) a description of the nature and purpose of each reserve.

The statement of comprehensive income

The statement of comprehensive income is a financial statement which shows an entity's income and expenses for the reporting period and summarises its financial performance for that period. As mentioned earlier in this chapter, IAS1 refers to this financial statement as the "statement of profit or loss and other comprehensive income". However, entities are permitted to use alternative titles for the financial statements if they so wish and the shorter title "statement of comprehensive income" is used throughout this book.

Most types of income and expenses are taken into account when calculating an entity's profit or loss for a reporting period. However, international standards require that certain classes of income or expense should be disregarded when calculating profit or loss and should instead be presented in the statement of comprehensive income under the heading "other comprehensive income". For instance:

(a) IAS16 *Property, Plant and Equipment* generally requires that surpluses arising on the revaluation of tangible non-current assets should be presented as other comprehensive income (see Chapter 5).

(b) IAS38 *Intangible Assets* makes a similar requirement in relation to surpluses arising on the revaluation of intangible assets (see Chapter 6).

Despite its name, "other comprehensive income" can include expenses as well as income and can therefore be negative.

Structure of the statement of comprehensive income

IAS1 requires that all items of income or expense that are recognised in an accounting period should be presented in *either*:

(a) a single statement of comprehensive income (with an "other comprehensive income" section following the calculation of profit or loss for the period), or

(b) two separate statements, comprising:

    (i)   a statement which shows the entity's profit or loss, and

    (ii) a second statement which begins with the profit or loss for the period and shows the entity's other comprehensive income.

In either case, the entity must present figures showing its profit or loss, the total of its other comprehensive income (if any) and its "total comprehensive income" for the period, which is equal to the sum of its profit or loss and its other comprehensive income.

Information presented in the statement of comprehensive income

As with the statement of financial position, IAS1 does not prescribe a specific format for the statement of comprehensive income. Instead, the standard provides a minimum list of line items that should be presented separately in this statement. Additional line items, headings and subtotals should be presented where relevant. The main items listed by IAS1 are as follows:

		Chapter of this book
(a)	revenue	13
(b)	finance costs	9,11
(c)	profits or losses accounted for by the equity method	20
(d)	tax expense	15
(e)	a single amount for the total of discontinued operations	8
(f)	each class of other comprehensive income	5,6,11,14,21

The order of the items and the descriptions used may be amended where this is necessary to explain the entity's financial performance. An important further requirement of IAS1 is that an entity should *not* present any items of income or expense as "extraordinary" items, either in the statement of comprehensive income or in the notes.

Classification of other comprehensive income

IAS1 requires that an entity's other comprehensive income (see above) should be presented in two categories. These are:

(a) items of other comprehensive income which, if certain conditions are satisfied, will be "reclassified to profit or loss" in a subsequent reporting period (i.e. they will take part in the calculation of the profit or loss for that period)

(b) items of other comprehensive income which will not be reclassified to profit or loss.

Items that may be reclassified to profit or loss are few and tend to be rather technical in nature (e.g. certain foreign exchange differences). The only items of other comprehensive income that will occur in practical exercises in this book are items which cannot be reclassified to profit or loss (e.g. revaluation surpluses).

Groups of companies

If the financial statements are for a group of companies, the statement of comprehensive income must also disclose:

(a) the amount of the profit or loss for the period which is attributable to non-controlling interests and the amount which is attributable to the owners of the parent company

(b) the amount of the total comprehensive income for the period which is attributable to non-controlling interests and the amount which is attributable to the owners of the parent company.

The financial statements of groups of companies and the meaning of terms such as "non-controlling interest" are explained in Chapters 18 and 19 of this book.

Information in the statement of comprehensive income or in the notes

In addition to the items which must be presented in the statement of comprehensive income, further items of income and expense should be disclosed separately (either in the statement itself or in the notes) if material. The entity must also present an analysis of expenses using a classification based on either:

(a) the nature of the expenses, or

(b) the function of the expenses within the entity.

Entities are encouraged to present this analysis in the statement of comprehensive income but it may be presented instead in the notes which accompany the financial statements. An analysis which is based on the nature of the expenses might include headings such as depreciation, employee benefits, motor expenses etc. An analysis based on function would normally classify expenses into cost of sales, distribution costs and administrative expenses. An entity which analyses expenses by function must also provide additional information on the nature of expenses, including depreciation and employee benefits.

Format of the statement of comprehensive income

The implementation guidance which accompanies IAS1 provides two illustrations of the statement of comprehensive income. One of these shows a single statement with expenses analysed by function and the other shows two separate statements with expenses analysed by nature. Simplified versions of these illustrations are shown in Figures 3.2a, 3.2b and 3.2c below. As with the statement of financial position, IAS1 makes it clear that these formats are only illustrations and that other formats may be used if appropriate.

XYZ plc - Statement of comprehensive income for year to 31 December 2013

	2013	2012
	£000	£000
Revenue	xxx	xxx
Cost of sales	(xxx)	(xxx)
Gross profit	xxx	xxx
Other income	xxx	xxx
Distribution costs	(xxx)	(xxx)
Administrative expenses	(xxx)	(xxx)
Other expenses	(xxx)	(xxx)
Finance costs	(xxx)	(xxx)
Profit before tax	xxx	xxx
Tax expense	(xxx)	(xxx)
PROFIT FOR THE YEAR	xxx	xxx
Other comprehensive income:		
***Items that will not be reclassified to profit or loss*:**		
Gains on property revaluation	xxx	xxx
Investments in equity instruments	xxx	xxx
Tax relating to items that will not be reclassified	(xxx)	(xxx)
Other comprehensive income for the year net of tax	xxx	xxx
TOTAL COMPREHENSIVE INCOME FOR THE YEAR	xxx	xxx

Figure 3.2a Single statement of comprehensive income (expenses analysed by function)

XYZ plc - Statement of profit or loss for year to 31 December 2013

	2013	2012
	£000	£000
Revenue	xxx	xxx
Other income	xxx	xxx
Changes in inventories of finished goods and WIP	(xxx)	(xxx)
Raw material and consumables used	(xxx)	(xxx)
Employee benefits expense	(xxx)	(xxx)
Depreciation and amortisation expense	(xxx)	(xxx)
Impairment of property, plant and equipment	(xxx)	(xxx)
Other expenses	(xxx)	(xxx)
Finance costs	(xxx)	(xxx)
Profit before tax	xxx	xxx
Tax expense	(xxx)	(xxx)
PROFIT FOR THE YEAR	xxx	xxx

Figure 3.2b Separate statement of profit or loss (expenses analysed by nature)

XYZ plc - Statement of comprehensive income for year to 31 December 2013

	2013	2012
	£000	£000
Profit for the year	xxx	xxx
Other comprehensive income:		
Items that will not be reclassified to profit or loss:		
Gains on property revaluation	xxx	xxx
Investments in equity instruments	xxx	xxx
Tax relating to items that will not be reclassified	(xxx)	(xxx)
Other comprehensive income for the year net of tax	xxx	xxx
TOTAL COMPREHENSIVE INCOME FOR THE YEAR	xxx	xxx

Figure 3.2c Separate statement of comprehensive income

The statement of changes in equity

A statement of changes in equity shows how each component of equity has changed during an accounting period. In the case of a company, the components of equity will be share capital and each of the company's reserves. IAS1 requires that the following items are presented in the statement of changes in equity:

(a) total comprehensive income for the period

(b) for each component of equity, the effects of any retrospective application of an accounting policy or retrospective restatement of items, in accordance with international standard IAS8 (see Chapter 4)

(c) for each component of equity, a reconciliation of the opening and closing balance of that component, separately disclosing changes resulting from:

   (i)   profit or loss

   (ii) other comprehensive income

   (iii) transactions with the owners of the entity, separately showing distributions to owners (e.g. dividends) and contributions by owners (e.g. share issues).

Further information must be provided either in the statement of changes in equity or in the notes. This information consists of:

(d) for each component of equity, an analysis of other comprehensive income by item

(e) the amount of dividends per share.

The implementation guidance to IAS1 provides an illustration of the statement of changes in equity. An amended version of this illustration is shown in Figure 3.3.

XYZ plc - Statement of changes in equity for the year to 31 December 2013

	Share capital £000	Retained earnings £000	Revaluation reserve £000	Total equity £000
Balance at 31 December 2011	xxx	xxx	xxx	xxx
Changes in equity for 2012				
Total comprehensive income		xxx		xxx
Dividends		(xxx)		(xxx)
Balance at 31 December 2012	xxx	xxx	xxx	xxx
Balance at 31 December 2012	xxx	xxx	xxx	xxx
Changes in equity for 2013				
Changes in accounting policy		xxx		xxx
Restated balance	xxx	xxx	xxx	xxx
Issue of share capital	xxx			xxx
Total comprehensive income		xxx	xxx	xxx
Dividends		(xxx)		(xxx)
Balance at 31 December 2013	xxx	xxx	xxx	xxx

Figure 3.3 Statement of changes in equity

Tutorial notes:

(a) This statement of changes in equity is for the year to 31 December 2013. The first few lines of the statement show comparative figures for 2012.

(b) In the year to 31 December 2012, the company's retained earnings were increased by the profit for the year but reduced by dividends paid to shareholders. There were no other changes in equity.

(c) The company changed an accounting policy in the year to 31 December 2013 and this necessitated an adjustment to retained earnings brought forward (see Chapter 4). Other changes in equity during 2013 were as follows:

   (i)   Share capital increased because of a share issue during the year.

   (ii) Retained earnings were increased by the profit for the year but were reduced by dividends paid to shareholders.

   (iii) The revaluation reserve increased (presumably because there was a revaluation gain during the year). This gain would have been presented in the statement of comprehensive income as "other comprehensive income".

The notes to the financial statements

As mentioned earlier in this chapter, the notes which accompany the statement of financial position, the statement of comprehensive income, the statement of cash flows and the statement of changes in equity are an integral part of the financial statements and so fall within the scope of international standards. IAS1 states that the notes should:

(a) present information about the basis of preparation of the financial statements and the accounting policies which have been used, including:

– the measurement bases used in preparing the financial statements
– other accounting policies relevant to an understanding of the financial statements

(b) disclose information required by international standards, to the extent that this is not presented elsewhere in the financial statements

(c) provide any additional information which is relevant to an understanding of any of the financial statements.

The notes should be presented in a systematic manner and should be cross-referenced to the four primary financial statements. The notes normally begin with a statement of compliance with international standards. There should then be a summary of significant accounting policies, followed by supporting information for line items presented in the four primary statements and further disclosures as necessary.

Sources of estimation uncertainty

When determining the amount at which assets or liabilities should be shown or "carried" in the financial statements, it may be necessary to estimate the effects of uncertain future events (such as technological change) and make assumptions. If there is a significant risk that these uncertain future events may cause a material adjustment to the carrying amount of assets or liabilities within the next financial year, IAS1 requires that the notes to the financial statements should explain the key sources of estimation uncertainty and disclose the assumptions that have been made.

Other disclosures

Other disclosures required in the notes include:

(a) the amount of any dividends proposed or declared before the financial statements were authorised for issue but not recognised during the period (see Chapter 12)

(b) the amount of any unrecognised cumulative preference dividends

(c) unless disclosed elsewhere, the entity's domicile and legal form, its country of incorporation, the address of its registered office and the nature of its operations.

If an entity is a subsidiary (see Chapter 18) it should disclose the name of its parent and the name of the ultimate parent of the group.

Interim financial reporting

IAS34 *Interim Financial Reporting* applies if an entity publishes an interim financial report that is stated to comply with international standards. An interim financial report is defined by IAS34 as "*a financial report containing either a complete set of financial statements ... or a set of condensed financial statements ... for an interim period*". An interim period is a period which is less than a full financial year.

The standards do not actually require entities to publish interim financial reports. But some entities whose shares are publicly traded might be required to do so by governments or stock exchanges. Other entities might do so voluntarily. In these cases, interim financial reports might be presented half-yearly or quarterly in addition to the main annual report. Interim financial reports that are stated to comply with international standards must satisfy the requirements of IAS34. A brief summary of these requirements is as follows:

(a) An interim financial report may consist of a complete set of financial statements as prescribed by IAS1. Alternatively, an entity may provide a condensed set of financial statements consisting of:

   – a condensed statement of financial position

   – a condensed statement of comprehensive income

   – a condensed statement of changes in equity

   – a condensed statement of cash flows

   – selected explanatory notes.

   These condensed financial statements should include, at a minimum, each of the headings and subtotals that were included in the entity's most recent annual financial statements. Additional items should be presented if their omission would make the condensed statements misleading. Unfortunately, the term "headings and subtotals" is not defined in IAS34 and so is open to interpretation. In practice, condensed financial statements tend to follow the same format as complete financial statements, so that the "condensed" nature of the statements is confined largely to the notes.

(b) Basic and diluted earnings per share figures (see Chapter 23) should be presented in the statement of comprehensive income, whether complete or condensed.

(c) The explanatory notes should include an explanation of any events or transactions that are significant to an understanding of changes in the entity's financial position or performance since the end of the last annual reporting period.

   Further explanatory notes which should be provided (if the information concerned is not disclosed elsewhere in the interim report) include:

   – a statement that the same accounting policies have been used in the interim financial statements as in the most recent annual statements, or a description of the nature and effect of any changes in policy

   – explanatory comments about the seasonality of the entity's operations

   – the nature and amount of any unusual items

- – the nature and amount of any changes made to estimates from previous periods
- – issues and repayments of debt securities (e.g. loan stock) or shares
- – dividends paid
- – certain segment information (see Chapter 24)
- – events after the interim period that have not been reflected in the interim financial statements
- – any changes to the composition of the entity during the interim period, including business combinations (see Chapter 18).

(d) The same accounting policies should be applied in the interim financial statements as in the annual financial statements, except for changes in accounting policy which are made after the most recent annual statements and which will be reflected in the next annual statements.

Management commentary

IFRS Practice Statement *Management Commentary* has been issued by the IASB to assist entities that wish to include a "management commentary" in their annual report. Such a commentary falls outside the scope of international standards and the Practice Statement is not itself a standard. However, the Statement provides a broad, non-binding framework for the presentation of a management commentary relating to financial statements prepared in accordance with international standards.

A management commentary is a narrative report which provides users with explanations of the amounts presented in the financial statements. It also provides commentary on the entity's future prospects. This information should help users to assess the performance of the entity and the actions of its management. A very brief summary of the guidance given in the Practice Statement is as follows:

(a) A management commentary should be clearly identified and distinguished from other information (e.g. the financial statements). The extent to which the Practice Statement has been followed should be explained. An assertion that a management commentary complies with the Practice Statement can be made only if it is complied with in full.

(b) A management commentary should provide a context for the financial statements. It should give management's view of what has happened, why it has happened and the implications for the future. It should also explain the main trends and factors that are likely to affect the entity's performance, position and progress in the future.

(c) The commentary should include forward-looking information that sets out management's objectives for the entity and strategies for achieving those objectives.

(d) A management commentary should also include information that is essential to an understanding of:

   (i)   the nature of the business

   (ii) the entity's most significant resources, risks and relationships

   (iii) the critical performance measures and indicators that are used by management to evaluate the entity's performance against its stated objectives.

(e) A management commentary should be clear and straightforward. The information provided should possess the qualitative characteristics described in the *Conceptual Framework* (see Chapter 2).

Summary

▶   A complete set of financial statements consists of a statement of financial position, a statement of comprehensive income, a statement of changes in equity, a statement of cash flows and a set of notes.

▶   The effects of transactions and other items should be faithfully represented in the financial statements. The application of international standards will normally ensure that this is the case.

▶   Financial statements should be prepared on the going concern basis (unless this does not apply) and on the accruals basis.

▶   The way in which items are presented and classified in the financial statements should generally be consistent from one accounting period to the next. Comparative information should normally be disclosed in respect of the previous period for all amounts reported in the financial statements.

▶   Financial statements should be clearly identified as such and each statement should be clearly labelled. Financial statements should normally be presented at least annually.

▶   IAS1 does not require any particular format for the financial statements but does provide some illustrative examples.

▶   In general, current and non-current assets and current and non-current liabilities should be shown separately in the statement of financial position. IAS1 defines the term "current" and "non-current" in each case.

▶   IAS1 lists the main line items that should be presented in the statement of financial position. The standard also lists further disclosures that should be made in the statement of financial position or in the notes.

▶   IAS1 also lists the main line items that should be presented in the statement of comprehensive income and requires an analysis of expenses (by nature or by function) to be shown in the statement itself or in the notes.

▸ The statement of changes in equity shows the changes in each component of equity during an accounting period. The statement shows total comprehensive income for the period and discloses transactions between the entity and its owners.

▸ The notes to the financial statements are within the scope of international standards. They provide information about measurement bases and accounting policies, together with supporting information for line items in the main financial statements and further information which is required by international standards or which is relevant to an understanding of the financial statements.

▸ International standard IAS34 prescribes the minimum content of an interim financial report (if one is published) but does not require entities to publish such a report.

▸ IFRS Practice Statement *Management Commentary* provides a broad, non-binding framework for the presentation of a management commentary relating to financial statements prepared in accordance with international standards.

Exercises

3.1 International standard IAS1 lists seven "general features" relating to the presentation of financial statements. These are:

(a) fair presentation and compliance with international standards

(b) going concern basis and accrual basis

(c) materiality and aggregation

(d) offsetting

(e) frequency of reporting

(f) comparative information

(g) consistency of presentation.

Explain the main requirements of IAS1 in relation to each of these considerations.

3.2 (a) Distinguish between current assets and non-current assets.

(b) Distinguish between current liabilities and non-current liabilities.

(c) Explain why these distinctions are useful.

3.3 Explain the purpose of a statement of changes in equity and list the main items that should be shown in this statement.

3.4   You have been asked to help prepare the financial statements of Tanhosier Ltd for the year ended 31 March 2014. A trial balance as at 31 March 2014 is shown below.

	£000	£000
Sales		50,332
Purchases	29,778	
Property, plant and equipment - cost	59,088	
Property, plant and equipment - accumulated depreciation		25,486
Inventories as at 1 April 2013	7,865	
Interest	200	
Accruals		426
Distribution costs	8,985	
Administrative expenses	7,039	
Retained earnings		23,457
Trade receivables	9,045	
Cash at bank	182	
8% bank loan repayable 2017		5,000
Share capital		10,000
Share premium		5,000
Trade payables		2,481
	122,182	122,182

The following further information is available:

(i)   The share capital of the company consists of ordinary shares with a nominal value of £1 each.

(ii)   No dividends are to be paid for the current year.

(iii)   The sales figure in the trial balance includes sales made on credit for April 2014 amounting to £3,147,000.

(iv)   The inventories at the close of business on 31 March 2014 cost £8,407,000. Included in this figure are inventories that cost £480,000, but which can be sold for only £180,000.

(v)   Transport costs of £157,000 relating to March 2014 are not included in the trial balance as the invoice was received after the year end.

(vi)   Interest on the bank loan for the last six months of the year has not been included in the trial balance.

(vii)   The corporation tax charge for the year has been calculated as £235,000.

Draft the statement of comprehensive income of Tanhosier Ltd for the year to 31 March 2014 and a statement of financial position at that date.   *(Amended from AAT)*

3.5   List the main types of information which should be provided in the notes which accompany and form an integral part of the financial statements.

3.6 The following trial balance has been extracted from the books of Walrus plc as at 31 March 2014:

	£000	£000
Land, at cost	120	
Buildings, at cost	250	
Equipment, at cost	196	
Vehicles, at cost	284	
Goodwill, at cost	300	
Accumulated depreciation at 1 April 2013:		
Buildings		90
Equipment		76
Vehicles		132
Inventory at 1 April 2013	107	
Trade receivables and payables	183	117
Allowance for receivables		8
Bank balance		57
Corporation tax		6
Ordinary shares of £1 each		200
Retained earnings at 1 April 2013		503
Sales		1,432
Purchases	488	
Directors' fees	150	
Wages and salaries	276	
General distribution costs	101	
General administrative expenses	186	
Dividend paid	20	
Rents received		30
Disposal of vehicle		10
	2,661	2,661

The following information is also available:

1. The company's non-depreciable land was valued at £300,000 on 31 March 2014 and this valuation is to be incorporated into the accounts for the year to 31 March 2014.

2. The company's depreciation policy is as follows:

Buildings	4% p.a. straight line
Equipment	40% p.a. reducing balance
Vehicles	25% p.a. straight line

   In all cases, a full year's depreciation is charged in the year of acquisition and no depreciation is charged in the year of disposal. None of the assets had been fully depreciated by 31 March 2013.

3. On 1 February 2014, a vehicle used entirely for administrative purposes was sold for £10,000. The sale proceeds were banked and credited to a disposal account but no other entries were made in relation to this disposal. The vehicle had cost £44,000 in August 2010. This was the only disposal of a non-current asset made during the year to 31 March 2014.

4. Depreciation is apportioned as follows:

	Distribution costs	Administrative expenses
Buildings	50%	50%
Equipment	25%	75%
Vehicles	70%	30%

5. The company's inventory at 31 March 2014 is valued at £119,000.

6. Trade receivables include a debt of £8,000 which is to be written off. The allowance for receivables is to be adjusted to 4% of the receivables which remain after this debt has been written off.

7. Corporation tax for the year to 31 March 2013 was over-estimated by £6,000. The corporation tax liability for the year to 31 March 2014 is estimated to be £30,000.

8. One-quarter of wages and salaries were paid to distribution staff and the remaining three-quarters were paid to administrative staff.

9. General administrative expenses include bank overdraft interest of £9,000.

10. A dividend of 10p per ordinary share was paid on 31 December 2013. No further dividends are proposed for the year to 31 March 2014.

Required:

Prepare the following financial statements for Walrus plc in accordance with the requirements of international standards:

(a) a statement of comprehensive income for the year to 31 March 2014

(b) a statement of financial position as at 31 March 2014

(c) a statement of changes in equity for the year to 31 March 2014.   *(CIPFA)*

*3.7   Chilwell Ltd prepares financial statements to 31 October each year. The company's trial balance at 31 October 2013 is as follows:

	£	£
Land at valuation	250,000	
Buildings at cost	300,000	
Equipment and motor vehicles at cost	197,400	
Allowances for depreciation at 1 November 2012:		
Buildings		60,000
Equipment and motor vehicles		105,750
Disposal of vehicle		18,000
Inventory at 1 November 2012	87,520	
Trade receivables and payables	71,500	103,290
Allowance for doubtful receivables at 1 November 2012		1,520
Bank balance		10,390
Taxation	8,400	
9% Loan stock (repayable 2017)		120,000
Purchases and sales	483,230	1,025,420
Returns inwards and outwards	27,110	12,570
Directors' fees	50,000	
Wages and salaries	102,400	
General administrative expenses	143,440	
General distribution costs	107,050	
Royalties received		10,270
Interest paid	6,220	
Dividends paid	35,000	
Ordinary shares of £1		80,000
Revaluation reserve		75,000
Retained earnings at 1 November 2012		247,060
	1,869,270	1,869,270

The following information is also available:

1. Land is non-depreciable and is to be revalued at £280,000 on 31 October 2013.

2. The buildings were acquired on 1 November 2002. At that time, their useful life was estimated to be 50 years and it was decided to adopt the straight-line method of depreciation, assuming no residual value. On 1 November 2012, it was determined that the useful life of the buildings would end on 31 October 2042. The estimate of residual value remains unchanged.

3. Equipment and vehicles are depreciated at 25% per annum on the reducing balance basis. A full year's depreciation is charged in the year of acquisition. No depreciation is charged in the year of disposal. In June 2013, a distribution vehicle which had cost £64,000 in February 2009 was sold for £18,000. This amount was debited to the bank account and credited to a disposal account, but no further entries have yet been made with regard to this disposal.

4. Depreciation of buildings should be split 70:30 between administrative expenses and distribution costs. Depreciation of equipment and vehicles should be split 40:60 between administrative expenses and distribution costs.

5.   The cost of inventory at 31 October 2013 is £92,280.

6.   Trade receivables include bad debts of £2,000 which should be written off. The allowance for doubtful receivables should then be adjusted to 2% of the remaining trade receivables.

7.   The company's tax liability for the year to 31 October 2012 was underestimated by £8,400. The liability for the year to 31 October 2013 is estimated to be £20,000 and falls due on 1 August 2014.

8.   The loan stock was issued on 1 January 2013. Interest is payable half-yearly on 30 June and 31 December. The interest due on 30 June 2013 was paid on the due date. Accrued interest at 31 October 2013 has not yet been accounted for.

9.   Directors' fees are to be treated as administrative expenses. Wages and salaries should be split 50:50 between administrative expenses and distribution costs.

10. A 1 for 2 bonus issue of ordinary shares was made on 1 July 2013, financed out of retained earnings. No entries have yet been made in relation to this issue.

Required:

Prepare the following financial statements for Chilwell Ltd in accordance with the requirements of international standards:

(a)   a statement of comprehensive income for the year to 31 October 2013

(b)   a statement of changes in equity for the year to 31 October 2013

(c)   a statement of financial position as at 31 October 2013.

Formal notes to the accounts are not required, but all workings should be shown.

(CIPFA)

Chapter 4

Accounting policies, accounting estimates and errors

Introduction

The purpose of this chapter is to explain the main features of international standard IAS8 *Accounting Policies, Changes in Accounting Estimates and Errors*. This standard lays down criteria for the selection of accounting policies and prescribes the circumstances in which an entity may change an accounting policy. The standard also deals with the accounting treatment and disclosure of changes in accounting policies, changes in accounting estimates and corrections of prior period errors.

Objectives

By the end of this chapter, the reader should be able to:

- define the term "accounting policy" and explain how an entity should select its accounting policies
- explain the circumstances in which an entity may change an accounting policy
- account for a change in an accounting policy and list the disclosures which must be made when an accounting policy is changed
- explain what is meant by an accounting estimate and account for a change in an accounting estimate
- define the term "prior period error"
- account for the correction of a prior period error and list the disclosures which must be made when a prior period error is corrected.

Accounting policies

IAS8 defines accounting policies as "*the specific principles, bases, conventions, rules and practices applied by an entity in preparing and presenting financial statements*". The use of the word "policies" suggests that entities are allowed to choose between alternative accounting treatments. However, some of an entity's accounting policies will be dictated by an international standard which permits no choice of treatment. For instance:

(a) IAS2 *Inventories* requires that inventories are measured at the lower of cost and net realisable value (see Chapter 10).

(b) IAS37 *Provisions, Contingent Liabilities and Contingent Assets* prevents entities from recognising contingent assets and liabilities (see Chapter 12).

(c) IAS38 *Intangible Assets* prevents entities from recognising internally-generated goodwill in their financial statements (see Chapter 6).

But some standards do permit a choice. For instance:

(a) IAS2 *Inventories* allows the cost of "interchangeable" inventory items to be assigned by using either the first-in, first out (FIFO) cost formula or the weighted average cost formula (see Chapter 10).

(b) IAS16 *Property, Plant and Equipment* allows items of property, plant and equipment to be measured using either the cost model or the revaluation model (see Chapter 5).

(c) Similarly, IAS38 *Intangible Assets* allows intangible assets to be measured using either the cost model or the revaluation model (see Chapter 6).

International standard IAS1 (see Chapter 3) requires entities to disclose their significant accounting policies in the notes which form a part of the financial statements. Guidance on the selection of accounting policies is given in IAS8.

Selection of accounting policies

IAS8 provides the following guidance on the selection of accounting policies:

(a) If an international standard (or an interpretation made by the IFRS Interpretations Committee) specifically applies to an item, the accounting policy which is applied to that item should be determined by applying the relevant standard or interpretation.

(b) If there is no international standard or interpretation which specifically applies to the item concerned, management should use its judgement in selecting an accounting policy that results in relevant and reliable information. In making this judgement, management should refer to:

(i) the guidance provided by international standards and interpretations which deal with similar and related issues

(ii) the definitions, recognition criteria and measurement concepts for assets, liabilities, income and expenses given in the IASB *Conceptual Framework*.

Management may also consider the pronouncements of other standard-setting bodies with a similar conceptual framework to the IASB *Conceptual Framework* and may refer to accounting literature and accepted industry practices, as long as these do not conflict with international standards, interpretations or the *Conceptual Framework*.

IAS8 also stresses the need for the *consistent* application of accounting policies. Having selected an accounting policy in relation to an item, that policy should be applied consistently to all similar items.

Changes in accounting policies

IAS8 allows an entity to change one of its accounting policies only if the change:

(a) is required by an international standard or interpretation; or

(b) results in the financial statements providing reliable and more relevant information than would be the case if the accounting policy were not changed.

The users of financial statements need to be able to compare an entity's financial statements from one accounting period to another. Therefore the same accounting policies should be used from one period to the next unless the above conditions are satisfied.

Accounting for a change in accounting policy

If a change in accounting policy results from the initial application of an international standard or interpretation, the change should be accounted for in accordance with the transitional provisions (if any) which are provided in that standard or interpretation.

However, if there are no transitional provisions or if the change in policy has been made voluntarily so as to improve the relevance of the financial statements, IAS8 requires that the change should be accounted for *retrospectively*. This means that comparative figures for the previous period (or previous periods if comparatives are provided for more than one period) must be adjusted and presented "*as if the new accounting policy had always been applied*". Retrospective application maintains comparability between accounting periods and this approach must usually be adopted unless it is impracticable to do so.

An important exception to this requirement arises in the case of property, plant and equipment (IAS16) and intangible assets (IAS38) where an entity changes from the cost model to the revaluation model. In this case, the relevant standards require that the change is accounted for prospectively rather than retrospectively (see Chapters 5 and 6).

Additional comparative information to be presented

An entity which accounts for a change in an accounting policy retrospectively must present a restated statement of financial position as at the *beginning* of the previous period (unless the change in policy does not have a material effect on that statement).

If the entity normally provides comparative figures for the previous period only, this represents an additional requirement. The statement of financial position as at the end of the current period will show restated comparative figures for both the end of the previous period and the beginning of the previous period.

EXAMPLE 1

A company began trading on 1 January 2011, preparing accounts to 31 December each year. As at 31 December 2013, the company adopted a new accounting policy with regard to the measurement of inventories. If the new policy had been applied in previous years, the company's inventory at 31 December 2011 would have been £150,000 higher than the amount originally calculated. Similarly, the inventory at 31 December 2012 would have been £400,000 higher than the amount originally calculated.

An extract from the draft statement of comprehensive income for the year to 31 December 2013 (before accounting retrospectively for the change in accounting policy) is as follows:

	2013 £000	2012 £000
Profit before taxation	2,600	1,900
Taxation	780	570
Profit after taxation	1,820	1,330

Retained earnings were originally reported to be £840,000 on 31 December 2011. No dividends were paid in 2011, 2012 or 2013. It may be assumed that the company's taxation expense is always equal to 30% of its profit before tax.

(a) Prepare an extract from the company's statement of comprehensive income for the year to 31 December 2013, showing restated comparative figures for 2012.

(b) Calculate the company's retained earnings at 31 December 2013. Also calculate the retained earnings figures which will be shown in the restated statements of financial position as at 31 December 2011 and 2012.

Solution

(a) If the new accounting policy had always been applied, opening inventory for the year to 31 December 2013 would have been £400,000 higher. This would have caused an increase of £400,000 in cost of sales for the year and a decrease of £400,000 in pre-tax profits. Similarly, pre-tax profits for the year to 31 December 2012 would have been increased by £400,000 but reduced by £150,000, giving an overall increase of £250,000. Therefore the extract from the company's statement of comprehensive income for the year to 31 December 2013 is as follows:

	2013 £000	(restated) 2012 £000
Profit before taxation	2,200	2,150
Taxation	660	645
Profit after taxation	1,540	1,505

Note that these figures show an increase in profit of approximately 2%, whereas the original figures (which were distorted by the change in accounting policy) suggested incorrectly that profit had risen by nearly 37%.

(b) In the year to 31 December 2011, the effect of increasing closing inventory by £150,000 is to increase pre-tax profit for the year by £150,000. The tax liability increases by £45,000 (30% of £150,000) and so retained earnings at the end of the year increase by £105,000. Retained earnings figures are as follows:

	£000
Balance at 31 December 2011, as previously reported	840
Change in accounting policy relating to inventories	105
Restated balance at 31 December 2011	945
Restated profit for the year to 31 December 2012	1,505
Restated balance at 31 December 2012	2,450
Profit for the year to 31 December 2013	1,540
Balance at 31 December 2013	3,990

If the change in accounting policy had not been accounted for retrospectively, the retained earnings figure at 31 December 2013 would still have been £3,990,000 (£840,000 + £1,330,000 + £1,820,000). However, the distribution of earnings over the three years concerned would have been different and misleading.

Disclosure of a change in accounting policy

If an entity changes any of its accounting policies, IAS8 requires that certain disclosures should be made in the notes to the financial statements. The main disclosures are:

(a) for a change in accounting policy which has been caused by the initial application of an international standard or interpretation:

– the title of the standard or interpretation

– if applicable, the fact that the change has been accounted for in accordance with transitional provisions specified in the relevant standard or interpretation and a description of those provisions

(b) for a voluntary change in accounting policy:

– the reasons which suggest that application of the new policy will provide reliable and more relevant information

(c) for all changes in accounting policy:

– the nature of the change

– for the current period and for each prior period presented, the amount of the adjustment made to each affected item in the financial statements and the amount of any adjustment to the entity's earnings per share (see Chapter 23)

– if retrospective application of the new policy would normally be required by IAS8 but this has proved to be impracticable, a description of the circumstances that have led to this condition and a description of how (and from when) the change in policy has been applied.

Accounting estimates

IAS8 states that "*many items in financial statements cannot be measured with precision but can only be estimated*". Estimates may be required in relation to items such as bad and doubtful receivables, the useful lives of depreciable non-current assets, the net realisable value of inventories and so forth. IAS8 also states that "*the use of reasonable estimates is an essential part of the preparation of financial statements and does not undermine their reliability*".

By definition, estimates cannot be precise. Therefore an estimate made in the past may need to be revised if changes occur to the conditions on which the original estimate was based or if new information becomes available. For instance, if new information is received concerning the solvency of a customer, a trade receivable which was previously estimated to be 50% collectible might now be estimated as being only 25% collectible.

IAS8 requires an entity which changes an accounting estimate to account for the change *prospectively*, not retrospectively. This means that the effect of the change should be dealt with in the entity's financial statements for the current period and (if applicable) future periods. But the standard does not require (or permit) the restatement of comparative figures for prior periods. This is totally different from the required treatment of changes in accounting policy. If it is difficult to distinguish a change in an accounting policy from a change in an accounting estimate, IAS8 requires that the change concerned should be treated as a change in an accounting estimate.

Disclosure of changes in accounting estimates

IAS8 requires disclosure of the nature and amount of a change in an accounting estimate which has an effect in the current period or is expected to have an effect in future periods. However, this requirement is subject to the materiality rule in IAS1. This rule states that a specific disclosure required by a standard or interpretation need not be provided "*if the information is not material*" (see Chapter 3).

Prior period errors

Financial statements do not comply with international standards if they contain material errors. Potential errors may be discovered before the financial statements are finalised, in which case they can be corrected before the statements are authorised for issue. However, it is possible that an error may not be detected until a subsequent accounting period. Such an error is referred to as a "prior period error".

IAS8 defines prior period errors as "*omissions from, and misstatements in, the entity's financial statements for one or more prior periods arising from a failure to use, or misuse of, reliable information that:*

(a) *was available when financial statements for those periods were authorised for issue; and (b)* *could reasonably be expected to have been obtained and taken into account in the preparation and presentation of those financial statements"*.

Such errors could be caused by mathematical mistakes, mistakes in applying accounting policies, oversights or misinterpretations of facts or by fraud. IAS8 requires that material prior period errors should be corrected *retrospectively*. The approach is similar to that adopted for a change in accounting policy and involves:

(a)   restating comparative figures for the prior period(s) in which the error occurred, or

(b)   if the error occurred before the earliest prior period for which comparatives are presented, restating the opening balances of assets, liabilities and equity for the earliest prior period presented.

In any case, an entity which corrects a prior period error retrospectively must present a statement of financial position as at the *beginning* of the previous period (unless the correction of the error does not have a material effect on that statement).

EXAMPLE 2

Whilst preparing its financial statements for the year to 31 December 2013, a company discovers that (because of an arithmetic error) its inventory at 31 December 2012 was overstated by £50,000. This is a material amount.

An extract from the company's draft statement of comprehensive income for the year to 31 December 2013 (before correcting the error) shows the following:

	2013 £000	2012 £000
Sales	940	790
Cost of goods sold	750	540
Gross profit	190	250
Other expenses	120	110
Profit before taxation	70	140
Taxation	14	28
Profit after taxation	56	112

Retained earnings were reported to be £270,000 on 31 December 2011. No dividends were paid in either 2012 or 2013. It may be assumed that the company's taxation expense is always equal to 20% of its profit before tax.

(a)   Prepare an extract from the company's statement of comprehensive income for the year to 31 December 2013, showing restated comparative figures for 2012.

(b)   Calculate the company's retained earnings at 31 December 2013 and the restated retained earnings at 31 December 2012.

Solution

(a) The extract from the statement of comprehensive income for the year to 31 December 2013 is as follows:

	2013	(restated) 2012
	£000	£000
Sales	940	790
Cost of goods sold	700	590
Gross profit	240	200
Other expenses	120	110
Profit before taxation	120	90
Taxation	24	18
Profit after taxation	96	72

(b) Retained earnings are as follows:

	£000
Balance at 31 December 2011	270
Restated profit for the year to 31 December 2012	72
Restated balance at 31 December 2012	342
Profit for the year to 31 December 2013	96
Balance at 31 December 2013	438

Note:

Retrospective adjustment of the prior period error reveals that profits after tax have risen in 2013. If the comparatives for 2012 had not been restated, the financial statements would have given the incorrect impression that profits after tax had fallen during 2013.

Disclosure of prior period errors

When an entity corrects a material prior period error, IAS8 requires that the following disclosures should be made in the notes to the financial statements:

(a) the nature of the prior period error

(b) for each prior period presented, the amount of the correction to each affected line item in the financial statements and, if applicable, the amount of any correction to the entity's earnings per share (see Chapter 23)

(c) the amount of the correction at the beginning of the earliest prior period presented

(d) if retrospective restatement is impracticable for a particular prior period, a description of the circumstances that have led to this condition and a description of how (and from when) the error has been corrected.

Summary

▸ IAS8 deals with accounting policies, changes in accounting estimates and the correction of prior period errors.

▸ Accounting policies are the specific principles, bases, conventions, rules and practices applied by an entity in preparing and presenting its financial statements.

▸ IFRSs issued by the IASB do not generally permit any choice of accounting treatment but some of the IASs which were adopted by the IASB on its inception do offer a choice. Therefore an entity's accounting policies will usually be a mixture of policies required by standards and policies chosen by the entity.

▸ IAS8 provides guidance on the selection of accounting policies.

▸ Accounting policies should be applied consistently and should be changed only if the change is required by an international standard or an interpretation, or if it results in reliable and more relevant information.

▸ A change in accounting policy should be accounted for retrospectively. This involves restating comparative figures for each prior period presented. Details of the change must be disclosed in the notes to the financial statements.

▸ A change in an accounting estimate should be accounted for prospectively and (if material) disclosed in the notes to the financial statements.

▸ Material prior period errors should be accounted for retrospectively and disclosed in the notes to the financial statements.

Exercises

4.1   (a)   Distinguish between accounting policies and accounting estimates.

(b)   Explain how a change in an accounting policy should be accounted for.

(c)   Explain how a change in an accounting estimate should be accounted for.

4.2   (a)   Explain how an entity should select its accounting policy in relation to an item if there is no applicable international standard or interpretation.

(b)   In what circumstances may an entity change one of its accounting policies?

4.3   List the disclosures which must be made if an accounting policy is changed.

4.4   (a)   Explain what is meant by a "material prior period error" and explain how such an error should be corrected.

(b)   List the disclosures which must be made when a material prior period error is corrected.

4.5   H Ltd began trading on 1 January 2010, preparing financial statements to 31 December each year. During 2013, the company decided to change its accounting policy with regard to the depreciation of property, plant and equipment. Depreciation charges calculated using the previous accounting policy and shown in the company's financial statements for the first three years of trading were as follows:

	£000
year to 31 December 2010	230
year to 31 December 2011	270
year to 31 December 2012	290

If the new accounting policy had been applied in previous years, depreciation charges would have been:

	£000
year to 31 December 2010	390
year to 31 December 2011	310
year to 31 December 2012	230

An extract from the company's statement of comprehensive income for the year to 31 December 2013 (before adjusting comparative figures to reflect the change in accounting policy) shows the following:

	2013	2012
	£000	£000
Profit before depreciation	2,510	2,450
Depreciation of property, plant and equipment	190	290
Profit before taxation	2,320	2,160
Taxation	696	648
Profit after taxation	1,624	1,512

Retained earnings were reported as £2,943,000 on 31 December 2011. No dividends have been paid in any year. It may be assumed that the company's tax expense is always equal to 30% of the profit before taxation.

Required:

(a)   Rewrite the extract from the statement of comprehensive income so as to reflect the change in accounting policy, in accordance with the requirements of IAS8.

(b)   Compute the company's retained earnings at 31 December 2013 and the restated retained earnings at 31 December 2011 and 2012.

4.6   Whilst preparing its financial statements for the year to 30 June 2014, a company discovers that (owing to an accounting error) the sales figure for the year to 30 June 2013 had been understated by £100,000. Trade receivables had been understated by the same amount. This error is regarded as material.

An extract from the company's draft statement of comprehensive income for the year to 30 June 2014, before correcting this error, is as follows:

	2014	**2013**
	£000	£000
Sales	1,660	1,740
Cost of goods sold	670	730
Gross profit	990	1,010
Expenses	590	560
Profit before taxation	400	450
Taxation	80	90
Profit after taxation	320	360

Retained earnings at 30 June 2012 were £860,000. No dividends were paid during the two years to 30 June 2014. It may be assumed that the company's tax expense is always equal to 20% of the profit before taxation.

Required:

(a)   Revise the extract from the statement of comprehensive income for the year to 30 June 2014, showing restated comparative figures for the year to 30 June 2013.

(b)   Compute the company's retained earnings at 30 June 2014 and the restated retained earnings at 30 June 2013.

*4.7   J Ltd has been trading for many years, preparing financial statements to 31 March each year. As from 1 April 2013, the company decided to adopt a new accounting policy in relation to revenue recognition.

If this policy had been adopted in previous years, the company's revenue for the year to 31 March 2012 would have been £300,000 higher than previously reported and trade receivables at 31 March 2012 would also have been £300,000 higher. Revenue for the year to 31 March 2013 would have been £600,000 higher than previously reported and trade receivables at 31 March 2013 would have been £900,000 higher. There would have been no effect in any earlier year.

An extract from the company's draft statement of comprehensive income for the year to 31 March 2014 (with comparatives for 2013 as originally stated) is as follows:

	2014	2013
	£000	£000
Revenue	5,200	4,800
Operating expenses	4,100	3,900
Profit before taxation	1,100	900
Taxation	275	225
Profit after taxation	825	675

The draft financial statements for the year to 31 March 2014 show only the revenue for that year (measured in accordance with the new accounting policy) and have not been adjusted to include the additional revenue of £900,000 from previous years which now needs to be accounted for.

The company's taxation expense is always equal to 25% of its profit before taxation. No dividends were paid in either 2013 or 2014 and retained earnings at 31 March 2012 were originally reported to be £925,000.

Required:

(a)   Explain the circumstances in which a company which complies with international standards may change an accounting policy. Also explain how such a change is accounted for in accordance with the requirements of IAS8.

(b)   Revise the extract from the statement of comprehensive income for the year to 31 March 2014 (with comparatives for 2013).

(c)   Calculate the company's retained earnings figure at 31 March 2014 and the restated retained earnings figures at 31 March 2012 and 31 March 2013.

(d)   Explain why the revised statement of comprehensive income is an improvement on the draft statement.

Part 2

FINANCIAL REPORTING IN PRACTICE

Chapter 5

Property, plant and equipment

Introduction

The main purpose of this chapter is to explain the requirements of international standard IAS16 *Property, Plant and Equipment*. This standard prescribes the accounting treatment of property, plant and equipment and deals with the following principal issues:

(a) the criteria which must be satisfied in order that an item of property, plant and equipment should be recognised as an asset

(b) the way in which items of property, plant and equipment should be measured in the financial statements, both at initial recognition and later

(c) the way in which depreciation charges should be calculated and accounted for.

The accounting treatment prescribed by IAS16 applies to most property, plant and equipment but does not apply if another standard requires or permits a different accounting treatment. In particular, IAS16 does not apply to property, plant and equipment which is classified as held for sale. This is dealt with in accordance with IFRS5 (see Chapter 8).

This chapter of the book also considers four other international standards which may be relevant when accounting for property, plant and equipment. These are:

(a) IFRS13 *Fair Value Measurement*

(b) IAS23 *Borrowing Costs*

(c) IAS20 *Accounting for Government Grants and Disclosure of Government Assistance*

(d) IAS40 *Investment Property*.

Objectives

By the end of this chapter, the reader should be able to:

• define the term "property, plant and equipment" in accordance with IAS16

• state the criteria which must be satisfied for an item of property, plant and equipment to be recognised as an asset

- determine the cost of an item of property, plant and equipment

- distinguish between the cost model and the revaluation model for the measurement of property, plant and equipment after initial recognition

- calculate and account for depreciation charges in accordance with IAS16

- list the main disclosures required by IAS16

- explain the requirements of IAS23 in relation to borrowing costs incurred for the acquisition, construction or production of a qualifying asset

- explain the requirements of IAS20 in relation to government grants

- define the term "investment property" and explain the requirements of IAS40 in relation to investment properties

- define the term "fair value" and outline the guidance provided by IFRS13 with regard to the measurement of fair value.

Definition of property, plant and equipment

IAS16 defines property, plant and equipment as "*tangible items that:*

(a) are held for use in the production or supply of goods or services, for rental to others, or for administrative purposes; and

(b) are expected to be used during more than one period."

This definition covers the majority of the tangible non-current assets that might normally be held by a business entity.

Definition of carrying amount

There are several other definitions in IAS16, most of which are covered in later sections of this chapter. But one definition which must be understood from the outset is the definition of an asset's carrying amount. The term "carrying amount" is used throughout the international standards to refer to the amount at which an item is "carried" or shown in the financial statements. In the case of property, plant and equipment, IAS16 defines carrying amount as "*the amount at which an asset is recognised after deducting any accumulated depreciation and accumulated impairment losses*". This amount could also be referred to as the asset's written down value, although this term is not used by the international standards. Impairment losses are dealt with in Chapter 7 of this book.

Recognition of property, plant and equipment

IAS16 states that an item of property, plant and equipment should be recognised as an asset if and only if:

(a) it is probable that future economic benefits associated with the item will flow to the entity concerned, and

(b) the cost of the item can be measured reliably.

These criteria are in accordance with the general recognition criteria for assets established in the IASB *Conceptual Framework* (see Chapter 2). Assessing the probability of future economic benefits will require the exercise of judgement but measuring the cost of an item will usually be straightforward. Further points made by IAS16 as regards the recognition of property, plant and equipment are as follows:

(a) An "item" generally consists of an individual piece of property, plant and equipment. However, it may sometimes be appropriate to group relatively insignificant items together (e.g. small tools) and apply the recognition criteria to the group.

(b) Spare parts should be recognised as property, plant and equipment if they meet the definition given earlier in this chapter. However, small parts may be treated as inventory (see Chapter 10) and accounted for as an expense when they are used in the repair and maintenance of property, plant and equipment.

(c) Items of property, plant and equipment acquired for safety or environmental reasons do not directly generate future economic benefits. However, such items qualify for recognition as assets because they enable the entity to derive future economic benefits from its other property, plant and equipment. For instance, a manufacturer might be obliged by law to instal certain safety equipment and would be unable to operate any production machinery at all if this safety equipment were not installed.

Subsequent costs

Routine servicing, repair and maintenance costs incurred after the initial recognition of an item of property, plant and equipment as an asset are not capital expenditure. These costs usually consist of labour costs and the cost of small parts (see above) and are accounted for as an expense in the period to which they relate.

However, it may be necessary to replace major parts of some items of property, plant and equipment at regular intervals (e.g. the interior fittings of an aircraft). IAS16 requires that the cost of major replacements should be treated as capital expenditure and recognised as an addition to the carrying amount of the asset concerned. The carrying amount of the part that has been replaced should simultaneously be derecognised (see below).

A similar procedure applies to the cost of major inspections. If an item of property, plant and equipment which has been recognised as an asset needs regular major inspections, the cost of each inspection is added to the carrying amount of the asset when it occurs. Any remaining carrying amount of the cost of the previous inspection is derecognised.

Derecognition

An item of property, plant and equipment previously recognised as an asset should be derecognised (i.e. removed from the statement of financial position) when:

(a)   it is disposed of, or

(b)   no future economic benefits are expected from its use or from its disposal.

IAS16 states that any gain or loss arising on the derecognition of an item of property, plant and equipment should be "included in profit or loss" when the item is derecognised. This means that the gain or loss should be included in the calculation of the entity's profit or loss for the period in which derecognition occurs.

The gain or loss arising on derecognition is equal to the difference between the disposal proceeds (if any) and the asset's carrying amount at the time of derecognition.

EXAMPLE 1

(a)   On 1 September 2013, a company paid £80,000 to replace the wall lining of one of its furnaces. The furnace had been acquired several years previously and its carrying amount on 1 September 2013 (before accounting for the replacement of the lining) was £320,000. Of this amount, £10,000 related to the original wall lining.

(b)   On 1 September 2013, a company paid £250,000 for a major inspection of one of its aircraft. It is a legal requirement that such an inspection is carried out at least once every three years. The previous inspection took place in March 2011 at a cost of £210,000. The carrying amount of the aircraft on 1 September 2013 (before accounting for the new inspection) was £1,200,000. Of this amount, £70,000 related to the previous inspection.

Explain how each of these transactions should be accounted for in accordance with the requirements of IAS16.

Solution

(a)   The cost of the replacement wall lining should be recognised as an asset and the carrying amount of the original lining should be derecognised. The carrying amount of the furnace becomes £390,000 (£320,000 + £80,000 − £10,000). The gain or loss arising on the disposal of the old lining is included in the calculation of the company's profit or loss for the accounting period in which derecognition occurs. This gain or loss is calculated as the difference between the £10,000 carrying amount of the old lining and any amount which is received on disposal.

(b)   The cost of the new inspection should be recognised as an asset and the carrying amount of the previous inspection should be derecognised. The carrying amount of the aircraft becomes £1,380,000 (£1,200,000 + £250,000 − £70,000). The £70,000 carrying amount of the previous inspection is written off as an expense.

Initial measurement of property, plant and equipment

On initial recognition, IAS16 requires that items of property, plant and equipment should be measured at cost. The cost of an item of property, plant and equipment comprises:

(a) the purchase price of the item, including import duties and non-refundable purchase taxes, less trade discounts or rebates

(b) costs that are directly attributable to bringing the item to the location and condition necessary for it to be operated as intended, including:

  (i) labour costs arising directly from the construction or acquisition of the item

  (ii) site preparation costs

  (iii) initial delivery and handling costs

  (iv) installation, assembly and testing costs

  (v) professional fees

(c) the estimated costs of dismantling and removing the item and restoring the site on which the item is located, as long as the obligation to meet these costs is incurred when the item is acquired (see Chapter 12).

In general, administrative costs and other general overhead expenses are not part of the cost of an item of property, plant and equipment.

EXAMPLE 2

On 31 July 2013, a company which prepares financial statements to 31 March each year bought a machine for £648,000. This amount was made up as follows:

	£
Manufacturer's list price	500,000
Less: Trade discount	30,000
	470,000
Delivery charge	4,300
Installation and testing charges	24,500
Small spare parts	5,200
Servicing contract for the year to 31 July 2014	36,000
	540,000
Value added tax at 20%	108,000
	648,000

The company is VAT-registered and reclaims VAT charged to it by its suppliers. Calculate the cost of the machine in accordance with the requirements of IAS16.

Solution

The machine's cost is £498,800 (£470,000 + £4,300 + £24,500). As regards the other amounts listed above:

(a) The small spare parts will probably be treated as inventory and should be accounted for as an expense when used.

(b) Eight-twelfths of the cost of the servicing contract (£24,000) should be accounted for as an expense in the year to 31 March 2014. The remaining four-twelfths (£12,000) is a prepayment of an expense for the year to 31 March 2015.

(c) VAT can be ignored since it is refunded to the company.

Self-constructed assets

The cost of a self-constructed asset (e.g. an office building constructed by a building firm for its own occupation) is determined in the same way as the cost of any other item of property, plant and equipment. If the entity sells similar assets to customers in the normal course of trade, the cost of the self-constructed asset will usually be the same as the cost of constructing an asset for sale. This should exclude any profit element and is calculated in accordance with IAS2 *Inventories* (see Chapter 10).

The accounting treatment of interest and other borrowing costs incurred in connection with the acquisition, construction or production of an asset is prescribed by international standard IAS23 *Borrowing Costs* (see later in this chapter).

Subsequent measurement of property, plant and equipment

IAS16 allows two different ways of measuring property, plant and equipment subsequent to its initial recognition as an asset. These are the "cost model" and the "revaluation model". A brief description of each model is as follows:

(a) **The cost model**. After initial recognition, items of property, plant and equipment are carried at cost less any accumulated depreciation and less any accumulated impairment losses. Impairment losses are dealt with in Chapter 7 of this book.

(b) **The revaluation model**. After initial recognition, items of property, plant and equipment are carried at a revalued amount. The revalued amount of an item consists of its fair value at the date of revaluation, less any subsequent accumulated depreciation and less any subsequent accumulated impairment losses. Note that:

(i) IAS16 defines fair value as "*the price that would be received to sell an asset or paid to transfer a liability in an orderly transaction between market participants at the measurement date*". This definition is derived from international standard IFRS13 *Fair Value Measurement*, which sets out a framework for measuring the fair value of an asset or liability. A brief summary of IFRS13 is provided in the appendix at the end of this chapter.

(ii) The revaluation model cannot be applied to an item of property, plant and equipment unless its fair value can be measured reliably.

(iii) If the revaluation model is applied to an item of property, plant and equipment, then it must be applied to the entire class to which the item belongs. A class of property, plant and equipment is a grouping of items of a similar nature. Typical classes might include land, buildings, machinery, motor vehicles etc.

(iv) Revaluations should be made with sufficient regularity to ensure that the carrying amount of an item is not materially different from its fair value at the end of the reporting period. All of the items within a class should be revalued simultaneously. This avoids selective revaluations and also avoids the reporting of amounts that are a mixture of valuations made on different dates.

Accounting for revaluation gains and losses

If the carrying amount of an item of property, plant and equipment is *increased* as a result of a revaluation, the increase must normally be credited to a revaluation reserve and shown as "other comprehensive income" in the entity's statement of comprehensive income. This accounting treatment ensures that unrealised revaluation gains (i.e. gains that have not been turned into cash) are excluded from profit and so are not available for payment as a dividend. If the carrying amount of an item of property, plant and equipment is *decreased* as a result of a revaluation, the decrease must normally be recognised as an expense when calculating the entity's profit or loss. But note that:

(a) a revaluation increase must be recognised as income when calculating the entity's profit or loss to the extent that it reverses any revaluation decrease in respect of the same item that was previously recognised as an expense

(b) a revaluation decrease must be debited to the revaluation reserve and shown (as a negative figure) in other comprehensive income to the extent of any credit balance previously existing in the revaluation reserve in respect of that same item.

Disposal of a revalued item of property, plant and equipment

When an item of property, plant and equipment is disposed of, any revaluation gain which is included in the revaluation reserve in respect of that item may be transferred to retained earnings. This transfer takes account of the fact that a previously unrealised gain has now been realised. The transfer is recorded in the statement of changes in equity and does not affect the statement of comprehensive income.

Note that a revaluation gain is an example of an item of other comprehensive income that will not be reclassified to profit or loss in a subsequent period (see Chapter 3). The fact that the transfer described above does not occur in the statement of comprehensive income means that the gain is excluded from profit both initially (when the asset is revalued) and subsequently (when it is disposed of).

EXAMPLE 3

(a) Company X prepares financial statements to 31 May each year. On 31 May 2013, the company acquired land for £400,000. This land was revalued at £450,000 on 31 May 2014 and at £375,000 on 31 May 2015.

(b) Company Y prepares financial statements to 30 June each year. On 30 June 2013, the company acquired land for £600,000. This land was revalued at £540,000 on 30 June 2014 and at £620,000 on 30 June 2015.

Assuming that both companies use the revaluation model, explain how each revaluation should be dealt with in the financial statements. Ignore depreciation.

Solution

(a) The £50,000 revaluation increase on 31 May 2014 should be credited to a revaluation reserve and shown as other comprehensive income in the company's statement of comprehensive income.

£50,000 of the £75,000 decrease on 31 May 2015 should be debited to revaluation reserve and shown (as a negative figure) in other comprehensive income in the statement of comprehensive income. The remaining £25,000 should be recognised as an expense when calculating the company's profit or loss for the year.

(b) The £60,000 revaluation decrease on 30 June 2014 should be recognised as an expense when calculating the company's profit or loss for the year.

£60,000 of the £80,000 increase on 30 June 2015 should be recognised as income when calculating the company's profit or loss for the year. The remaining £20,000 should be credited to a revaluation reserve and shown as other comprehensive income in the statement of comprehensive income.

Depreciation

IAS16 defines depreciation as "*the systematic allocation of the depreciable amount of an asset over its useful life*". This definition makes it clear that the purpose of depreciation is simply to allocate an expense between accounting periods. The depreciation process makes no attempt to show assets at their current values. Nor does it guarantee that there will be funds available to replace those assets when they come to the end of their useful lives. Depreciation charges reduce profits but have no direct effect on an entity's cash resources and do not ensure that cash is "saved up" to buy replacement assets.

IAS16 also defines a number of key terms which are used in the section of the standard which deals with depreciation. These are as follows:

(a) Depreciable amount is "*the cost of an asset, or other amount substituted for cost, less its residual value*".

(b) The residual value of an asset is "*the estimated amount that an entity would currently obtain from disposal of the asset, after deducting the estimated costs of disposal, if the asset were already of the age and in the condition expected at the end of its useful life*".

(c) Useful life is "*the period over which an asset is expected to be available for use by an entity ... or the number of production or similar units expected to be obtained from the asset by an entity*".

The definition of depreciable amount makes it clear that depreciation does not cease if an asset is revalued. All that happens is that a valuation is substituted for the asset's carrying amount, resulting in a revaluation gain or loss. Depreciable amount is now equal to the amount of the valuation less the asset's residual value. Subsequent depreciation charges will be based upon this revised depreciable amount and will continue for the remainder of the asset's useful life.

If an item of property, plant and equipment is revalued upwards and a revaluation gain in relation to that item is credited to revaluation reserve, subsequent depreciation charges will exceed depreciation based on the item's original cost. In these circumstances, the amount of excess depreciation in each accounting period may be transferred from revaluation reserve to retained earnings. This transfer takes place in the statement of changes in equity and does not affect the statement of comprehensive income.

IAS16 requirements with regard to depreciation

IAS16 establishes a number of general requirements with regard to the depreciation of property, plant and equipment and then deals with depreciation methods. The main general requirements are as follows:

(a) Each part of an item of property, plant and equipment with a cost that is significant in relation to the item's total cost should be depreciated separately. However, parts of an item may be grouped for depreciation purposes if they have the same useful life and if the same depreciation method is applicable to each part. An example of the need to depreciate the parts of an item separately arises in the case of an aircraft, where the airframe and the engines may have very different useful lives.

(b) The depreciation charge for an accounting period should normally be recognised as an expense when calculating profit or loss. However, if an item of property, plant and equipment is used to produce other assets, then the depreciation of that item should be included in the cost of those other assets. For instance, the depreciation of factory machines may be included in the cost of inventories (see Chapter 10).

(c) The residual value and useful life of property, plant and equipment should be reviewed at least at the end of each financial year. If expectations differ from previous estimates, the revised estimates should be accounted for prospectively, as required by IAS8 (see Chapter 4). The asset's remaining depreciable amount should be amended to reflect any change in residual value and then this amount should be allocated as depreciation over the remainder of the asset's expected useful life.

(d) A number of factors should be taken into account when judging the useful life of an asset. These include expected usage of the asset, expected physical wear and tear and the likelihood of technical or commercial obsolescence. Useful life is defined in terms of the usefulness of the asset to the entity concerned and this may be shorter than the asset's full economic life.

(e) If the residual value of an asset is greater than or equal to its carrying amount, then the asset's depreciable amount is zero. This means that depreciation charges will also be zero until such time as the asset's residual value becomes less than its carrying amount. This may or may not happen.

(f) Depreciation should begin when an asset is available for use and then continue until the asset is derecognised or classified as held for sale (see Chapter 8). Depreciation should not cease simply because an asset has become idle. However, some methods of depreciation (see below) are based on an asset's usage and would give a zero depreciation charge whilst the asset is not being used.

(g) Land and buildings should be dealt with separately from one another for depreciation purposes. In most cases, land has an unlimited useful life and is not depreciated for that reason. But an exception arises in the case of quarries, mines etc. which generally have finite useful lives and so should be depreciated.

Depreciation methods

IAS16 states that a variety of depreciation methods may be used to allocate the depreciable amount of an item of property, plant and equipment over its useful life. These include (but are not limited to) the following well-known methods:

(a) **Straight-line method**. The asset's depreciable amount is spread evenly over its useful life, so giving a constant depreciation charge in each accounting period.

(b) **Diminishing balance (or reducing balance) method**. The depreciation charge for an accounting period is calculated by applying a constant percentage to the carrying amount of the asset brought forward from the previous period. This method gives a decreasing depreciation charge in each successive period.

(c) **Units of production method**. This method is typically applied to machines used in a factory. The useful life of the asset is measured in units of production rather than years and the depreciation charge for an accounting period is calculated in accordance with the number of units of production achieved in that period.

This is very similar to the machine hours method, where the useful life of a machine is measured in working hours and the depreciation charge for an accounting period is calculated in accordance with the number of hours for which the machine has been used during the period.

In principle, the chosen method should be the one which most closely matches the usage pattern of the asset concerned. This is what IAS16 requires.

The depreciation method applied to an asset should be reviewed at least at the end of each financial year and changed if there has been a change in usage pattern. Such a change should be accounted for as a change in an accounting estimate in accordance with the requirements of IAS8 (see Chapter 4). This standard requires the new depreciation method to be applied prospectively over the remainder of the asset's useful life.

EXAMPLE 4

On 1 January 2013, a company which prepares financial statements to 31 December each year buys a machine at a cost of £46,300. The machine's useful life is estimated at four years with a residual value of £6,000. The machine is expected to achieve 50,000 units of production over its useful life, as follows:

	2013	2014	2015	2016
Number of units	10,000	20,000	15,000	5,000

Calculate depreciation charges for each of these four years using:

(a) the straight-line method
(b) the diminishing balance method (at a rate of 40%)
(c) the units of production method.

Solution

(a) The machine's depreciable amount is £40,300. Allocating this evenly over the four years gives an annual depreciation charge of £10,075.

(b)
Year	Carrying amount b/f	Depreciation at 40%	Carrying amount c/f
	£	£	£
2013	46,300	18,520	27,780
2014	27,780	11,112	16,668
2015	16,668	6,667	10,001
2016	10,001	4,001	6,000
		40,300	

(c) Depreciation per unit of production is 80.6p (£40,300 ÷ 50,000). Depreciation charges in each year are as follows:

Year	Units of production	Depreciation at 80.6p
	£	£
2013	10,000	8,060
2014	20,000	16,120
2015	15,000	12,090
2016	5,000	4,030
		40,300

Disclosure requirements

The disclosure requirements of IAS16 are very extensive. The main disclosures required are as follows:

(a) for each class of property, plant and equipment:

    (i) the measurement bases used

    (ii) the depreciation methods used

    (iii) the useful lives or depreciation rates used

    (iv) the gross carrying amount and accumulated depreciation at the beginning and end of the accounting period

    (v) a reconciliation of the carrying amount at the beginning and end of the period, showing additions, disposals, revaluation increases and decreases, depreciation, impairment losses and any other movements

(b) the amount of any property, plant and equipment pledged as security for liabilities

(c) the amount of any contractual commitments for the acquisition of property, plant and equipment

(d) for items of property, plant and equipment stated at revalued amounts (in addition to the disclosures required by IFRS13 *Fair Value Measurement*):

    (i) the date of the revaluation

    (ii) whether or not an independent valuer was involved

    (iii) for each revalued class of property, plant and equipment, the carrying amount that would have been recognised if the cost model had been used.

IAS16 also encourages (but does not require) entities to disclose additional information which may be relevant to the needs of users. This additional information might include:

(e) the carrying amount of temporarily idle property, plant and equipment

(f) the gross carrying amount of any fully-depreciated property, plant and equipment that is still in use

(g) the fair value of property, plant and equipment to which the cost model has been applied, if this is materially different from the carrying amount.

Borrowing costs

The objective of IAS23 *Borrowing Costs* is to prescribe the accounting treatment of interest and other borrowing costs, especially those which are incurred in connection with the acquisition of assets such as property, plant and equipment.

The "core principle" of IAS23 is that borrowing costs that are directly attributable to the acquisition, construction or production of a "qualifying asset" should be capitalised as part of the cost of that asset. Other borrowing costs should be recognised as an expense. The standard provides the following definitions:

(a) Borrowing costs are "*interest and other costs that an entity incurs in connection with the borrowing of funds*". Borrowing costs include:

   (i) costs calculated using the "effective interest method" (see Chapter 11) such as:
   - interest on bank overdrafts and on short-term and long-term borrowings
   - discounts and premiums related to borrowings
   - ancillary costs incurred in connection with the arrangement of borrowings

   (ii) finance charges in respect of finance leases (see Chapter 9).

(b) A qualifying asset is "*an asset that necessarily takes a substantial period of time to get ready for its intended use or sale*". Depending on the circumstances, any of the following may be qualifying assets:
   - inventories
   - manufacturing plants and power generation facilities
   - intangible assets
   - investment properties.

Inventories produced over a short period of time are not qualifying assets. Nor are assets which are ready for their intended use or sale as soon as they are acquired.

Borrowing costs eligible for capitalisation

The borrowing costs that are directly attributable to the acquisition, construction or production of a qualifying asset are those borrowing costs which would have been avoided if the expenditure on the asset had not occurred. Identifying these costs is straightforward if funds are borrowed specifically for this purpose. In these circumstances, the borrowing costs eligible for capitalisation are the actual borrowing costs incurred on the borrowed funds during the "period of capitalisation" (see below).

If a qualifying asset is funded out of a pool of general borrowings, the borrowing costs that may be capitalised are calculated by applying a "capitalisation rate" to the expenditure on the asset. The capitalisation rate is the weighted average of the borrowing costs that are applicable to the general borrowings outstanding during the period of capitalisation.

Period of capitalisation

The capitalisation of borrowing costs incurred in relation to a qualifying asset should begin as soon as *all* of the following conditions are satisfied:

(a) expenditure is being incurred on the asset, and

(b) borrowing costs are being incurred, and

(c) activities are in progress that are necessary to prepare the asset for its intended use.

Capitalisation of borrowing costs ceases when substantially all of the activities necessary to prepare the asset for its intended use are complete.

Disclosure requirements

An entity is required to disclose:

(a) the amount of borrowing costs capitalised during the accounting period

(b) the capitalisation rate used to calculate the amount of general borrowing costs that are eligible for capitalisation.

EXAMPLE 5

A company which prepares financial statements to 30 June each year has the following general borrowings outstanding throughout the year to 30 June 2014:

	£000
7.5% Bank loan	800
9% Bank loan	500
8.5% Loan stock	1,200
	2,500

On 1 October 2013, the company began construction of a qualifying asset and incurred expenditure of £300,000. A further £240,000 was spent on 1 February 2014. Both of these amounts were financed out of general borrowings. Construction of the asset was still underway at 30 June 2014.

Calculate the amount of borrowing costs that should be capitalised as part of the cost of the qualifying asset during the year to 30 June 2014.

Solution

The total borrowing costs incurred in relation to general borrowings during the year to 30 June 2014 were (£800,000 x 7.5%) + (£500,000 x 9%) + (£1,200,000 x 8.5%) = £207,000.

On total borrowings of £2.5 million, this represents a weighted average rate of 8.28%. The borrowing costs which should be capitalised are therefore (£300,000 x 8.28% x 9/12) + (£240,000 x 8.28% x 5/12) = £26,910.

Government grants

The main objective of international standard IAS20 *Accounting for Government Grants and Disclosure of Government Assistance* is to prescribe the accounting treatment of government grants. IAS20 defines government grants as "*assistance by government in the form of transfers of resources to an entity in return for past or future compliance with certain conditions relating to the operating activities of the entity*". Government grants are of two main types:

(a) **Grants related to assets**. These are government grants which are made on condition that the entity should purchase, construct or otherwise acquire long-term assets such as property, plant and equipment. The purpose of such a grant is to help the entity to pay for the asset or assets concerned.

(b) **Grants related to income**. These are government grants other than grants related to assets. The usual purpose of a grant related to income is to help the entity to pay some of its operating expenses.

The first requirement of IAS20 is that government grants should not be recognised in the financial statements until there is reasonable assurance that the entity will comply with the relevant conditions and the grant will in fact be received. Once this assurance exists, government grants should be "*recognised in profit or loss on a systematic basis over the periods in which the entity recognises as expenses the related costs for which the grants are intended to compensate*".

This means that a grant for the acquisition of an asset should be recognised as income when calculating the entity's profit or loss for the accounting periods in which depreciation is charged on that asset. In each period, the proportion of the grant which is recognised as income should be the same as the proportion of the asset's depreciable amount which is charged as depreciation in that period. IAS20 permits two ways of achieving this effect:

(a) The grant may be credited to a deferred income account and then systematically transferred to the statement of comprehensive income over the useful life of the asset.

(b) The grant may be deducted from the carrying amount of the asset. This will result in reduced depreciation charges over the asset's useful life.

The two methods are equivalent but give a different presentation in the statement of comprehensive income and in the statement of financial position.

EXAMPLE 6

On 1 April 2013, a company which prepares financial statements to 31 March acquires an item of property, plant and equipment and receives a government grant of 40% towards the item's cost. The item costs £250,000 and has a useful life of four years. Its residual value is £60,000.

(a) Calculate the amount of the grant that should be recognised as income for each of the four years to 31 March 2017 if the asset is depreciated:

(i)   on the straight-line basis

(ii)   on the diminishing balance basis (at a rate of 30%).

(b) Assuming that the straight-line basis is used, explain how the grant will be dealt with in the financial statements if:

(i)   the grant is treated as deferred income

(ii)   the grant is deducted from the cost of the asset.

Solution

(a) The grant is £100,000 and the asset's depreciable amount is £190,000. The amount of the grant that should be recognised as income each year is calculated as follows:

(i)   **Straight-line basis**

	Depreciation charge	Grant recognised as income
	£	£
year to 31 March 2014	47,500	25,000
year to 31 March 2015	47,500	25,000
year to 31 March 2016	47,500	25,000
year to 31 March 2017	47,500	25,000
	190,000	100,000

Since the asset is depreciated on the straight-line basis, the grant is recognised as income on the straight-line basis.

(ii)   **Diminishing balance basis**

	Carrying amount b/f	Depreciation charge	Grant recognised as income
	£	£	£
year to 31 March 2014	250,000	75,000	39,474
year to 31 March 2015	175,000	52,500	27,632
year to 31 March 2016	122,500	36,750	19,342
year to 31 March 2017	85,750	25,750	13,552
		190,000	100,000

Each year's depreciation charge is 30% of the carrying amount brought forward, except that the charge for 2017 has been rounded to ensure that the sum of the depreciation charges is exactly equal to the depreciable amount.

In 2014, the depreciation charge of £75,000 is approximately 39.474% of the depreciable amount of £190,000, so 39.474% of the grant is recognised as income in that year. A similar calculation is used in the remaining three years to calculate the amount of the grant recognised as income.

(b) (i) The grant of £100,000 is credited to a deferred income account and transferred in equal instalments to the statement of comprehensive income. The figures appearing in the statement of comprehensive income and in the statement of financial position are as follows:

	2014 £	2015 £	2016 £	2017 £
Statement of comprehensive income:				
Depreciation charge	47,500	47,500	47,500	47,500
Grant income	25,000	25,000	25,000	25,000
Statement of financial position:				
Asset carrying amount	202,500	155,000	107,500	60,000
Deferred income a/c	75,000	50,000	25,000	0

(ii) In this case, the cost of the asset (net of the grant) is £150,000. Residual value is £60,000, so depreciable amount is £90,000. This is written off as an expense on the straight-line basis over the four years, as follows:

	2014 £	2015 £	2016 £	2017 £
Statement of comprehensive income:				
Depreciation charge	22,500	22,500	22,500	22,500
Statement of financial position:				
Asset carrying amount	127,500	105,000	82,500	60,000

Disclosure requirements of IAS20

IAS20 requires that entities should disclose:

(a) the accounting policy adopted in relation to government grants, including the method of presentation adopted in the financial statements

(b) the nature and extent of government grants recognised in the financial statements.

(c) any unfulfilled conditions attaching to government grants that have been recognised.

Investment property

There is a presumption in IAS16 that property, plant and equipment is acquired for use in an entity's operations and is generally used up or "consumed" over the period of its useful life. Depreciation charges are made so as to match the cost of consuming an asset against the revenues which it helps to generate. But property which is acquired as an investment rather than for use is not consumed in the entity's operations and does not have a useful life. This means that the accounting treatment required by IAS16 is generally inappropriate for such property. The objective of IAS40 *Investment Property* is to offer a more suitable accounting treatment for property held as an investment.

Definition of investment property

IAS40 defines investment property as "*property (land or a building or part of a building or both) held ... to earn rentals or for capital appreciation or both, rather than:*

(a) for use in the production or supply of goods or services, or

(b) for administrative purposes, or

(c) for sale in the ordinary course of business".

Examples of investment property given in IAS40 include the following:

(a)   land held for long-term capital appreciation

(b)   land held for a currently undetermined future use

(c)   a building that is leased out under one or more operating leases (see Chapter 9)

(d)   a building that is vacant but is held to be leased out under operating leases

(e)   property that is being constructed or developed for future use as investment property.

The standard also provides examples of items that are *not* investment property and are not within the scope of IAS40. These include:

(a)   property intended for sale in the ordinary course of business; the applicable standard is IAS2 *Inventories* (see Chapter 10)

(b)   property being constructed or developed on behalf of third parties; the applicable standard is IAS11 *Construction Contracts* (see Chapter 10)

(c)   owner-occupied property (including property held for future use as owner-occupied property); the applicable standard is IAS16 *Property, Plant and Equipment*

(d)   property leased to another entity under a finance lease; the applicable standard is IAS17 *Leases* (see Chapter 9).

Measurement of investment property

Investment property should be measured initially at cost. This includes transaction costs such as legal fees and property transfer taxes. As regards the measurement of investment property subsequent to its initial recognition, IAS40 requires an entity to choose between two models. Whichever model is adopted as the entity's accounting policy must normally be applied to all of the entity's investment property. The two models are as follows.

(a) **The fair value model**. Investment property is measured at its fair value at the end of each reporting period. As stated earlier in this chapter, IFRS13 defines fair value as "*the price that would be received to sell an asset or paid to transfer a liability in an orderly transaction between market participants at the measurement date*".

    A gain or loss arising from a change in the fair value of investment property must be recognised in the calculation of profit or loss for the period in which it arises. This is different from the IAS16 treatment of revaluation gains and losses, since IAS16 requires revaluation gains to be excluded from profit (see earlier in this chapter).

(b) **The cost model**. This is the cost model as defined in IAS16. Investment property is measured at cost, less any accumulated depreciation and less any accumulated impairment losses. The *Basis for Conclusions* for IAS40 suggests that this model might be used in countries with less-developed property markets and valuation professions.

An entity which generally adopts the fair value model in relation to investment property must nonetheless apply the cost model to a specific investment property if the fair value of that property cannot be determined reliably.

Disclosure requirements

The general disclosure requirements of IAS40 (which are in addition to the disclosures required by IFRS13) are as follows:

(a) whether the entity has adopted the fair value model or the cost model

(b) the extent to which fair values have been determined by an independent valuer who holds a recognised and relevant professional qualification

(c) the amounts of any rental income from investment property and related expenses that have been recognised when calculating the entity's profit or loss for the period.

If the fair value model is adopted, the entity must also provide a reconciliation between the carrying amounts of investment property at the beginning and end of the period, showing additions, disposals, gains or losses from fair value adjustments and any other movements.

    If the cost model is adopted, the entity must disclose similar information to that required by IAS16 for property, plant and equipment measured using the cost model. The entity must also disclose the fair value of its investment property (unless this cannot be determined reliably). This means that fair values will normally have to be determined whether or not the entity has actually adopted the fair value model.

Summary

▸ Property, plant and equipment consists of tangible non-current assets that are held for use in the production or supply of goods or services, or for rental to others or for administrative purposes.

▸ Property, plant and equipment is recognised as an asset when it is probable that it will yield future economic benefits and its cost can be measured reliably. It should be derecognised on disposal or when no future economic benefits are expected from it.

▸ Property, plant and equipment is measured initially at cost. Subsequently, an entity may apply either the cost model or the revaluation model.

▸ In general, revaluation gains are credited to a revaluation reserve and recognised as other comprehensive income in the statement of comprehensive income. Revaluation losses are recognised as an expense when calculating profit or loss for the period.

▸ The purpose of depreciation is to allocate the depreciable amount of an asset over its useful life. Residual values and lengths of useful lives should be reviewed at regular intervals. A depreciation method should be chosen that best matches the usage pattern of the asset concerned.

▸ Borrowing costs that are directly attributable to the acquisition, construction or production of a qualifying asset must be capitalised as part of the cost of that asset. Other borrowing costs must be recognised as an expense.

▸ Government grants relating to the acquisition of an asset are recognised as income over the useful life of that asset. The grant may be credited to a deferred income account and then systematically transferred to the statement of comprehensive income. Alternatively, the grant may be deducted from the carrying amount of the asset, resulting in reduced depreciation charges over the asset's useful life.

▸ Investment property consists of land or buildings held for the purpose of earning rental income or for capital appreciation or both.

▸ Investment property is measured initially at cost. Subsequently, an entity may apply either the fair value model or the cost model.

Appendix

IFRS13 *Fair Value Measurement*

The objectives of IFRS13 are to define "fair value", to set out a framework for measuring fair value, and to specify the required disclosures about fair value measurements.

Definition of fair value

IFRS13 defines fair value as "*the price that would be received to sell an asset or paid to transfer a liability in an orderly transaction between market participants at the measurement date*". This definition makes it clear that fair value is an "exit price" from the perspective of the entity that holds the asset or has the liability.

Measurement of fair value

IFRS13 states that the fair values of assets and liabilities should be determined by using appropriate valuation techniques. Three techniques identified in IFRS13 are:

(a) the "market approach", which uses prices generated by market transactions involving identical or comparable assets (e.g. quoted prices of listed shares)

(b) the "cost approach", which is based upon current replacement costs

(c) the "income approach", which converts future amounts (e.g. cash flows) into a single current discounted amount (e.g. present value).

IFRS13 also establishes a fair value hierarchy which categorises into three levels the inputs to the techniques used to measure fair value. These levels are as follows:

(a) "Level 1 inputs" are quoted prices in active markets for identical assets or liabilities.

(b) "Level 2 inputs" are inputs (other than Level 1 inputs) that are observable for the asset or liability, either directly or indirectly. Examples of such inputs include quoted prices for similar assets or liabilities in active markets and inputs other than quoted prices that are observable for the asset or liability, such as interest rates.

(c) "Level 3 inputs" are unobservable inputs for the asset or liability (i.e. inputs for which market data is not available). Such inputs use the best information available about the assumptions that market participants would make when pricing the asset or liability.

IFRS13 gives the highest priority to Level 1 inputs and gives the lowest priority to Level 3 inputs. Entities are required to maximise the use of observable inputs and minimise the use of unobservable inputs when making fair value measurements.

Fair value disclosures

Entities are required to disclose information which helps users to assess:

(a) for assets and liabilities measured at fair value in the entity's financial statements, the valuation techniques and inputs used to determine those measurements

(b) for fair value measurements made using Level 3 inputs, the effect of those measurements on the entity's profit or loss or other comprehensive income for the period.

Exercises

5.1   (a)   Define the term "property, plant and equipment".

(b)   When should an item of property, plant and equipment be recognised as an asset and when should it be derecognised?

(c)   Which of the following costs should be included in the cost of an item of property, plant and equipment at initial recognition?

- the purchase price of the item
- import duties incurred in relation to the item
- delivery charges
- small spare parts for the item
- the cost of a maintenance contract
- non-refundable purchase taxes relating to the item.

5.2   (a)   Distinguish between the cost model and the revaluation model for the measurement of property, plant and equipment subsequent to its initial recognition.

(b)   If the revaluation model is used, explain how revaluation gains and losses should be accounted for.

(c)   A company which uses the revaluation model and prepares financial statements to 31 December each year acquired an item of property on 1 February 2013 at a cost of £5 million. On 31 December 2013, this property was revalued at £5.2 million. On 31 December 2014, it was revalued at £4.7 million.

Explain how these revaluations should be accounted for. Also explain what would have happened if the valuations at 31 December 2013 and 2014 had been reversed.

5.3   (a)   In relation to property, plant and equipment, define the terms "depreciation", "depreciable amount", "useful life" and "residual value".

(b)   On 1 July 2013, a company which prepares financial statements to 30 June each year acquires an item of equipment at a cost of £59,500. The item's useful life is expected to be five years with a residual value of £10,000. Calculate depreciation charges for each of the five years of the item's useful life, using:

- the straight-line method
- the diminishing balance method (at a rate of 30%)

How should the company choose between these methods?

5.4 (a) Define the term "borrowing costs" and explain the accounting treatment of such costs which is required by international standard IAS23.

(b) During the year to 31 December 2013, a company started work on the construction of a manufacturing plant and incurred expenditure as follows:

	£000
1 April 2013	1,500
1 August 2013	2,400
1 December 2013	1,800

All of these payments were made out of general borrowings. Construction work was still underway at 31 December 2013. The company had the following general borrowings outstanding throughout the year 2013:

	Amount of loan	Interest for the year
	£000	£000
Loan A	10,000	1,150
Loan B	8,000	720
Loan C	5,000	430

Calculate the amount of borrowing costs that should be capitalised in relation to the construction of the manufacturing plant during the year.

5.5 (a) Define the term "investment property" and explain the two models permitted by international standard IAS40 for the measurement of investment property after its initial recognition.

(b) How do these two models differ from the two models permitted by IAS16 in relation to the measurement of property, plant and equipment?

5.6 Elite Leisure is a private limited liability company that operates a single cruise ship. The ship was acquired on 1 October 2005. Details of the cost of the ship's components and their estimated useful lives are:

component	original cost (£million)	depreciation basis
ship's fabric (hull, decks etc.)	300	25 years straight-line
cabins and entertainment area fittings	150	12 years straight-line
propulsion system	100	useful life of 40,000 hours

At 30 September 2013 no further capital expenditure had been incurred on the ship.

In the year ended 30 September 2013 the ship had experienced a high level of engine trouble which had cost the company considerable lost revenue and compensation costs. The measured expired life of the propulsion system at 30 September 2013 was 30,000 hours. Due to the unreliability of the engines, a decision was taken in early October 2013 to replace the whole of the propulsion system at a cost of £140 million. The expected life of the new propulsion system was 50,000 hours and in the year ended 30 September 2014 the ship had used its engines for 5,000 hours.

At the same time as the propulsion system replacement, the company took the opportunity to do a limited upgrade to the cabin and entertainment facilities at a cost of £60 million and repaint the ship's fabric at a cost of £20 million. After the upgrade of the cabin and entertainment area fittings it was estimated that their remaining life was five years (from the date of the upgrade). For the purpose of calculating depreciation, all the work on the ship can be assumed to have been completed on 1 October 2013. All residual values can be taken as nil.

Required:

Calculate the carrying amount of Elite Leisure's cruise ship at 30 September 2014 and the related amounts which should be recognised as expenses for the year ended 30 September 2014. Your answer should explain the treatment of each item.

(ACCA)

*5.7 Accounting standard IAS16 *Property, Plant and Equipment* makes a number of recognition, measurement and disclosure requirements with regard to tangible non-current assets. The term "non-current asset" is defined in accounting standard IAS1 *Presentation of Financial Statements*. The information given below relates to two companies, both of which prepare accounts to 31 December.

Alpha Ltd

Alpha Ltd bought a factory machine on 30 June 2013 and paid a total of £420,000. The supplier's invoice showed that this sum was made up of the following items:

	£
Manufacturer's list price	380,000
Less: Trade discount	38,000
	342,000
Delivery charge	6,800
Installation costs	29,600
Maintenance charge for year to 30 June 2014	27,000
Small spare parts	14,600
	420,000

Beta Ltd

On 1 January 2003, Beta Ltd bought freehold property for £800,000. This figure was made up of land £300,000 and buildings £500,000. The land was non-depreciable but it was decided to depreciate the buildings on the straight-line basis, assuming a useful life of 40 years and a residual value of £nil.

On 1 January 2013, the land was revalued at £400,000 and the buildings were revalued at £450,000. The company decided to incorporate these valuations into its accounts. The previous estimates of the buildings' useful life and residual value remain unchanged.

Required:

(a) Distinguish between current assets and non-current assets, giving TWO examples of each type of asset.

(b) Explain, with appropriate examples, the difference between capital expenditure and revenue expenditure.

(c) If a company incorrectly classified an item of capital expenditure as revenue expenditure, what effect would this have on the company's accounts in the year of the expenditure and in subsequent years?

(d) In accordance with the rules of IAS16, calculate the cost figure at which the machine bought by Alpha Ltd should initially be measured. Also explain the correct accounting treatment of any component of the £420,000 expenditure which cannot be treated as part of the machine's cost.

(e) Write journal entries for the revaluation of Beta Ltd's freehold property on 1 January 2013. Also calculate the amount of depreciation which should be charged in relation to the buildings for the year to 31 December 2013.

(CIPFA)

*5.8 (a) Define the term "investment property". Explain why it is not generally appropriate to charge depreciation in relation to such a property.

(b) Give three examples of properties (land or buildings) that should be classified as investment properties.

(c) Explain the "fair value model" which is permitted by IAS40 for the measurement of investment property.

(d) A company's investment property at 31 December 2013 is shown in the statement of financial position at its fair value of £23m. Explain the accounting treatment which should be applied in the financial statements for the year to 31 December 2014 if the property has risen in value by 10% during the year. Also explain the accounting treatment if the property has fallen in value by 10% during the year.

Chapter 6

Intangible assets

Introduction

The main purpose of this chapter is to explain the requirements of international standard IAS38 *Intangible Assets*. Basically, intangible assets are those without physical substance, such as patents and trademarks. IAS38 applies to all intangible assets except for those which fall within the scope of another international standard. The main exceptions and the applicable standards are:

(a) intangible assets held for sale in the ordinary course of trade (IAS2 *Inventories*)

(b) deferred tax assets (IAS12 *Income Taxes*)

(c) leases (IAS17 *Leases*)

(d) assets arising from employee benefits (IAS19 *Employee Benefits*)

(e) financial assets (IAS32 *Financial Instruments: Presentation*)

(f) goodwill acquired in a business combination (IFRS3 *Business Combinations*)

(g) non-current intangible assets classified as held for sale (IFRS5 *Non-current Assets Held for Sale and Discontinued Operations*).

The requirements of IFRS3 with regard to goodwill acquired in a business combination are explained later in this chapter. All of the other standards mentioned above are dealt with in later chapters of this book.

Objectives

By the end of this chapter, the reader should be able to:

• define the term "intangible asset" in accordance with IAS38

• state and explain the criteria which must be satisfied for an item to be recognised as an intangible asset

• determine the cost of an intangible asset

- distinguish between the cost model and the revaluation model for the measurement of intangible assets after initial recognition

- explain the requirements of IAS38 with regard to the amortisation of intangible assets

- list the main disclosure requirements of IAS38

- explain the requirements of IFRS3 in relation to goodwill.

Definition of an intangible asset

IAS38 defines an intangible asset as "*an identifiable, non-monetary asset without physical substance*". The main features of this definition are as follows:

(a) **Asset**. An item cannot be an intangible asset unless it is an asset in the first place. The IASB *Conceptual Framework* defines an asset as "*a resource controlled by the entity as a result of past events and from which future economic benefits are expected to flow to the entity*" (see Chapter 2). This definition is repeated in IAS38. The standard makes the point that expenditure on intangible resources (e.g. research) does not necessarily mean that an intangible asset has been acquired. This can only be the case if the expenditure results in the acquisition of an item which qualifies as an asset. The criteria which may be difficult to satisfy are:

   (i) **Future economic benefits**. There must be an expectation of future economic benefits, such as revenue from the sale of goods or services, or cost savings.

   (ii) **Control**. The entity must have the power to obtain the future economic benefits flowing from the resource. This power will usually (but not necessarily) stem from legally enforceable rights. In the absence of such rights, it is much more difficult to demonstrate control and therefore much more difficult to prove that an asset exists. For example:

   – Technical knowledge which gives rise to future economic benefits may be protected by a patent or copyright. This would demonstrate that the entity has the power to obtain the future benefits associated with that knowledge.

   – Expenditure on staff training may result in improved staff skills which are expected to generate future economic benefits. However, the entity incurring this expenditure may have little or no control over the staff, who could decide to move to a different employer and take their skills with them. It would be difficult in such a case to demonstrate that the entity has the power to obtain the future benefits associated with the training.

(b) **Without physical substance**. Intangible assets are distinguished from property, plant and equipment by the fact that they are without physical substance. IAS38 gives examples of items that have no physical substance and which would therefore qualify as intangible assets if all of the other necessary conditions were met. These examples include computer software, patents and copyrights, import quotas, franchises etc.

(c) **Non-monetary**. Monetary assets are defined as "*money held and assets to be received in fixed or determinable amounts of money*". Intangible assets must be non-monetary. Therefore, items such as cash, bank deposits and trade receivables are not intangible assets. Such items are in fact financial assets (see Chapter 11).

(d) **Identifiable**. IAS38 states that an asset is identifiable when it arises from contractual or other legal rights or when it is "separable". An asset is separable if it "*is capable of being separated or divided from the entity and sold, transferred, licensed, rented or exchanged*". The definition of an intangible asset requires the asset to be identifiable so as to distinguish it from goodwill, which is outside the scope of IAS38. Goodwill arises from factors such as an entity's good reputation and, by definition, is not identifiable (see later in this chapter).

Initial recognition and measurement of intangible assets

An item is recognised as an intangible asset if it meets the definition of an intangible asset and also satisfies the usual recognition criteria for an asset which are given in the IASB *Conceptual Framework* (see Chapter 2). These criteria are listed in IAS38 as follows:

(a) it is probable that the expected future economic benefits that are attributable to the asset will flow to the entity, and

(b) the cost of the asset can be measured reliably.

The probability of expected future economic benefits should be assessed using reasonable and supportable assumptions that represent management's best estimate of the economic conditions that will exist during the asset's useful life.

IAS38 states that intangible assets should be measured initially at their cost. The cost of an intangible asset is the cost incurred to acquire it or internally generate it (see below).

Separately acquired intangible assets

If an intangible asset is acquired in a separate transaction, the fact that a price has been paid for the asset is a reflection of the expectation that future economic benefits will flow to the entity. Furthermore, the asset's cost can usually be measured reliably. Therefore both of the recognition criteria listed above will usually be satisfied in the case of separately acquired intangible assets. The cost of such an asset includes:

(a) the purchase price of the asset, including import duties and non-refundable purchase taxes, after deducting trade discounts and rebates, and

(b) any directly attributable costs of preparing the asset for its intended use, including employee costs, professional fees and testing costs (but excluding advertising costs, staff training costs and administrative or other general overhead costs).

Once an intangible asset is in working condition, any further costs incurred in relation to that asset are not recognised as part of its cost. Therefore, costs incurred in using or redeploying an intangible asset should be recognised as an expense.

Intangible assets acquired as part of a business combination

An intangible asset may be acquired in a business combination. International standard IFRS3 *Business Combinations* defines a business combination as "*a transaction or other event in which an acquirer obtains control of one or more businesses*".

If an intangible asset is acquired in a business combination, the cost of that asset is specified by IAS38 (in accordance with IFRS3) to be the asset's fair value on the date of acquisition. Fair value is defined by international standard IFRS13 as "*the price that would be received to sell an asset or paid to transfer a liability in an orderly transaction between market participants at the measurement date*" (see Chapter 5).

The fact that a price has been paid for an intangible asset which is acquired in a business combination is accepted as evidence that future economic benefits are expected to flow to the entity. Furthermore, sufficient information will always exist to measure the asset's fair value reliably. Therefore both of the required recognition criteria will be satisfied for an intangible asset acquired in a business combination.

Internally generated intangible assets

Internally generated intangible assets are those which have been developed by the entity itself rather than purchased from another entity. The first point made by IAS38 in relation to internally generated assets is that "*internally generated goodwill shall not be recognised as an asset*". Goodwill which is purchased when one business entity acquires another is dealt with by IFRS3 *Business Combinations* (see below).

IAS38 then states that it may be difficult to assess whether an internally generated intangible asset qualifies for recognition because of:

(a) the problem of establishing whether or not there is an identifiable asset which will generate future economic benefits, and

(b) the problem of determining the cost of the asset reliably.

To resolve these problems, IAS38 requires that the internal generation of an intangible asset should be classified into a "research phase" and a "development phase". The standard then provides guidance with regard to the accounting treatment of each phase.

The research phase

Research is defined as "*original and planned investigation undertaken with the prospect of gaining new scientific or technical knowledge and understanding*". Examples of research activities include:

(a) activities aimed at gaining new knowledge

(b) the search for applications of research findings

(c)   the search for alternatives to materials, products, processes etc.

(d)   the formulation, design, evaluation and selection of possible alternatives for new or improved materials, products, processes etc.

IAS38 takes the view that, in the research phase of an internal project, it is not possible to demonstrate that an asset exists which will probably generate future economic benefits. In consequence, entities are not allowed to recognise an intangible asset arising from research work. All research expenditure must be written off as an expense when it is incurred.

The development phase

Development is defined as "*the application of research findings or other knowledge to a plan or design for the production of new or substantially improved materials, devices, products, processes, systems or services before the start of commercial production or use*". Examples of development activities include:

(a)   the design, construction and testing of pre-production prototypes and models

(b)   the design of tools, jigs, moulds and dies involving new technology

(c)   the design, construction and operation of a pilot plant

(d)   the design, construction and testing of a chosen alternative for new or improved materials, products, processes etc.

Since the development phase of an internal project is further advanced than the research phase, it may be possible to identify an intangible asset arising from this phase and to demonstrate that this asset will probably generate future economic benefits.

IAS38 requires that an intangible asset arising from the development phase of an internal project *must* be recognised if all of the following can be demonstrated:

(a)   the technical feasibility of completing the asset so that it will be ready for use or sale

(b)   the entity's intention to complete the asset and use or sell it

(c)   the entity's ability to use or sell the asset

(d)   the fact that the asset will probably generate future economic benefits

(e)   the availability of adequate technical, financial and other resources to complete the development work and use or sell the asset

(f)   the entity's ability to measure reliably the expenditure attributable to the asset during its development.

If any of these cannot be demonstrated, the development expenditure concerned must be written off as an expense when it is incurred. Past development expenditure which was previously written off an expense (because one or more of the above matters could not be demonstrated at that time) cannot be capitalised at a later date.

Expenditure on internally generated brands, mastheads, publishing titles, customer lists and similar items must always be written off.

Cost of an internally generated intangible asset

The cost of an internally generated intangible asset is the sum of the directly attributable costs incurred in relation to the asset as from the date when it first meets the recognition criteria listed above. Examples of directly attributable costs include:

(a) costs of materials and services used or consumed in generating the asset

(b) labour costs arising from the generation of the asset

(c) fees to register legal rights

(d) amortisation of patents and licenses used to generate the asset (see below).

Selling, administrative and other general overhead costs are usually excluded, as are staff training costs.

EXAMPLE 1

During the year to 31 March 2014, a company incurred the following expenditure with regard to the development of a new production process:

	£000
1 April 2013 to 31 October 2013	230
1 November 2013 to 31 March 2014	410

The criteria for the recognition of an internally generated intangible asset were satisfied as from 1 November 2013. Explain the accounting treatment of the development costs.

Solution

The £230,000 must be written off as an expense in the statement of comprehensive income for the year to 31 March 2014. The £410,000 must be capitalised and recognised as an intangible asset in the statement of financial position. The £230,000 cannot be reinstated as capital expenditure.

Recognition of an expense

IAS38 provides a number of examples of expenditure on intangible resources that must be recognised as an expense when the expenditure is incurred. These examples include:

(a) start-up costs

(b) training expenditure

(c) expenditure on advertising and promotional activities

(d) expenditure on relocating or reorganising part or all of an entity.

Such expenditure cannot be treated as giving rise to the acquisition of an intangible asset.

Subsequent measurement of intangible assets

IAS38 allows entities to choose between the "cost model" and the "revaluation model" for the measurement of intangible assets subsequent to initial recognition. These two models are very similar to those which are permitted by IAS16 in relation to property, plant and equipment (see Chapter 5). A brief description of each model is as follows:

(a) **The cost model**. After initial recognition, intangible assets are carried at cost less any accumulated amortisation and accumulated impairment losses (see Chapter 7). Note that the allocation of the depreciable amount of an intangible asset over its useful life is normally referred to as "amortisation" rather than "depreciation".

(b) **The revaluation model**. After initial recognition, intangible assets are carried at a revalued amount. The revalued amount of an intangible asset consists of its fair value at the date of revaluation, less any subsequent accumulated amortisation and less any subsequent accumulated impairment losses. Note that:

   (i) For this purpose, the fair value of an intangible asset must always be determined by reference to an active market in that type of asset. The revaluation model cannot be applied to an intangible asset if there is no active market. However, it is unusual for such a market to exist, since many intangible assets are unique.

   (ii) If the revaluation model is applied to an intangible asset, the same model should normally be applied to all of the other assets in its class. A class of intangible assets is a grouping of assets of a similar nature and use. However, if there is no active market for a specific intangible asset which belongs to a class of revalued intangible assets, this particular asset should be measured using the cost model.

   (iii) Revaluations should be made with sufficient regularity to ensure that the carrying amount of an intangible asset does not differ materially from fair value. The items within a class of intangible assets should all be revalued simultaneously. This avoids selective revaluations and also avoids the reporting of amounts that are a mixture of valuations made on different dates.

Accounting for revaluation gains and losses

If the carrying amount of an intangible asset is *increased* as a result of a revaluation, the increase must normally be credited to a revaluation reserve and recognised as "other comprehensive income" in the statement of comprehensive income. This treatment ensures that unrealised revaluation gains are excluded from profit and so are not available for payment as a dividend. If the carrying amount of an intangible asset is *decreased* as a result of a revaluation, the decrease must normally be recognised as an expense when calculating the entity's profit or loss. But note that:

(a) a revaluation increase must be recognised as income when calculating the entity's profit or loss to the extent that it reverses any revaluation decrease in respect of the same asset that was previously recognised as an expense

(b) a revaluation decrease must be debited to the revaluation reserve and shown (as a negative figure) in other comprehensive income to the extent of any credit balance previously existing in the revaluation reserve in respect of that same asset.

These rules are of course identical to the corresponding rules in IAS16 with regard to the revaluation of property, plant and equipment (see Chapter 5).

Disposal of a revalued intangible asset

When an intangible asset is disposed of, any revaluation gain included in the revaluation reserve in respect of that asset may be transferred to retained earnings. This recognises the fact that a previously unrealised gain has now been realised. The transfer is recorded in the statement of changes in equity and does not affect the statement of comprehensive income.

Note that revaluation gains recognised initially in other comprehensive income cannot be reclassified to profit or loss in a subsequent period (see Chapter 3).

EXAMPLE 2

(a) Company R prepares financial statements to 31 May each year. On 31 May 2013, the company acquired an intangible asset for £50,000. This asset was revalued at £60,000 on 31 May 2014 and at £35,000 on 31 May 2015.

(b) Company S prepares financial statements to 31 March each year. On 31 March 2013, the company acquired an intangible asset for £70,000. The asset was revalued at £55,000 on 31 March 2014 and at £75,000 on 31 March 2015.

(c) Company T prepares financial statements to 30 April each year. On 30 April 2014, the company disposed of an intangible asset that had been acquired some years ago and which had been revalued since acquisition. The company's revaluation reserve at 30 April 2014 included a £100,000 revaluation gain in relation to this asset.

Assuming that all three companies use the revaluation model, explain how each of the above transactions should be dealt with in the financial statements. Ignore amortisation.

Solution

(a) The £10,000 revaluation increase on 31 May 2014 should be credited to a revaluation reserve and recognised as other comprehensive income.

£10,000 of the £25,000 decrease on 31 May 2015 should be debited to revaluation reserve and recognised (as a negative figure) in other comprehensive income. The remaining £15,000 should be recognised as an expense.

(b) The £15,000 decrease on 31 March 2014 should be recognised as an expense.

£15,000 of the £20,000 increase on 31 March 2015 should be recognised as income. The remaining £5,000 should be credited to a revaluation reserve and recognised as other comprehensive income.

(c) £100,000 may be transferred from revaluation reserve to retained earnings. This transfer should be shown in the statement of changes in equity.

Amortisation of intangible assets

The accounting treatment of an intangible asset is dependent upon the length of its useful life. Intangible assets with finite useful lives are amortised (i.e. depreciated). Intangible assets with indefinite useful lives are not. Therefore it is important to be able to determine the useful life of an intangible asset and IAS38 lists a number of factors which should be taken into account when doing this. These include:

(a) the expected usage of the asset by the entity concerned

(b) public information on estimates of useful lives of similar assets used in similar ways

(c) technological, commercial or other types of obsolescence

(d) the stability of the industry in which the asset is being used

(e) expected actions by competitors

(f) the level of maintenance expenditure required so as to ensure that the asset generates the expected economic benefits (and whether the entity has the ability and intention to fund that level of expenditure)

(g) the period of control over the asset and any legal (or similar) limits on the length of time for which it can be used.

If an intangible asset arises from contractual or other legal rights, the useful life of the asset cannot exceed the period of those rights, but may be shorter than this if the entity intends to use the asset for a shorter period.

An intangible asset should be regarded as having an indefinite useful life only if there is no foreseeable limit to the period over which the asset is expected to generate net cash inflows for the entity.

Intangible assets with finite useful lives

IAS38 requires that the depreciable amount of an intangible asset with a finite useful life should be amortised on a systematic basis over its useful life. An intangible asset's depreciable amount is defined as "*the cost of an asset, or other amount substituted for cost, less its residual value*". Note the following points:

(a) Amortisation of an intangible asset should begin when the asset is available for use and should then continue until the asset is derecognised or classified as held for sale (see Chapter 8). Various amortisation methods are available, including the straight-line and diminishing balance methods. The chosen method should reflect the asset's usage pattern and should be applied consistently unless there is a change in that pattern. If the asset's usage pattern cannot be estimated reliably, the straight-line method should be used.

(b) Amortisation should normally be recognised as an expense. But if an intangible asset is used in the production of other assets (e.g. inventories), the amortisation of that intangible asset should be included in the cost of those assets.

(c)   As with property, plant and equipment, amortisation does not stop simply because an intangible asset is revalued. In these circumstances, the asset's depreciable amount is reset to the amount of the valuation (less residual value) and amortisation charges for the rest of the asset's useful life are based upon this revised depreciable amount.

(d)   If an intangible asset is revalued upwards and a revaluation gain in relation to that asset is credited to revaluation reserve, subsequent amortisation charges will exceed amortisation based on the asset's original cost. In these circumstances, the amount of excess amortisation in each accounting period may be transferred from revaluation reserve to retained earnings. This transfer takes place in the statement of changes in equity and does not affect the statement of comprehensive income.

Residual value

The residual value of an intangible asset with a finite useful life is normally assumed to be zero. However, this will not be the case if:

(a)   a third party is committed to buy the asset at the end of its useful life, or

(b)   residual value can be determined by reference to an active market for the type of asset concerned and that market will probably still exist at the end of the asset's useful life.

The residual value of an intangible asset should be reviewed at least at the end of each financial year. Any change in residual value is accounted for as a change in an accounting estimate in accordance with the requirements of IAS8 (see Chapter 4).

If the residual value of an intangible asset becomes greater than or equal to its carrying amount, the asset's depreciable amount is zero. Amortisation charges will then also be zero until such time as the asset's residual value becomes less than its carrying amount.

Review of useful life and amortisation method

The useful life of an intangible asset and the amortisation method used for that asset should be reviewed at least at the end of each financial year. If the asset's expected useful life has changed, the amortisation period should be changed accordingly. If the expected usage pattern of the asset has changed, the amortisation method should be changed accordingly. These changes should be accounted for as changes in accounting estimates in accordance with the requirements of IAS8 (see Chapter 4).

Intangible assets with indefinite useful lives

Intangible assets with indefinite useful lives are not amortised. However, the useful life of such an asset should be reviewed in every accounting period. If circumstances now indicate that the asset's useful life has become finite, it should be amortised over the remainder of that life. This change is accounted for as a change in an accounting estimate in accordance with the requirements of IAS8 (see Chapter 4).

International standard IAS36 *Impairment of Assets* explicitly states that intangible assets with indefinite useful lives should be reviewed for impairment every year (see Chapter 7).

Derecognition

An item previously recognised as an intangible asset should be derecognised (i.e. removed from the statement of financial position) when:

(a) it is disposed of, or

(b) no future economic benefits are expected from its use or from its disposal.

IAS38 states that any gain or loss arising on the derecognition of an intangible asset should be "recognised in profit or loss" when the asset is derecognised. This means that the gain or loss should be included in the calculation of the entity's profit or loss for the period in which derecognition occurs.

The gain or loss arising on derecognition is equal to the difference between the disposal proceeds (if any) and the asset's carrying amount at the time of derecognition.

Disclosure requirements

The main disclosures required by IAS38 are as follows:

(a) for each class of intangible asset, distinguishing between internally generated intangible assets and other intangible assets:

    (i) whether the useful lives are indefinite or finite and, if finite, the useful lives or amortisation rates used

    (ii) the amortisation methods used

    (iii) the gross carrying amount and accumulated amortisation at the beginning and end of the accounting period

    (iv) the line item(s) in the statement of comprehensive income in which amortisation of intangible assets is included

    (v) a reconciliation of the carrying amount at the beginning and end of the period, showing additions, disposals, revaluation increases and decreases, amortisation, impairment losses and any other movements

(b) the carrying amount of each intangible asset which is assessed as having an indefinite useful life and the reasons for that assessment

(c) the description, carrying amount and remaining amortisation period of any individual intangible asset which is material to the entity's financial statements

(d) the carrying amounts of any intangible assets pledged as security for liabilities

(e) the amount of any contractual commitments for the acquisition of intangible assets

(f)   for intangible assets stated at revalued amounts:

   (i)   for each revalued class, the date of the revaluation, the carrying amount of the revalued assets and the carrying amount that would have been recognised if the cost model had been used

   (ii) the amount of the revaluation surplus at the beginning and end of the period

(g)   the amount of research and development expenditure recognised as an expense during the accounting period.

IAS38 also encourages (but does not require) entities to disclose additional information which may be relevant to the needs of users. This additional information might include:

(h)   a description of any fully-amortised intangible asset that is still in use

(i)   a brief description of any significant intangible assets which were not recognised as assets because they did not meet the IAS38 recognition criteria.

Goodwill

As stated earlier in this chapter, goodwill arises from factors such as an entity's good reputation and strong customer relationships. Goodwill is a very significant asset to many entities, but accounting for goodwill raises two main difficulties:

(a)   It is usually impossible to determine reliably the cost or value of internally generated goodwill. Therefore internally generated goodwill fails one of the recognition criteria specified in the *Conceptual Framework* (see Chapter 2). This difficulty does not arise if goodwill is purchased when an entity acquires an established business, since the cost of the goodwill can be measured reliably in these circumstances.

(b)   Goodwill is a very vulnerable asset and may easily be damaged or destroyed.

Because of the first of these difficulties, IAS38 does not allow internally generated goodwill to be recognised as an asset. However, purchased goodwill is recognised as an asset in accordance with IFRS3 *Business Combinations*. The requirements of this standard insofar as they relate to goodwill are explained below.

IFRS3 *Business Combinations*

In general, entities are required to apply the requirements of IFRS3 when accounting for "business combinations". As mentioned earlier in this chapter, a business combination occurs when an entity acquires control of a business. This may happen when:

(a) the acquirer buys net assets which together form a business, or

(b) the acquirer buys the shares of another entity and so establishes a parent-subsidiary relationship (see Chapter 18).

In each case, it is necessary to measure the amount of any goodwill acquired as a result of the business combination. IFRS3 defines goodwill as "*an asset representing the future economic benefits arising from ... assets acquired in a business combination that are not individually identified and separately recognised*" and requires that goodwill acquired in a business combination should be recognised as an asset. In case (a) above, this goodwill is recognised as an asset in the financial statements of the acquirer. In case (b), the goodwill is recognised in the acquirer's consolidated financial statements (see Chapter 18).

IFRS3 also prescribes the way in which such goodwill should be measured at initial recognition. This measurement can involve a number of factors (see Chapter 18). But in a straightforward case the amount of the goodwill to be recognised is the excess of:

(a) the price paid by the acquirer in the business combination, over

(b) the acquirer's interest in the net fair value of the acquiree's identifiable assets and liabilities at the acquisition date.

Therefore the measurement of goodwill acquired in a business combination depends upon ascertaining the net fair value of the identifiable assets and liabilities acquired and then comparing this with the price paid by the acquirer. IFRS3 repeats the IFRS13 definition of fair value as "*the price that would be received to sell an asset or paid to transfer a liability in an orderly transaction between market participants at the measurement date*".

Negative goodwill

If the price (or "consideration") paid by the acquirer in a business combination is *less* than the net fair value of the identifiable assets and liabilities acquired, it would appear that there is "negative goodwill" (though this term is not used in IFRS3). This situation could arise for two main reasons:

(a) Errors might have been made when determining the fair value of the consideration or the fair values of the identifiable assets and liabilities acquired.

(b) The acquirer may have made a "bargain purchase".

Accordingly, the first requirement of IFRS3 if negative goodwill arises is that there should be a reassessment of the fair value of the consideration and the fair values of the identifiable assets and liabilities acquired. Any negative goodwill which remains after this reassessment should be treated as income and included in the acquirer's profit or loss.

Subsequent measurement of goodwill

After initial recognition, goodwill acquired in a business combination should <u>not</u> be amortised. Instead, IFRS3 requires that such goodwill should be measured at the amount initially recognised less any accumulated "impairment losses". In very general terms, an impairment loss arises when an asset's value falls below its carrying amount.

IAS36 *Impairment of Assets* prescribes the accounting treatment of impairment losses. This standard states that goodwill acquired in a business combination should be tested for impairment every year (see Chapter 7).

Disclosure requirements of IFRS3

The main disclosure requirements of IFRS3 in relation to goodwill are as follows:

(a) a reconciliation of the carrying amount of goodwill at the beginning and end of the accounting period, showing:

    (i) the gross amount of goodwill and any accumulated impairment losses at the beginning of the period

    (ii) additional goodwill recognised in the period

    (iii) goodwill now derecognised because it has been disposed of or because it is included in a disposal group classified as held for sale (see Chapter 8)

    (iv) impairment losses for the period

    (v) any other movements

    (vi) the gross amount of goodwill and any accumulated impairment losses at the end of the period

(b) in the case of a bargain purchase:

    (i) the amount of any gain which has been included in the entity's profit or loss for the period and the line item in the statement of comprehensive income in which this gain is included, and

    (ii) an explanation of the reasons that caused this gain to occur.

Summary

▸ IAS38 defines intangible assets as identifiable, non-monetary assets without physical substance. An asset is identifiable if it arises from legal rights or is capable of being separated from the entity and sold, transferred, licensed, rented or exchanged.

▸ Goodwill is not identifiable and is therefore outside the scope of IAS38.

▸ The cost of a separately acquired intangible asset includes its purchase price and any directly attributable costs of preparing the asset for use. General administrative or other overhead costs are excluded. The cost of an intangible asset acquired in a business combination is its fair value on the date of acquisition.

▸ All research expenditure is written off an expense when it is incurred. Development expenditure incurred in relation to an internally generated intangible asset must be recognised as an asset if certain conditions are satisfied.

▸ Entities may choose between the cost model and the revaluation model for measuring intangible assets after initial recognition. But the revaluation method cannot be used unless there is an active market for the assets concerned.

▸ If the revaluation model is used, it must be applied to entire classes of intangible assets and regular revaluations must be made.

▸ In general, revaluation gains are credited to a revaluation reserve and recognised as other comprehensive income in the statement of comprehensive income. Revaluation losses are recognised as an expense when calculating profit or loss for the period.

▸ Intangible assets with finite useful lives should be systematically amortised over those lives. Intangible assets with indefinite useful lives are not amortised but are subject to annual impairment reviews.

▸ Internally generated goodwill cannot be recognised as an asset.

▸ Goodwill acquired in a business combination is recognised as an asset and measured initially at the excess of the price paid by the acquirer over the net fair value of the assets and liabilities acquired. Negative goodwill is treated as income and is included in the acquirer's profit or loss.

▸ Subsequent to its initial recognition, goodwill acquired in a business combination is measured at the amount at which it was initially recognised less any accumulated impairment losses. Goodwill must be tested for impairment every year.

▸ Intangible assets are derecognised on disposal or if they are expected to yield no more economic benefits.

▸ IAS38 and IFRS3 make disclosure requirements with regard to intangible assets and goodwill respectively.

Exercises

6.1   (a)   Define the term "intangible asset" and explain the main features of this definition.

        (b)   Explain how an intangible asset should be measured at its initial recognition if it is acquired in a separate transaction.

        (c)   Explain how an intangible asset should be measured at its initial recognition if it is acquired in a business combination.

6.2   (a)   Distinguish between research expenditure and development expenditure.

        (b)   Explain the accounting treatment required by IAS38 in relation to each of these types of expenditure.

        (c)   During the year to 31 July 2014, a pharmaceuticals company spent a total of £830,000 on research and development. Of this amount, £370,000 was spent on an unsuccessful attempt to find a cure for the common cold. The remaining £460,000 was spent on the development of a new range of cosmetic products. How should this expenditure be accounted for in the company's financial statements?

6.3   A company has purchased the following intangible assets in separate transactions:

        (a)   a patent which expires after ten years; the company expects to make use of this patent for six years and then dispose of it

        (b)   a copyright which expires after 40 years; the company intends to use this copyright for 30 years, after which it is expected to be of no further value

        (c)   a trademark relating to a product; this trademark has an unlimited legal life but the company expects to cease manufacture of the product within three years.

    Determine the useful life of each of these assets. Assuming that the company does not use the revaluation model, explain how each asset should be treated in the company's financial statements.

6.4   Distinguish between the cost model and the revaluation model for the measurement of intangible assets subsequent to their initial recognition.

6.5   (a)   Define the term "goodwill" and distinguish between internally generated goodwill and goodwill acquired in a business combination.

        (b)   Identify the main features of goodwill which distinguish it from other intangible assets and which warrant a special accounting treatment.

        (c)   Why is not logical to amortise purchased goodwill?

6.6   On 1 January 2014, A Ltd bought all of the assets and liabilities of B Ltd for a price of £500,000. B Ltd then went into liquidation. The statements of financial position of the two companies just <u>before</u> this purchase were as follows:

		A Ltd		B Ltd
	£000	£000	£000	£000
Assets				
Non-current assets				
Property, plant and equipment		4,320		460
Current assets				
Inventories	1,210		220	
Trade receivables	940		90	
Cash at bank	1,650	3,800	-	310
		8,120		770
Equity				
Ordinary share capital		1,000		200
Retained earnings		3,650		390
		4,650		590
Liabilities				
Non-current liabilities		2,500		-
Current liabilities		970		180
		8,120		770

The fair values of the assets and liabilities of B Ltd as at 1 January 2014 were agreed to be as follows:

	£000
Property, plant and equipment	390
Inventories	160
Trade receivables	80
Current liabilities	180

Required:

(a)   Calculate the amount paid by A Ltd for the goodwill of B Ltd.

(b)   Prepare a statement of financial position for A Ltd as it would be immediately after the purchase of the net assets of B Ltd, assuming that A Ltd paid for this purchase out of its bank account.

6.7   (a)   Distinguish between *research* and *development* within the context of IAS38 *Intangible Assets*.

    (b)   State, with reasons, how the following expenditure would be dealt with in the financial statements of Prebnez plc to conform with IAS38:

       (i)   Money spent on a joint project with a university investigating the potential use of carbon nanotubes for the storage of digital data.

      (ii)   Expenditure on developing a new high speed hard disk which, in the opinion of Prebnez plc, has an assured and profitable market. Work has been suspended pending the development of a new glue suitable for the construction of the disk drives.   *(CIPFA)*

*6.8   The following information relates to three companies that use the revaluation model in relation to intangible assets and prepare annual financial statements to 31 December:

    (a)   Company W acquired an intangible asset for £250,000 on 31 December 2012. This asset was revalued at £225,000 on 31 December 2013 and at £270,000 on 31 December 2014.

    (b)   Company X disposed of an intangible asset on 31 December 2014. This asset had been acquired some years previously at a cost of £100,000 and had a carrying amount of £160,000 on the date of disposal. Disposal proceeds were £195,000.

    (c)   Company Y acquired an intangible asset for £80,000 on 31 December 2012. This asset was revalued at £90,000 on 31 December 2013 and at £65,000 on 31 December 2014.

Describe the circumstances in which the revaluation model may be used (in accordance with the requirements of IAS38) and explain how each of the above matters should be dealt with in the financial statements of the company concerned.

*6.9   There are two international standards which deal with goodwill. IAS38 does not allow internally generated goodwill to be recognised as an asset. Goodwill acquired in a business combination is dealt with by IFRS3.

    (a)   Define the term "goodwill" and explain why internally generated goodwill may not be recognised as an asset.

    (b)   Explain how goodwill acquired in a business combination should be measured at initial recognition and in subsequent accounting periods.

    (c)   Explain the accounting treatment which should be applied if goodwill acquired in a business combination appears to have a negative value.

    (d)   List the main disclosures required by IFRS3 in relation to goodwill.

Chapter 7

Impairment of assets

Introduction

This chapter explains the main requirements of international standard IAS36 *Impairment of Assets*. The objective of this standard is to ensure that assets are not carried in the financial statements at more than their recoverable amounts. The recoverable amount of an asset is the amount that can be obtained by either using it or selling it and an asset is said to be "impaired" if its recoverable amount falls beneath its carrying amount. IAS36 applies to all assets other than those for which other standards prescribe the required accounting treatment. The main exceptions and the applicable standards are:

(a) inventories (IAS2 *Inventories*)

(b) assets arising from construction contracts (IAS11 *Construction Contracts*)

(c) deferred tax assets (IAS12 *Income Taxes*)

(d) assets arising from employee benefits (IAS19 *Employee Benefits*)

(e) most financial assets (IFRS9 *Financial Instruments*)

(f) investment property measured at fair value (IAS40 *Investment Property*)

(g) non-current assets classified as held for sale (IFRS5 *Non-current Assets Held for Sale and Discontinued Operations*).

All of the standards on this list are dealt with in other chapters of this book.

In principle, IAS36 applies to assets in general, not just non-current assets. However, the exclusion of inventories and most financial assets (including receivables and cash) means that, in practice, the standard is mainly applicable to non-current assets.

Objectives

By the end of this chapter, the reader should be able to:

- define the term "impairment loss"
- list the main factors which may indicate that an asset is impaired
- calculate the recoverable amount of an asset and the amount of any impairment loss
- explain the accounting treatment of impairment losses

- define the term "cash-generating unit" and explain how such units are identified
- allocate an impairment loss amongst the assets of a cash-generating unit
- account for the reversal of an impairment loss
- list the main disclosure requirements of IAS36.

Indications of impairment

IAS36 defines an impairment loss as *"the amount by which the carrying amount of an asset or cash-generating unit exceeds its recoverable amount"*. A cash-generating unit is a group of assets which are judged for impairment collectively (see later in this chapter).

This definition suggests that it might be necessary to determine the recoverable amount of every asset every time that financial statements are prepared, so as to discover which assets have suffered impairment losses. However, this would involve a great deal of effort and much of that effort would be wasted, since in normal circumstances it is unlikely that many of an entity's assets will actually be impaired. In general, therefore, IAS36 requires entities to determine the recoverable amount of an asset only if there is some indication that the asset might be impaired. Examples of such indications listed by IAS36 include:

(a) **External sources of information**:

  (i) there are observable indications that an asset's value has declined during the period by significantly more than expected

  (ii) significant and adverse changes have occurred (or will occur in the near future) in the technological, market, economic or legal environment in which the entity operates or in the market to which an asset is dedicated

  (iii) interest rate increases have occurred which are likely to increase the discount rate used in calculating an asset's value in use (see later in this chapter) and so cause a material decrease in the asset's recoverable amount

  (iv) the carrying amount of the entity's net assets exceeds its market capitalisation (i.e. the market value of its entire share capital, in the case of a company).

(b) **Internal sources of information**:

  (i) there is evidence of obsolescence of an asset or physical damage to an asset

  (ii) significant and adverse changes have occurred (or are expected to occur in the near future) in the extent to which an asset is used or the manner in which it is used; such changes include:

    – the asset becoming idle
    – plans to discontinue the operation in which the asset is used
    – plans to dispose of the asset earlier than expected
    – reassessing the asset's useful life as finite rather than indefinite

  (iii) there is evidence that the economic performance of an asset is (or will be) worse than expected.

If any of these indications are present, the asset concerned must be tested for impairment by comparing its recoverable amount with its carrying amount. IAS36 stresses that the above list is not exhaustive and there could be other indications that an asset might be impaired. These indications would also require the entity to determine the recoverable amount of the asset concerned.

IAS36 also points out that if there are indications that an asset might be impaired, these indications may also suggest that the entity should review the asset's useful life and residual value and the depreciation or amortisation method being used, in accordance with the requirements of standards IAS16 (see Chapter 5) and IAS38 (see Chapter 6).

Intangible assets and goodwill

As stated above, the recoverable amount of most assets need not be determined unless there is some indication that impairment might have occurred. However, there are two types of asset for which the recoverable amount must be determined every year, regardless of whether or not there are any indications of impairment. These are:

(a) intangible assets which have an indefinite useful life or which are not yet available for use (see Chapter 6)

(b) goodwill acquired in a business combination (see Chapter 6).

Recoverable amount

IAS36 defines the recoverable amount of an asset (or cash-generating unit) as "*the higher of its fair value less costs of disposal and its value in use*". This definition depends upon three further definitions also given in IAS36. These are:

(a) Fair value (as defined by IFRS13) is "*the price that would be received to sell an asset or paid to transfer a liability in an orderly transaction between market participants at the measurement date*".

(b) Costs of disposal are "*incremental costs directly attributable to the disposal of an asset or cash-generating unit, excluding finance costs and income tax expense*".

(c) Value in use is "*the present value of the future cash flows expected to be derived from an asset or cash-generating unit*".

If it is not possible to determine an asset's fair value, then the asset's value in use may be used as its recoverable amount. Conversely, if there is no reason to suppose that an asset's value in use is materially higher than its fair value less costs of disposal, then the asset's fair value less costs of disposal may be used as its recoverable amount.

In any case, it is not always necessary to determine both fair value less costs of disposal and value in use for an asset. If either of these two amounts can be shown to be greater than the asset's carrying amount, it follows that the asset cannot be impaired and so there is no need to determine the other of the two amounts.

EXAMPLE 1

A company has seven assets (labelled A to G) for which there are indications of possible impairment. The carrying amount, fair value less costs of disposal and value in use for each asset are as shown below. Determine the amount of any impairment loss arising in relation to each asset.

	Carrying amount	Fair value less costs of disposal	Value in use
	£	£	£
Asset A	10,000	12,000	18,000
Asset B	11,000	9,000	13,000
Asset C	7,000	11,500	n/d
Asset D	8,500	6,500	7,000
Asset E	12,750	n/d	16,800
Asset F	10,000	14,000	12,000
Asset G	21,000	15,000	10,000

Note: n/d = not determined

Solution

	Carrying amount	Recoverable amount	Impairment loss
	£	£	£
Asset A	10,000	18,000	0
Asset B	11,000	13,000	0
Asset C	7,000	11,500 (at least)	0
Asset D	8,500	7,000	1,500
Asset E	12,750	16,800 (at least)	0
Asset F	10,000	14,000	0
Asset G	21,000	15,000	6,000

Notes:

(i) In each case, recoverable amount is the higher of fair value less costs of disposal and value in use. For assets C and E, one of these figures has not been determined, so recoverable amount cannot be calculated. However, recoverable amount must be at least equal to the one figure which is known (and may be higher).

(ii) For most of the assets, carrying amount is less than recoverable amount, so there is no impairment loss. However, assets D and G are impaired.

(iii) Although value in use has not been determined for asset C and fair value less costs of disposal has not been determined for asset E, it is still clear that these assets are not impaired. Therefore, it is not necessary to expend further accounting effort in trying to determine the missing figures.

Fair value less costs of disposal

An asset's fair value should be determined in accordance with the requirements of IFRS13 (see Chapter 5). If the type of asset in question is traded in an active market involving identical assets, then the "market approach" can be used and the quoted price in that market will provide a Level 1 input. Otherwise, the fair value of the asset will have to be determined by using one of the other valuation techniques listed in IFRS13. Note that:

(a) An asset's fair value normally differs from its value in use because value in use may reflect factors that are specific to the entity concerned and not applicable to market participants in general.

(b) The costs of disposal which are deducted when calculating fair value less costs of disposal include items such as legal costs, stamp duty, costs of removing the asset and direct costs that would be incurred to bring the asset into a condition suitable for sale.

Value in use

As stated above, an asset's value in use is calculated by discounting the future cash flows which the asset is expected to generate. These future cash flows should include:

(a) projections of future cash inflows from the use of the asset

(b) projections of future cash outflows that will be necessarily incurred so as to generate cash inflows from the use of the asset (e.g. servicing and maintenance costs)

(c) net cash flows (if any) to be received or paid on disposal of the asset at the end of its useful life.

Future cash flows should be estimated for the asset in its current condition and should not take into account any cash flows that are expected to arise from improving or enhancing the asset's performance. Furthermore, estimates of future cash flows should *not* include:

(a) cash inflows or outflows from financing activities (e.g. interest payable)

(b) tax receipts or payments.

It is clear that the calculation of value in use will involve making estimates of future cash flows. IAS36 states that these estimates should be based on reasonable and supportable assumptions and that greater weight should be given to external evidence than to internal evidence. IAS36 also states that cash flow projections should be based on management's most recent financial budgets or forecasts. Short-term budgets may be extrapolated into the future using a steady or declining growth rate (unless an increasing rate can be justified).

The discount rate used in calculating an asset's value in use should be a pre-tax interest rate which reflects current market assessments of the time value of money.

EXAMPLE 2

A company estimates that an asset is expected to generate the following cash flows over its useful life of four years:

	Inflows	Outflows
	£000	£000
Year 1	75	6
Year 2	100	7
Year 3	90	7
Year 4	60	6

All cash flows will occur at the end of the year concerned. At the end of the four-year period, the asset is expected to be sold for £50,000. Assuming a discount rate of 12% and working to the nearest £000, calculate the asset's value in use.

Solution

	Inflows	Outflows	Net cash flow	Discount factor	Present value
	£000	£000	£000		£000
Year 1	75	6	69	0.893	62
Year 2	100	7	93	0.797	74
Year 3	90	7	83	0.712	59
Year 4	110	6	104	0.636	66
Value in use					261

Notes:

(i)   The cash inflow for year 4 includes the £50,000 disposal proceeds of the asset.

(ii) The discount factor for the first year is $1/1.12 = 0.893$. The discount factor for the second year is $1/(1.12)^2$ and so forth (see Chapter 2).

(iii) The asset's value is use is £261,000.

Recognition and measurement of an impairment loss

If the recoverable amount of an asset is less than its carrying amount, IAS36 requires that the asset's carrying amount should be reduced to its recoverable amount. This reduction is an impairment loss. In general, an impairment loss should be recognised as an expense. However, if the asset is carried at a revalued amount, the impairment loss is accounted for in the same way as a revaluation decrease. This means that:

(a)   the impairment loss is debited to the revaluation reserve and shown (as a negative figure) in other comprehensive income to the extent of any credit balance previously existing in the revaluation reserve in respect of that same asset

(b) any excess is then recognised as an expense.

After an impairment loss has been recognised, subsequent depreciation or amortisation charges should allocate the asset's revised carrying amount (less residual value) over the remainder of its useful life on a systematic basis.

Cash-generating units

If there is any indication that an asset might be impaired, the asset's recoverable amount should be determined and compared with its carrying amount. But a problem arises if it is not possible to determine an individual asset's recoverable amount. This would occur if:

(a) the asset does not generate cash inflows that are largely independent of those from other assets, so value in use cannot be determined, and

(b) fair value less costs of disposal cannot be used as the asset's recoverable amount since its value in use might be materially more than its fair value less costs of disposal.

In these circumstances, IAS36 requires that impairment testing should be performed at the cash-generating unit (CGU) level. IAS36 defines a cash-generating unit as "*the smallest identifiable group of assets that generates cash inflows that are largely independent of the cash inflows from other assets or groups of assets*". An entity's CGUs should be identified consistently from period to period unless a change can be justified.

If the recoverable amount of an individual asset which might be impaired cannot be determined, the recoverable amount of the CGU to which the asset belongs should be determined instead and an impairment loss should be recognised if the CGU's recoverable amount is less than its carrying amount. A CGU should also be tested for impairment if there is any indication that the CGU as a whole is impaired.

EXAMPLE 3

This example is based upon one provided in IAS36.

A mining company owns a private railway to support its mining activities. This railway could be sold only for scrap value and does not generate cash inflows that are largely independent of the cash inflows from the other assets of the mine. Would it be possible to determine the recoverable amount of the railway?

Solution

The railway's value in use cannot be estimated and is probably materially more than its scrap value. Therefore the recoverable amount of the railway cannot be determined. If there is any indication of impairment, the company should determine the recoverable amount of the CGU to which the railway belongs (i.e. the mine as a whole).

Recoverable amount and carrying amount of a CGU

The recoverable amount of a CGU is the higher of its fair value less costs of disposal and its value in use. The carrying amount of a CGU should be determined on a basis that is consistent with the way in which its recoverable amount has been determined. This means that a CGU's carrying amount:

(a) includes the carrying amount of only those assets that can be attributed directly to the CGU (or can be allocated to it on a reasonable and consistent basis) and which will generate the future cash inflows used in determining the CGU's value in use

(b) excludes the carrying amount of the CGU's liabilities, unless the CGU's recoverable amount cannot be determined without taking these liabilities into account.

Assets which are not within the scope of IAS36 (e.g. inventories) should be excluded when determining a CGU's carrying amount and recoverable amount.

EXAMPLE 4

One of a company's cash-generating units is being tested for impairment. The carrying amount of the CGU's assets on the date of the test is £25 million. The carrying amount of its liabilities on that date is £8 million.

It has been established that the CGU could be sold to a buyer for £15 million, in which case the buyer would take over all of the CGU's assets and liabilities. Disposal costs would be immaterial. The value in use of the CGU is estimated to be £24 million. This figure ignores future cash outflows relating to payment of the CGU's existing liabilities.

Calculate the CGU's recoverable amount and carrying amount. Also calculate the amount of any impairment loss.

Solution

Normally, existing liabilities are ignored when determining the carrying amount and value in use of a CGU. However, the figure which is given for fair value less costs of disposal takes into account the CGU's liabilities as well as its assets. Therefore, to ensure that meaningful comparisons are made, these liabilities must also be taken into account when determining the CGU's carrying amount and its value in use. The calculations are as follows:

(i) Fair value less costs of disposal is stated to be £15 million. Value in use (subtracting the existing liabilities) is £16 million. Therefore recoverable amount is £16 million.

(ii) Carrying amount (again subtracting the existing liabilities) is £17 million. This exceeds recoverable amount by £1 million and so there is an impairment loss of £1 million.

Goodwill

As mentioned earlier in this chapter, goodwill acquired in a business combination must be tested for impairment every year, regardless of whether or not there are any indications of impairment. However, goodwill does not generate cash flows independently of other assets and so must be allocated between CGUs for impairment testing purposes. If goodwill cannot be allocated between individual CGUs, it is allocated between groups of CGUs to which the goodwill relates. Impairment testing then proceeds as follows:

(a) An individual CGU to which goodwill has been allocated should be tested annually for impairment by comparing its carrying amount (including goodwill) with its recoverable amount.

(b) A group of CGUs to which goodwill has been allocated should be tested annually for impairment by comparing the carrying amount of the group (including goodwill) with the group's recoverable amount.

(c) An individual CGU to which no goodwill has been allocated should be tested only if there are indications of impairment. This applies whether or not the CGU belongs to a group of CGUs to which goodwill has been allocated. The impairment test compares the CGU's carrying amount (excluding goodwill) with its recoverable amount.

Corporate assets

IAS36 defines corporate assets as *"assets other than goodwill that contribute to the future cash flows of both the cash-generating unit under review and other cash-generating units"*. Corporate assets include items such as a headquarters building or research centre. Like goodwill, corporate assets do not generate cash inflows independently of other assets and so must be allocated between CGUs (or groups of CGUs) for impairment testing purposes. This allocation must be done on a reasonable and consistent basis. If it becomes necessary to test a CGU (or group of CGUs) for impairment, the testing procedure is as follows:

(a) An individual CGU to which a portion of corporate assets has been allocated should be tested for impairment by comparing its carrying amount (including the allocation of corporate assets) with its recoverable amount.

(b) A group of CGUs to which a portion of corporate assets has been allocated should be tested for impairment by comparing the carrying amount of the group (including the allocation of corporate assets) with the group's recoverable amount.

(c) An individual CGU to which no portion of corporate assets has been allocated should be tested by comparing the CGU's carrying amount (excluding corporate assets) with its recoverable amount, in the usual way.

Allocation of an impairment loss for a CGU

An impairment loss must be recognised if the recoverable amount of a CGU (or group of CGUs) is less than its carrying amount. This loss is recognised by reducing the carrying amount of the CGU's assets. An impairment loss is allocated between assets as follows:

(a) first, to any goodwill which has been allocated to the CGU

(b) next, to the other assets of the CGU, in proportion to their carrying amounts.

These allocations are then treated as if they were impairment losses on individual assets (see earlier in this chapter). When allocating an impairment loss between the assets of a CGU, the carrying amount of an asset should not be reduced below the highest of:

(a) the asset's fair value less costs of disposal (if measurable)

(b) the asset's value in use (if this can be determined)

(c) zero.

If any of these restrictions apply, the amount of the impairment loss that would otherwise have been allocated to the asset concerned should be allocated pro rata between the other assets of the CGU.

EXAMPLE 5

The carrying amounts of the assets of a cash generating unit are as follows:

	£000
Goodwill acquired in a business combination	200
Development costs	300
Property, plant and equipment	600
	1,100

The recoverable amount of this CGU is only £780,000. The fair value less costs of disposal of the property, plant and equipment is £500,000.

(a) Calculate the amount of the impairment loss and show how this should be allocated between the assets of the CGU.

(b) Explain how the allocation of the impairment loss would change if the fair value less costs of disposal of the property, plant and equipment were £550,000.

Solution

(a) The impairment loss is £320,000 (£1,100,000 – £780,000). Of this loss, £200,000 is used to eliminate the goodwill. The remaining £120,000 is split between the other two assets in the ratio 300:600. Development costs are reduced by £40,000 and property, plant and equipment is reduced by £80,000.

The carrying amounts of the assets in the CGU are now £260,000 for development costs and £520,000 for property, plant and equipment (a total of £780,000).

(b) The carrying amount of the property, plant and equipment cannot be reduced to less than £550,000. So £30,000 of the impairment loss that would have been allocated to this asset must be allocated instead to the development costs (the only remaining asset of the CGU).

The carrying amounts of the assets in the CGU are now £230,000 for development costs and £550,000 for property, plant and equipment (a total of £780,000).

Reversal of impairment losses

If impairment losses have been recognised in previous accounting periods, IAS36 requires the entity to assess (at the end of each reporting period) whether there are any indications that these impairment losses have now decreased or no longer exist. Examples of such indications listed by IAS36 include:

(a) **External sources of information**:

(i) there are observable indications that an asset's value has increased significantly during the period

(ii) significant and favourable changes have occurred (or will occur in the near future) in the technological, market, economic or legal environment in which the entity operates or in the market to which an asset is dedicated

(iii) interest rate decreases have occurred which are likely to reduce the discount rate used in calculating an asset's value in use and so cause a material increase in the asset's recoverable amount.

(b) **Internal sources of information**:

(i) significant and favourable changes have occurred (or are expected to occur in the near future) in the extent to which or the manner in which an asset is used

(ii) there is evidence that the economic performance of an asset is (or will be) better than expected.

If any of these indications exist, the recoverable amount of the asset or CGU concerned must be determined again, with a view to reversing all or part of the previously recognised impairment loss. However, there is one exception to this general rule. IAS36 states that "*an impairment loss recognised for goodwill shall not be reversed in a subsequent period*".

The following points should be noted with regard to the reversal of impairment losses:

(a) A previously recognised impairment loss cannot be reversed unless there has been a change in the estimates used when the impairment loss was recognised. If this is the case and the recoverable amount of the asset or CGU concerned is now greater than its carrying amount, then the carrying amount of that asset or CGU should generally be increased to its recoverable amount.

(b) The reversal of an impairment loss for a CGU should be allocated between the assets of the CGU (other than goodwill) pro rata to the carrying amounts of those assets.

(c) When an impairment loss in relation to an asset is reversed, the asset's increased carrying amount should not exceed the carrying amount that would have applied if there had been no impairment loss in the first place. Any further increase beyond that amount is a revaluation and should be dealt with in accordance with the relevant standard (IAS16 *Property, Plant and Equipment* or IAS38 *Intangible Assets*).

(d) The reversal of a previously recognised impairment loss is usually recognised as income. But if the asset is carried at a revalued amount, the reversal is accounted for in the same way as a revaluation gain.

(e) After the reversal of an impairment loss, subsequent depreciation or amortisation charges should allocate the asset's revised carrying amount (less residual value) over the remainder of its useful life. It may also be necessary to review the asset's useful life and residual value and the depreciation or amortisation method being used.

Disclosure requirements

The disclosure requirements of IAS36 are extremely extensive. A summary of the main disclosures that are required is as follows:

(a) For each class of assets, the entity should disclose:

    (i) the amount of impairment losses recognised as expenses during the period and the line items in the statement of comprehensive income in which these impairment losses are included

    (ii) the amount of reversals of impairment losses recognised as income during the period and the line items in the statement of comprehensive income in which these reversals are included

    (iii) the amount of impairment losses (and reversals) on revalued assets recognised in other comprehensive income during the period.

(b) For each material impairment loss or reversal recognised during the period, the entity should disclose:

    (i) the events that led to the recognition of the impairment loss or reversal

(ii) the amount of the impairment loss or reversal

(iii) the nature of the impaired asset or a description of the impaired CGU

(iv) whether the recoverable amount of the asset or CGU is its fair value less costs of disposal or its value in use

(v) if recoverable amount is fair value less costs of disposal, the basis on which this has been determined (e.g. by reference to a quoted price for an identical asset in an active market)

(vi) if recoverable amount is value in use, the discount rate used when calculating the value in use figure.

Summary

▸ An impairment loss is the amount by which the carrying amount of an asset or cash-generating unit exceeds its recoverable amount. Impairment testing must be carried out annually for goodwill and for intangible assets with indefinite useful lives. Other assets should be tested if there are indications of impairment.

▸ The recoverable amount of an asset or CGU is the higher of its fair value less costs of disposal and its value in use. Value in use is calculated by discounting the future cash flows which the asset or CGU is expected to generate.

▸ Impairment losses are usually recognised as an expense. But if an asset is carried at a revalued amount, impairment losses are treated in the same way as revaluation losses.

▸ A cash-generating unit is the smallest identifiable group of assets that generates cash inflows that are largely independent of the cash inflows from other assets or groups of assets. Goodwill and corporate assets are allocated between CGUs for impairment testing purposes.

▸ An impairment loss for a CGU first reduces (or eliminates) any goodwill which has been allocated to the CGU. Any remaining part of the loss then reduces the CGU's other assets.

▸ Impairment losses are reversed (partly or wholly) if the recoverable amount of the asset or CGU concerned is now greater than its carrying amount. But impairment losses recognised for goodwill cannot be reversed.

▸ IAS36 makes extensive disclosure requirements. The required disclosures provide users with information about the impairment losses recognised or reversed during the accounting period.

Exercises

7.1   (a)   Define the term "impairment loss".

(b)   List the main indications which would suggest that an asset might be impaired.

(c)   Identify the two types of asset which must always be tested for impairment, even if there are no indications that impairment has occurred.

(d)   Explain how the recoverable amount of an asset is determined.

7.2   Determine the recoverable amount of each of the following four assets and state the amount of any impairment loss which should be recognised in each case:

	Carrying amount	Fair value less costs of disposal	Value in use
	£	£	£
Asset 1	25,000	22,500	27,500
Asset 2	6,500	3,750	4,800
Asset 3	18,250	17,500	15,000
Asset 4	11,400	13,400	12,750

7.3   An asset (which has never been revalued) has a carrying amount of £100,000. The asset is being depreciated on the straight-line basis, with a remaining useful life of three years and a residual value of £10,000.

The asset is expected to generate net cash inflows of £20,000 per year for the next three years and then to be sold for £10,000. Disposal costs are expected to be negligible.

At present, the asset could be sold for £50,000. Disposal costs would be £2,000.

Required:

(a)   Assuming a discount rate of 10% and that all cash flows occur at the end of the year concerned, determine the asset's value in use.

(b)   Calculate the amount of the impairment loss which has occurred and explain how this should be accounted for.

(c)   Calculate the amount of depreciation that should be charged in relation to the asset for each of the next three years, assuming that the straight-line method will continue to be used.

7.4   (a)   Define the term "cash-generating unit" (CGU).

(b)   Explain the circumstances in which a CGU should be tested for impairment.

7.5   The carrying amounts of the assets of a cash-generating unit are as follows:

	£m
Goodwill	25
Patents and copyrights	50
Property, plant and equipment	200
	275

There are indications that this CGU is impaired and therefore its recoverable amount has been determined. The CGU's recoverable amount is £195 million. Value is use cannot be ascertained for any of the assets, but fair value less costs of disposal is £20 million for the patents and copyrights and £160 million for the property, plant and equipment.

Calculate the amount of the impairment loss and show how this should be allocated between the assets of the CGU.

7.6   IAS36 *Impairment of Assets* was issued in June 1998 and subsequently revised in March 2004. Its main objective is to prescribe the procedures that should ensure that an entity's assets are carried at no more than their recoverable amounts. Where an asset is carried at an amount in excess of its recoverable amount, it is said to be impaired and IAS36 requires an impairment loss to be recognised.

Wilderness owns and operates an item of plant that cost £640,000 and had accumulated depreciation of £400,000 at 1 October 2013. It is being depreciated at 12.5% on cost. On 1 April 2014 (exactly half way through the year) the plant was damaged when a factory vehicle collided into it. Due to the unavailability of replacement parts, it is not possible to repair the plant, but it still operates, albeit at a reduced capacity. Also it is expected that as a result of the damage the remaining life of the plant from the date of the damage will be only two years.

Based on its reduced capacity, the estimated present value of the plant in use is £150,000. The plant has a current disposal value of £20,000 (which will be nil in two years' time), but Wilderness has been offered a trade-in value of £180,000 against a replacement machine which has a cost of £1 million (there would be no disposal costs for the replaced plant). Wilderness is reluctant to replace the plant as it is worried about the long-term demand for the product produced by the plant. The trade-in value is only available if the plant is replaced.

Required:

(a)   Define an impairment loss, explaining the relevance of an asset's fair value less costs of disposal and its value in use. State how frequently assets should be tested for impairment.

(b)   Explain how an impairment loss is accounted for after it has been calculated.

(c)   Prepare extracts from the financial statements of Wilderness in respect of the plant for the year ended 30 September 2014. Your answer should explain how you arrived at your figures.   *(ACCA)*

*7.7   An asset which cost £200,000 on 1 January 2012 is being depreciated on the straight line basis over a five year period with an estimated residual value of £40,000. The company which owns the asset has conducted an impairment review at 31 December 2013 and estimates that the asset will generate the following cash flows over the remainder of its useful life:

Year	Inflows	Outflows
	£000	£000
2014	45	5
2015	35	5
2016	60	5

The cash inflow for 2016 includes the estimated residual value of £40,000. The asset could be sold on 31 December 2013 for £110,000. Disposal costs would be £6,000.

(a)   Determine the asset's value in use, assuming that all cash flows occur at the end of the year concerned and using a discount rate of 8%.

(b)   Determine the asset's recoverable amount.

(c)   Calculate the amount of the impairment loss that has occurred and explain how this should be accounted for.

(d)   Calculate the amount of depreciation that should be charged in relation to the asset for each of the remaining years of its useful life.

*7.8   Stenberg plc is preparing its financial statements for the year ended 30 November 2014. On 1 May 2014, the company purchased a factory for the manufacture of optical disks, paying £24,000,000. The factory will be depreciated over its estimated life of 10 years using the straight line method on a full year basis with no residual value.

The asking price for the factory had been £30,000,000. However, Stenberg plc estimated the net present value of the factory's future expected net cash flows at £28,500,000 and the price eventually agreed with the vendor was £24,000,000.

During October 2014 a rival company announced that it had patented a new technology which has been enthusiastically greeted by the major players in the industry. Stenberg plc now feels that it may be necessary to revise downwards its expectations for the factory. It now believes that the net present value of the expected net cash flows from the factory as at 30 November 2014 was £20,500,000. The net realisable value of the factory was estimated at £14,000,000 as at 30 November 2014.

Required:

Discuss whether or not there is evidence of impairment and describe how the factory should be treated in the financial statements for the year ended 30 November 2014.

(CIPFA)

Chapter 8

Non-current assets held for sale and discontinued operations

Introduction

Non-current assets such as property, plant and equipment are generally held for use, rather than for sale. In other words, an entity which holds non-current assets normally intends to use them in its business operations. In these circumstances, it is appropriate to spread the cost (or revalued amount) of the assets over their useful lives in the form of depreciation charges which are then matched against the revenue which use of the assets has helped to generate. Importantly, the realisable value of such assets (i.e. the amount for which they could be sold) is usually of no interest.

However, if a non-current asset is held for sale rather than use, the notion of "useful life" is inapplicable and it is no longer appropriate to make depreciation charges or to carry the asset at its cost (or revalued amount) less depreciation to date. A more suitable accounting treatment for such assets is prescribed by IFRS5 *Non-current Assets Held for Sale and Discontinued Operations* and the first purpose of this chapter is to explain that accounting treatment.

A non-current asset held for sale may originally have been acquired for use in a business operation that has now been discontinued. It is logical, therefore, that IFRS5 should deal with discontinued operations as well as with non-current assets held for sale. The standard establishes certain presentation and disclosure requirements with regard to discontinued operations and the second purpose of this chapter is to explain those requirements.

Objectives

By the end of this chapter, the reader should be able to:

- correctly classify non-current assets as either held for use or held for sale, in accordance with the requirements of IFRS5

- explain the concept of a "disposal group"

- correctly measure non-current assets (or disposal groups) held for sale

- define the term "discontinued operation"

• state the main presentation and disclosure requirements of IFRS5 with regard to non-current assets held for sale and discontinued operations.

Classification of non-current assets as held for sale

IFRS5 states that a non-current asset should be classified as held for sale if its carrying amount (the amount at which it is "carried" in the financial statements) "*will be recovered principally through a sale transaction rather than through continuing use*". For this to be the case, the asset must be available for immediate sale in its present condition, subject only to terms that are usual and customary for sales of such assets. The sale must also be highly probable. A sale is usually regarded as "highly probable" if:

(a) management is committed to a plan to sell the asset and an active programme has been initiated to locate a buyer and complete the plan; and

(b) the asset is being actively marketed at a sale price that is reasonable in relation to its current fair value; and

(c) a completed sale is expected within one year from the date of classification (although this period may be extended if any delay is caused by circumstances beyond the entity's control); and

(d) it is unlikely that there will be any significant changes to the plan or that the plan will be withdrawn.

If these criteria are not satisfied at the end of the reporting period, the asset should not be classified as held for sale. If the criteria are satisfied after the reporting period but before the financial statements are authorised for issue, the fact that the asset is now classified as held for sale should be disclosed in the notes to the financial statements.

Disposal groups

IFRS5 also applies if an entity disposes of a group of assets (possibly with some directly associated liabilities) in a single transaction. Such a group is known as a "disposal group" and may consist of a number of cash-generating units, a single cash-generating unit or part of a cash-generating unit. A cash-generating unit is defined as "*the smallest identifiable group of assets that generates cash inflows that are largely independent of the cash inflows from other assets or groups of assets*" (see Chapter 7).

As with individual non-current assets, a disposal group should be classified as held for sale if its carrying amount will be recovered principally through a sale transaction rather than through continuing use. The criteria which are used to determine whether or not a disposal group is held for sale are the same as those which apply in the case of individual non-current assets (see above).

EXAMPLE 1

This example is based upon implementation guidance provided with IFRS5.

(a) Company A is committed to a plan to sell its headquarters building and has initiated a an active programme to find a buyer and complete the plan. The building is being marketed at a reasonable price and a completed sale is expected within 12 months. It is unlikely that this plan will change significantly. The company will not actually vacate the building until a buyer is found but then the time taken to vacate the building will not exceed what is regarded as usual and customary for such buildings.

(b) Company B is also committed to a plan to sell its headquarters building and is in precisely the same situation as Company A except that it will not vacate the building and transfer it to a buyer until a new headquarters building has been constructed.

(c) Company C is committed to a plan to sell a factory and has initiated actions to find a buyer. However, there is currently a backlog of uncompleted orders and the company does not intend to transfer the factory to a buyer until it has dealt with this backlog.

(d) Company D is also committed to a plan to sell a factory and is in precisely the same situation as Company C except that the backlog of orders will be transferred to the buyer of the building along with the building itself. Therefore the existence of this backlog will not delay the sale.

(e) Company E is committed to a plan to sell a disposal group. All of the criteria which must normally be met in order for a disposal group to be classified as held for sale are satisfied except that the sale is not expected to take place within one year. It is highly probable that a buyer will be found within that time but the sale will then require Government approval. The approval process is a lengthy one and cannot begin until a buyer has been found. Therefore completion of the sale is unlikely to occur within 12 months.

In each case, determine whether or not the asset or disposal group in question should be classified as held for sale.

Solution

(a) Strictly speaking, the building is not immediately available since it will take time for the company to move out once a buyer is found. However, the time taken will be "usual and customary". Furthermore, all of the other criteria for classification as held for sale are satisfied. Therefore this building should be classified as held for sale.

(b) The building is not available for immediate sale since the sale cannot be completed until a new HQ building has been constructed. This building should not be classified as held for sale.

(c) The factory is not available for immediate sale since the sale cannot be completed until the backlog of orders has been dealt with. This is a similar situation to (b) above and the factory should not be classified as held for sale.

(d) The factory is immediately available and should be classified as held for sale so long as all of the other classification criteria specified in IFRS5 are satisfied.

(e) Sale of the disposal group is not expected to be completed within one year. However, a buyer is expected to be found within that time and any delay in completion will be caused by circumstances outside the company's control. The disposal group should be classified as held for sale.

Measurement of non-current assets held for sale

IFRS5 requires that a non-current asset or a disposal group which is held for sale should be measured at the lower of its carrying amount when it was initially classified as held for sale and its "fair value less costs to sell", where:

(a) fair value (as defined by IFRS13) is "*the price that would be received to sell an asset or paid to transfer a liability in an orderly transaction between market participants at the measurement date*", and

(b) costs to sell are "*... costs directly attributable to the disposal of an asset (or disposal group), excluding finance costs and income tax expense*".

When an asset or disposal group is initially classified as held for sale, an impairment loss should be recognised (see Chapter 7) if the fair value less costs to sell of the asset or group at that time is lower than its carrying amount. Subsequently, a further impairment loss should be recognised if there is a decrease in fair value less costs to sell and a gain should be recognised if there is an increase in fair value less costs to sell. However, gains which exceed the cumulative impairment losses that have already been recognised in relation to the asset or disposal group (if any) are not recognised.

In the case of a disposal group, impairment losses and any subsequent gains are generally allocated between the non-current assets in the group in the order set out in international standard IAS36 *Impairment of Assets* (see Chapter 7). However, no allocation is made to assets that are outside the scope of the measurement requirements of IFRS5 (see below).

It is important to appreciate that depreciation should cease with regard to non-current assets or disposal groups which are held for sale and that such assets should instead be measured as described above.

EXAMPLE 2

(a) On 1 July 2013, a company which prepares financial statements to 31 December classifies a non-current asset as held for sale. The asset's carrying amount on that date is £10,000 and its fair value less costs to sell is £9,500. The asset is sold in May 2014 for £9,400 (net of costs). Calculate any impairment losses (or gains) that should be recognised if the asset's fair value less costs to sell at 31 December 2013 is:

(i) £9,200   (ii) £9,700   (iii) £10,100

In each case, also calculate the gain or loss that should be recognised on the disposal of the asset.

(b) On 1 October 2013, a company which prepares financial statements to 31 December classifies a non-current asset as held for sale. The asset's carrying amount on that date is £50,000 and its fair value less costs to sell is £55,000. The asset is sold in June 2014 for £53,000 (net). Calculate any impairment losses (or gains) that should be recognised if the asset's fair value less costs to sell at 31 December 2013 is:

(i)   £52,500   (ii)   £49,000

In each case, also calculate the gain or loss that should be recognised on the disposal of the asset.

Solution

(a) An impairment loss of £500 should be recognised on 1 July 2013, writing the asset down to its fair value (less costs to sell) of £9,500. On 31 December 2013:

(i)   the asset is remeasured at £9,200 and an impairment loss of £300 is recognised

(ii)   the asset is remeasured at £9,700 and a gain of £200 is recognised

(iii) the asset is remeasured at £10,000 and a gain of £500 is recognised (the gain cannot be £600 since this would exceed the previously recognised impairment losses in relation to the asset).

The gain or loss on the sale in May 2014 (recognised in the financial statements for the year to 31 December 2014) is:

(i)   gain £200 (£9,400 – £9,200)

(ii)   loss £300 (£9,400 – £9,700)

(iii) loss £600 (£9,400 – £10,000).

(b) There is no impairment loss on 1 October 2013, since the asset's fair value less costs to sell exceeds its carrying amount. The asset continues to be measured at £50,000. On 31 December 2013:

(i)   the asset is still measured at £50,000 and no gain is recognised (since there were no previous impairment losses in relation to this asset)

(ii)   the asset is remeasured at £49,000 and an impairment loss of £1,000 is recognised.

The gain or loss on the sale in June 2014 (recognised in the financial statements for the year to 31 December 2014) is:

(i)   gain £3,000 (£53,000 – £50,000)

(ii)   gain £4,000 (£53,000 – £49,000).

Scope of the measurement requirements of IFRS5

The measurement requirements of IFRS5 apply only to non-current assets and do not apply at all to the following types of asset, whether these are to be sold individually or as part of a disposal group:

		Chapter of this book
(a)	deferred tax assets (IAS12 *Income Taxes*)	15
(b)	employee benefits assets (IAS19 *Employee Benefits*)	14
(c)	financial assets (IFRS9 *Financial Instruments*)	11
(d)	investment properties at fair value (IAS40 *Investment Property*)	5

If an asset on this list is classified as held for sale, it should continue to be measured in accordance with the applicable standard. But the asset should be presented in the financial statements as an asset held for sale (see later in this chapter).

In the case of a disposal group held for sale, the carrying amount of all assets not within the scope of IFRS5 (and the carrying amount of any liabilities) should be remeasured in accordance with the applicable standard on each occasion that the carrying amount of the disposal group is compared with its fair value less costs to sell.

EXAMPLE 3

On 1 September 2013, a company which prepares financial statements to 31 December each year classifies a disposal group as held for sale. This disposal group is still unsold at 31 December 2013. The carrying amounts of the disposal group's assets and liabilities at 1 September 2013 are shown below, along with the carrying amounts at which these assets and liabilities would have been measured at 31 December 2013 (in accordance with applicable standards) if the group had not been classified as held for sale.

	1 September 2013	31 December 2013
	£000	£000
Goodwill	2,000	1,900
Property, plant and equipment (PPE)	4,300	3,900
Inventories	850	800
Financial assets	1,500	1,750
Liabilities	(900)	(900)

The fair value (less costs to sell) of the disposal group is £8 million at 1 September 2013 and £7.5 million at 31 December 2013. Calculate the amount of any impairment losses (or gains) that should be recognised at:

(a)   1 September 2013

(b)   31 December 2013.

Also show how these impairment losses or gains should be allocated amongst the assets and liabilities in the group.

Solution

(a) On 1 September 2013, the total carrying amount of all the assets and liabilities in the disposal group is £7.75m. This is less than fair value less costs to sell (£8m). So the group is measured at its carrying amount. There are no impairment losses.

(b) The measurement requirements of IFRS5 do not apply to the inventories, the financial assets or the liabilities. Therefore the carrying amounts of these three items must be remeasured on 31 December 2013 in accordance with the applicable standards. The carrying amount of the disposal group becomes £7.95m, as follows:

	£000
Goodwill	2,000
Property, plant and equipment	4,300
Inventories	800
Financial assets	1,750
Liabilities	(900)
	7,950

This exceeds fair value less costs to sell (£7.5m) so there is an impairment loss of £450,000. This loss is allocated to non-current assets to which the measurement requirements of IFRS5 apply (goodwill and PPE). IAS36 requires the loss to be set first against the goodwill, reducing that asset from £2 million to £1.55 million. This absorbs the whole of the loss so there is nothing left to set against the PPE. The assets and liabilities in the disposal group are now measured as follows:

	£000
Goodwill	1,550
Property, plant and equipment	4,300
Inventories	800
Financial assets	1,750
Liabilities	(900)
	7,500

The gain on remeasurement of £200,000 (£7.95m – £7.75m) and the impairment loss of £450,000 are recognised in the company's statement of comprehensive income for the year to 31 December 2013.

Measurement of assets no longer classified as held for sale

If an asset or disposal group has been classified as held for sale but then the criteria for this classification are no longer met, the asset or disposal group should cease to be classified as held for sale. A non-current asset that ceases to be classified as held for sale (or ceases to be part of a disposal group classified as such) should be measured at the *lower* of:

(a) its carrying amount before being classified as held for sale, less any depreciation that would have been charged in the meantime if it had not been held for sale, and

(b) its recoverable amount at the date of the decision not to sell, which is the *higher* of:

   (i) the asset's fair value less costs to sell

   (ii) the asset's value in use, which is defined as "*the present value of estimated future cash flows expected to arise from the continuing use of an asset and from its disposal at the end of its useful life*".

The effect of this measurement rule is that an impairment review is required whenever an asset ceases to be classified as held for sale (see Chapter 7).

Presentation of non-current assets held for sale

Non-current assets held for sale and the assets of a disposal group held for sale should be presented separately from other assets in the statement of financial position. Similarly, the liabilities of a disposal group should be presented separately from other liabilities. It is not permissible to offset these assets and liabilities. The major classes of assets and liabilities classified as held for sale should be disclosed either in the statement of financial position or in the notes.

Additional disclosures

In the accounting period in which a non-current asset or a disposal group is classified as held for sale (or is sold) the following additional disclosures should be made in the notes to the financial statements:

(a) a description of the asset or disposal group

(b) a description of the facts and circumstances of the expected disposal (or the sale) and the expected manner and timing of that disposal

(c) any impairment loss recognised when the asset or disposal group was classified as held for sale and any further loss or gain recognised subsequently

(d) if applicable, the reportable segment in which the asset or disposal group is presented (see Chapter 24).

If an asset or disposal group which was previously classified as held for sale is no longer held for sale, the facts and circumstances of this decision should also be disclosed.

ILLUSTRATION

This illustration is based upon implementation guidance provided with IFRS5.

A company which prepares financial statements to 31 December each year has classified a disposal group as held for sale. At 31 December 2013, this group's assets consist of non-current assets with a carrying value of £8 million and liabilities with a carrying value of £3.3 million. These assets and liabilities could be presented in the statement of financial position at 31 December 2013 as follows:

Statement of financial position as at 31 December 2013

	£000	£000
Assets		
Non-current assets		
Property, plant and equipment		xxx
Current assets		
Inventories	xxx	
Trade receivables	xxx	
Cash at bank	xxx	
	xxx	
Non-current assets held for sale	8,000	xxx
		xxx
Equity		
Share capital		xxx
Retained earnings		xxx
		xxx
Liabilities		
Non-current liabilities		
Long-term loans		xxx
Current liabilities		
Trade payables	xxx	
Liabilities directly associated with non-current assets held for sale	3,300	xxx
		xxx

Discontinued operations

IFRS5 requires that entities should present and disclose information that enables users of the financial statements to evaluate the effects of discontinued operations. Two definitions are important here:

(a) A discontinued operation is "*a component of an entity that either has been disposed of or is classified as held for sale ...*".

(b) A component of an entity comprises "*operations and cash flows that can be clearly distinguished ... from the rest of the entity*". Whilst held for use, a component will usually be a single cash-generating unit or a group of such units (see Chapter 7).

In general, a discontinued operation will represent "*a separate major line of business or geographical area of operations*". The presentation and disclosure requirements of IFRS5 in relation to discontinued operations are outlined below.

Presentation and disclosure of discontinued operations

With regard to discontinued operations, an entity should disclose:

(a) a single amount in the statement of comprehensive income, comprising the total of:

  (i) the post-tax profit or loss of discontinued operations, and

  (ii) the post-tax gain or loss recognised on the measurement to fair value less costs to sell (or on the disposal) of the assets constituting the discontinued operation

(b) an analysis of this single amount, either in the statement of comprehensive income or in the notes to the financial statements, into:

  (i) the revenue, expenses and pre-tax profit or loss of discontinued operations

  (ii) the related income tax expense

  (iii) the pre-tax gain or loss recognised on the measurement to fair value less costs to sell (or on the disposal) of the assets constituting the discontinued operation

  (iv) the related income tax expense

(c) the net cash flows attributable to the operating, investing and financing operations of discontinued operations (either in the statement of cash flows or in the notes).

ILLUSTRATION

This illustration is based upon implementation guidance provided with IFRS5.

A company discontinued an operation during the year to 31 March 2014 and sold the corresponding disposal group. The revenue and expenses of the discontinued operation for the year to 31 March 2014 were as follows:

	£000
Revenue	432
Expenses	295
Pre-tax profit	137
Tax expense	41
Post-tax profit	96

The fair value of the disposal group when it was initially classified as held for sale was in excess of its carrying amount, so there was no impairment loss at that time. A pre-tax gain of £20,000 arose when the disposal group was sold (tax expense £6,000). Therefore the total profit from discontinued operations is £110,000 (£96,000 + £20,000 − £6,000).

This information could be presented in the statement of comprehensive income for the year to 31 March 2014 in the following manner:

Statement of comprehensive income for the year to 31 March 2014

	£000
Continuing operations	
Revenue	xxx
Cost of sales	(xxx)
Gross profit	xxx
Other income	xxx
Distribution costs	(xxx)
Administrative expenses	(xxx)
Finance costs	(xxx)
Profit before tax	xxx
Taxation	(xxx)
Profit for the year from continuing operations	xxx
Discontinued operations	
Profit for the period from discontinued operations	110*
Profit for the year	xxx
Other comprehensive income for the year	xxx
Total comprehensive income for the year	xxx

*An analysis of this figure would be given in the notes.

Summary

▸ Non-current assets or disposal groups should be classified as held for sale if their value will be recovered principally through sale rather than through use. The asset or group must be available for immediate sale and the sale must be highly probable.

▸ A disposal group is a group of assets (together with any associated liabilities) which is to be disposed of in a single transaction.

▸ Non-current assets and disposal groups held for sale should be measured at the lower of their carrying amount when initially classified as held for sale and their fair value less costs to sell. Depreciation should cease.

▸ The measurement requirements of IFRS5 do not apply to deferred tax assets, assets arising from employee benefits, financial assets or investment properties.

▸ Non-current assets held for sale should be presented separately in the statement of financial position. The liabilities of a disposal group should also be presented separately.

▶ A discontinued operation is a component of an entity that has been disposed of or is held for sale. A component comprises an operation that can be clearly distinguished from the rest of the entity.

▶ The results of discontinued operations should be presented separately in the statement of comprehensive income and in the statement of cash flows.

Exercises

8.1 (a) Explain what is meant by a non-current asset "held for sale" and list the criteria which must be satisfied in order for an asset to be classified as held for sale.

(b) Explain why it is not appropriate to measure non-current assets held for sale in the same way as non-current assets held for use.

(c) Explain how non-current assets held for sale should be measured.

8.2 Wilbern Ltd prepares financial statements to 30 June each year. On 1 March 2013, the company classifies a non-current asset as held for sale. The asset is eventually sold in July 2013. Calculate:

(i) any impairment losses (or gains) that should be recognised in the financial statements for the year to 30 June 2013, and

(ii) any gain or loss on disposal that should be recognised in the financial statements for the year to 30 June 2014

if the carrying amount of the asset at 1 March 2013, its fair value (less costs to sell) on that date and on 30 June 2013 and its disposal proceeds are as follows::

	Carrying amount at 1 March 2013 £	Fair value at 1 March 2013 £	Fair value at 30 June 2013 £	Disposal proceeds £
(a)	6,000	5,400	5,200	5,140
(b)	6,000	6,800	6,750	6,630
(c)	6,000	5,900	5,950	5,920
(d)	6,000	5,900	6,050	6,080

8.3 (a) Explain what is meant by a "discontinued operation".

(b) Explain why IFRS5 requires the results of discontinued operations to be presented separately in the financial statements.

8.4   Varnay Ltd is a manufacturing company which prepares annual financial statements to 31 December. In November 2013, the company announced a plan to close down one of its manufacturing operations and to sell off the assets of that operation. The operation will be closed down over a period of approximately nine months and closure is expected to be complete by the end of July 2014. Sale of the operation's assets is expected to take place in September 2014.

Explain how this closure and sale should be dealt with in the financial statements of Varnay Ltd for the year to 31 December 2013 and for the year to 31 December 2014.

8.5   Yeng and Sons Ltd prepares financial statements to 31 May each year. On 25 January 2014, the company classifies a disposal group as held for sale. This disposal group is eventually sold in August 2014. The carrying amounts of the assets and liabilities in the disposal group at 25 January 2014 and the carrying amounts at which these assets and liabilities would have been measured at 31 May 2014 if the group had not been held for sale are as follows:

	25 January 2014	31 May 2014
	£000	£000
Goodwill	200	150
Property, plant and equipment	2,100	1,900
Investment properties	700	760
Inventories	420	380
Liabilities	(360)	(360)

The fair value (less costs to sell) of the disposal group is £3 million at 25 January 2014 and £2.85 million at 31 May 2014. The group is sold in August 2014 for £2.8 million.

(a)   Calculate the amount of any impairment losses (or gains) that should be recognised at 25 January 2014 and at 31 May 2014.

(b)   Calculate the gain or loss arising on the sale of the disposal group.

8.6   An extract from the draft statement of comprehensive income of Andisson Ltd for the year to 30 April 2014 is as follows:

	£000	£000
Sales revenue		558
Cost of sales		184
Gross profit		374
Other income		12
		386
Distribution costs	59	
Administrative expenses	148	207
Profit before tax		179
Taxation		45
Profit for the year		134

In January 2014, the company sold one of its business operations, incurring a loss of £17,000 on the sale. This loss is included in administrative expenses. The associated tax relief of £4,000 has been deducted when computing the tax expense shown in the draft statement of comprehensive income.

The operation sold in January 2014 yielded sales revenue of £103,000 during the year to 30 April 2014. Related costs were cost of sales £38,000, distribution costs £2,000 and administrative expenses £20,000. The tax expense shown in the draft statement of comprehensive income includes £11,000 in relation to the profit made by this operation.

Re-draft the extract from the statement of comprehensive income in accordance with the requirements of IFRS5 and draft a suitable note relating to discontinued operations which could appear in the notes to the financial statements.

*8.7   Bakerwell Ltd prepares annual financial statements to 31 December. On 1 August 2013 the company closed down one of its operations and classified the corresponding cash-generating unit (CGU) as held for sale. All of the assets in this CGU were within the scope of the measurement requirements of IFRS5. There were no associated liabilities.

The carrying amount of the CGU on 1 August 2013 was £3m and its fair value on that date was estimated to be £2.7m. Estimated disposal costs were £100,000. The CGU remained unsold on 31 December 2013. On this date, its estimated fair value had fallen to £2.5m and estimated disposal costs had risen to £150,000.

The operation which was closed down generated sales revenue of £400,000 between 1 January 2013 and 1 August 2013. Costs of the operation during this period totalled £520,000. This total comprised cost of sales £360,000, distribution costs £70,000 and administrative expenses £90,000.

(a) Explain what is meant by a "disposal group" and explain why the CGU referred to above qualifies as a disposal group. Also list the criteria which determine whether or not a disposal group may be classified as held for sale.

(b) Explain what is meant by a "discontinued operation" and explain why the operation referred to above qualifies as a discontinued operation.

(c) Explain how the transactions referred to above will affect the financial statements of Bakerwell Ltd for the year to 31 December 2013. (Ignore taxation).

Chapter 9

Leases

Introduction

The IASB *Conceptual Framework* (see Chapter 2) states that financial information cannot faithfully represent transactions and other events unless it represents their underlying economic substance rather than just their legal form. This principle is embodied in international standard IAS17 *Leases*, which deals with the accounting treatment of leased items such as property, plant and equipment.

The legal form of a lease is that ownership of the leased item remains with the *lessor* (the supplier) and is not transferred to the *lessee* (the user). However, the underlying substance of certain leases is that the lessee does, in effect, acquire the item and that this acquisition is financed by means of a loan from the lessor. In such cases, IAS17 requires that the item should be shown as an asset in the lessee's financial statements along with a corresponding liability to the lessor. The lessor's financial statements should not show the item itself but should instead show a receivable for the amount owing by the lessee.

The main purpose of this chapter is to distinguish between the types of lease identified by IAS17 and to explain the requirements of IAS17 in relation to each type of lease.

However, the IASB has issued an exposure draft of a leases standard which would supersede IAS17 and make significant changes to the accounting treatment of leases. This exposure draft is considered briefly at the end of this chapter.

Objectives

By the end of this chapter, the reader should be able to:

*   distinguish between finance leases and operating leases
*   account for an operating lease in accordance with the requirements of IAS17
*   account for a finance lease in accordance with the requirements of IAS17
*   allocate finance charges over the term of a finance lease, using the level spread method, the actuarial method and the sum of digits method
*   outline the disclosure requirements of IAS17.

Classification of leases

IAS17 begins by defining a lease as "*an agreement whereby the lessor conveys to the lessee in return for a payment or series of payments the right to use an asset for an agreed period of time*". The standard then distinguishes between "finance leases" and "operating leases" and prescribes a different accounting treatment for each. Finance leases and operating leases are defined as follows:

- A finance lease is "*a lease that transfers substantially all the risks and rewards incidental to ownership of an asset. Title may or may not eventually be transferred*".

- An operating lease is "*a lease other than a finance lease*".

As these definitions make clear, the classification of a lease ignores the legal form of the arrangement but concentrates instead on the extent to which the "risks and rewards" that are normally associated with ownership lie with either the lessor or the lessee. Risks which are incidental to ownership of an asset include the possibility of losses from idle capacity or technological obsolescence. Rewards include the expectation of profitable operation over the asset's useful life and gain from any appreciation in the asset's value. IAS17 gives examples of situations which would normally lead to a lease being classified as a finance lease. These include:

(a) the lease transfers ownership of the asset to the lessee by the end of the lease term

(b) the lessee has the option to purchase the asset at a price expected to be sufficiently lower than the asset's fair value on the date that the option is exercised, so as to make it reasonably certain as from the inception of the lease (i.e. the start of the lease) that this option will be exercised

(c) the lease term is for the major part of the economic life of the asset, even if legal title is not transferred

(d) at the inception of the lease, the present value of the minimum lease payments which the lessee is required to make over the lease term amounts to (at least) substantially all of the fair value of the leased asset

(e) the leased assets are of such a specialised nature that only the lessee can use them without major modifications.

However, the factors illustrated by these examples are not always conclusive. If it is clear from other features of the lease agreement that a lease does not transfer substantially all of the risks and rewards of ownership, then the lease will be classified as an operating lease.

Leases of land

Leases of land are classified as either finance leases or operating leases in the same way as any other assets. However, land has an indefinite economic life and so a lease of land cannot be for "the major part of the economic life of the asset". Nonetheless, the risks and rewards incidental to the ownership of land can be transferred to a lessee if legal title to the land is expected to be transferred by the end of the lease term or if the lease is for such a long period (e.g. 999 years) that all significant risks and rewards are transferred to the lessee even if title is not. In such cases, a lease of land is classified as a finance lease.

In the case of a lease of both land and buildings, the land element and the buildings element should be considered separately for the purposes of lease classification. The lease payments are then allocated between the elements of the lease in proportion to the fair values of the land element and the buildings element at the inception of the lease.

Accounting for operating leases

Operating leases are straightforward and present no major accounting problems. Since the lessee has not taken on the risks and rewards of ownership, the leased item is not shown as an asset in the lessee's financial statements. The lease payments are simply recognised as an expense, generally on a straight-line basis over the lease term.

The lessor has retained the risks and rewards of ownership, so the leased item is shown as an asset in the lessor's financial statements and depreciated as usual. The lease payments are recognised as income, generally on a straight-line basis over the lease term. Any direct costs incurred by the lessor on arranging an operating lease should be added to the carrying amount of the asset concerned and then written off over the lease term.

Accounting for finance leases

In the case of a finance lease, the lessee has (by definition) acquired the risks and rewards of ownership and therefore the leased item should be shown as an asset in the lessee's financial statements along with a corresponding liability to the lessor. At the commencement of the lease term, IAS17 requires that both the asset and the liability to the lessor should be recognised at the *lower* of:

(a) the fair value of the leased item, and

(b) the present value of the minimum lease payments.

Any initial direct costs incurred by the lessee (e.g. arrangement costs) are added to the amount recognised as an asset. If there are no such costs, the asset and the corresponding liability will initially be recognised at the same amount. The asset should be included in a suitable category of assets in the lessee's statement of financial position (usually property, plant and equipment) and the liability to the lessor should be split between current and non-current liabilities, as appropriate. IAS17 does not allow the liability to the lessor to be shown as a deduction from the leased asset.

Subsequent measurement

The asset which was established at the inception of a finance lease should be depreciated in accordance with the lessee's normal depreciation policy. This policy should comply with the requirements of the relevant standard, which is usually IAS16 *Property, Plant and Equipment* (see Chapter 5). If it is reasonably certain that the lessee will obtain ownership of the asset by the end of the lease term, then the asset should be depreciated over its useful life. Otherwise, the asset should be fully depreciated over the *shorter* of its useful life and the lease term.

As regards the liability to the lessor, each lease payment must be apportioned between the finance charge element (which is recognised as an expense in the lessee's statement of comprehensive income) and the amount which reduces the outstanding liability. The total finance charge is equal to the difference between:

(a)   the total of the minimum lease payments, and

(b)   the liability to the lessor which was established at the inception of the lease.

IAS17 requires that this finance charge should be allocated to accounting periods "*so as to produce a constant periodic rate of interest on the remaining balance of the liability*". In practice, however, some form of approximation may be used so as to simplify the calculations. Methods which could be used for allocating the finance charge between accounting periods include:

(a)   **The actuarial method**. The rate of interest implicit in the lease is used to calculate the finance charge element of each lease payment. This method is preferred by IAS17 but cannot be used unless the interest rate is known. If necessary, this rate can usually be derived with the aid of present value tables.

(b)   **The sum of digits method**. The "sum of digits" method provides a reasonable approximation to the actuarial method if the interest rate implicit in the lease is not known. An outline of the method is as follows:

   (i)   A digit is assigned to each lease payment. Digit 1 is assigned to the final lease payment, digit 2 to the penultimate (next-to-last) payment and so on. If the first lease payment is payable in advance at the inception of the lease, it does not contain a finance charge element and so is not assigned a digit.

   (ii)   The digits are totalled to give the "sum of digits". If there are twelve payments (perhaps monthly payments over a one-year period) the sum will be 78. For this reason the sum of digits method is sometimes referred to as the "rule of 78".

   (iii) The finance charge element of each lease payment is calculated by dividing the total finance charge by the sum of the digits and then multiplying by the digit assigned to that payment.

The method is illustrated further in the worked example which follows.

(c) **The level spread method**. The level spread method simply allocates the finance charge to lease payments on a straight-line basis over the lease term. This is unrealistic, since the amount of the finance charge allocated to each payment should fall as the liability to the lessor also falls. However, this method might be used if the amounts concerned are not material.

EXAMPLE

On 1 January 2013, a company acquires an item of equipment on a finance lease. The fair value of the equipment on 1 January 2013 is £20,000 and the company is required to make four lease payments of £6,654 each. These payments fall due on 31 December 2013, 2014, 2015 and 2016. The rate of interest implicit in the lease is 12.5% per annum.

Calculate the total finance charge payable by the company and show how this is allocated over the lease term using:

(a) the level spread method

(b) the sum of digits method

(c) the actuarial method.

Assuming that the actuarial method is used, calculate the amount of the liability to the lessor which should be shown in the company's statement of financial position at the end of each year of the lease. Also show how the liability outstanding at 31 December 2013 should be split between current and non-current liabilities.

Solution

Total lease payments are 4 × £6,654 = £26,616, so the total finance charge is £6,616.

(a) **Level spread method**

The finance charge of £6,616 is spread evenly over the four years of the lease term, giving an annual finance charge of £1,654.

(b) **Sum of digits method**

Year	Digit	Finance charge (£)	
2013	4	4/10 × £6,616 =	2,646
2014	3	3/10 × £6,616 =	1,985
2015	2	2/10 × £6,616 =	1,323
2016	1	1/10 × £6,616 =	662
	10		£6,616

(c) **Actuarial method**

Year	Liability b/f £		Finance charge @ 12.5% £		Lease payment £		Liability c/f £
2013	20,000	+	2,500	−	(6,654)	=	15,846
2014	15,846	+	1,981	−	(6,654)	=	11,173
2015	11,173	+	1,396	−	(6,654)	=	5,915
2016	5,915	+	739	−	(6,654)	=	0

Notes:

(i)   The liability is set initially to the fair value of the asset acquired (£20,000).

(ii) The finance charge each year is equal to 12.5% of the liability brought forward.

(iii) The annual finance charges calculated by the sum of digits method are indeed a reasonable approximation to those calculated by the actuarial method.

The liability outstanding at the end of 2013 is £15,846. The payment due during 2014 is £6,654 but this includes the 2014 finance charge of £1,981, so only £4,673 will be paid off the capital sum. Therefore the liability of £15,846 at the end of 2013 should be split into a current liability of £4,673 and a non-current liability of £11,173.

Accounting for a finance lease by the lessor

The lessor of a finance lease has relinquished the risks and rewards of ownership of the leased asset. Therefore the asset should be removed from the lessor's statement of financial position and replaced by a receivable which represents the amount owed by the lessee. In general, this receivable is initially recognised at the present value of the minimum lease payments that the lessee is required to make.

Subsequently, the rate of interest implicit in the lease is used to calculate the finance income element of each payment made by the lessee. This finance income is recognised in the lessor's statement of comprehensive income. The remainder of the lease payment is subtracted from the amount owed by the lessee.

Any direct costs incurred by the lessor in setting up the lease are added to the initial carrying amount of the receivable. This automatically reduces the interest rate implicit in the lease, since the lease payments must now cover these direct costs as well as the cost of the asset itself. This also reduces the finance income recognised over the lease term.

Disclosure requirements

IAS17 makes a number of disclosure requirements in relation to leases, both for the lessee and for the lessor. A summary of the main disclosure requirements is as follows:

(a) **Operating leases**

The *lessee* should disclose:

(i) the amount of operating lease payments recognised as an expense in the period

(ii) the total of the future minimum lease payments payable under non-cancellable operating leases, analysed into amounts falling due within one year, within two to five years and after more than five years

(iii) a general description of the lessee's significant leasing arrangements.

Similarly, the *lessor* should disclose:

(i) the total of the future minimum lease payments receivable under non-cancellable operating leases, analysed into amounts receivable within one year, within two to five years and after more than five years

(ii) a general description of the lessor's leasing arrangements.

(b) **Finance leases**

The *lessee* should disclose:

(i) for each class of asset, the net carrying amount of assets held under finance leases at the end of the reporting period

(ii) the total of the future minimum lease payments (and their present value) payable under finance leases, analysed into payments due within one year, within two to five years and after more than five years

(iii) a general description of the lessee's material leasing arrangements.

In general terms, the *lessor* should disclose:

(i) the total of future minimum lease payments (and their present value) receivable under finance leases, analysed into amounts receivable within one year, within two to five years and after more than five years

(ii) unearned finance income (i.e. finance income to be earned over the remaining term of finance leases outstanding at the end of the reporting period)

(iii) a general description of the lessor's material leasing arrangements.

It should be noted that leases are a form of financial instrument and are therefore also subject to the disclosure requirements specified by international standard IFRS7 *Financial Instruments: Disclosures* (see Chapter 11).

Proposed new leases standard

At the time of writing, the IASB (jointly with the US FASB) is developing a new leases standard which would supersede IAS17 and make significant changes to the accounting treatment of leases. It seems likely that the new standard would remove the distinction between finance leases and operating leases and require that most leases should be dealt with in (broadly) the same way as is currently required by IAS17 for finance leases.

However, lessors and lessees would be allowed to elect that "short-term" leases should be accounted for in a way which is similar to the IAS17 treatment of operating leases. A short-term lease is a lease with a lease term not exceeding twelve months.

An exposure draft of the new standard is expected by the end of June 2013. Further information may be obtained from website www.ifrs.org.

Summary

▸ IAS17 distinguishes between finance leases and operating leases and prescribes a different accounting treatment for each type of lease.

▸ A finance lease is one which transfers substantially all of the risks and rewards of ownership to the lessee. IAS17 lists a number of situations in which a lease would normally be classified as a finance lease.

▸ An operating lease is one that does *not* transfer substantially all of the risks and rewards of ownership to the lessee.

▸ In the case of an operating lease, the leased item is shown as an asset in the lessor's statement of financial position. The lease payments are recognised as income in the lessor's financial statements and as an expense in the lessee's financial statements.

▸ In the case of a finance lease, the leased item is shown as an asset in the lessee's statement of financial position, with a corresponding liability to the lessor. In the lessor's statement of financial position, the leased asset is replaced by a receivable which represents the amount owed by the lessee.

▸ The finance charge in relation to a finance lease is generally equal to the difference between the total of the minimum lease payments and the fair value of the asset at the inception of the lease. This charge is spread over the lease term using either the actuarial method or another method which gives a reasonable approximation.

▸ IAS17 makes numerous disclosure requirements in relation to leases, both for the lessee and for the lessor.

Exercises

9.1   International standard IAS17 distinguishes between finance leases and operating leases and prescribes the accounting treatment for each type of lease.

    (a)   Define the terms "finance lease" and "operating lease".

    (b)   List the main situations in which a lease would normally be classified as a finance lease.

    (c)   Conston Ltd is the lessee of the following leases:

        (i)   Item A is leased at a cost of £5,000 per annum with a minimum lease term of five years. The item has a useful life of five years and would cost £18,000 if bought for cash.

        (ii)   Item B is leased at a cost of £500 per month. The leased item has a useful life of ten years and would cost £40,000 to buy outright. The lease may be terminated at any time.

    Determine whether each of these leases is an operating lease or a finance lease.

9.2   On 1 January 2014, Crimmock Ltd leases a machine from Derrent plc. The lease is for a term of three years and lease payments of £1,000 per month are required. The machine has a useful life of eight years and would cost £50,000 if bought for cash.

    (a)   Explain why this lease is an operating lease.

    (b)   Explain how the machine itself and the lease payments should be dealt with in the financial statements of Crimmock Ltd, assuming that the company prepares accounts to 30 June each year.

9.3   Ennidale Ltd prepares accounts to 31 March each year. On 1 April 2013, the company acquired an asset by means of a finance lease. The fair value of the asset on this date was £40,000 and the company was required to make six half-yearly lease payments of £7,674 each. The first payment was payable on 1 April 2013. The rate of interest implicit in the lease was 6% per half-year.

    Calculate the finance charge which should be recognised as an expense in the company's financial statements for each of the years to 31 March 2014, 2015 and 2016, using:

    (a)   the actuarial method (*prepare a table with one row for each half-year*)

    (b)   the sum of digits method

    (c)   the level spread method.

9.4   On 1 July 2013, Granitor Ltd entered into a finance lease to acquire a machine. The cash price of the machine would have been £132,000. The lease agreement specified that the company would make four lease payments, each of £45,303, on 30 June 2014, 2015, 2016 and 2017. The interest rate implicit in the lease was 14% per annum. Granitor Ltd prepares accounts to 30 June each year.

Using the actuarial method to allocate finance charges over the lease period, calculate the finance charge which should be shown as an expense in the company's financial statements for each of the years to 30 June 2014, 2015, 2016 and 2017. Also show how the liability to the lessor should be represented in the statement of financial position of Granitor Ltd on 30 June 2014.

9.5 Glassmere Ltd prepares accounts to 31 December each year. On 1 January 2013, the company acquired an asset by means of a finance lease. Details of the lease agreement are as follows:

Cash price of leased asset	£27,500
Lease term	5 years
Payments due annually in advance	£6,595 each
Useful life of asset	7 years
Residual value	£3,000
Rate of interest implicit in lease	10% per annum

Glassmere Ltd will obtain legal ownership of the asset at the end of the lease term. The company calculates depreciation on the straight-line basis.

Assuming that the actuarial method is used to allocate the finance charge over the lease term, calculate the finance charge and depreciation charge which should be shown in the company's financial statements for each of the years to 31 December 2013, 2014, 2015, 2016 and 2017.

Also calculate the liability to the lessor at the end of each of these years and show how this liability should be split between current liabilities and non-current liabilities.

9.6 Lees Ltd is about to lease an assembly machine on a finance lease. The terms of the lease require Lees Ltd to make five rental payments of £18,000 annually in advance. The fair value of the assembly machine is £75,000 and its economic life is five years with no residual value. The rate of interest implicit in the lease is 10.05%.

Required:

(a) Explain why this lease is a finance lease and not an operating lease.

(b) Prepare a table showing how the finance charge in this lease would be allocated to each of the five years using each of the following methods:

(i) straight line method

(ii) sum of digits ("rule of 78") method

(iii) actuarial method.

(c) State with reasons which of the above methods best achieves the objectives of IAS17 *Leases*.

(d) Show how the finance lease would be reported in the financial statements of Lees Ltd for the first and second years of the lease using the actuarial method. *(CIPFA)*

*9.7 International standard IAS17 defines the term "lease" and distinguishes between finance leases and operating leases. The standard also prescribes the accounting treatment of each type of lease, both by the lessor and by the lessee.

(a) Define the terms "lease", "finance lease" and "operating lease".

(b) Explain why IAS17 requires different accounting treatments for finance leases and for operating leases.

(c) Summarise the required accounting treatment by the lessor and by the lessee of:

    (i)   operating leases

    (ii) finance leases.

(d) List the main disclosure requirements of IAS17.

*9.8 On 1 December 2013, Gebouw plc entered into a finance lease requiring the payment of five annual rental payments of £785,000 payable in advance on 1 December 2013, 2014, 2015, 2016 and 2017.

The fair value of the leased asset on 1 December 2013 was £2,997,000 and it was expected to have a five-year economic life as from 1 December 2013 with no residual value. The rate of interest implicit in the lease is 15.65% a year. Taxation implications are to be ignored.

In the financial statements for the year ended 30 November 2014 the rental paid on 1 December 2013 has been recorded as a payment and reported as an operating expense for the year. No other entries have been made.

Required:

Prepare detailed calculations showing how this lease should have been reported in the financial statements for the year to 30 November 2014 in order to conform with the requirements of IAS17 *Leases*. State the difference that the appropriate treatment would make to the following totals reported in the draft financial statements:

(i)   profit before tax

(ii) total assets

(iii) current liabilities

(iv) non-current liabilities.   *(CIPFA)*

Chapter 10

Inventories and construction contracts

Introduction

In general terms, inventories are stocks of goods. For a manufacturing business, these will usually consist of raw materials, partly-completed products (work in progress) and finished products awaiting sale to customers. For a retailer or wholesaler, inventories will comprise mainly stocks of goods acquired for resale.

The value placed on inventories affects the cost of sales figure shown in the statement of comprehensive income and so has a direct impact on reported profit. Furthermore, the value of inventories is often very significant, so that even a small percentage error in their valuation could lead to a material mis-statement of profit. International standard IAS2 *Inventories* provides guidance on the valuation of inventories and this chapter explains the main requirements of that standard.

IAS2 applies to most inventories but does not apply to work in progress arising under construction contracts. This specialised topic is dealt with by international standard IAS11 *Construction Contracts* which is also explained in this chapter.

Objectives

By the end of this chapter, the reader should be able to:

- define the term "inventories" and measure the value of inventories in accordance with the requirements of IAS2 *Inventories*
- apply cost formulas such as first-in, first-out and weighted average cost
- define the term "construction contract"
- calculate the revenue and expenses which should be recognised in an accounting period in relation to a construction contract, in accordance with the requirements of IAS11 *Construction Contracts*
- list the main disclosures that should be made in the financial statements in relation to inventories and construction contracts.

Inventories

International standard IAS2 defines inventories as "*assets:*

(a) *held for sale in the ordinary course of business;*

(b) *in the process of production for such sale; or*

(c) *in the form of materials or supplies to be consumed in the production process or in the rendering of services*".

The standard also prescribes a well-known rule for the valuation of inventories. This rule is that "*inventories shall be measured at the lower of cost and net realisable value*". The remainder of IAS2 provides guidance on the determination of the cost and net realisable value of inventories and makes certain disclosure requirements.

Cost of inventories

IAS2 states that the cost of inventories "*shall comprise all costs of purchase, costs of conversion and other costs incurred in bringing the inventories to their present location and condition*". Note the following points:

(a) Costs of purchase consist of the purchase price of inventories, including import duties and other taxes (if these are irrecoverable), transport and handling costs and any other costs directly attributable to the acquisition of the goods concerned. Trade discounts are deducted when calculating costs of purchase.

(b) Costs of conversion are relevant mainly to manufacturing businesses and consist of direct costs of production (such as direct labour) together with a systematic allocation of fixed and variable overheads incurred in converting materials into finished goods.

   Fixed production overheads are indirect production costs that remain relatively constant regardless of the volume of production (e.g. factory rent and rates). Variable production overheads are indirect production costs that vary more or less in line with the volume of production, such as indirect materials and some indirect labour costs.

(c) The allocation of fixed production costs to units of production should be based upon the normal capacity of the production facilities.

   (i) If production is abnormally low, there will be unallocated fixed production overheads. These should be recognised as an expense in the period in which they are incurred and should *not* be included in the cost of inventories.

   (ii) If production is abnormally high, the amount of fixed production overheads allocated to each item of production should be decreased so as to ensure that the cost of inventories is not overstated.

(d) Certain costs are explicitly excluded from the cost of inventories. The main items are:

    (i) the costs of abnormal wastage of materials, labour or other production costs

    (ii) storage costs, unless these costs are necessary in the production process before a further production stage

    (iii) administrative overheads that do not contribute to bringing inventories to their present location or condition

    (iv) selling costs.

(e) Techniques such as standard costing and the retail method may be used to determine the cost of inventories, so long as they provide a reasonable approximation to cost.

    (i) Standard costs are computed in accordance with normal prices and usage of materials, labour etc. and normal levels of efficiency. Standard costs should be reviewed regularly and revised if necessary.

    (ii) The retail method is often used in the retail industry for measuring inventories which consist of large numbers of rapidly changing items with similar profit margins. This method determines the cost of inventories by reducing their sales value by the appropriate percentage profit margin.

EXAMPLE 1

A manufacturing company's inventory at the end of an accounting period includes a finished product with the following costs to date:

	£
Purchase price of materials	9,000
Less: 5% trade discount	450
	8,550
Import duty at 10%	855
Direct labour costs	5,850
Allocation of fixed production overheads	2,840
Storage costs since product completed	225
Advertising costs	317
Total cost	18,637

Notes:

(i) All of these costs exclude VAT. The company is able to recover any VAT which it is charged by its suppliers but cannot recover import duties.

(ii) One-third of the materials included above were wasted as the result of an abnormal machine malfunction.

(iii) Fixed production overheads are allocated to products on the assumption that production is running at normal capacity. In fact, production was unusually low during the period in which this product was made and a further allocation of £820 would be required if fixed overheads were allocated on the basis of actual production.

(iv) The advertising costs were incurred whilst trying to find a buyer for the product. No buyer had been found by the end of the accounting period.

Calculate the cost of this product in accordance with the requirements of IAS2.

Solution

For inventory valuation purposes, the cost of the product is as follows:

	£
Purchase price of materials, net of trade discount	5,700
Import duty at 10%	570
Direct labour costs	5,850
Allocation of fixed production overheads	2,840
Total cost	14,960

Notes:

(i)   Recoverable VAT is not a cost to the company and is therefore excluded from the cost of inventories.

(ii)   The cost of abnormal wastage is also excluded from the cost of inventories. The cost of the remaining two-thirds of the materials was £5,700 (2/3 x £8,550).

(iii)   The further £820 of fixed production overheads is treated as an expense and is not included in the cost of inventories.

(iv)   The storage costs were incurred after production was complete. The advertising costs are selling costs. Neither of these can be included in the cost of inventories. Furthermore, the failure to find a buyer for the product may cast doubt on its net realisable value (see later in this chapter).

Cost formulas

In general, IAS2 requires that the cost of inventory items should be ascertained "*by using specific identification of their individual costs*". In other words, each item of inventory should be considered separately and its cost should be individually established.

However, it is not always possible to distinguish one inventory item from another. For instance, a business may have an inventory of identical machine parts which have been bought on different dates and at different prices. In such a case, it is frequently impossible to determine the cost of each individual item with any certainty. IAS2 refers to such items as "interchangeable" and requires that their cost should be ascertained by means of a cost formula. Two cost formulas are allowed. These are:

(a)   **First-in, first-out (FIFO)**. The FIFO formula assumes that inventory items which are purchased or produced first are sold or used first, so that the items remaining at the end of an accounting period are those most recently purchased or produced.

(b) **Weighted average cost (AVCO)**. Use of the AVCO formula generally involves computing a new weighted average cost per item after each acquisition takes place. The cost of the items remaining at the end of an accounting period is then calculated by using the most recently-computed weighted average cost per item.

IAS2 allows either of these cost formulas to be used and there is no requirement that the choice of formula should mirror the actual physical flow of the items concerned. However, there is a requirement that the same cost formula should be used for all inventories having a similar nature and use.

LIFO not allowed

It is important to note that IAS2 does *not* allow the use of last-in, first-out (LIFO). This cost formula assumes that the newest inventory items are sold or used first, so that the items remaining at the end of an accounting period are the oldest. IAS2 objects to the LIFO formula for a number of reasons:

(a) LIFO is generally not a reliable representation of actual inventory flows.

(b) The use of LIFO is often tax-driven, since it matches sales revenue against the cost of the newest items acquired. In times of rising prices, this will result in lower reported profits and a lower tax liability (so long as the tax authorities will accept LIFO for tax purposes). However, the IASB takes the view that tax considerations do not provide an adequate conceptual basis for the selection of an accounting treatment.

(c) The use of LIFO results in inventories being shown in the financial statements at values which bear little relation to recent cost levels.

Even though the use of LIFO has been eliminated, IAS2 does not rule out "*specific cost methods that reflect inventory flows that are similar to LIFO*". For instance, inventories may be held in piles or bins which are both depleted and replenished from the top. In such a case, it could be argued that there is no need to apply a cost formula at all, since the items remaining on the pile or in the bin can be clearly identified. A specific costing approach which reflected the physical flow of items in these circumstances would not be ruled out purely because it gave similar results to LIFO.

EXAMPLE 2

On 1 April 2013, a company's inventory included 12,000 bricks which had been acquired for £140 per thousand. Purchases and sales of bricks during the year to 31 March 2014 were as follows:

Purchases	Number bought	Cost per thousand	Sales	Number sold
		£		
14 July 2013	10,000	142	26 August 2013	16,000
11 October 2013	8,000	145	5 November 2013	7,000
19 January 2014	15,000	147	12 March 2014	17,000

Calculate the cost of the bricks sold during the year and the cost of the inventory of bricks remaining at 31 March 2014, using:

(a)   first-in, first-out (FIFO)

(b)   last-in, first-out (LIFO)

(c)   weighted average cost (AVCO).

Which of these three cost formulas should the company use?

Solution

(a)   **FIFO**

	Number of bricks			Cost (£)
Sold 26 August	16,000	12,000 @ 14.0p	1,680	
		4,000 @ 14.2p	568	2,248
Sold 5 November	7,000	6,000 @ 14.2p	852	
		1,000 @ 14.5p	145	997
Sold 12 March	17,000	7,000 @ 14.5p	1,015	
		10,000 @ 14.7p	1,470	2,485
Cost of goods sold				5,730
Inventory at 31 March	5,000	5,000 @ 14.7p		**735**

(b)   **LIFO**

	Number of bricks			Cost (£)
Sold 26 August	16,000	10,000 @ 14.2p	1,420	
		6,000 @ 14.0p	840	2,260
Sold 5 November	7,000	7,000 @ 14.5p		1,015
Sold 12 March	17,000	15,000 @ 14.7p	2,205	
		1,000 @ 14.5p	145	
		1,000 @ 14.0p	140	2,490
Cost of goods sold				5,765
Inventory at 31 March	5,000	5,000 @ 14.0p		**700**

(c) **AVCO**

	Number of Bricks		Total cost	Weighted average	Cost (£)
Opening inventory	12,000	@ 14.0p	1,680		
Bought 14 July	10,000	@ 14.2p	1,420		
	22,000		3,100	14.09p	
Sold 26 August	16,000	@ 14.09p	2,254		2,254
	6,000		846		
Bought 11 October	8,000	@ 14.5p	1,160		
	14,000		2,006	14.33p	
Sold 5 November	7,000	@ 14.33p	1,003		1,003
	7,000		1,003		
Bought 19 January	15,000	@ 14.7p	2,205		
	22,000		3,208	14.58p	
Sold 12 March	17,000	@ 14.58p	2,479		2,479
Cost of goods sold					5,736
Inventory at 31 March	5,000	@ 14.58p	729		**729**

The company may use either FIFO or AVCO but must use the same cost formula for all inventories of a similar nature and use. The business is not allowed to use LIFO.

Net realisable value

As stated above, IAS2 requires that inventories should be measured at the lower of cost and net realisable value. Net realisable value (NRV) is defined as "*estimated selling price in the ordinary course of business less the estimated costs of completion and the estimated costs necessary to make the sale*". The effect of measuring inventories at the lower of cost and NRV is that any loss expected on the sale of items at less than cost is accounted for immediately rather than when the items are sold. Note that:

(a) The costs and NRV of inventories are normally compared item by item. However, IAS2 accepts that it may sometimes be appropriate to group similar or related items together and to compare the total cost of the group with its total NRV.

(b) Materials and other supplies held for use in production are not written down below cost so long as the finished products in which they will be incorporated are expected to be sold at cost or above.

EXAMPLE 3

The inventory of a motor vehicles dealer at the end of an accounting period includes the following used vehicles:

	Costs incurred to date	Expected further costs before sale	Expected selling price
	£	£	£
Vehicle A	14,200	1,250	18,000
Vehicle B	17,500	1,000	20,000
Vehicle C	11,900	1,240	14,000
Vehicle D	13,000	2,760	15,000

The dealer's sales staff are paid a commission when they sell a vehicle. This commission is calculated at 5% of selling price. Calculate the value at which these items should be shown in the dealer's financial statements.

Solution

	Cost	NRV	Lower of cost and NRV
	£		£	£
Vehicle A	14,200	(18,000 x 95%) − 1,250 = 15,850	14,200
Vehicle B	17,500	(20,000 x 95%) − 1,000 = 18,000	17,500
Vehicle C	11,900	(14,000 x 95%) − 1,240 = 12,060	11,900
Vehicle D	13,000	(15,000 x 95%) − 2,760 = 11,490	11,490
	56,600	57,400	55,090

For vehicles A, B and C, cost is less than NRV, so these vehicles are valued at cost. But the cost of vehicle D exceeds its NRV, so this vehicle must be valued at NRV. The closing inventory should be valued at a total of £55,090. It would not be permissible to value the vehicles at the lower of total cost and total NRV (i.e. £56,600).

Disclosures relating to inventories

The main disclosures required by IAS2 are as follows:

(a) the accounting policies adopted in measuring inventories, including the cost formula used (if any)

(b) the total carrying amount of inventories (i.e. the amount at which the inventories are shown or "carried" in the entity's financial statements) together with an analysis into appropriate categories

(c) the amount of inventories recognised as an expense during the period

(d) the amount of any write-down to net realisable value during the period and the amount of any reversal of previous write-downs.

These disclosures will be made in the notes which form part of the financial statements.

Construction contracts

The scope of international standard IAS2 specifically excludes work in progress arising under construction contracts. This is for a good reason. By their very nature, construction contracts are often long-term, so that construction work may begin in one accounting period but not end until a later period. If IAS2 applied to such contracts, it would be necessary at the end of each period to measure work in progress at the lower of cost and net realisable value. This would mean that none of the profit arising on a construction contract would be recognised until the contract had ended. In an extreme case, a business engaged upon a construction contract might report zero profits for several years followed by a very large profit in the final year of the contract. It would obviously be fairer to spread contract revenue, expenses and profit over the accounting periods in which the construction work is performed and international standard IAS11 *Construction Contracts* prescribes an accounting treatment which achieves this aim.

IAS11 defines a construction contract as "*a contract specifically negotiated for the construction of an asset or a combination of assets that are closely interrelated or inter-dependent in terms of their design, technology and function or their ultimate purpose or use*". For the purposes of IAS11, construction contracts include:

(a) contracts for the rendering of services that are directly related to the construction of assets (e.g. contracts for the services of project managers and architects)

(b) contracts for the destruction or restoration of assets and for the restoration of the environment after the demolition of assets.

Combining and segmenting construction contracts

The requirements of IAS11 are usually applied separately to each construction contract on which a business is engaged. But note that:

(a) a group of contracts should be treated as a single contract when:

    (i)   the group of contracts is negotiated as a single package; and

    (ii) the contracts are so closely related that they are, in effect, a single project; and

    (iii) the contracts are performed concurrently or in a continuous sequence.

(b) a single contract which covers the construction of a number of assets should be treated as several separate contracts (one for each asset) when:

    (i)   separate proposals have been submitted for each asset; and

    (ii) each asset has been subject to separate negotiation; and

    (iii) the costs and revenues for each asset can be separately identified.

Contract revenue and costs

In order to spread contract revenue and costs over the accounting periods in which the construction work is performed, it is first necessary to estimate the total revenue expected from the contract and the expected total costs. These estimates may need to be revised from time to time in the light of events as the contract work proceeds. Note that:

(a) Contract revenue comprises:

    (i) the initial amount of revenue agreed in the contract

    (ii) plus or minus the revenue associated with agreed variations in the contract work

    (iii) plus amounts claimed by the contractor as reimbursement for costs not included in the contract price (e.g. costs arising from delays caused by the customer)

    (iv) plus incentive payments to which the contractor is entitled for meeting or for exceeding specified performance targets

    (v) minus penalties arising from delays or other problems caused by the contractor.

In general, amounts should be included in contract revenue only if is probable that the revenue will arise and if the amount concerned can be measured reliably.

(b) Contract costs comprise:

    (i) costs that relate directly to the specific contract (e.g. materials, labour, plant hire, depreciation of equipment used in the construction work)

    (ii) costs that relate to contract activity in general and can be allocated to the contract (e.g. insurance, construction overheads)

    (iii) such other costs as are specifically chargeable to the customer under the terms of the contract (e.g. general administration costs for which reimbursement is specified in the terms of the contract).

Costs that relate to contract activity in general should be allocated using methods which are systematic, rational and consistent.

Certain costs are excluded from the cost of a construction contract. The main items are general administration or research and development costs for which reimbursement is not specified in the terms of the contract and selling costs.

Recognition of contract revenue and expenses

When the outcome of a construction contract can be estimated reliably, IAS11 requires that contract revenue and costs are "*recognised as revenue and expenses respectively by reference to the stage of completion of the contract activity at the end of the reporting period*". The stage of completion may be determined in a number of ways. For example:

(a) by comparing the costs incurred for the work performed to date with the estimated total contract costs

(b)   by carrying out a survey of the work performed to date

(c)   by considering the physical proportion of the contract work completed.

If the stage of completion is determined by reference to the proportion of total contract costs incurred to date, only those costs that reflect work performed are included in costs incurred to date. Costs which relate to future activity (e.g. the cost of inventory which has been acquired in readiness for future work) are excluded from the calculation.

EXAMPLE 4

A company which prepares accounts to 31 December each year began work on a construction contract on 17 February 2013. The contract price was originally agreed to be £19 million but during 2014 the customer requested a substantial variation to the contract work and this increased the price to £25 million. The contract was completed on 2 May 2015. Cost information is as follows:

	31/12/2013	31/12/2014	31/12/2015
	£m	£m	£m
Expected total contract costs	16	20	21
Total costs incurred to date	5	14	21
Costs relating to future activity	1	-	-

The costs incurred to date of £5 million at 31 December 2013 included £1 million spent on acquiring materials for use during future work on the contract. The company's accounting policy is to determine the stage of completion of a construction contract by comparing the costs incurred for the work performed to date with the estimated total contract costs.

Calculate the revenue and expenses arising from this contract which should be recognised in the statement of comprehensive income for each of the years to 31 December 2013, 2014 and 2015.

Solution

(i)   At 31 December 2013, costs incurred for work performed to date were £4 million and expected total contract costs were £16 million, so the stage of completion was 25%.

(ii)   At 31 December 2014, costs incurred for work performed to date were £14 million and expected total contract costs were £20 million, so the stage of completion was 70%.

(iii) At 31 December 2015, the contract was 100% complete.

Revenue and expenses which should be recognised in the statement of comprehensive income for each of the three years are as follows:

	Cumulative total	Recognised in prior years	Recognised this year
	£m	£m	£m
year to 31/12/2013			
Contract revenue			
25% x £19m	4.75	-	4.75
Contract expenses	4.00	-	4.00
Contract profit	0.75	-	0.75
year to 31/12/2014			
Contract revenue			
70% x £25m	17.50	4.75	12.75
Contract expenses	14.00	4.00	10.00
Contract profit	3.50	0.75	2.75
year to 31/12/2015			
Contract revenue			
100% x £25m	25.00	17.50	7.50
Contract expenses	21.00	14.00	7.00
Contract profit	4.00	3.50	0.50

No reliable estimate of contract outcome

During the early stages of a construction contract, it is often not possible to make a reliable estimate of the contract outcome. In these circumstances, IAS11 does not permit any profit to be recognised. However, sufficient contract revenue may be recognised to cover the costs incurred to date, so long as it is thought probable that these costs will be recovered.

If no reliable estimate can be made of the contract outcome but it is thought probable that the total costs of the contract will exceed total contract revenue, the expected loss should immediately be recognised as an expense (see below).

Recognition of expected losses

If at any stage it is probable that total contract costs will exceed total contract revenue, the expected loss must be recognised immediately. Although expected profits are spread over the period of the contract, expected losses are accounted for as soon as they become probable.

Presentation and disclosure for construction contracts

In the statement of financial position, contractors are required to present the gross amount due *from* customers for contract work as an asset. The total amount due *to* customers for contract work should be presented as a liability. Note that:

(a) The gross amount due *from* customers for contract work is equal to:

    (i) costs incurred to date plus recognised profits, *less*

    (ii) amounts billed to date ("progress billings") and any recognised losses

    for all contracts in progress at the end of the reporting period for which costs incurred to date plus recognised profits less recognised losses exceed progress billings.

(b) The gross amount due *to* customers for contract work is equal to:

    (i) progress billings plus any recognised losses, *less*

    (ii) costs incurred to date and recognised profits

    for all contracts in progress at the end of the reporting period for which progress billings exceed costs incurred to date plus recognised profits less recognised losses.

The effect of these presentation rules is that items such as inventories of materials and amounts due from customers (but not yet billed) are included in the gross amount which is due to/from customers, rather than being shown under separate headings in the statement of financial position. Amounts already billed to customers (but not yet received) are of course included in trade receivables.

Disclosures

The main disclosures required by IAS11 are as follows:

(a) the amount of contract revenue recognised during the accounting period

(b) the methods used to determine contract revenue for the period

(c) the methods used to determine the stage of completion of contracts in progress

(d) for contracts in progress at the end of the reporting period:

    (i) the total of costs incurred to date and total recognised profits/losses to date

    (ii) the amount of any "advances" received; advances are amounts received by the contractor before the related work is performed

    (iii) the amount of any "retentions"; retentions are amounts that have been billed to the customer but which are not payable until certain conditions specified in the contract have been satisfied.

These disclosures will be made in the notes which form part of the financial statements.

EXAMPLE 5

This example is based upon an illustration which is provided with IAS11.

A company which operates as a construction contractor has reached the end of its first year of operations. There are five contracts in progress at the end of the year. Contracts A, B and C are expected to be profitable. Contracts D and E are expected to result in overall losses of £90,000 and £30,000 respectively.

The stage of completion of each contract has been determined and this has been used to calculate the amount of revenue which may be recognised in the year. These revenue figures (and other contract data) are as follows:

	A £000	B £000	C £000	D £000	E £000	Total £000
Revenue recognised in year	**145**	**520**	**380**	**200**	**55**	**1,300**
Costs incurred in year	110	510	450	250	100	1,420
Less: Inventory c/f	-	60	100	-	45	205
Costs relating to the year	110	450	350	250	55	1,215
Add: Additional costs recognised	-	-	-	40	30	70
Costs recognised in year	**110**	**450**	**350**	**290**	**85**	**1,285**
Profit/(loss) for the year	**35**	**70**	**30**	**(90)**	**(30)**	**15**
Revenue recognised in year	145	520	380	200	55	1,300
Less: Billed to customers	100	520	380	180	55	1,235
Unbilled at year end	45	-	-	20	-	65

Notes:

(a) In the case of contracts B, C and E, some of the costs incurred during the year relate to the purchase of inventories for use during future work on those contracts.

(b) In the case of contracts D and E, additional costs have been recognised so as to account for the expected overall losses on those contracts. For each contract, these additional costs have been set at amounts which ensure that the costs recognised in the year exceed revenue for the year by the amount of the expected loss.

(c) Contract revenue of £1,300,000 and contract costs of £1,285,000 have been included in the company's statement of comprehensive income for the year, contributing a net amount of £15,000 towards the company's pre-tax profit.

Explain how these contracts will be presented in the company's statement of financial position at the end of the year and list the main disclosures which will appear in the notes which form part of the company's financial statements.

Solution

The amounts presented in the statement of financial position are calculated as follows:

	A	B	C	D	E	Total
	£000	£000	£000	£000	£000	£000
Costs incurred in year	110	510	450	250	100	1,420
Recognised profits/(losses)	35	70	30	(90)	(30)	15
	145	580	480	160	70	1,435
Progress billings	100	520	380	180	55	1,235
	45	60	100	(20)	15	200
Due from customers	45	60	100	-	15	220
Due to customers	-	-	-	(20)	-	(20)

The company's statement of financial position should show an asset of £220,000 for the amount due from customers for contract work and a liability of £20,000 for the amount due to customers for contract work. The main <u>disclosures</u> required are:

	£000
Contract revenue recognised during the accounting period	1,300
Costs incurred to date plus recognised profits (less losses) to date for contracts in progress at the end of the reporting period	1,435

Tutorial notes:

An alternative way of computing the amounts due to/from customers is as follows:

	A	B	C	D	E	Total
	£000	£000	£000	£000	£000	£000
Inventory	-	60	100	-	45	205
Unbilled at year end	45	-	-	20	-	65
Provision for additional costs	-	-	-	(40)	(30)	(70)
	45	60	100	(20)	15	200

(i) **Contract A**. The amount due from customers consists solely of the unbilled revenue of £45,000 (£145,000 – £100,000).

(ii) **Contracts B and C**. In each case, the amount due from customers relates solely to inventory which has been purchased by the company and earmarked for contract use but has not yet been paid for by the customer.

(iii) **Contract D**. Unbilled revenue is £20,000 (£200,000 – £180,000). But additional costs of £40,000 must be provided for, giving rise to a £40,000 liability. The £20,000 asset and £40,000 liability are offset, giving an overall liability of £20,000.

(iv) **Contract E**. The customer owes the company £45,000 for inventory but there is a liability for additional costs of £30,000, giving an overall asset of £15,000.

Proposed new standard

In June 2010, the IASB issued an exposure draft of a new international standard *Revenue from Contracts with Customers* which would change the way in which revenue from construction contracts is recognised. This draft standard proposes that contract revenue should not be recognised until the customer obtains control of the asset which is being constructed. For an incomplete contract, revenue would be recognised only if the customer had control of the partially-completed asset. This contrasts with the current "stage of completion" method, whereby revenue is recognised as work is performed, regardless of whether or not control of the asset has passed to the customer.

A revised version of the exposure draft was issued in November 2011 and still further amendments may be made before the finalised standard is published. The progress of this project may be followed on website www.ifrs.org.

Summary

▶ International standard IAS2 defines "inventories" and requires that inventories are measured at the lower of cost and net realisable value.

▶ The cost of inventories comprises costs of purchase, conversion costs and any other costs incurred in bringing the inventories to their present location and condition.

▶ The cost of interchangeable inventory items should be established by use of a cost formula. Permitted formulas are first-in, first-out and weighted average cost. The use of last-in, first-out is not permitted.

▶ The net realisable value of inventories is their estimated selling price in the ordinary course of business, less estimated costs of completion and selling costs.

▶ IAS2 makes certain disclosure requirements with regard to inventories.

▶ International standard IAS11 defines the term "construction contract" and prescribes an accounting treatment for contract revenue and contract costs.

▶ In general, contract revenue and costs are recognised as revenue and expenses in the statement of comprehensive income by reference to the stage of completion of contract activity. Any expected losses must be accounted for immediately.

▶ IAS11 makes certain presentation and disclosure requirements with regard to construction contracts.

Exercises

10.1   (a)   Explain the term "inventories" as defined by international standard IAS2.

(b)   List the costs which should be included when measuring the cost of inventories and identify any costs which should be excluded.

(c)   Explain the term "net realisable value" in relation to inventories.

10.2   (a)   Identify the circumstances in which a cost formula may be used to establish the cost of inventories.

(b)   A company's inventories at 30 April 2014 include 11,000kg of a chemical which is used in the company's manufacturing processes. Purchases and issues of this chemical during the year to 30 April 2014 were as follows:

		Number of kg	*Cost per kg*
May 2013	Opening inventory	32,000	£7.50
June 2013	Issued to production	25,000	
August 2013	Purchased	15,000	£8.75
September 2013	Issued to production	12,000	
October 2013	Issued to production	5,000	
January 2014	Purchased	10,000	£9.50
February 2014	Issued to production	4,000	

Calculate the cost of the company's inventory of the chemical at 30 April 2014 using each of the following cost formulas:

(i)   first-in, first-out (FIFO)

(ii)   weighted average cost (AVCO).

10.3   (a)   Explain why international standard IAS2 does not apply to construction contracts.

(b)   Explain how the stage of completion of a construction project can be determined.

10.4   Madderley plc prepares financial statements to 31 December each year. The company began work on a construction contract on 21 June 2012 and completed the contract work on 13 August 2014. The contract price was initially set at £500,000 and this figure did not change throughout the duration of the contract. Cost information is as follows:

	31/12/2012	*31/12/2013*	*31/12/2014*
	£000	£000	£000
Expected total costs	400	480	475
Total costs incurred to date	250	440	475
Costs relating to future activity	10	8	-

The costs incurred to date of £250,000 at 31 December 2012 and £440,000 at 31 December 2013 included £10,000 and £8,000 respectively for materials to be used in the following year's contract work.

The company determines the stage of completion of a contract by comparing the costs incurred for the work performed to date with the estimated total contract costs.

Compute the revenue and expenses which would be shown in relation to this contract in the company's financial statements for each of the years to 31 December 2012, 2013 and 2014.

10.5 Kellerstone Ltd buys used machines which it reconditions and sells on to customers. The company's inventory at the end of its most recent accounting period included the following machines:

	Purchase price	Reconditioning costs incurred to date	Expected further costs before sale	Expected selling price
	£	£	£	£
Machine W	10,300	650	-	12,500
Machine X	15,750	850	400	17,500
Machine Y	18,450	500	2,100	23,000
Machine Z	8,300	-	900	9,500
	52,800	2,000	3,400	62,500

Selling expenses are expected to absorb 4% of the expected selling price.

(a) Explain why it is not permissible to value the inventory of machines at their total purchase price of £52,800 or at their total selling price of £62,500.

(b) Compute the value at which the inventory of machines should be measured in the company's financial statements.

10.6 Laidlow plc is a construction contractor which prepares financial statements to 31 May each year. The following information relates to a contract which began during the year to 31 May 2014 and which was still in progress on that date:

	£000
Contract price	600
Costs incurred to date:	
- for work performed up to 31 May 2014	190
- to acquire inventories for use in future work	30
Estimated further costs to completion	280
Progress billings to date	175

The company's accounting policy is to determine the stage of completion of a contract by comparing the costs incurred for the work performed to date with the estimated total contract costs.

(a) Show how this contract would be reflected in the company's financial statements for the year to 31 May 2014.

(b) How would the accounting treatment differ if the contract price was £480,000 but all of the other figures remained unaltered?

10.7 A company which makes only one type of product incurs fixed production overheads of £240,000 during the year to 31 March 2014. Normal production capacity is 80,000 units per annum. Calculate the amount of fixed production overheads that should be allocated to each unit of production when determining the cost of inventories at 31 March 2014 if actual production for the year is:

(a) 80,000 units   (b) 100,000 units   (c) 60,000 units.

10.8 Klinibild plc has three contracts to build new clinics for NHS trusts. The three projects are the Tyne, the Tees and the Wear. The following information as at 31 October 2014 is available for each of the three contracts:

	Tyne £m	Tees £m	Wear £m
Contract price	19.80	24.83	15.50
Certified value of work completed	10.30	1.25	10.00
Value of work invoiced	8.30	1.00	10.00
Payments received	6.50	1.00	9.00
Costs incurred to date	7.52	1.33	12.93
Estimated future costs to complete	6.56	9.45	5.27
Recognised in previous financial year:			
Contract revenue	5.25	-	-
Contract costs	3.85	-	-
Contract profit	1.40	-	-

Work on both the Tees contract and the Wear contract commenced during the financial year ended 31 October 2014. The Tyne contract commenced during the financial year ended 31 October 2013.

Klinibild plc accounts for its contracts in accordance with IAS11 *Construction Contracts* using a revenue approach to calculate the percentage of work completed. Revenue is to be based on independent surveyors' certificates.

All of the amounts invoiced to the contractees are expected to be collected and no allowance is to be made for doubtful debts.

Required:

(a) Calculate the estimated total profit or loss on each of the three contracts.

(b) Calculate the profit or loss to date on each of the three contracts.

(c) Calculate the figures to be reported in Klinibild plc's statement of comprehensive income for the year ended 31 October 2014 for contract revenue, contract costs, and profit or loss for each of the three contracts.

(d) Calculate the figures which will be reported in Klinibild plc's statement of financial position as at 31 October 2014 for each of the three contracts. *(CIPFA)*

*10.9   Parrison Ltd is a manufacturing company. The company's inventory at 30 June 2014 includes the following items of work in progress:

	Product X	Product Y
Number of units held at 30 June 2014	6,400	3,800
Costs incurred per unit to date	£8	£12
Estimated further costs per unit to completion	£7	£8
Estimated selling costs per unit	£2	£4
Estimated selling price per unit	£15	£30

The company complies with IAS2 *Inventories*.

(a)   Define the term "inventories".

(b)   Explain how the cost of inventories should be determined.

(c)   Define the term "net realisable value".

(d)   Explain how inventories should be measured in accordance with IAS2.

(e)   Calculate the figure at which the work in progress of Parrison Ltd should be shown in the company's financial statements for the year to 30 June 2014.

*10.10   Beetie is a construction company that prepares its financial statements to 31 March each year. During the year ended 31 March 2014 the company commenced two construction contracts that are expected to take more than one year to complete. The position of each contract at 31 March 2014 is as follows:

	Contract 1	Contract 2
	£000	£000
Agreed contract price	5,500	1,200
Estimated total cost of contract at commencement	4,000	900
Estimated total cost at 31 March 2014	4,000	1,250
Agreed value of work completed at 31 March 2014	3,300	840
Progress billings invoiced and received at 31 March 2014	3,000	880
Contract costs incurred to 31 March 2014	3,900	920

The agreed value of the work completed at 31 March 2014 is considered to be equal to the revenue earned in the year ended 31 March 2014. The percentage of completion is calculated as the agreed value of work completed to the agreed contract price.

Required:

Calculate the amounts which should appear in the financial statements of Beetie for the year to 31 March 2014 in respect of the above contracts.   *(ACCA)*

Chapter 11

Financial instruments

Introduction

Broadly speaking, a "financial instrument" is a means of raising finance. In practice, the term covers a wide range of highly complex financial arrangements, but simple examples include loans of various types and share issues. There are four international standards which deal with financial instruments. These are:

IAS32 *Financial Instruments: Presentation*

IAS39 *Financial Instruments: Recognition and Measurement*

IFRS7 *Financial Instruments: Disclosures*

IFRS9 *Financial Instruments*

These standards define the term "financial instrument", identify several different types of financial instrument and prescribe the accounting treatment of each type.

This area of accounting is renowned for its complexity. In fact, the four standards listed above (together with implementation guidance and other documentation) occupy over 500 pages of fine print. A detailed coverage of financial instruments is well beyond the scope of this book and therefore this chapter provides only a basic introduction to the topic.

Objectives

By the end of this chapter, the reader should be able to:

- define the term "financial instrument"
- define the terms "financial asset", "financial liability" and "equity instrument"
- correctly classify financial instruments as either liabilities or equity
- explain the circumstances in which a financial asset or liability should be recognised
- calculate the amounts at which financial assets and financial liabilities should be measured on initial recognition and subsequently
- list the main disclosures required in relation to financial instruments.

Definitions

IAS32 *Financial Instruments: Presentation* provides four key definitions which apply throughout all of the standards which deal with financial instruments. The main features of these definitions are as follows:

- A financial instrument is "*any contract that gives rise to a financial asset of one entity and a financial liability or equity instrument of another entity*".

- A financial asset is "*any asset that is:*

  (a) cash;

  (b) an equity instrument of another entity;

  (c) a contractual right to receive cash or another financial asset from another entity".

- A financial liability is "*any liability that is a contractual obligation to deliver cash or another financial asset to another entity*".

- An equity instrument is "*any contract that evidences a residual interest in the assets of an entity after deducting all of its liabilities*". Ordinary shares are the most common instance of an equity instrument.

The full definitions given in IAS32 are actually longer and more complex than this, but the versions given above are sufficient for most purposes. These definitions are illustrated in the following example.

EXAMPLE 1

Explain why each of the transactions listed below gives rise to a financial instrument as defined by international standard IAS32:

(a) a company makes an issue of loan stock

(b) a company sells goods to a customer on credit

(c) a company buys goods from a supplier on credit

(d) a company deposits money into its bank account

(e) a company overdraws its bank account

(f) a company makes an issue of ordinary shares

(g) a company invests in newly-issued ordinary shares of another company.

Solution

(a) The issue of loan stock creates a contractual obligation on the part of the company to repay the loan at some time in the future. The contract between the company and the lenders is a financial instrument because:

    (i) the lenders now have the right to be repaid (a financial asset)

    (ii) the company is now under an obligation to repay the loan (a financial liability)

(b) A sale on credit creates a contractual obligation on the part of the customer to pay for the goods. The contract with the customer is a financial instrument because:

    (i) the company now has a trade receivable (a financial asset)

    (ii) the customer now has a trade payable (a financial liability).

(c) A purchase on credit creates a contractual obligation on the part of the company to pay for the goods. The contract with the supplier is a financial instrument because:

    (i) the supplier now has a trade receivable (a financial asset)

    (ii) the company now has a trade payable (a financial liability).

(d) In effect, a bank deposit is a loan to the bank and the bank is contractually obliged to repay this money. The contract with the bank is a financial instrument because:

    (i) the company now has the right to withdraw its cash (a financial asset)

    (ii) the bank is now under an obligation to repay the cash (a financial liability).

(e) A bank overdraft is a form of bank loan and the company is contractually obliged to repay this loan. The contract with the bank is a financial instrument because:

    (i) the bank now has the right to be repaid (a financial asset)

    (ii) the company is now under an obligation to repay the bank (a financial liability).

(f) Ordinary shares are an equity instrument, as defined by IAS32. The issue of ordinary shares creates a contract between the company and its shareholders. This contract is a financial instrument because:

    (i) the shareholders now own the shares (a financial asset)

    (ii) the company now has extra share capital (an equity instrument).

(g) This purchase of ordinary shares creates a contract between the investing company and the issuing company. This contract is a financial instrument because:

    (i) the investing company now owns the shares (a financial asset)

    (ii) the issuing company now has extra share capital (an equity instrument).

Classification of financial instruments

The objective of IAS32 is to clarify the distinction between liabilities and equity and so ensure that financial liabilities and equity instruments are correctly identified in financial statements. If IAS32 did not exist, an entity might be able to incur a financial liability but present this liability as equity. This would artificially increase the company's net assets and improve its gearing ratio (see Chapter 22) thus reducing the extent to which the financial statements provided a faithful representation of the entity's financial position.

IAS32 takes a "substance over form" approach to distinguishing between liabilities and equity. Even though the legal form of a financial instrument might be a share issue, the instrument could still be regarded as giving rise to a financial liability if the underlying substance of the transaction indicates that this is the case. IAS32 states that a financial instrument should be classified as an equity instrument if and only if:

"the instrument includes no contractual obligation ... to deliver cash or another financial asset to another entity ... ".

Ordinary shares are an example of an equity instrument, since the company which issues the shares is under no contractual obligation to pay dividends and is usually prevented by law from repaying the share capital. Ordinary shareholders may in fact receive dividends from time to time but the important point is that the company cannot be *required* to deliver cash or any other financial asset to these shareholders. This situation should be contrasted with a loan, where the borrower is generally obliged to make interest payments throughout the period of the loan and to repay the loan itself at the end of that period.

Redeemable preference shares

As stated above, IAS32 adopts a substance over form approach to distinguishing between liabilities and equity. This approach is illustrated by the required treatment of redeemable preference shares. These are preference shares which either:

(a)   provide for mandatory repayment of the share capital at a future date, or

(b)   give the shareholders the right to require repayment of the share capital on or after a particular date, for a fixed or determinable amount.

In these circumstances, it is clear that the issuing company has a contractual obligation to deliver cash. Therefore redeemable preference shares must be classified as liabilities rather than equity, despite their legal form. Furthermore, IAS32 states that interest and dividends relating to financial liabilities should be recognised as an expense when calculating the issuing company's profit or loss. Therefore dividends paid to the holders of redeemable preference shares must be treated as an expense. Any accrued dividends unpaid at the end of an accounting period must be treated in the same way as accrued interest. Dividends that are classified as an expense are presented in the statement of comprehensive income either together with interest on other liabilities or as a separate item.

It may seem strange to treat shares as if they were liabilities and to treat dividends as if they were interest, but this is simply a logical consequence of the IAS32 requirement that the accounting treatment of a financial instrument should follow its substance rather than its legal form.

Compound financial instruments

Some financial instruments (known as "compound financial instruments") contain both a liability component and an equity component. For example, loan stock that is convertible to ordinary shares at the option of the holder is a compound financial instrument. IAS32 requires that compound financial instruments should be separated into their two components and that each of these components should then be recognised separately, one as a financial liability and the other as equity. The separation of a compound financial instrument into its two components is achieved as follows:

(a) The fair value of the liability component is determined first. This is equal to the fair value of a similar instrument without an associated equity component. In the case of convertible loan stock, IAS32 states the fair value of the liability component should be determined by calculating the present value of the scheduled payments of interest and principal, ignoring the conversion option.

(b) The fair value of the equity component is then determined by deducting the fair value of the liability component from the fair value of the whole instrument. The fair value of the whole instrument is normally equal to the amount of the consideration which was received when the instrument was issued.

IAS32 repeats the IFRS13 definition of fair value as "*the price that would be received to sell an asset or paid to transfer a liability in an orderly transaction between market participants at the measurement date*" (see Chapter 5).

EXAMPLE 2

On 1 January 2013, a company issues £200,000 of 7% loan stock at par. Interest on this loan stock is payable on 31 December each year. The stock is due for redemption at par on 31 December 2016 but may be converted into ordinary shares on that date instead.

Calculate the fair value of the liability component and the equity component of this loan stock, assuming that the fair value of the liability component is to be determined by cash flow analysis using a discounting rate of 9% per annum.

Solution

Ignoring the conversion option, the company will pay interest of £14,000 on 31 December 2013, 2014, 2015 and 2016 and will then make a £200,000 repayment of the loan stock on 31 December 2016. Using a discounting rate of 9%, the present value of these cash flows may be calculated as follows:

	Workings	*Present value* £
Payment due 31 December 2013	£14,000 ÷ 1.09	12,844
Payment due 31 December 2014	£14,000 ÷ $(1.09)^2$	11,784
Payment due 31 December 2015	£14,000 ÷ $(1.09)^3$	10,811
Payment due 31 December 2016	£214,000 ÷ $(1.09)^4$	151,603
Total present value		187,042

This calculation shows that the fair value on 1 January 2013 of the right to receive £14,000 on 31 December for each of the next three years, followed by £214,000 at the end of the fourth year is £187,042. This is the fair value of the liability component of the loan stock.

The lenders are paying £200,000 to buy this stock and this exceeds the fair value of the liability component by £12,958. The extra £12,958 must be the price that the lenders are paying for the option to convert and this is the value of the equity component.

Recognition and measurement

The recognition and measurement rules relating to financial instruments are currently to be found in IAS39 *Financial Instruments: Recognition and Measurement*. The recognition rules determine when a financial asset or liability should be shown in an entity's statement of financial position. The measurement rules determine the amount at which a financial asset or liability should be shown.

However, it should be noted that IAS39 is gradually being replaced by IFRS9 *Financial Instruments*. This project is being conducted in three phases, as follows:

Phase 1: Classification and measurement of financial assets and financial liabilities

Phase 2: Impairment methodology

Phase 3: Hedge accounting (which is outside the scope of this book).

The first phase was completed in October 2010 but, at the time of writing, the IASB is still working on the remaining phases. As usual, the progress of this project may be followed on website www.ifrs.org.

IFRS9 applies for accounting periods which begin on or after 1 January 2015 (although earlier application is permitted). IAS39 is generally applicable until that date. This chapter explains the main requirements of both of these standards.

Recognition of financial assets and liabilities

The recognition principles which relate to financial assets and liabilities are fairly straight-forward. IAS39 and IFRS9 both state that a financial asset or a financial liability should be recognised when (and only when) the entity "*becomes party to the contractual provisions of the instrument*". In other words, recognition occurs when the financial instrument becomes binding. As regards derecognition:

(a) A financial asset is derecognised (removed from the statement of financial position) when the entity's contractual rights to receive cash flows from the asset expire.

(b) A financial liability is derecognised when the entity's contractual obligations expire or are discharged or cancelled.

Initial measurement of financial assets and liabilities

IAS39 and IFRS9 both require that financial assets and liabilities should be measured initially at their fair value, which is normally equal to the amount of the consideration which was given or received when the asset was acquired or the liability incurred.

In general, transaction costs that are directly attributable to the acquisition of a financial asset (e.g. fees and commissions) should be added to the initial carrying amount of that asset. Similarly, transaction costs that are directly attributable to the issue of a financial liability should be subtracted from the initial carrying amount of that liability.

Subsequent measurement of financial assets

IAS39 classifies financial assets into four categories and then prescribes the way in which assets falling into each category should be measured after initial recognition. The four categories and the associated measurement rules are as follows:

(a) **Financial assets at fair value through profit or loss**. These are usually financial assets that are held for trading. But any financial asset may be designated as "at fair value through profit or loss" if this would result in more relevant information.

   After initial recognition, financial assets which fall into this category should be measured at their fair value. Gains or losses arising from fluctuations in fair value are recognised in the calculation of profit or loss for the period in which they arise.

(b) **Held-to-maturity investments**. These are financial assets with fixed or determinable payments and fixed maturity dates that the entity intends to hold until maturity.

   After initial recognition, held-to-maturity investments should be measured at their amortised cost using the effective interest method (see below).

(c) **Loans and receivables**. These are financial assets with fixed or determinable payments that are not quoted in an active market.

   After initial recognition, loans and receivables should usually be measured at their amortised cost using the effective interest method. This method involves discounting the amounts expected to be received when the loan or the receivable is settled. But short-term receivables (e.g. most trade receivables) may be measured at the original invoice amount if the effect of discounting is not material.

(d) **Available-for-sale financial assets**. These are financial assets which do not fall into any of the other three categories. An example of an available-for-sale financial asset is a long-term investment in ordinary shares. After initial recognition, available-for-sale financial assets should usually be measured at fair value. Gains or losses arising from fluctuations in fair value are recognised in other comprehensive income but are reclassified to profit or loss when the asset concerned is derecognised (see Chapter 3).

IFRS9 classifies financial assets into only two categories. These are financial assets which are subsequently measured at fair value and financial assets which are subsequently measured at amortised cost. A financial asset is normally measured at amortised cost if:

(a) the contractual terms of the asset give rise on specified dates to cash flows that are solely payments of principal and interest on the principal amount outstanding, and

(b) the asset is held by the entity in order to collect these cash flows.

All other financial assets are measured at fair value. Furthermore, an entity may elect that certain financial assets which would otherwise be measured at amortised cost should instead be measured at fair value. Gains and losses arising from fluctuations in fair value are usually recognised in the calculation of profit or loss. But an entity may elect that gains and losses arising in relation to an investment in an equity instrument may be recognised in other comprehensive income (as long as the instrument is not held for trading). Such gains and losses cannot be subsequently reclassified to profit or loss.

The effective interest method

As stated above, certain financial assets should be measured after initial recognition at their amortised cost using the effective interest method. In simple terms:

(a) The "amortised cost" of a financial asset is equal to the amount at which the asset was initially recognised, plus the amount of interest earned to date, minus any repayments received to date.

(b) The "effective interest method" is a way of calculating the amount of interest earned to date. This method uses an interest rate that exactly discounts estimated future cash receipts to the initial carrying amount of the asset. The calculation takes into account not only interest receivable, but also items such as premiums and discounts.

The technique is very similar to the actuarial method which is used in connection with finance leases (see Chapter 9) and is illustrated in the following example.

EXAMPLE 3

On 1 January 2013, a company buys £100,000 of 6% loan stock for £93,930. Interest will be received on 31 December each year and the stock will be redeemed at par on 31 December 2017. The effective interest rate is 7.5% per annum. Financial statements are prepared to 31 December each year.

(a) State the amount at which this loan stock should be measured on 1 January 2013.

(b) Calculate the amount at which the loan stock should be measured on 31 December 2013, 2014, 2015, 2016 and 2017.

(c) Show that the effective rate of 7.5% exactly discounts estimated future cash receipts to the initial carrying amount of the asset.

Solution

(a) The loan stock is measured initially at £93,930.

(b) The amortised cost of the loan stock at the end of each year is calculated as follows:

Year	Balance b/f	Interest @ 7.5%	Amount received	Amortised cost
	£	£	£	£
2013	93,930	7,045	(6,000)	94,975
2014	94,975	7,123	(6,000)	96,098
2015	96,098	7,207	(6,000)	97,305
2016	97,305	7,298	(6,000)	98,603
2017	98,603	7,397	(106,000)	0
		36,070		

Notes:

(i) The interest earned each year is 7.5% of the balance brought forward. This is recognised as income in the company's financial statements. Interest at 7.5% for 2017 would in fact be £7,395 but this has been adjusted to £7,397 to ensure that the balance remaining at the end of the year is £nil.

(ii) The effective interest rate (7.5%) is higher than the rate (6%) at which annual interest payments are calculated because the company will receive a premium of £6,070 (£100,000 – £93,930) when the loan stock is redeemed. The effective interest method spreads this premium fairly over the life of the loan stock.

(iii) Total income is £36,070. This amount is equal to annual interest of £6,000 for five years plus the premium of £6,070.

(c) If the amounts receivable during the life of the loan stock are discounted at an annual rate of 7.5%, the present value of each amount is as follows:

	Workings	Present value £
Receivable 31 December 2013	£6,000 ÷ 1.075	5,581
Receivable 31 December 2014	£6,000 ÷ $(1.075)^2$	5,192
Receivable 31 December 2015	£6,000 ÷ $(1.075)^3$	4,830
Receivable 31 December 2016	£6,000 ÷ $(1.075)^4$	4,493
Receivable 31 December 2017	£106,000 ÷ $(1.075)^5$	73,835
Total present value		93,931

Apart from a small rounding difference, an effective rate of 7.5% does indeed discount estimated future cash receipts to the initial carrying amount of £93,930.

Impairment of financial assets carried at amortised cost

If there is objective evidence that an impairment loss (see Chapter 7) has been incurred on a financial asset carried at amortised cost, IAS39 requires that the amount of this loss should be measured as the difference between:

(a) the current carrying amount of the asset, and

(b) the present value of the estimated future cash flows relating to the asset, discounted at the effective rate of interest which was calculated at initial recognition.

The carrying amount of the asset should then be reduced by the amount of the impairment loss, either directly or through the use of an allowance account. The loss itself should be written off as an expense.

A common example of an impairment loss arises if a trade receivable becomes wholly or partly uncollectible, in which case the loss is either written off as a bad debt or dealt with through an allowance for doubtful receivables. If a short-term receivable is measured at the original invoice amount rather than amortised cost, the amount of any impairment loss is simply the difference between the current carrying amount of the receivable and the undiscounted cash flows expected to be received in relation to it.

Subsequent measurement of financial liabilities

IAS39 states that, after initial recognition, financial liabilities should usually be measured at amortised cost using the effective interest method. This is precisely the same method as is used for certain types of financial asset (see above). There are some exceptions to this general rule, but these are mainly beyond the scope of this book. However, there are two important exceptions which must be mentioned here. These are:

(a) **Financial liabilities at fair value through profit or loss**. This category of financial liabilities is similar to the equivalent category of financial assets and consists mainly of financial liabilities that are held for trading. However, as with financial assets, any financial liability may be designated as "at fair value through profit or loss" if this would result in more relevant information.

　　After initial recognition, financial liabilities which fall into this category should be measured at fair value. Gains or losses arising from fluctuations in fair value are recognised in the calculation of profit or loss for the period in which they arise.

(b) **Trade payables**. Short-term payables (e.g. most trade payables) may be measured at the original invoice amount if the effect of discounting is not material.

IFRS9 retains most of these requirements. However, in the case of a financial liability at fair value through profit or loss, any gain or loss that is attributable to changes in the credit risk of that liability (see later in this chapter) is usually recognised in other comprehensive income.

EXAMPLE 4

On 1 July 2013, a company issues £1million of 8% loan stock. The stock is issued at a 10% discount (so only £900,000 is received from the lenders) and issue costs of £39,300 are incurred. Interest is payable in arrears on 30 June each year and the loan stock is redeemable at par on 30 June 2016. The effective interest rate is 14% p.a. The company prepares financial statements to 30 June each year.

(a) State the amount at which this loan stock should be measured on 1 July 2013.

(b) Calculate the amount at which the loan stock should be measured on 30 June 2014, 2015 and 2016.

Solution

(a) The loan stock should be measured initially at £860,700 (£900,000 − £39,300). This is the amount of the consideration received when the stock was issued, less directly attributable transaction costs.

(b) The loan stock should be measured at amortised cost using the effective interest method. Amortised cost at the end of each year is calculated as follows:

Year to 30 June	Balance b/f £	Interest @ 14% £	Amount paid £	Amortised cost £
2014	860,700	120,498	(80,000)	901,198
2015	901,198	126,168	(80,000)	947,366
2016	947,366	132,634	(1,080,000)	0
		379,300		

Notes:

(i) The interest each year is 14% of the balance brought forward. This is recognised as an expense in the company's financial statements. Interest at 14% for 2016 is actually £132,631 but this has been adjusted to £132,634 to ensure that the balance remaining at the end of 2016 is £nil.

(ii) The effective interest rate (14%) is higher than the rate (8%) at which annual interest payments are calculated because the loan was issued at a discount and the company has had to pay transaction costs. The effective interest method spreads these two items fairly over the life of the loan stock.

(iii) Total expenses are £379,300. This amount is equal to annual interest of £80,000 for three years plus the discount of £100,000 and issue costs of £39,300.

Disclosure requirements

International standard IFRS7 *Financial Instruments: Disclosures* requires entities to make a number of disclosures relating to financial instruments. The purpose of these disclosures is to enable users to evaluate two things. These are:

(a) the significance of financial instruments for the financial position and the financial performance of the entity concerned, and

(b) the nature and extent of risks to which the entity is exposed in relation to financial instruments, and the way in which those risks are being managed.

These two matters are considered separately below.

Significance of financial instruments

The main disclosures required by IFRS7 to enable users to evaluate the significance of financial instruments for an entity's financial position and performance are as follows:

(a) **Carrying amounts**. The carrying amount of each of the following categories of financial asset and liability should be disclosed either in the statement of financial position or in the notes:

    (i)   financial assets measured at fair value through profit or loss

    (ii) held-to-maturity investments

    (iii) loans and receivables

    (iv) available-for-sale financial assets

    (v) financial liabilities measured at fair value through profit or loss

    (vi) financial liabilities measured at amortised cost.

When an entity applies IFRS9, categories (ii), (iii) and (iv) do not apply. Instead, the entity should disclose the carrying amounts of financial assets measured at amortised cost and financial assets measured at fair value through other comprehensive income.

(b) **Allowance for credit losses**. If financial assets are impaired by credit losses and the amount of the impairment is recorded in an allowance account (e.g. an allowance for doubtful receivables) then the entity should disclose a reconciliation of changes in this allowance account during the accounting period for each class of financial assets.

(c) **Fair value**. The fair value of each class of financial asset and liability should be disclosed in a way that facilitates comparison with carrying amounts. This disclosure is not required if the carrying amount is a reasonable approximation of fair value.

(d) **Items of income, expense, gains and losses**. The entity should disclose the following items, either in the statement of comprehensive income or in the notes:

    (i)   net gains or losses on each class of financial assets and liabilities (e.g. gains or losses arising from fair value fluctuations)

    (ii) total interest income and total interest expense for financial assets and liabilities measured at amortised cost

    (iii) the amount of any impairment loss for each class of financial asset.

(e) **Accounting policies**. The entity should disclose the measurement bases and other accounting policies used in relation to financial instruments, where these are relevant to an understanding of the financial statements.

Nature and extent of risks

IFRS7 defines three main types of risk associated with financial instruments. These are:

(a) **Credit risk**. Credit risk is "*the risk that one party to a financial instrument will cause a financial loss for the other party by failing to discharge an obligation*".

(b) **Liquidity risk**. Liquidity risk is "*the risk that an entity will encounter difficulty in meeting obligations associated with financial liabilities*".

(c) **Market risk**. Market risk is "*the risk that the fair value or future cash flows of a financial instrument will fluctuate because of changes in market prices*". Such changes may occur because of changes in exchange rates ("currency risk"), changes in market interest rates ("interest rate risk") or for other reasons ("other price risk").

In general, IFRS7 requires entities to disclose information which enables the users of the financial statements to evaluate the nature and extent of the risks arising from financial instruments. This information should include:

(a) a description of the risks concerned

(b) a description of the methods used to measure risk

(c) a description of the entity's policies for managing risk

(d) quantitative data about the exposure to risk at the end of the reporting period.

Specific detailed disclosures are also required in relation to credit risk, liquidity risk and market risk. The main disclosures are as follows:

(a) **Credit risk**. For each class of financial asset, the entity should disclose:

    (i) the amount of the maximum exposure to credit risk and a description of any collateral held as security

    (ii) an age analysis of financial assets that are overdue but not impaired

    (iii) an analysis of financial assets that are impaired.

(b) **Liquidity risk**. The entity should disclose a maturity analysis for financial liabilities and a description of how any inherent liquidity risk is managed.

(c) **Market risk**. The entity should disclose a sensitivity analysis for each type of market risk to which the entity is exposed. This analysis should show how profit or loss and equity would be affected by changes in the relevant risk variable (e.g. exchange rates or market interest rates).

Summary

▸ A financial instrument is a contract which gives rise to a financial asset for one entity and a financial liability (or equity instrument) for another. Financial instruments are dealt with in international standards IAS32, IAS39, IFRS7 and IFRS9.

▸ IAS32 establishes rules for distinguishing between financial liabilities and equity instruments. The standard adopts a substance over form approach and states that an equity instrument is one which includes no contractual obligation to deliver cash (or any other financial asset) to another entity.

▸ Redeemable preference shares are generally classed as financial liabilities. Dividends relating to such shares are treated as an expense.

▸ A compound financial instrument is separated into its two components by evaluating the liability component first and then deducting this from the fair value of the whole instrument to give the equity component.

▸ Financial assets and liabilities are recognised when the relevant financial instrument becomes binding and are derecognised when the entity's contractual rights or obligations under the instrument cease.

▸ Financial assets and liabilities are measured initially at their fair value.

▸ IAS39 requires that (subsequent to initial recognition) financial assets at fair value through profit or loss and available-for-sale financial assets are measured at fair value. Held-to-maturity investments and loans and receivables are measured at amortised cost using the effective interest method.

▸ IFRS9 (which applies as from 1 January 2015) requires that all financial assets are measured at fair value other than those measured at amortised cost. A financial asset is measured at amortised cost if it gives rise to cash flows that are solely payments of principal and interest and the asset is held in order to collect these cash flows.

▸ Subsequent to initial recognition, financial liabilities at fair value through profit or loss are measured at fair value. Most other financial liabilities are measured at amortised cost using the effective interest method.

▸ The disclosure requirements of IFRS7 enable users of the financial statements to evaluate the significance of an entity's financial instruments and the nature and extent of any risks to which the entity is exposed in relation to financial instruments.

Exercises

11.1   (a)   Define the terms "financial instrument", "financial asset", "financial liability" and "equity instrument".

       (b)   Explain the way in which international standard IAS32 distinguishes between financial liabilities and equity instruments.

       (c)   Explain the accounting treatment of redeemable preference shares required by IAS32.

11.2   (a)   Explain what is meant by a "compound" financial instrument. Also explain the required accounting treatment of such an instrument.

       (b)   On 1 April 2012, a company issues a £500,000 4% convertible bond at par. Interest is payable on 31 March each year. The bond is redeemable at par on 31 March 2017 but may be converted into ordinary shares at any time before maturity. The market rate of interest to be used in discounting calculations is 6.5%.

           Calculate the liability component and the equity component of this bond.

11.3   (a)   International standard IAS39 classifies financial assets into four categories. IFRS9 (which applies as from 1 January 2015) lists only two categories.

           Identify and explain each of these categories. Also explain the way in which each category of financial asset should be measured subsequent to initial recognition.

       (b)   On 1 January 2014, a company which prepares financial statements to 30 June each year buys £400,000 of 5% loan notes for £411,225. Interest will be received half-yearly on 30 June and 31 December and the loan notes will be repaid at a premium of 10% on 31 December 2016. The effective rate of interest is 3.5% per half year.

           Calculate the amount of interest income that should be recognised in the company's financial statements for each of the years to 30 June 2014, 2015, 2016 and 2017. Also calculate the amount at which the loan notes should be shown in the statement of financial position at the end of each of these years.

11.4   (a)   Explain the terms "credit risk", "liquidity risk" and "market risk" which are used in international standard IFRS7.

       (b)   List the main disclosures required by IFRS7 in relation to each of these risks.

11.5   On 1 May 2013, a company which prepares financial statements to 30 April each year issues £750,000 of 3% loan stock at a discount of 5%. Issue costs are £13,175. Interest is payable on 30 April each year and the stock is redeemable on 30 April 2017 at a premium of 10%. The effective rate of interest is 7.25% per annum.

       (a)   State the amount at which the loan stock should be measured on 1 May 2013.

       (b)   Calculate the amount at which the loan stock should be shown in the company's statement of financial position on 30 April 2014, 2015, 2016 and 2017.

*11.6   Querk plc prepares financial statements to 31 December each year. On 1 January 2013 the company bought £500,000 of 6% loan stock for £490,420. Interest is receivable on 31 December each year and the loan stock will be redeemed at a 15% premium on 31 December 2017. The effective rate of interest is 9% per annum and Querk plc intends to hold the loan stock until it is redeemed.

(a)   Define the term "financial instrument". Explain why the loan stock referred to above falls within this definition.

(b)   Define the terms "financial asset" and "financial liability". Explain why the loan stock is a financial asset for Querk plc but is a financial liability for the borrower.

(c)   Identify the category of financial asset to which the loan stock belongs. Explain how financial assets of this type should be measured, both at initial recognition and subsequently.

(d)   Calculate the amount of interest income that should be recognised in the financial statements of Querk plc for each of the years to 31 December 2013, 2014, 2015, 2016 and 2017. Also calculate the amount at which the loan stock should be shown in the statement of financial position at each of those dates.

(e)   Explain why the accounting treatment required for this loan stock by international standards gives a fair measure of the interest income for each year.

Chapter 12

Provisions and events after the reporting period

Introduction

The main purpose of this chapter is explain the requirements of international standard IAS37 *Provisions, Contingent Liabilities and Contingent Assets*. The aims of IAS37 are:

(a) to ensure that all necessary provisions are recognised and properly measured in the financial statements of business entities

(b) to prevent the recognition of unjustified provisions

(c) to prescribe an accounting treatment for contingent liabilities and contingent assets

(d) to ensure that sufficient disclosures are made so as to enable users to understand the nature, timing and amount of provisions, contingent liabilities and contingent assets.

IAS37 defines a provision to be a type of liability (see below) and this usage of the word "provision" should be carefully distinguished from other usages. In particular, IAS37 is *not* concerned with provisions for depreciation or for doubtful debts, since these are reductions in the carrying amounts of assets and are not a type of liability. Such reductions are in fact more properly referred to as "allowances" rather than "provisions".

This chapter also covers IAS10 *Events after the Reporting Period*, which prescribes the accounting treatment of events which occur after the end of the reporting period but before the date on which the financial statements are authorised for issue.

Scope of IAS37

IAS37 does not apply to certain types of provisions, contingent liabilities and contingent assets which are dealt with in other standards. These standards include:

(a) IAS11 *Construction Contracts* (see Chapter 10)

(b) IAS12 *Income Taxes* (see Chapter 15)

(c) IAS17 *Leases* (see Chapter 9)

(d) IAS19 *Employee Benefits* (see Chapter 14).

Furthermore, IAS37 does not apply to financial instruments which are within the scope of international standards IAS39 and IFRS9 (see Chapter 11).

Objectives

By the end of this chapter, the reader should be able to:

- define the terms "provision", "contingent liability" and "contingent asset" in accordance with international standard IAS37

- state the conditions under which a provision should be recognised and explain how the amount of a provision should be measured

- explain the required accounting treatment of contingent assets and liabilities

- explain the requirements of IAS37 with regard to future operating losses, onerous contracts and restructuring costs

- list the main disclosure requirements of IAS37

- distinguish between adjusting and non-adjusting events after the reporting period

- explain the main requirements of international standard IAS10.

Recognition of a provision

IAS37 defines a provision as "*a liability of uncertain timing or amount*" and states that a provision should be recognised when all of the following conditions are satisfied:

(a) the entity has a present obligation (legal or constructive) as a result of a past event

(b) it is probable that an outflow of resources embodying economic benefits will be required to settle the obligation

(c) a reliable estimate can be made of the amount of the obligation.

If any of these conditions are not satisfied, a provision must *not* be recognised. It should be noted that the first two conditions stem from the definition of a liability which is given in the IASB *Conceptual Framework* (see Chapter 2) and which is repeated in IAS37. This reinforces the point that a provision is simply a kind of liability and the only difference between a provision and any other liability is the degree of uncertainty involved. Although many liabilities might involve some uncertainty (e.g. the amount of an accrued expense) this will generally be much less than the uncertainty in the case of a provision.

IAS37 also states that the amount of a provision should be equal to "*the best estimate of the expenditure required to settle the present obligation at the end of the reporting period*".

EXAMPLE 1

A company gives warranties at the time of sale to customers who buy the company's products. These warranties commit the company to make good any manufacturing defects that become apparent within three years from the date of sale. On past experience, it is probable that some valid warranty claims will arise.

When preparing its financial statements for the year to 30 June 2014, should the company make a provision for warranty claims? If so, how should this be measured?

Solution

It is clear that the company is obliged at 30 June 2014 to meet any valid claims which arise under warranties given in the previous three years. Therefore there is a present obligation arising from a past event. It is also clear that such claims will probably occur and so it is probable that an outflow of resources will be required to settle this obligation. If the amount and timing of the claims was certain, a liability could be recognised in the usual way. But there is considerable uncertainty with regard to both the timing and the amount of this liability and therefore a provision is required.

The amount of the provision should be the company's best estimate of the cost of meeting warranty claims arising in relation to products sold in the last three years. This estimate will be based on past experience.

Obligating events

A past event which leads to a present obligation is known as an "obligating event". For a past event to be an obligating event, the business entity involved must have no realistic alternative but to settle the obligation created by the event. This will be the case if:

(a)   the obligation is legally enforceable, or

(b)   the event has given rise to a "constructive obligation", where the entity has created a valid expectation in other parties that it will discharge the obligation, even though this is not legally enforceable.

For instance, a business entity which operates in a country with environmental legislation may have a legal obligation to decontaminate land which it has contaminated by its past actions. An entity which operates in a country with no such legislation may nonetheless have a widely-published policy of cleaning up all contamination which it causes and a record of honouring this policy, in which case there is a constructive obligation.

Without an obligating event, there cannot be a provision. Whether or not such an event has occurred is usually a matter of fact but in rare cases this may not be clear. For instance, if an entity is involved in a law suit at the end of a reporting period, there may be some dispute as to whether certain events have occurred, or whether past events have resulted in a present obligation. In these circumstances, the entity should consider all available evidence (possibly including expert opinion) and then:

(a)   if it is more likely than not that a present obligation exists at the end of the reporting period (and if the other recognition criteria are met) a provision should be recognised

(b)   if it is more likely that there is no present obligation at the end of the reporting period, a contingent liability should be disclosed (see below) unless there is only a remote possibility of an outflow of economic benefits.

It should be stressed that a provision is recognised only if the obligation in question exists independently of the entity's future actions. For this reason, no provision can be made in relation to future operating costs, since these could be avoided by changing the method of operation or by ceasing the operations concerned.

Probable outflow of economic benefits

As stated above, a provision cannot be recognised unless it is probable that an outflow of economic benefits will be required to settle the obligation in question. For this purpose, the word "probable" means "more likely than not".

If a number of similar obligations (e.g. product warranties) exist at the end of a reporting period, IAS37 requires that the probability of an outflow of benefits should be assessed by considering the class of obligations as a whole. Even though it may not be probable that any one obligation will result in an outflow of benefits, it may indeed be probable that an outflow will be needed to settle the entire class of obligations.

Reliable estimate of the obligation

The final condition which must be satisfied in order for a provision to be recognised is that a reliable estimate can be made of the amount of the obligation. IAS37 takes the view that it will usually be possible to determine a range of possible outcomes and then make an estimate that is sufficiently reliable for this purpose.

If (rarely) a reliable estimate cannot be made, a liability exists but a provision cannot be recognised. This liability must be disclosed as a contingent liability (see below).

Measurement of a provision

As mentioned earlier in this chapter, the amount of a provision should be the best estimate of the expenditure required to settle the obligation concerned. This is of course a matter of judgement and may require advice from independent experts. Note that:

(a) The "best estimate" of the required expenditure is the amount that the entity would rationally pay to settle the obligation or transfer it to a third party.

(b) If the effect of the time value of money is material, the amount of a provision should be calculated as the present value of the expenditure required to settle the obligation.

(c) Future events that may affect the amount required to settle an obligation should be taken into account when measuring a provision, so long as there is sufficient objective evidence that these events will occur. For instance, the estimated costs of cleaning up environmental damage might be reduced by anticipated changes in technology.

If a single obligation is being measured and there are several possible outcomes, the best estimate of the required expenditure is usually the cost of the most likely outcome. But if most of the other possible outcomes would involve a higher cost, the best estimate of the expenditure will be a higher amount. Similarly, if most of the other possible outcomes would involve a lower cost, the best estimate of the expenditure will be a lower amount.

In cases where a provision relates to a large population of items, the amount of the provision should be estimated by calculating the "expected value" of the obligation at the end of the reporting period. This statistical method of estimation involves weighting all possible outcomes by their associated probabilities and is illustrated in the next example.

EXAMPLE 2

This example is based upon an example provided in IAS37.

A company sells goods with a six-month warranty. If minor defects were detected in all of the goods covered by warranties at the end of the reporting period, the company would incur costs of £1 million. If major defects were detected in all of these goods, the company would incur costs of £4 million. Experience shows that 75% of goods sold have no defects, 20% have minor defects and 5% have major defects.

What is the expected value of the cost of repairs under warranties?

Solution

The expected value of the cost of repairs is:

(75% × £nil) + (20% × £1m) + (5% × £4m) = £400,000.

Changes in provisions and use of provisions

IAS37 requires that provisions should be reviewed at the end of each reporting period and adjusted to reflect the current best estimate of the required expenditure. If it is no longer probable that an outflow of economic benefits will be required to settle an obligation, the related provision should be reversed.

IAS37 also requires that a provision should be used only for the purpose for which it was originally established. It is not permitted to set unrelated expenditure against a provision that was initially set up for a different purpose.

Application of the recognition and measurement rules

Having established the recognition and measurement rules described above, IAS37 then explains how these general rules should be applied in three specific cases. The three cases identified are future operating losses, onerous contracts and restructuring costs. A brief summary of the requirements of IAS37 in relation to each of these is given below.

(a) **Future operating losses**. Future operating losses are not present obligations and so do not satisfy the recognition criteria for a provision. Therefore, provisions should not be recognised for future operating losses.

However, the fact that future operating losses are expected indicates that the assets used in the operation concerned may be impaired. Therefore these assets should be tested for impairment (see Chapter 7).

(b) **Onerous contracts**. An onerous contract is a contract "*in which the unavoidable costs of meeting the obligations under the contract exceed the economic benefits expected to be received under it*". If an entity has a contract that is onerous, the present obligation under that contract should be measured and recognised as a provision.

(c) **Restructuring costs**. A provision for restructuring costs should be recognised only if the general recognition criteria set out in IAS37 are satisfied. In particular:

(i) A constructive obligation to restructure arises only when the entity has a detailed formal plan for the restructuring and has raised a valid expectation in those affected that it will carry out the restructuring, either by beginning to implement the plan or by announcing its main features.

(ii) If the restructuring involves the sale of an operation, no obligation for that sale arises until there is a binding sale agreement.

(iii) A provision for restructuring costs should include only the direct costs arising from the restructuring. These costs must be necessarily incurred and must not be associated with the ongoing activities of the entity.

Staff retraining and relocation costs, marketing costs and the cost of investment in new systems cannot be included in the amount of a provision for restructuring costs.

EXAMPLE 3

The following information relates to a company which prepares financial statements to 31 December each year:

(a) On 1 January 2013, the company acquired new plant costing £10 million. This plant will require a complete overhaul after five years of use, at an estimated cost of £1 million. Accordingly, the company wishes to make a provision of £200,000 for plant overhaul costs in its financial statements for the year to 31 December 2013 and then to increase this provision by £200,000 in each of the next four years. This will have the effect of spreading the overhaul costs evenly over the years 2013 to 2017.

(b) On 31 December 2013, the company moved from leased premises into new freehold premises. The lease on the old premises will continue for three more years at an annual cost of £100,000. The lease cannot be cancelled and the premises cannot be sublet or used for any other purpose. The company wishes to make a provision of £300,000 in its financial statements for the year to 31 December 2013.

(c) In November 2013, the company decided to sell off one of its operations. No buyer had been found at 31 December 2013, but the sale is expected to result in a loss of £500,000 when it occurs. The company wishes to provide for this loss in the financial statements for the year to 31 December 2013.

Accordingly to the rules of IAS37, may any of these three provisions be made?

Solution

(a) At 31 December 2013, there is no present obligation to undertake the overhaul that is due in four years time. The plant could in fact be sold before the overhaul is required. Therefore no provision can be made for the overhaul costs. International standard IAS16 *Property, Plant and Equipment* prescribes the accounting treatment of this type of expenditure (see Chapter 5).

(b) In general, IAS37 does not apply to leases (see above). But this is an example of an onerous contract and IAS37 does apply to such contracts. The obligation of £300,000 is unavoidable and should be provided for.

(c) IAS37 states that there is no present obligation in relation to the sale of an operation until a binding sale agreement exists. There is no such agreement at 31 December 2013 and so there is no present obligation on that date. A provision cannot be made.

However, depending on the circumstances, the non-current assets of the operation might be classified as "held for sale" and measured in accordance with the requirements of IFRS5 (see Chapter 8). Assets of the operation that are not classified as held for sale should be tested for impairment under IAS36 (see Chapter 7).

Contingent liabilities and contingent assets

IAS37 defines a contingent liability as:

"(a) a possible obligation that arises from past events and whose existence will be confirmed only by the occurrence or non-occurrence of one or more uncertain future events not wholly within the control of the entity; or

(b) a present obligation that arises from past events but is not recognised because:

    (i) it is not probable that an outflow of resources embodying economic benefits will be required to settle the obligation; or

    (ii) the amount of the obligation cannot be measured with sufficient reliability."

An example of a "possible obligation" may arise when an entity is involved in a legal case and will be required to pay damages if the case is lost. If it is probable that the case will be lost, the entity should recognise a provision. But if it is merely possible that the case will be lost, the entity should treat the obligation as a contingent liability.

IAS37 requires that contingent liabilities should not be recognised in the statement of financial position but should instead be disclosed in the notes, unless the possibility of an outflow of economic benefits is remote.

Contingent assets

A contingent asset is defined as "*a possible asset that arises from past events and whose existence will be confirmed only by the occurrence or non-occurrence of one or more uncertain future events not wholly within the control of the entity*". An example of such an asset may arise if an entity is involved in a legal case and will receive damages if the case is won. If it is virtually certain that the case will be won, the entity should treat the damages as an asset in the usual way. Otherwise, the entity should treat the damages as a contingent asset.

IAS37 requires that contingent assets should not be recognised in the statement of financial position. However, contingent assets should be disclosed in the notes if the inflow of economic benefits is judged to be probable.

EXAMPLE 4

In May 2013, ABC plc (which prepares financial statements to 31 December) guaranteed a £100,000 bank loan provided to DEF Ltd. DEF Ltd was in a strong financial position at 31 December 2013, but this had worsened by 31 December 2014 and it seemed likely on that date that ABC plc would be required to honour its guarantee.

Explain how this guarantee should be treated in the financial statements of ABC plc at 31 December 2013 and 2014.

Solution

At 31 December 2013, there is a present obligation arising from a past event. However, an outflow of economic benefits does not seem probable, so no provision can be made. The guarantee falls within the definition of a contingent liability and should be disclosed in the notes to the financial statements, unless the possibility of an outflow of benefits is judged to be remote.

At 31 December 2014, there is still a present obligation arising from a past event, but now it seems probable that there will be an outflow of economic benefits. As long as a reliable estimate of the obligation can be made (which will almost certainly be the case) a provision should be made in relation to this obligation.

Disclosure requirements

The following disclosures are required for each class of provision that is recognised in the financial statements:

(a) the carrying amount at the beginning and end of the accounting period

(b) additional provisions made in the period, including increases in existing provisions

(c) amounts used and amounts reversed during the period

(d) a brief description of the nature of the obligation, the expected timing of any resulting expenditure and an indication of the uncertainties involved.

Unless the possibility of an outflow of benefits is remote, the following disclosures are required for each class of contingent liability:

(a) a brief description of the nature of the contingent liability

(b) an estimate of its financial effect

(c) an indication of the uncertainties involved.

Finally, in cases where an inflow of benefits is probable, the entity should disclose a brief description of the nature of any contingent assets at the end of the reporting period, with an estimate of their financial effect.

Events after the reporting period

IAS10 *Events after the Reporting Period* defines events after the reporting period as:

"*those events, favourable and unfavourable, that occur between the end of the reporting period and the date when the financial statements are authorised for issue*".

Such events are classified into two types. These are:

(a) **Adjusting events**. Adjusting events are defined as "*those that provide evidence of conditions that existed at the end of the reporting period*". An example is the sale of inventories which were held at the end of the reporting period. This event provides useful evidence of the net realisable value of those inventories. Further examples of adjusting events listed in IAS10 include:

   (i)   the settlement of a court case in which the company was involved at the end of the reporting period

   (ii) the bankruptcy of a customer who owed money to the company at the end of the reporting period

   (iii) the discovery of fraud or errors which show that the financial statements for the period are incorrect.

(b) **Non-adjusting events**. Non-adjusting events are defined as "*those that are indicative of conditions that arose after the reporting period*". An example of a non-adjusting event is a decline in the fair value of investments held at the end of the reporting period. Such a decline does not usually relate to the condition of the investments at the end of the period but reflects circumstances that have arisen subsequently.

IAS10 requires that the financial statements should be adjusted to reflect adjusting events that occur after the reporting period. The financial statements should *not* be adjusted to reflect non-adjusting events. However, material non-adjusting events should be disclosed in the notes to the financial statements. For each such event, the notes should disclose the nature of the event and (if possible) an estimate of its financial effect. Note that:

(a) IAS10 does not specifically state that the financial statements should be adjusted to reflect only *material* adjusting events, but this is implied by the materiality principle established in the IASB *Conceptual Framework* (see Chapter 2).

(b) Dividends to equity shareholders which are declared after the end of the reporting period but before the financial statements are authorised for issue do not qualify as a "present obligation" at the end of the period and so should not be recognised as a liability. Such dividends should be disclosed in the notes in accordance with the requirements of IAS1 (see Chapter 3).

Summary

▸ A provision is defined by IAS37 as a liability of uncertain timing or amount. To recognise a provision, there must be a present obligation arising from a past event, it must be probable that an outflow of benefits will be required to settle this obligation and it must be possible to make a reliable estimate of the amount involved.

▸ An obligation may be legally enforceable or it may be constructive. A constructive obligation is one which arises because the entity has created a valid expectation that it will discharge the obligation and has no realistic alternative but to do so.

▸ The amount of a provision should be the best estimate of the expenditure involved.

▸ Provisions should be reviewed at the end of each reporting period and adjusted or reversed if necessary. A provision should be used only for the purpose for which it was established.

▸ A contingent liability is either a possible obligation or a present obligation that does not satisfy all of the conditions necessary to recognise a provision. Contingent liabilities are not recognised in the financial statements but are disclosed in the notes unless the possibility of an outflow of benefits is remote.

▸ A contingent asset is a possible asset. Contingent assets are not recognised in the financial statements but are disclosed in the notes if an inflow of benefits is judged to be probable.

▸ IAS37 makes a number of disclosure requirements with regard to provisions and with regard to contingent liabilities and assets.

▸ IAS10 requires that financial statements should be adjusted to reflect adjusting events that occur after the end of the reporting period but before the date on which the financial statements are authorised for issue. Non-adjusting events that occur during this interval should be noted if material.

Exercises

12.1   Hullman Ltd prepares financial statements to 31 March each year. Consider each of the following situations and determine in each case whether or not a provision should be recognised in the company's financial statements for the year to 31 March 2014.

(a)   On 23 January 2014, the board of directors decided to close down one of the company's operations. By 31 March 2014, this decision had been announced to the workforce and a detailed plan had been drawn up for its implementation. The closure would involve redundancy payments of £375,000.

(b)   On 12 March 2014, the directors decided to close down another of the company's operations. This would involve redundancy payments of £250,000. At 31 March 2014, the decision had not been announced and had not yet been acted upon.

(c)   For the past few years, the company has been conducting two operations which cause environmental damage. One of these operations is in a country with legislation which requires companies to rectify any environmental damage which they cause. The other is in a country with no such legislation. The costs of rectifying the damage caused to date by these two operations are estimated at £5 million and £10 million respectively.

(d)   At 31 March 2014, the company owns a fleet of motor lorries, all of which require an annual service. This servicing work is expected to occur in the first few months of the year to 31 March 2015, at an estimated cost of £50,000.

12.2   (a)   Explain how the amount of a provision should be measured.

(b)   A company needs to make a provision for the cost of repairing a faulty product supplied to a customer some weeks previously. The company estimates that there is a 60% chance that this repair will cost £100,000. However, there is a 30% chance that the cost will be £150,000 and a 10% chance that the cost will be £200,000. How should the amount of the provision be measured?

12.3   At the end of an accounting period, a company has each of the following:

(a)   a present obligation which will probably require an outflow of resources

(b)   a present obligation which will probably not require an outflow of resources

(c)   a possible obligation arising from a disputed past event; the company denies that this event occurred and a legal case is currently proceeding; it seems likely that the company will win the case and that an outflow of resources will not be required

(d)   a possible obligation arising from another disputed past event; the company again denies that this event occurred and again a legal case is currently proceeding; it seems likely that the company will lose this case and that an outflow of resources will be required.

State, for each of these obligations, whether the company should recognise a provision, disclose a contingent liability or do nothing. Assume that all of the obligations arise from past events and that reliable estimates can be made of the amounts concerned.

12.4 Kenston Ltd prepares financial statements to 30 April each year. At 30 April 2014, the company is being sued by a customer who claims to have been harmed by one of the company's products. The case will come before the courts in late 2014. Explain how this matter should be dealt with in the financial statements for the year to 30 April 2014 if:

(a) the company's lawyers advise that the company will probably be found liable

(b) the company's lawyers advise that the company will probably not be found liable.

12.5 The annual accounting date of Lawston plc is 31 May. The following matters need to be dealt with before the financial statements for the year to 31 May 2014 can be finalised:

(a) The company is currently suing one of its suppliers for failure to supply goods according to contract. Legal advice suggests that Lawston plc will probably win the case and will probably be awarded damages.

(b) The company operates an open-cast mine and is legally obliged to restore the environment when mine workings are complete. This is expected to occur in the year 2024. The estimated cost of rectifying the environmental damage caused so far is £3 million. The estimated total cost of rectifying the damage caused until mine workings are complete is £25 million.

Explain how these two matters should be dealt with in the financial statements for the year to 31 May 2014.

12.6 A company prepares financial statements to 31 December each year. The following events occurred after 31 December 2013 but before the financial statements for the year to 31 December 2013 were authorised for issue:

(a) Inventory held at 31 December 2013 was sold to a customer.

(b) The company made a major investment in plant and equipment.

(c) The company made a take-over bid for another company.

(d) A customer who owed an amount of money to the company on 31 December 2013 was declared bankrupt.

(e) The company announced a major restructuring plan.

(f) It was discovered that cash shown as an asset in the statement of financial position at 31 December 2013 had been stolen on 28 December 2013.

(g) It was discovered that a item of equipment shown as an asset in the statement of financial position at 31 December 2013 had been stolen on 12 January 2014.

(h) The government announced a change in tax rates that will have a significant effect on the company's tax liability at 31 December 2013.

Classify each of these events as either an adjusting event or a non-adjusting event and explain how each event should be dealt with in the company's financial statements for the year to 31 December 2013. It may be assumed that all of the events are material.

12.7   Triangle, a public listed company, is in the process of preparing its draft financial statements for the year to 31 March 2014. The following matters have been brought to your attention:

(i)   On 1 April 2013 the company brought into use a new processing plant that had cost £15 million to construct and had an estimated life of ten years. The plant uses hazardous chemicals which are put into containers and shipped abroad for safe disposal after processing. The chemicals have also contaminated the plant itself and this occurred as soon as the plant was used. It is a legal requirement that the plant is decontaminated at the end of its life. The estimated present value of the cost of this decontamination, using a discount rate of 8% per annum, is £5 million. The financial statements have been charged with £1·5 million (£15 million/10 years) for plant depreciation and a provision of £500,000 (£5 million/10 years) has been made towards the cost of the decontamination.

(ii)   On 15 May 2014 the company's auditors discovered a fraud in the material requisitions department. A senior member of staff who took up employment with Triangle in August 2013 had been authorising payments for goods that had never been received. The payments were made to a fictitious company that cannot be traced. The member of staff was immediately dismissed. Calculations show that the total amount of the fraud to the date of its discovery was £240,000 of which £210,000 related to the year to 31 March 2014. (Assume the fraud is material).

(iii) The company has contacted its insurers in respect of the above fraud. Triangle is insured for theft, but the insurance company maintains that this is a commercial fraud and is not covered by the theft clause in the insurance policy. Triangle has not yet had an opinion from its lawyers.

Required:

Explain how the items in (i) to (iii) above should be treated in Triangle's financial statements for the year to 31 March 2014 in accordance with current international accounting standards. Your answer should quantify the amounts where possible.

(ACCA)

*12.8   (a)   Sparkling Pictures plc is a company which specialises in video production. The company is preparing its financial statements for the financial year ended 30 April 2014.

During the financial year ended 30 April 2013 Sparkling Pictures plc was responsible for videoing an important prize awards ceremony for subsequent broadcast on television. Shortly after the ceremony twenty-two people who had been there became seriously ill. They claimed that Sparkling Pictures plc was responsible because a poisonous chemical used in the manufacture of digital video tapes had been found in a soup tureen which had been used during the ceremony.

Legal proceedings seeking damages from Sparkling Pictures plc were started during the financial year ended 30 April 2013. Sparkling Pictures plc denied liability and up to the date of authorisation of the financial statements for the year ended 30 April 2013 the company's lawyers were confident that the evidence against the company was weak and circumstantial and that it was probable that Sparkling Pictures plc would not be found liable.

However, additional evidence emerged during the year ended 30 April 2014 which has caused Sparkling Pictures plc's lawyers to change their advice. They are now of the opinion that it is probable that Sparkling Pictures plc will be found liable.

Required:

Explain, with reasons, how this matter would have been reported in the financial statements for the year ended 30 April 2013 and how it should be reported in the financial statements for the year ended 30 April 2014.

(b)   Stenberg plc is preparing its financial statements for the year ended 30 November 2014.

An employee is claiming damages of £15,000 against Stenberg plc because of injuries received while driving one of the company's delivery vans in September 2014. The employee is claiming that Stenberg plc was negligent in its maintenance of the van and that the van crashed because of poor maintenance. Stenberg plc's lawyer is of the opinion that the probability of the employee winning the case is 80%.

Stenberg plc is making a claim for damages of £25,000 against a contractor to cover the additional costs of making good faulty work on a contract. The contractor had refused to make good the work because they were too busy with work on other contracts. Stenberg plc's lawyer is of the opinion that the probability of winning this claim is 85%.

Required:

For each of the two legal claims Stenberg plc is involved in discuss whether or not a provision should be made in the financial statements for the year ended 30 November 2014.

(CIPFA)

Chapter 13

Revenue

Introduction

The IASB *Conceptual Framework* (see Chapter 2) defines an entity's income for a period in terms of increases in economic benefits arising during that period and states that income encompasses both revenue and gains. Revenue consists of income which arises in the course of the ordinary activities of an entity and may include items such as sales, fees, interest, dividends, royalties and rents.

The main problem in accounting for revenue is that of determining when it should be recognised. This problem is addressed by international standard IAS18 *Revenue*, which:

(a) sets out criteria for the recognition of revenue

(b) identifies the circumstances in which these criteria are met, and

(c) provides practical guidance on the application of these criteria.

The purpose of this chapter is to explain the main requirements of IAS18.

Objectives

By the end of this chapter, the reader should be able to:

- define the term "revenue" in accordance with IAS18 *Revenue*

- explain how revenue should be measured

- state and apply the conditions which must be satisfied in order that revenue arising from a sale of goods should be recognised

- state and apply the conditions which must be satisfied in order that revenue arising from the rendering of services should be recognised

- explain and apply the recognition bases identified in IAS18 in relation to interest, royalties and dividends

- state the main disclosure requirements of IAS18.

Definition of revenue

Revenue is defined by IAS18 as "*the gross inflow of economic benefits during the period arising in the course of the ordinary activities of an entity when those inflows result in increases in equity, other than increases relating to contributions from equity participants*". This definition makes it clear that:

(a) revenue arises from ordinary activities (e.g. the selling of goods or services)

(b) revenue excludes borrowings, since borrowings increase liabilities, not equity

(c) revenue excludes amounts contributed by shareholders (e.g. share issues).

IAS18 also makes it clear that revenue includes only amounts collected by an entity on its own account. Amounts that are collected on behalf of third parties (e.g. VAT collected from customers on behalf of the tax authorities) do not yield economic benefits for the entity and so do not rank as revenue. Similarly, amounts collected by an agent on behalf of a principal are not revenue for the agent. In this case, the agent's revenue is the amount of any commission which is earned from the principal.

Scope of IAS18

IAS18 applies to revenue arising from:

(a) the sale of goods

(b) the rendering of services

(c) the use by others of an entity's assets, yielding interest, royalties and dividends.

However, IAS18 does *not* apply to rental income, since this is dealt with by IAS17 *Leases* (see Chapter 9).

Measurement of revenue

IAS18 states that revenue should be measured "*at the fair value of the consideration received or receivable*". In most cases, the consideration (or price) for a sale transaction takes the form of cash and the amount of revenue is simply equal to the amount of cash receivable, net of any trade discounts or volume rebates allowed. However, if the inflow of cash is deferred until some time after the transaction has occurred, the fair value of the consideration is determined by discounting future receipts to their present value (although this is not required if the effect of discounting is immaterial).

If goods are sold or services are rendered in exchange for other goods or services, the amount of revenue will usually be measured at the fair value of the goods or services received. Fair value is defined by IAS18 (in accordance with IFRS13) as "*the price that would be received to sell an asset or paid to transfer a liability in an orderly transaction between market participants at the measurement date*" (see Chapter 5).

Recognition of revenue: Sale of goods

IAS18 states that revenue from a sale of goods should be recognised when *all* of the following conditions have been satisfied:

(a) the seller has transferred to the buyer the significant risks and rewards of ownership of the goods

(b) the seller retains neither continuing managerial involvement with the goods (to the degree usually associated with ownership) nor effective control over them

(c) the amount of revenue can be measured reliably

(d) it is probable that the economic benefits associated with the transaction will flow to the seller

(e) the costs incurred (or to be incurred) in respect of the transaction can be measured reliably.

Risks and rewards of ownership

In most cases (and especially in the case of most retail sales) the transfer to the buyer of the significant risks and rewards of ownership will coincide with the transfer of legal title in the goods. However, it is necessary to examine the circumstances of each transaction in order to assess when these risks and rewards are actually transferred. There are a number of situations in which the seller may retain significant risks or rewards of ownership even after legal title has passed. For example:

(a) if the seller retains an obligation for unsatisfactory performance of the goods and this is not covered by normal warranty provisions

(b) if the receipt of revenue from the sale depends upon the buyer being able to sell the goods on to a third party

(c) if the goods are shipped subject to installation by the seller and the installation is not yet complete

(d) if the buyer has the right to rescind the purchase and the seller is uncertain about the probability of the goods being returned.

It is important to note the use of the word "significant" here. If the seller retains only insignificant risks or rewards of ownership, then revenue can be recognised (assuming that the other conditions listed above are satisfied). An example of this arises where a retailer offers refunds to dissatisfied customers. In this case, revenue may be recognised at the time of sale, provided that the retailer also recognises a liability for returns, based upon previous experience.

Probability that economic benefits will flow

As stated above, revenue is recognised only when it is probable that the economic benefits associated with a sale will flow to the seller. This will usually be so but uncertainty might arise in some cases. For instance, if goods are sold to an overseas customer, there may be some doubt as to whether the foreign government concerned will give permission for the sale consideration to be remitted to the seller. If a significant uncertainty exists, revenue should not be recognised until the uncertainty is removed.

If revenue is recognised in relation to a sale but then a bad debt occurs, the uncollectible amount should be treated as an expense rather than as a reduction in revenue.

Recognition of revenue: Rendering of services

When the outcome of a transaction involving the rendering of services can be estimated reliably, IAS18 states that the revenue associated with the transaction should be recognised by reference to the stage of completion of the transaction at the end of the reporting period. IAS18 also states that the outcome of such a transaction can be estimated reliably when *all* of the following conditions are satisfied:

(a) the amount of revenue can be measured reliably

(b) it is probable that the economic benefits associated with the transaction will flow to the entity

(c) the stage of completion of the transaction at the end of the reporting period can be measured reliably

(d) the costs incurred for the transaction and the costs to complete the transaction can be measured reliably.

If a transaction involving the rendering of services is 100% complete by the end of the reporting period (and all of the above conditions are satisfied) then all of the revenue associated with the transaction may be recognised. Otherwise, it will be necessary to determine the stage of completion of the transaction and recognise only a proportion of the revenue. There are several ways of determining the stage of completion. These include:

(a) calculating the proportion that the services performed to date bear to the total services to be performed, or

(b) calculating the proportion that the costs incurred to date bear to the total costs expected to be incurred in relation to the transaction.

The chosen method should be one which reliably measures the services which have been performed by the end of the reporting period. In practice, if a contract for the rendering of services specifies that the services should be performed over a specified period, revenue will often be recognised on a straight-line basis over that period (unless some other method better indicates the stage of completion).

Recognition of revenue: Interest, royalties and dividends

IAS18 states that revenue arising from the use (by others) of an entity's assets, yielding either interest, royalties or dividends, should be recognised when both of the following conditions are satisfied:

(a) it is probable that the associated economic benefits will flow to the entity

(b) the amount of the revenue can be measured reliably.

If these conditions are satisfied, revenue consisting of interest, royalties or dividends is recognised on the following bases:

(a) Interest is recognised using the "effective interest method" which is set out in IAS39 (see Chapter 11). This means that interest is recognised on the accruals basis, using an interest rate which takes into account all of the amounts to be paid and received over the life of the financial instrument concerned.

(b) Royalties are recognised on the accruals basis.

(c) Dividends are recognised when the right to receive payment is established.

Disclosure requirements

IAS18 requires that entities should disclose:

(a) accounting policies adopted for revenue recognition, including the methods used to determine the stage of completion of transactions involving the rendering of services

(b) the amount of each significant category of revenue recognised during the accounting period, including revenue arising from the sale of goods, the rendering of services, interest, royalties and dividends.

(c) the amount of revenue arising from exchanges of goods or services included in each significant category of revenue.

Proposed new standard

In November 2011, the IASB issued a revised exposure draft of a new standard entitled *Revenue from Contracts with Customers*. This standard would make certain changes to the way in which revenue is recognised. In particular, revenue would be recognised only when (or as) an entity satisfied a performance obligation by transferring goods or services to a customer. This transfer would occur only when (or as) the customer obtained control of the goods or services concerned. Furthermore, impairment losses relating to contracts with customers (e.g. bad debts) would be presented in the statement of comprehensive income as a separate line item adjacent to the revenue line item.

However, this is only a draft standard and amendments may be made before the final standard is issued. Further information is available on website www.ifrs.org.

Guidance to the implementation of IAS18

IAS18 is accompanied by a number of illustrative examples which relate to revenue recognition. Some of these examples are outlined below. All of the examples assume that the amount of revenue can be measured reliably, the costs incurred (or to be incurred) can also be measured reliably and that it is probable that the economic benefits concerned will flow to the seller. Although these examples offer useful practical guidance, they are not actually part of IAS18.

Examples relating to the sale of goods

(a) *Bill and hold sales*. These are sales in which delivery is delayed (at the buyer's request) but the buyer takes over legal title to the goods and accepts billing. In such cases, revenue should be recognised when the buyer takes legal title, so long as:

(i) it is probable that delivery will be made

(ii) the goods are ready for delivery at the time that the sale is recognised

(iii) the buyer acknowledges the deferred delivery instructions, and

(iv) the usual payment terms apply.

Revenue should not be recognised in cases where a buyer has been billed for goods but these goods are not available for delivery because they have not yet been acquired (or manufactured) by the seller.

(b) *Goods shipped subject to conditions*:

(i) *Installation and inspection*. If goods are sold subject to satisfactory installation and inspection, revenue should normally be recognised only when the buyer has accepted delivery and both installation and inspection are complete. But revenue may be recognised immediately that the buyer accepts delivery if:

– the installation is fairly simple in nature (e.g. the unpacking and connection of a factory-tested TV receiver)

– the inspection is performed only for price-determination purposes.

(ii) *Goods sold on approval*. If goods are sold on approval, revenue should not be recognised until either:

– the goods have been formally accepted by the buyer, or

– the goods have been delivered to the buyer and the time period for rejection and return has elapsed.

(iii) *Consignment sales*. If goods are shipped to a recipient who undertakes to sell those goods on behalf of the shipper, revenue should not be recognised by the shipper until the goods have been sold to a third party.

(iv) *Cash on delivery sales*. Revenue should be recognised only when the goods have been delivered and cash has been received.

(c) *Lay away sales*. These are sales where delivery is delayed until the buyer makes the final payment in a series of instalments. In such cases, revenue should not usually be recognised until the goods are delivered. However, revenue may be recognised when a significant deposit is received, so long as the goods are ready for delivery and experience indicates that most such sales do in fact go ahead.

(d) *Orders where payment is received in advance*. If payment is received in advance for goods which are not currently held in inventory (perhaps because they have not yet been manufactured) revenue should not be recognised until the goods have been delivered to the buyer.

(e) *Sale and repurchase agreements*. These are sales of goods where the seller has agreed (or has the right) to repurchase the goods at a later date or where the buyer can require such repurchase. In these circumstances, it is necessary to consider the substance of the agreement to determine whether or not the risks and rewards of ownership have been passed to the buyer. If so, revenue should be recognised. If not, revenue should not be recognised (even if legal title to the goods has been transferred) and the agreement should be treated as a financing arrangement. This approach is an application of the "substance over form" principle (see Chapter 2).

(f) *Sales to intermediate parties for resale*. If goods are sold to intermediate parties (such as distributors or dealers) for resale, revenue should normally be recognised when the risks and rewards of ownership have passed. However, if the substance of the arrangement is that the buyer is acting as an agent for the seller, the sale is treated as a consignment sale (see above).

(g) *Subscriptions to publications and similar items*. Revenue is normally recognised on a straight-line basis over the period in which the items are despatched. However, if the items to be despatched during the period vary in value, revenue should be recognised on the basis of the sales value of each item in relation to the total sales value of all the items covered by the subscription.

(h) *Instalment sales*. If goods are sold and the consideration for the sale is receivable by instalments, revenue equal to the sale price of the goods (excluding interest) should be recognised at the date of sale. The sale price is equal to the present value of the instalments to be received. The interest element of the instalments is recognised as revenue as it is earned.

Examples relating to the rendering of services

(a) *Installation fees*. Installation fees are usually recognised by reference to the stage of completion of the installation work. However, if such fees are incidental to the sale of goods, they are recognised when the goods are sold.

(b) *Servicing fees included in the price of a product*. If the selling price of a product includes an amount for after-sales servicing and support, this amount is deferred and recognised as revenue over the period in which the services are performed. The amount deferred is the amount which will cover the expected costs of providing the services, plus a reasonable profit margin.

(c) *Financial services fees*. Financial services fees (e.g. investment management fees) are generally recognised as revenue as the services are provided. However, if financial services fees are an integral part of the effective interest rate of a financial instrument, they should be dealt with in accordance with IAS39 and IFRS9 (see Chapter 11).

(d) *Admission fees*. Revenue from an artistic performance or similar event is recognised when the event takes place. A subscription which covers a number of such events is allocated between the events on a basis which reflects the extent to which services are performed at each event.

(e) *Tuition fees*. Revenue from tuition fees is recognised over the period of tuition.

(f) *Membership fees*. If a membership fee permits only membership and all other services or products are paid for separately (or if there is a separate annual subscription) then the membership fee is recognised as revenue when it is received or when there is no significant doubt as to its collectibility. However, if a membership fee entitles the member to services, it should be recognised on a basis that reflects the timing and value of those services.

(g) *Franchise fees*. Franchise fees may cover the supply of initial or subsequent services, equipment, know-how etc. and are recognised as revenue on a basis that reflects the purpose for which the fees are charged.

   If the fees charged for the provision of subsequent services do not cover the cost of providing those services (together with a reasonable profit) part of the initial franchise fee should be deferred and should be recognised as revenue as the subsequent services are provided. The amount deferred should be sufficient to cover the cost of the subsequent services and give a reasonable profit.

Summary

▸ Revenue arises from the ordinary activities of an entity and results in an increase in equity. Increases in equity caused by contributions from equity participants are not revenue. International standard IAS18 sets out rules relating to the measurement and recognition of revenue.

▸ Revenue should be measured at the fair value of the consideration receivable.

▸ The revenue arising from a sale of goods is recognised when the significant risks and rewards of ownership have passed to the buyer, so long as it is probable that the economic benefits associated with the sale will pass to the seller and both the amount of the revenue and the amount of the costs incurred can be measured reliably.

▸ The revenue arising from a transaction for the rendering of services is recognised by reference to the stage of completion of those services, so long as it is probable that the economic benefits associated with the transaction will pass to the provider of the services and both the amount of the revenue and the amount of the costs incurred can be measured reliably.

▸ Revenue arising in the form of interest, royalties or dividends is recognised on the appropriate basis when it is probable that the economic benefits concerned will flow to the entity concerned and the amount of the revenue can be measured reliably.

▸ IAS18 makes a number of disclosure requirements relating to an entity's revenue and the accounting policies adopted for the recognition of revenue.

▸ IAS18 is accompanied by a large number of illustrative examples which indicate how and when revenue should be recognised in a wide variety of situations.

Exercises

13.1   (a)   Define the term "revenue" and explain how revenue should be measured in accordance with the requirements of international standard IAS18.

        (b)   Identify the amount of revenue arising in each of the following cases:

            (i)   A company sells goods for £1,000 plus VAT at 20%, so that the customer is charged a total of £1,200.

            (ii) A company sells goods for £500 less a trade discount of £25. The customer is offered a further cash discount of £19 if payment is made within 30 days and does in fact pay within this period of time. The company acquired the goods at a cost of £350.

            (iii) A company issues 100,000 £1 ordinary shares at par.

            (iv) A manufacturing company which is moving to a new factory sells its old factory for £450,000. The company acquired the factory 20 years previously at a cost of £300,000.

13.2   (a)   State the conditions which must be satisfied in order for the revenue relating to a sale of goods to be recognised.

        (b)   Explain when revenue should be recognised in each of the following situations:

            (i)   A company sells goods on "sale or return" terms. The customer is entitled to return the goods to the company (and obtain a full refund) if they cannot be sold to a third party within three months.

            (ii) A company delivers goods to an agent who undertakes to sell these goods on behalf of the company.

            (iii) A company sells goods on approval. The customer has one month in which to decide whether or not to accept the goods.

13.3   (a)   State the conditions which must be satisfied in order for the revenue relating to the rendering of services to be recognised.

        (b)   Explain when revenue should be recognised in each of the following situations:

            (i)   A company which prepares financial statements to 31 December each year has a contract with a customer for the provision of certain services. These services are to be supplied evenly over the two-year period from 1 July 2013 to 30 June 2015. The agreed contract price is £45,000.

            (ii) The above company has another two-year contract (again covering the period from 1 July 2013 to 30 June 2015) for the provision of services to a customer but these services are *not* to be supplied evenly over the two-year period. The agreed contract price is £80,000. It is estimated that 10% of the services have been rendered by the end of 2013 and that 65% of the services have been rendered by the end of 2014.

13.4   Identify whether (and when) the "significant risks and rewards" of ownership pass from seller to buyer in each of the following situations:

(a)   A retailer has a "no questions asked" returns policy. Customers may return goods for any reason within one month of purchase and obtain a full refund. Experience shows that less than 1% of sales result in such returns and refunds.

(b)   A company sells a machine to a customer and also undertakes to instal the machine on the customer's premises. The installation will take approximately three days, after which the customer will inspect the installed machine and decide whether or not to accept it.

13.5   A company sells goods to a customer on the understanding that the customer will pay £5,000 immediately and will then pay two further instalments of £5,000 each at annual intervals. Assuming an effective interest rate of 10% per annum, calculate the amount of revenue which should be recognised at the date of the sale.

13.6   On 1 July 2013, Ashtor Ltd sells goods worth £800,000 to Bokker plc for £500,000. The sales agreement states that Ashtor Ltd is entitled to repurchase the goods on 30 June 2016 for £500,000 plus compound interest calculated at 10% per annum and it is expected that repurchase will in fact occur.

Taking into account the substance of this transaction, how much revenue should Ashtor Ltd recognise on 1 July 2013?

*13.7   Triangle, a public listed company, is in the process of preparing its draft financial statements for the year to 31 March 2014.

On 1 April 2013, Triangle sold maturing inventory that had a carrying value of £3m (at cost) to Factorall, a finance house, for £5m. Its estimated market value at this date was in excess of £5m. The inventory will not be ready for sale until 31 March 2017 and will remain on Triangle's premises until this date. The sale contract includes a clause allowing Triangle to repurchase the inventory at any time up to 31 March 2017 at a price of £5m plus interest at 10% per annum compounded from 1 April 2013. The inventory will incur storage costs until maturity. The cost of storage for the current year of £300,000 has been included in trade receivables (in the name of Factorall). If Triangle chooses not to repurchase the inventory, Factorall will pay the accumulated storage costs on 31 March 2017. The proceeds of the sale have been debited to the bank and the sale has been included in Triangle's sales revenue.

Required:

Explain how this item should be treated in Triangle's financial statements for the year to 31 March 2014 in accordance with current international accounting standards. Your answer should quantify the amounts where possible.   *(ACCA)*

Chapter 14

Employee benefits

Introduction

This chapter is concerned with IAS19 *Employee Benefits*, which lays down accounting and disclosure requirements in relation to all forms of benefits provided by employers to their employees. The main categories of employee benefits identified in the standard are:

(a)   short-term employee benefits

(b)   post-employment benefits (e.g. pensions)

(c)   other long-term employee benefits

(d)   termination benefits.

This chapter covers all of these categories and explains the accounting treatment required for each of them. However, the majority of the chapter is concerned with post-employment benefits, for which the required accounting treatment can be quite complex.

Objectives

By the end of this chapter, the reader should be able to:

*   define each of the main categories of employee benefits which are identified in international standard IAS19 *Employee Benefits*

*   explain and apply the required accounting treatment for short-term employee benefits

*   explain the term "post-employment benefit plan" and distinguish between defined contribution plans and defined benefit plans

*   explain and apply the required accounting treatment for defined contribution plans and for defined benefit plans

*   outline the requirements of IAS19 relating to other long-term benefits and termination benefits

*   list the main disclosures that should be made in the financial statements in relation to employee benefits.

Short-term employee benefits

IAS19 defines short-term employee benefits as "*employee benefits (other than termination benefits) that are expected to be settled wholly before twelve months after the end of the annual reporting period in which the employees render the related service*". This means that short-term employee benefits are those which fall due either during the period in which the employee provides services to the employer or within twelve months of the end of that period. The definition of short-term employee benefits covers items such as:

(a)   wages, salaries and employer's social security contributions

(b)   short-term holiday pay and sick pay

(c)   profit-sharing payments and bonuses payable within twelve months of the end of the period in which the related employee services are performed

(d)   non-monetary benefits (e.g. medical care, company cars) for current employees.

In general, accounting for short-term employee benefits presents no great difficulties. If an employee has rendered services to an employer during an accounting period, the employer's financial statements for that period should usually recognise:

(a)   an expense equal to the amount of the short-term employee benefits due in exchange for those services, and

(b)   a liability (accrued expense) equal to any part of this expense that has not been paid by the end of the period.

An exception to the requirement to recognise an expense arises if another standard requires or permits the cost of the benefits to be recognised as an asset. For instance, IAS16 requires employee benefits to be capitalised if they arise directly from the construction or acquisition of an item of property, plant or equipment (see Chapter 5).

Note that short-term employee benefits are measured on an undiscounted basis, since the required payments are made either during the relevant accounting period or within twelve months of its end, so that the effect of discounting would be minimal.

Short-term paid absences

IAS19 uses the expression "short-term paid absences" to refer to paid employee absences (e.g. paid holidays and paid sick leave) which occur during the period in which the related employee services are performed or which are expected to occur within twelve months of the end of that period. Entitlement to paid absences falls into two categories:

(a)   "accumulating" paid absences, which can be carried forward and used in a future period if the current period's entitlement is not used in full

(b)   "non-accumulating" paid absences, which cannot be carried forward.

In the case of accumulating short-term paid absences, the employer's statement of financial position should show a liability equal to the expected amount payable during the following twelve months as a result of unused entitlement carried forward.

EXAMPLE 1

A company has 1,000 employees, each of whom is entitled to ten days of paid sick leave in each calendar year. Unused sick leave at the end of each year may be carried forward for up to one further calendar year. Sick leave is taken first out of the current year's ten-day entitlement and then out of any unused entitlement brought forward.

At 31 December 2013, the average unused entitlement is six days per employee. Based on past experience, the company expects that 85% of employees will take no more than ten days sick leave in the forthcoming year but that the remaining 15% of employees will each take an average of twelve days.

Assuming an average cost to the company of £120 per day of paid sick leave, calculate the liability which should appear in the company's statement of financial position at 31 December 2013 in relation to paid sick leave.

Solution

850 employees are not expected to make use of their unused entitlement and therefore the amount expected to be paid in relation to these employees is £nil. The remaining 150 employees are each expected to use two days of their unused entitlement. Therefore the liability which should appear in the company's statement of financial position as at 31 December 2013 is £36,000 (150 x 2 x £120).

Profit-sharing and bonus payments

Profit-sharing and bonus payments payable within twelve months of the end of the period in which the employees render the related services are short-term employee benefits and should be recognised as an expense in that period, so long as:

(a) there is a present obligation to make the payments as a result of past events, and

(b) a reliable estimate of the obligation can be made.

A "present obligation" exists when the employer has no realistic alternative but to make the payments concerned. This may be a legal or a constructive obligation. A constructive obligation is not legally enforceable but derives from the entity's actions (see Chapter 12).

Profit-sharing and bonus payments which fall due more than twelve months after the end of the period are treated as "other long-term employee benefits" (see later in this chapter).

Disclosures relating to short-term employee benefits

IAS19 makes no specific disclosure requirements relating to short-term employee benefits. However, certain disclosures are required by other standards. For instance:

(a) IAS1 *Presentation of Financial Statements* requires disclosure of the total employee benefits expense for each accounting period (see Chapter 3), and

(b) IAS24 *Related Party Disclosures* requires disclosures relating to benefits provided for key management personnel (see Chapter 21).

Post-employment benefits

Post-employment benefits consist mainly of retirement benefits, such as pensions. In some cases, the post-employment benefits scheme is administered directly by the employer. In other cases, a separate entity (a pension fund) is set up to receive contributions and pay employee benefits. In either case, the requirements of IAS19 should be applied.

IAS19 distinguishes between two types of pension scheme or "plan":

(a) **Defined contribution plans**. Defined contribution plans are post-employment benefit plans where an employer pays fixed contributions into a pension fund each year and is not obliged to make any further contributions, even if the pension fund's assets are insufficient to pay the expected level of employee benefits. The risk that benefits will be less than expected falls upon the employees, not the employer.

(b) **Defined benefit plans**. Defined benefit plans are post-employment benefit plans where the employer is obliged (either legally or constructively) to provide an agreed level of post-employment benefits. The employer's contributions are not limited to any fixed amount and these contributions may need to be increased if the pension fund has insufficient assets to pay the agreed level of benefits. The risk of having to make further contributions is borne by the employer, not the employee.

Accounting for defined contribution plans

Accounting for defined contribution plans is straightforward and the required accounting treatment is very similar to that required for short-term benefits. In general, if an employee has rendered services to an employer during an accounting period, the employer's financial statements for that period should recognise:

(a) an expense equal to the amount of the contributions payable by the employer into the defined contribution plan in exchange for those services, and

(b) a liability (accrued expense) equal to any part of this expense that has not been paid by the end of the period.

If the contributions already paid exceed the amount due to date, the excess should be recognised as an asset (prepaid expense) to the extent that this prepayment will lead to either a reduction in future payments or a cash refund. Note also that:

(a) As for short-term employee benefits, the requirement to recognise an expense may be over-ruled by another standard which requires or permits the contributions to be included in the cost of an asset.

(b) Contributions to a defined contribution plan are measured on an undiscounted basis unless they fall due more than twelve months after the end of the period in which employees render the related services.

(c) The amount recognised as an expense in relation to defined contribution plans should be disclosed in the notes which form part of the employer's financial statements.

Accounting for defined benefit plans

Accounting for defined benefit plans is a complex matter and much of IAS19 is devoted to this topic. The complexity arises because the expense recognised in each accounting period should be the cost to the employer of the retirement benefits that will eventually be paid to employees as a result of the services that they have provided during that period. The problem is that these benefits may be payable in many years' time and their cost will depend upon a number of factors which are difficult to determine in advance, such as employee mortality rates and future returns on investments. The employer is exposed to both the "actuarial risk" that employees will live longer than expected (which increases the cost of providing benefits) and the "investment risk" that assets invested in the plan will be insufficient to pay the required benefits.

In these circumstances, the calculation of the expense which should be recognised in an accounting period in relation to a defined benefit plan is not straightforward. Furthermore, a liability (or asset) must be shown in the employer's financial statements in relation to the plan and the amount of this liability or asset also has to be calculated. A simplified summary of the main features of these calculations is given below.

Main steps in the defined benefit calculations

Accounting for defined benefit plans in accordance with the requirements of IAS19 involves the following main steps:

(a) At the end of each accounting period, reliable estimates must be made of:

(i) the amount of the accumulated benefits which past and present employees have earned in return for their services to date and which will be payable to them in the future ("the defined benefit obligation")

(ii) the extra amount of such benefits that employees have earned in return for their services during the current period (the "current service cost").

These estimates involve the making of assumptions with regard to such matters as employee mortality rates and future salary increases. Employers are encouraged (but not required) by IAS19 to engage a qualified actuary to make the necessary estimates.

(b) These estimates are discounted so as to determine the present value of the defined benefit obligation and the present value of the current service cost.

(c) The "interest cost" for the period is calculated. This is equal to the increase during the current accounting period of the present value of the defined benefit obligation which was calculated at the end of the previous period (adjusted if part of that obligation has now been discharged as a result of benefit payments). This increase arises because the accumulated benefits which employees had earned at the end of the previous period are now one period closer to being paid.

(d)   "Actuarial gains and losses" with regard to the defined benefit obligation may now be calculated. These are caused by:

(i)   differences between actuarial assumptions which were made at the end of the previous period and events that actually occurred during the current period

(ii)   changes in actuarial assumptions between the start and end of the period.

The overall actuarial gain or loss with regard to the defined benefit obligation for an accounting period is calculated by summarising the changes in that obligation during the period and inserting a balancing figure, as illustrated below:

	£000
Present value of DB obligation at start of period	xxx
Add: Interest cost	xxx
Present value of current service cost	xxx
Less: Benefits paid during the period	(xxx)
	xxx
Actuarial losses/(gains)	xxx (balancing figure)
Present value of DB obligation at end of period	xxx

(e)   The final step in the process is to determine the fair value of the plan assets (if any) at the end of the accounting period and to reconcile this figure with the fair value of plan assets at the start of the period. The reconciliation is as follows:

	£000
Fair value of plan assets at start of period	xxx
Add: Interest income	xxx
Return on plan assets	xxx
Contributions received from employer	xxx
Contributions received from employees	xxx
Less: Benefits paid during the period	(xxx)
Fair value of plan assets at end of period	xxx

Note that:

(i)   The "interest income" for the period is obtained by multiplying the fair value of plan assets at the start of the period by the interest rate used when calculating the interest cost (but taking account of changes in plan assets during the period).

(ii)   Return on plan assets is defined as "*interest, dividends and other income derived from the plan assets, together with realised and unrealised gains or losses*", less interest income for the period.

These calculations provide all the figures required in order to compute the defined benefit expense for the period and the defined benefit liability (or asset) at the end of the period. The way in which these amounts are derived is explained below.

The defined benefit expense and the defined benefit liability

The defined benefit expense which is shown in the statement of comprehensive income when calculating profit or loss for an accounting period is arrived at by *adding*:

(a)   the present value of the current service cost for the period

(b)   interest cost for the period

and then *subtracting*:

(c)   the amount of any employee contributions made during the period (since these have helped to fund the current service cost)

(d)   interest income for the period.

IAS19 requires that any actuarial gains or losses and the return on plan assets (less interest income) should be shown in other comprehensive income. These amounts may not be reclassified to profit or loss in a subsequent accounting period (see Chapter 3).

The defined benefit liability (i.e. deficit) shown in the statement of financial position is equal to the present value of the defined benefit obligation at the end of the period, less the fair value of the plan assets at that date. A surplus is recognised as an asset.

EXAMPLE 2

A company which prepares annual accounts to 31 December has operated a defined benefit pension scheme for many years. The scheme is non-contributory (i.e. employees are not required to make contributions). At 31 December 2012, the company's statement of financial position showed a defined benefit liability of £575,000, made up as follows:

	£000
Present value of defined benefit obligation	2,430
Fair value of plan assets	1,855
Defined benefit liability	575

The following figures relate to the year to 31 December 2013:

	£000
Present value of current service cost for the year	415
Interest cost	170
Interest income	130
Return on plan assets (before deducting interest income)	235
Employer contributions	450
Benefits paid	375
Present value of defined benefit obligation at end of year	2,760
Fair value of plan assets at end of year	2,165

Calculate the defined benefit expense for the year to 31 December 2013. Also calculate the defined benefit liability (or asset) which should be shown in the company's statement of financial position as at that date.

Solution

Calculation of actuarial gains or losses:

	£000
Present value of DB obligation at start of year	2,430
Interest cost	170
Present value of current service cost for the year	415
Benefits paid during the year	(375)
	2,640
Actuarial losses (balancing figure)	120
Present value of defined benefit obligation at end of year	2,760

Reconciliation of the fair value of plan assets:

	£000
Fair value of plan assets at start of year	1,855
Interest income	130
Return on plan assets (after deducting interest income)	105
Employer contributions	450
Benefits paid during the year	(375)
Fair value of plan assets at end of year	2,165

The amounts which should be shown in the company's financial statements for the year to 31 December 2013 are as follows:

Defined benefit expense:

	£000
Present value of current service cost for the year	415
Interest cost	170
Interest income	(130)
Expense recognised in profit or loss	455
Actuarial losses	120
Return on plan assets	(105)
Expense recognised in other comprehensive income	15

Defined benefit liability:

	£000
Present value of defined benefit obligation at end of year	2,760
Fair value of plan assets at end of year	2,165
DB liability in statement of financial position	595

The defined benefit expense for the year is £470,000 in total, but employer contributions were only £450,000. This is why the defined benefit liability (i.e. deficit) has increased by £20,000 during the year, from £575,000 to £595,000.

Disclosures relating to defined benefit plans

IAS19 makes extensive disclosure requirements with regard to defined benefit plans. The main disclosures required are as follows:

(a) Information which explains the characteristics of each of the entity's defined benefit plans and the risks associated with that plan:

    (i) the nature of the benefits provided by the plan

    (ii) a description of the regulatory framework within which the plan operates

    (iii) a description of any other entity's responsibilities for governance of the plan

    (iv) a description of the risks to which the entity is exposed because of the plan.

(b) Information which identifies and explains the amounts in the entity's financial statements which relate to defined benefit plans:

    (i) a reconciliation between the opening and closing balances of the defined benefit liability (or asset), showing separate reconciliations for the plan assets and for the present value of the defined benefit obligation

    (ii) an analysis of the fair value of the plan assets into classes which distinguish the nature and risks of those assets, subdividing each class into assets which have a quoted price in an active market and those that do not

    (iii) the fair value of the entity's own financial instruments held as plan assets and the fair value of any plan assets consisting of property occupied by the entity or other assets used by the entity

    (iv) the significant actuarial assumptions used to determine the present value of the defined benefit obligation.

(c) Information which describes how the entity's defined benefit plans may affect the amount, timing and uncertainty of its future cash flows:

    (i) a sensitivity analysis for each significant actuarial assumption used to determine the present value of the defined benefit obligation, showing how the obligation would have been affected by changes in each assumption

    (ii) a description of funding arrangements that affect future contributions

    (iii) the expected contributions to the plan for the next annual accounting period

    (iv) information about the maturity profile of the defined benefit obligation, such as a maturity analysis of benefit payments.

Other long-term employee benefits

"Other long-term employee benefits" include items such as:

(a) long-term paid absences such as long-service leave and sabbatical leave

(b) long-term disability benefits

(c) profit-sharing and bonus payments

as long as these are not expected to be settled wholly before twelve months after the end of the period in which the employees render the related services.

The accounting treatment of these benefits is similar to the treatment required for defined benefit post-employment plans. The employer's financial statements for an accounting period should recognise:

(a) a liability equal to the present value at the end of the period of the accumulated long-term benefits to which employees are entitled in return for their services to date, less the fair value of any assets out of which this obligation is to be settled

(b) an expense, equal to the extra amount of such benefits that employees have earned in return for their services during the current period (the current service cost) adjusted for interest cost, interest income, return on assets and actuarial gains/losses.

IAS19 requires that the whole of the above expense should be taken into account when calculating the employer's profit or loss, with none of it recognised in other comprehensive income. However, as is the case for short-term employee benefits and post-employment benefits, the requirement to recognise an expense may be over-ruled by another standard which requires or permits the cost of the benefits to be included in the cost of an asset.

IAS19 does not contain any specific disclosure requirements with regard to other long-term employee benefits. However, certain other standards (e.g. IAS1 and IAS24) require a number of disclosures relating to employee benefits (see earlier in this chapter).

Termination benefits

Termination benefits are defined by IAS19 as "*employee benefits provided in exchange for the termination of an employee's employment* ...". These may arise because an entity decides to terminate an employee's employment or because of an employee's decision to accept an offer of benefits in exchange for the termination of employment.

IAS19 requires that an entity should recognise a liability and an expense for termination benefits at the earlier of the following dates:

(a)   when the entity can no longer withdraw the offer of those benefits

(b)   when the entity recognises costs for a restructuring that is within the scope of IAS37 (see Chapter 12) and which involves the payment of termination benefits.

Termination benefits that are expected to be settled wholly before twelve months after the end of the period in which they are recognised should be measured in the same way as short-term benefits (i.e. on an undiscounted basis). Otherwise, termination benefits should be measured in the same way as other long-term employee benefits.

IAS19 does not contain any specific disclosure requirements with regard to termination benefits. However, as mentioned above, certain other standards (e.g. IAS1 and IAS24) require a number of disclosures relating to employee benefits.

Summary

▸   Short-term employee benefits are those employee benefits that are expected to be settled wholly before twelve months after the end of the period in which they are earned. They are recognised as an expense in that period.

▸   An employer's statement of financial position should show a liability for the expected amount payable in relation to employees' unused entitlement to accumulating short-term paid absences.

▸   Post-employment benefits consist largely of pensions. A pension scheme or plan may be a defined contribution plan or a defined benefit plan.

▸   A defined contribution plan is one where the employer's contributions are fixed. The employer's financial statements should show an expense equal to the agreed amount of contributions for the period.

▸   A defined benefit plan is one where the employer is obliged to provide an agreed level of post-employment benefits. In order to account for defined benefit plans, it is necessary to make actuarial estimates of the accumulated post-employment benefits which employees have earned to date and the extra amount of such benefits that employees have earned during the current accounting period.

▸ Actuarial gains or losses may arise with regard to the defined benefit obligation. These may be caused by experience adjustments (i.e. differences between previous actuarial assumptions and actual events) or by changes in actuarial assumptions.

▸ The defined benefit expense for an accounting period is basically equal to the present value of the extra benefits that employees have earned during that period. But this figure is adjusted to reflect interest cost, interest income and any contributions made in the period by employees.

▸ Actuarial gains or losses and the return on plan assets (excluding interest income) are shown in other comprehensive income.

▸ The defined benefit liability at the end of an accounting period is equal to the present value of the defined benefit obligation less the fair value of the plan assets.

▸ The accounting treatment of other long-term employee benefits (e.g. long-term paid absences) is similar to the treatment required for defined benefit plans.

▸ Termination benefits should be recognised as a liability and an expense when the employer can no longer withdraw the offer of those benefits, or when the employer provides for restructuring costs which involve the payment of termination benefits.

Exercises

14.1 List the four main categories of employee benefits which are identified by international standard IAS19 and give examples of each category.

14.2 A company has 10,000 employees. Each employee is entitled to twenty days of paid holiday per calendar year. Up to five days of this entitlement may be carried forward and taken in the following year but cannot be carried forward any further. Employees are not paid for any holidays which they fail to take.

As at 31 December 2013, a total of 9,130 employees had used their full holiday entitlement for 2013. The remaining employees are carrying forward an average of three days per employee. Based on past experience, it is expected that these employees will each use an average of two of these three days before the end of 2014.

Each day of paid holiday costs the company an average of £150. Calculate the liability which should appear in the company's statement of financial position at 31 December 2013 with regard to paid holiday entitlement.

14.3 (a) Distinguish between defined contribution pension plans and defined benefit pension plans.

(b) A company's agreed contributions to a defined contribution plan for 2013 are £350,000. Of this sum, the company had paid £320,000 by the end of the year. It is becoming clear that the pension fund assets will be insufficient to finance the expected level of employee benefits and that the company would have to increase its annual contributions by 50% if employee expectations were to be met.

Calculate the expense which should be shown in the statement of comprehensive income for the year to 31 December 2013 in relation to this plan. Also calculate the amount of the liability which should appear in the statement of financial position.

(c) Explain why accounting for a defined benefit plan is much more difficult than accounting for a defined contribution plan.

14.4 (a) With regard to defined benefit pension plans, explain each of the following terms:
- defined benefit obligation
- current service cost
- interest cost
- actuarial gains and losses.

(b) Identify the main components of the defined benefit expense which should be shown in an employer's statement of comprehensive income.

(c) Identify the main components of the defined benefit liability which should appear in the employer's statement of financial position.

14.5 Northerley plc prepares accounts to 31 December each year and has operated a defined benefit pension scheme for many years. At 31 December 2012, the present value of the defined benefit obligation was calculated to be £22.5m and the fair value of plan assets was £21.9m. The following information relates to the year to 31 December 2013:

(a) The present value of the current service cost for the year is £3.7m. This is before deducting employee contributions.

(b) Interest cost and interest income for the year have been calculated at £1.8m and £2.1m respectively.

(c) The return on plan assets (before deducting interest income) was £2.9m.

(d) Northerley plc made contributions of £3.8m into the plan. Employees contributed a further £1.5m.

(e) The plan paid out benefits to past employees amounting to £1.9m.

(f) At 31 December 2013, the present value of the defined benefit obligation is £27.4m and the fair value of plan assets is £28.2m.

Calculate the defined benefit expense which should appear in the company's statement of comprehensive income for the year to 31 December 2013 and the defined benefit asset or liability which should appear in the statement of financial position at that date. Also reconcile the expense for the year to the employer contributions made during the year.

*14.6   Prentiss plc operates a defined benefit pension plan and prepares financial statements to 31 March each year. The financial statements for the year to 31 March 2013 showed that the present value of the defined benefit obligation on 31 March 2013 was £140m and the fair value of the plan assets on that date was £147m. The following information relates to the year to 31 March 2014:

(i)   The company made contributions of £18.4m into the plan. Employee contributions were £7.3m.

(ii)   Benefits paid in the year were £19.6m.

(iii)   The return on plan assets (before deducting interest income) was £5.9m.

(iv)   The present value of the current service cost for the year is estimated at £19.2m.

(v)   The interest cost for the year was £9.8m and interest income was £10.3m.

At 31 March 2014, the company's actuary estimated that the present value of the defined benefit obligation was £158m. The fair value of plan assets was £159m.

Required:

(a)   Identify the main difference between a defined benefit pension plan and a defined contribution pension plan.

(b)   Explain the terms "defined benefit obligation" and "current service cost" in relation to defined benefit pension plans. Also explain why the amounts of these items can only be estimated.

(c)   Explain the terms "interest cost" and "actuarial gains and losses".

(d)   Calculate the defined benefit expense which should be shown in the company's statement of comprehensive income for the year to 31 March 2014. Explain why the amount of this expense is not equal to the £18.4m contributed by the company during the year.

(e)   Calculate the defined benefit asset or liability which should be shown in the company's statement of financial position at 31 March 2014. Reconcile this amount to the equivalent amount at 31 March 2013.

Chapter 15

Taxation in financial statements

Introduction

This chapter is concerned with the treatment of taxation in financial statements. The applicable standard is IAS12 *Income Taxes*, which sets out rules for the accounting treatment of "current tax" and "deferred tax". Both of these terms are defined in this chapter and the requirements of IAS12 are explained.

It is important to appreciate that IAS12 is solely concerned with accounting for taxation and is *not* concerned with the actual calculation of tax liabilities. The tax system differs widely between countries and it would be beyond the scope of international standards (and beyond the scope of this book) to try to explain how an entity's tax liability for an accounting period is calculated. IAS12 assumes throughout that the tax calculations have already been done and that the problem now is how to account for taxation in the financial statements of the entity concerned.

Despite its title, IAS12 deals with any taxes payable on the profits of an entity, no matter what those taxes might be called in different countries. For example, the corporation tax payable on the profits of UK companies falls within the scope of IAS12.

Objectives

By the end of this chapter, the reader should be able to:

- define the term "current tax" and account for current tax in accordance with the requirements of IAS12 *Income Taxes*
- define the term "temporary differences" and distinguish between taxable temporary differences and deductible temporary differences
- explain the meaning of the "tax base" of an asset or liability
- calculate the deferred tax assets and liabilities arising from deductible and taxable temporary differences
- account for deferred tax in accordance with the requirements of IAS12.

Current tax

IAS12 defines current tax as "*the amount of income taxes payable (recoverable) in respect of the taxable profit (tax loss) for a period*". As mentioned earlier, the term "income taxes" refers to any tax which is payable on an entity's profits, regardless of the name given to that tax in the country concerned. The main requirements of IAS12 with regard to current tax may be summarised as follows:

(a)   The amount of current tax for an accounting period should generally be recognised as an expense (or as income in the case of tax recoverable) and should be included in the calculation of profit or loss. IAS1 requires that the tax expense should be presented separately in the statement of comprehensive income (see Chapter 3). However:

   (i)   Any current tax that arises from an item which is recognised in "other comprehensive income" in the statement of comprehensive income should also be recognised in other comprehensive income. Examples of such items include:

   – revaluation surpluses arising in relation to property, plant and equipment or intangible assets (see Chapters 5 and 6)

   – certain foreign exchange differences (see Chapter 21).

   (ii)   Any current tax that arises from an item which is recognised directly in the statement of changes in equity should also be recognised in the statement of changes in equity. One example of such an item is an adjustment to the opening balance of retained earnings resulting from the retrospective application of an accounting policy or the correction of a prior period error (see Chapter 4).

(b)   Any current tax that remains unpaid at the end of the period should be recognised as a liability. If the amount already paid exceeds the amount due, the excess should be recognised as an asset. The benefit relating to a tax loss that can be carried back to recover current tax of a previous period should also be recognised as an asset.

   Current tax assets and liabilities should not be offset in the statement of financial position unless there is a legally enforceable right to set off the amounts concerned and the entity intends to do so. This would not apply if (for example) the entity owed tax in one country and was due to a refund of tax from another country.

(c)   Current tax should be measured using tax rates and tax laws "*that have been enacted or substantively enacted by the end of the reporting period*". Tax rates and tax laws which have been announced but not enacted by the end of the period can be treated as "substantively enacted" if their enactment is regarded as more or less a formality.

   Tax rates and laws announced after the end of the reporting period are dealt with as non-adjusting events in accordance with the requirements of IAS10 (see Chapter 12).

(d)   Any adjustments necessary so as to reflect underestimates or overestimates of current tax in previous periods should be included in the tax expense for the current period and then (if material) disclosed separately in the notes. This is in accordance with the requirements of IAS8 (see Chapter 4).

EXAMPLE 1

The following information relates to a company which prepares accounts to 30 June each year and is now completing its financial statements for the year to 30 June 2014:

(a) The company estimates that current tax for the year to 30 June 2014 is £750,000. This figure takes into account new tax rates which were announced in March 2014 and which are confidently expected to be enacted in August 2014. If the new tax rates were disregarded, the amount due would be £810,000.

(b) Payments on account totalling £390,000 have been made during the year to 30 June 2014 in relation to the current tax for the year.

(c) Current tax for the year to 30 June 2013 was overestimated by £30,000.

Calculate the amount of the current tax expense which should be shown in the statement of comprehensive income for the year to 30 June 2014 and the amount of the current tax liability which should be shown in the statement of financial position at that date.

Solution

The new tax rates can be regarded as substantively enacted, so that current tax for the year is £750,000. But the statement of comprehensive income should show a current tax expense of only £720,000, so as to adjust for the previous year's overestimate.

Payments on account of £390,000 reduce the current tax liability shown in the statement of financial position to £360,000 (£750,000 − £390,000).

Tax deducted at source and tax credits on dividends (UK)

From time to time, UK companies may receive certain forms of income net of UK income tax, although this is now rare. Similarly, UK companies may occasionally make certain payments net of income tax. In these circumstances, any income tax suffered by deduction at source is reclaimed from the tax authorities and any income tax withheld from payments is remitted to the tax authorities. The overall tax effect is nil and so there is no impact on the tax expense for the year. The company's financial statements should show the relevant income and payments *gross* (i.e. at the amount before income tax was deducted).

Another UK-specific tax point is concerned with dividends. An individual who receives a dividend is usually entitled to deduct a "tax credit" (equal to one-ninth of the amount of the dividend) from his or her tax liability in relation to that dividend. But a *company* which receives a dividend cannot make use of this tax credit. Therefore, tax credits on dividends are ignored when preparing a company's financial statements. Dividends received and paid are shown at the amounts actually received or paid, with no adjustment for tax credits.

Deferred tax

The amount of current tax payable by an entity for an accounting period depends upon the entity's taxable profit for that period. However, this taxable profit will often be different from the profit shown in the financial statements (the "accounting profit"). There are two main reasons for this discrepancy:

(a) **Permanent differences**. Some of the income shown in the financial statements may not be chargeable to tax and some of the expenses shown in the financial statements may not be deductible for tax purposes. In such cases, there will be a "permanent difference" between the accounting profit and the taxable profit (i.e. a difference that will not reverse itself in a future accounting period).

(b) **Temporary differences**. Some of the income or expenses shown in the financial statements for an accounting period may be dealt with for tax purposes in a different accounting period. In the UK, for example, the depreciation charges shown in the financial statements are disregarded for tax purposes and are replaced by standardised depreciation charges known as "capital allowances". Total depreciation charges will usually equal total capital allowances over the entire lifespan of the entity, but there may be a significant difference between depreciation and capital allowances in any one period. This is an example of a "temporary difference" (i.e. a difference that will reverse itself in a future accounting period).

Permanent differences cause no accounting problems and can be ignored. But temporary differences may lead to a significant distortion of the reported figures for profit after tax and so give a misleading impression of the entity's performance. For a company, this distortion also affects the important earnings per share ratio (see Chapter 23). The problem is illustrated by the following example.

EXAMPLE 2

A company with an issued share capital of 1,000,000 ordinary shares has the following results for the three years to 31 December 2014:

	2012	2013	2014
	£000	£000	£000
Profit before tax	800	800	800
Depreciation charged in the year	200	200	200
Depreciation for tax purposes	400	150	50

Assuming that there are no other permanent or temporary differences and that the rate of tax is 20% throughout, compute the company's profit after tax for each of the three years.

Also calculate the earnings per share ratio for each year. (This ratio is equal to the profit after tax divided by the number of issued ordinary shares).

Solution

The <u>tax expense</u> for each year is calculated as follows:

	2012 £000	2013 £000	2014 £000
Profit before tax	800	800	800
Add: Depreciation charged in the year	200	200	200
	1,000	1,000	1,000
Less: Depreciation for tax purposes	400	150	50
Taxable profit	600	850	950
Tax expense (20% of taxable profit)	120	170	190

The <u>profit after tax</u> calculation for each year is:

	2012	2013	2014
Profit before tax	800	800	800
Tax expense	120	170	190
Profit after tax	680	630	610
Earnings per share	68p	63p	61p

These figures give the impression that profit after tax and earnings per share are on a downward trend (which may deter investors) when in fact the company's profits have been identical in each of the three years. Total depreciation charges in the accounts and total depreciation charges for tax purposes are both £600,000 but temporary differences have caused the reported figures for profits after tax and earnings per share to be misleading.

Accounting for deferred tax

IAS12 solves the problem illustrated above by requiring entities to account for "deferred tax". The broad approach is as follows:

(a) In an accounting period in which temporary differences cause taxable profits to be lower than accounting profits, the tax expense which is shown in the statement of comprehensive income is increased by a transfer *to* a deferred tax account.

(b) In an accounting period in which temporary differences cause taxable profits to be higher than accounting profits, the tax expense which is shown in the statement of comprehensive income is reduced by a transfer *from* the deferred tax account.

IAS1 *Presentation of Financial Statements* (see Chapter 3) requires that the balance on the deferred tax account should be shown as a non-current liability (or asset) in the entity's statement of financial position.

EXAMPLE 3

Rework Example 2, showing the necessary transfers to and from the company's deferred tax account. As before, assume that the applicable rate of tax is 20% in all years.

Solution

	2012 £000		2013 £000		2014 £000	
Profit before tax		800		800		800
Tax expense:						
Current tax	120		170		190	
Deferred tax	40	160	(10)	160	(30)	160
Profit after tax		640		640		640
Earnings per share		64p		64p		64p

Notes:

(i)   In 2012, taxable profits are £200,000 lower than accounting profits and this is caused by a temporary difference. Therefore £40,000 (20% x £200,000) is transferred to a deferred tax account and is shown as part of the tax expense for the year.

(ii)   In 2013, taxable profits are £50,000 higher than accounting profits and this is caused by the reversal of a temporary difference. So £10,000 (20% x £50,000) is transferred back from the deferred tax account, reducing the tax expense for the year.

(iii) In 2014, taxable profits are £150,000 higher than accounting profits and this is caused by the reversal of a temporary difference. So £30,000 (20% x £150,000) is transferred back from the deferred tax account, again reducing the tax expense for the year.

By the end of 2014, the temporary difference which occurred in 2012 has been totally reversed, and so the balance on the deferred tax account is £nil. The overall effect over the three years is to show profit after tax at a constant £640,000 and earnings per share at a constant 64p per share. This is a much fairer presentation of the company's results than the presentation which was given in Example 2 (without a deferred tax account).

The tax base concept

The approach adopted by IAS12 in relation to deferred tax requires that the "tax base" of each asset and liability at the end of the reporting period should be calculated and then compared with its "carrying amount" (i.e. the amount at which the item is shown in the financial statements). If the tax base of an asset or liability is not the same as its carrying amount, a temporary difference exists and a deferred tax adjustment is required.

IAS12 defines the tax base of an asset or liability as "*the amount attributed to that asset or liability for tax purposes*". In particular:

(a) The tax base of an asset is "*the amount that will be deductible for tax purposes against any taxable economic benefits that will flow to an entity when it recovers the carrying amount of the asset. If those economic benefits will not be taxable, the tax base of the asset is equal to its carrying amount.*".

(b) The tax base of a liability is "*its carrying amount, less any amount that will be deductible for tax purposes in respect of that liability in future periods*".

Furthermore, IAS12 defines temporary differences as "*differences between the carrying amount of an asset or liability in the statement of financial position and its tax base*". The definition continues by stating that:

(a) Taxable temporary differences are temporary differences "*that will result in taxable amounts in determining taxable profit ... of future periods when the carrying amount of the asset or liability is recovered or settled*". Taxable temporary differences result in deferred tax liabilities.

(b) Deductible temporary differences are temporary differences "*that will result in amounts that are deductible in determining taxable profit ... of future periods when the carrying amount of the asset or liability is recovered or settled*". Deductible temporary differences result in deferred tax assets.

These definitions (which may seem very complex at first) are explained below.

The tax base of an asset

As the *Conceptual Framework* definition of an asset makes clear (see Chapter 2) entities hold assets so as to generate future economic benefits. These benefits might arise through:

(a) selling the asset (e.g. inventories)

(b) using the asset (e.g. property, plant and equipment)

(c) realising the asset (e.g. trade receivables).

In each case, the benefits obtained might or might not be taxable. If they are, the entity will usually expect the tax system to recognise that an asset has been sacrificed in order to earn those benefits and so allow a deduction when calculating the tax due. If the deduction allowed is the same as the carrying amount of the asset concerned, the tax system and the accounting system are in harmony and there is no deferred tax problem. But if the deduction allowed is not the same as the carrying amount of the asset, the difference will give rise to a deferred tax adjustment. This is why IAS12 defines the tax base of an asset in terms of the amount of the deduction that will be allowed for tax purposes against the economic benefits generated by that asset.

If the benefits obtained from an asset are not taxable, there is no deferred tax problem. In these circumstances, the tax base of the asset is regarded as being the same as its carrying amount, so that there is no need for a deferred tax adjustment.

EXAMPLE 4

Consider each of the following assets which appear in a company's statement of financial position as at 31 March 2014.

(a)   A machine which cost £40,000 is shown at its written down value of £16,000. For tax purposes, its written down value is £11,250. The machine's residual value at the end of its useful life is expected to be £nil.

(b)   Trade receivables are shown at £75,000. The revenue to which these relate was included in taxable profit for the year to 31 March 2014.

(c)   Interest receivable is shown at £3,000. This interest has been included in accounting profit but will not be taxed until it is actually received. It will then be fully taxable.

For each of these assets:

(i)   Compute the tax base of the asset and determine whether a temporary difference exists with respect to it. If so, state whether this is a taxable temporary difference or a deductible temporary difference.

(ii)   Assuming a tax rate of 30%, calculate the amount of the deferred tax liability or asset which should be shown in the statement of financial position in relation to the asset.

Solution

This solution relies heavily on the IAS12 definitions given above and should be read with those definitions firmly in mind.

(a)   (i)   Use of the machine in future periods will generate taxable revenue. Deductions totalling £11,250 will be allowed against that revenue for tax purposes, so the tax base of the machine is £11,250. The carrying amount is £16,000 and this is the amount that will be deductible when computing accounting profits in future periods as the machine is used. Since only £11,250 will be deducted for tax purposes, there is a taxable temporary difference of £4,750.

      (ii)   The deferred tax liability is £1,425 (30% x £4,750).

(b)   When the receivables are realised, the amount received will not be taxable, so the tax base of the receivables is the same as their carrying amount (i.e. £75,000). There is no temporary difference and so there are no deferred tax implications.

(c)   (i)   When the interest is received, taxable revenue of £3,000 will occur. There will be no deduction from this revenue for tax purposes so the tax base is £nil. There is a taxable temporary difference of £3,000.

      (ii)   The deferred tax liability is £900 (30% x £3,000).

The tax base of a liability

The settlement of a liability has no effect on accounting profit and usually has no effect on taxable profit either, so liabilities tend not to cause deferred tax problems. However, the settlement of a liability might in some cases trigger a deduction from taxable profits. In these circumstances, the amount of the deduction will give rise to a deferred tax adjustment. This is why IAS12 defines the tax base of a liability in terms of the amount of the deduction that will be allowed for tax purposes when the liability is settled.

EXAMPLE 5

Consider each of the following liabilities which appear in a company's statement of financial position as at 31 March 2014.

(a) Current liabilities include accrued expenses of £5,000. These expenses have already been deducted when computing both accounting profit and taxable profit.

(b) Current liabilities include further accrued expenses of £8,000. These expenses have been deducted when computing accounting profit but will not be deducted for tax purposes until they are actually paid.

For each of these liabilities:

(i) Compute the tax base of the liability and determine whether a temporary difference exists with respect to it. If so, state whether this is a taxable temporary difference or a deductible temporary difference.

(ii) Assuming a tax rate of 30%, calculate the amount of the deferred tax liability or asset which should be shown in the statement of financial position in relation to the liability.

Solution

Once again, this solution relies heavily on the IAS12 definitions given above and should be read with those definitions firmly in mind.

(a) When these accrued expenses are paid, the payment will not be deductible for tax purposes. Therefore their tax base is the same as their carrying amount (i.e. £5,000). There is no temporary difference and so there are no deferred tax implications.

(b) (i) When these accrued expenses are paid, the payment will be deductible for tax purposes. Therefore their tax base is £nil (£8,000 − £8,000) and there is a deductible temporary difference of £8,000.

    (ii) The deferred tax asset is £2,400 (30% x £8,000).

EXAMPLE 6

Here is a reminder of the basic data given in Example 2/3 earlier in this chapter:

A company with an issued share capital of 1,000,000 ordinary shares has the following results for the three years to 31 December 2014:

	2012	2013	2014
	£000	£000	£000
Profit before tax	800	800	800
Depreciation charged in the year	200	200	200
Depreciation for tax purposes	400	150	50

The applicable tax rate is 20% throughout.

Now use the tax base concept to rework this example and to calculate the necessary transfers to and from the company's deferred tax account. Assume that the depreciation charges relate to an asset acquired for £600,000 on 1 January 2012 and depreciated on the straight-line basis over three years, with an estimated residual value of £nil.

Solution

At the end of 2012, the asset has a carrying value of £400,000 but its tax base is only £200,000 (cost £600,000 – depreciation of £400,000 for tax purposes). There is a taxable temporary difference of £200,000, giving rise to a deferred tax liability of £40,000 (20% x £200,000). Setting up this liability increases the tax expense for 2012 by £40,000.

At the end of 2013, the asset's carrying value is £200,000 but its tax base is only £50,000 (cost £600,000 – depreciation of £550,000 for tax purposes). There is a taxable temporary difference of £150,000, giving rise to a deferred tax liability of £30,000 (20% x £150,000). This is £10,000 less than the liability which was set up in 2012, so £10,000 must be transferred from the deferred tax account, reducing the tax expense for 2013 by £10,000.

At the end of 2014, the asset's carrying value and tax base are both £nil. There is no temporary difference so the £30,000 deferred tax liability from 2013 is no longer required. Transferring this £30,000 back from the deferred tax account reduces the tax expense for 2014 by £30,000.

Note:
As expected, the results obtained by using the tax base concept are identical to those which were obtained originally in the solution to Example 3.

Unused tax losses

The tax law of the country in which an entity resides may allow trading and other losses to be carried forward and deducted from future taxable profits, so reducing the tax due on those profits. In these circumstances, IAS12 states that a deferred tax asset should be recognised to the extent that it is probable that future taxable profits will be available against which the losses can be utilised.

IAS12 requirements with regard to deferred tax

IAS12 makes a number of detailed requirements with regard to deferred tax. Broadly, the main points are as follows:

(a) A deferred tax liability must be recognised for all taxable temporary differences.

(b) A deferred tax asset must be recognised for all deductible temporary differences to the extent that it is probable that taxable profits will be available in the future against which these deductible temporary differences can be utilised.

(c) The carrying amount of deferred tax assets must be reviewed at the end of each reporting period and reduced to the extent that it is no longer probable that taxable profits will arise against which they can be utilised.

(d) A deferred tax asset or liability must be measured at the tax rates that are expected to apply to the period in which the asset is realised or the liability is settled. These tax rates should be based upon tax rates and laws that have been enacted or substantively enacted by the end of the reporting period (see earlier in this chapter).

(e) Deferred tax assets and liabilities must not be discounted, even though they might not be realised or settled for many years. IAS12 regards it as inappropriate to require or permit discounting because of the uncertain timing of the reversal of each temporary difference.

(f) Transfers to or from the deferred tax account should generally be recognised in the calculation of profit or loss. However, a deferred tax transfer that arises from an item which is recognised in other comprehensive income or directly in equity should also be recognised in other comprehensive income or directly in equity.

(g) Deferred tax assets and liabilities should not be offset in the statement of financial position unless the entity has a legally enforceable right to do so.

Disclosure requirements

The disclosure requirements of IAS12 are very extensive. A brief summary of the main disclosures that must be made in the notes to the financial statements is as follows:

(a) The tax expense shown in the calculation of profit or loss for the accounting period must be analysed into its main components. These may include:

   (i) the current tax expense (or income) for the period

   (ii) any adjustments relating to underestimates or overestimates of current tax in previous accounting periods

   (iii) the amount of any transfers to or from the deferred tax account relating to the origination or reversal of temporary differences.

(b) The following must also be disclosed separately:

(i) the amounts of current and deferred tax relating to items that are recognised in other comprehensive income or directly in equity

(ii) an explanation of the relationship between the accounting profit for the period and the tax expense for the period

(iii) for each type of temporary difference, the amount of the deferred tax asset or liability recognised in the statement of financial position and the amount of the deferred tax expense or income recognised in the period.

Summary

▸ Current tax is the amount of tax payable or recoverable in respect of the taxable profit or loss for an accounting period. Current tax is generally shown as an expense in the statement of comprehensive income. Any amount which remains unpaid at the end of the reporting period is shown as a liability in the statement of financial position.

▸ The current tax expense may be adjusted so as to reflect any underestimates or overestimates of current tax in previous periods.

▸ A temporary difference arises if an item of income or expense is recognised in the financial statements in one accounting period but is dealt with for tax purposes in a different period. Temporary differences would distort the reported figures for profit after tax and earnings per share if deferred tax were not taken into account.

▸ In general, transfers to the deferred tax account are made in periods in which taxable profits are lower than accounting profits. Transfers from the deferred tax account are made in periods in which taxable profits exceed accounting profits.

▸ IAS12 deals with deferred tax by comparing the tax base of each asset and liability at the end of the reporting period with its carrying amount. The tax base of an item is the amount attributed to that item for tax purposes.

▸ Temporary differences arise if the tax base of an asset or liability is different from its carrying amount. Taxable temporary differences result in deferred tax liabilities. Deductible taxable differences result in deferred tax assets.

▸ In general, IAS12 requires that deferred tax liabilities must be recognised for all taxable temporary differences. Deferred tax assets must be recognised for deductible temporary differences if it is probable that they will be utilised in the future.

▸ The tax laws and rates used when accounting for taxation should be those which have been enacted or substantively enacted by the end of the reporting period.

▸ IAS12 makes extensive disclosure requirements. These include an analysis of the tax expense for the accounting period and details of deferred tax assets and liabilities.

Exercises

15.1   Otlay Ltd prepares accounts to 31 July each year. The company's financial statements for the year to 31 July 2013 showed a liability for current tax of £120,000. This was an estimate of the current tax due for the year to 31 July 2013. The following information is also available:

(a)   The current tax due for the year to 31 July 2013 was finally agreed with the tax authorities to be £127,000 and this sum was paid on 1 May 2014.

(b)   On 15 June 2014, the company received a dividend of £9,000. This dividend had an attached tax credit of £1,000 but Otlay Ltd can make no use of this tax credit.

(c)   The company estimates the amount of current tax due for the year to 31 July 2014 to be £140,000.

Prepare a current tax ledger account for the year to 31 July 2014, showing the amount of the current tax expense for that year and the amount of the current tax liability as at the end of the year.

15.2   (a)   Distinguish between current tax and deferred tax.

(b)   Distinguish between permanent differences and temporary differences.

(c)   Explain how temporary differences between accounting profits and taxable profits would affect the tax expense shown in an entity's financial statements unless deferred tax were taken into account.

15.3   The pre-tax profits of Radfern Ltd for the last three years (as reported in its financial statements) have been as follows:

	£
year to 31 August 2012	125,000
year to 31 August 2013	130,000
year to 31 August 2014	135,000

In the year to 31 August 2012, there was a taxable temporary difference of £50,000 between accounting profits and taxable profits. £10,000 of this difference was reversed in the year to 31 August 2013 and the remaining £40,000 was reversed in the year to 31 August 2014.

(a)   Assuming a tax rate of 20% throughout, demonstrate that if the company did not account for deferred tax, its profits after tax would appear to be on a downward trend, even though pre-tax profits are rising and tax rates have remained unchanged.

(b)   Show the transfers that should be made to or from the deferred tax account in each year.

15.4   Explain the concept of the "tax base" of an asset or liability. Explain how this concept helps to identify situations in which deferred tax adjustments are required.

15.5 Consider each of the following assets and liabilities which appear in a company's statement of financial position at 30 April 2014:

(a) A motor lorry which cost £100,000 is shown at its written down value of £20,000. For tax purposes, its written down value is £30,000.

(b) A loan payable is shown at £60,000. The repayment of the loan will have no tax consequences.

(c) An amount receivable is shown at £45,000. Of this amount, £25,000 has already been taxed but the remaining £20,000 will be taxed in the accounting period in which it is received. The whole £45,000 has already been included in accounting profit.

(d) An amount payable is shown at £3,000. This relates to an expense which has already been deducted when computing accounting profit but which will not be deducted for tax purposes until it is paid.

Compute the tax base of each of these assets and liabilities and identify any taxable or deductible temporary differences.

15.6 The draft statement of comprehensive income of Harrington, a public company, for the year to 31 March 2014 shows an income tax expense of £55,000. The draft statement of financial position shows a non-current liability of £280,000 for deferred tax but does not show a current tax liability.

Tax on the profit for the year to 31 March 2014 is estimated at £260,000. The figure in the draft statement of comprehensive income is the underestimate for the year to 31 March 2013. The carrying amount of Harrington's net assets at 31 March 2014 is £1.4m more than their tax base on that date. The tax rate is 25%.

Required:

Restate the figures which should appear in relation to taxation in the company's financial statements for the year to 31 March 2014.   *(ACCA)*

*15.7   Petersford plc prepares accounts to 31 December each year. On 1 January 2010, the company acquired a non-current asset at a cost of £256,000 and decided to depreciate this asset on the straight-line basis over a five-year period, assuming a residual value of £nil. Depreciation allowed for tax purposes with regard to this asset in the first five years of ownership are as follows:

	£
year to 31 December 2010	102,400
year to 31 December 2011	38,400
year to 31 December 2012	28,800
year to 31 December 2013	21,600
year to 31 December 2014	16,200

The company's pre-tax profit (after charging depreciation) was £500,000 in the year to 31 December 2010 and remained at a consistent £500,000 per annum for each of the next four years.

There are no other non-current assets and there are no differences between taxable profit and accounting profit other than those relating to depreciation. A tax rate of 20% applies throughout.

(a)   Without making use of the "tax base" concept, show the necessary transfers to and from the deferred tax account for each of the five years to 31 December 2014. Also calculate and explain the closing balance on this account at 31 December 2014.

(b)   Re-work this exercise using the tax base concept.

Chapter 16

Statement of cash flows

Introduction

It has often been said that cash is the "lifeblood" of a business. This is very true. Without cash, a business cannot pay its employees or its suppliers and will soon fail. Therefore a financial statement which focuses on the flows of cash in and out of a business (and draws attention to any cash problems) serves a useful purpose. This is the function of a statement of cash flows and IAS7 *Statement of Cash Flows* requires that all entities which comply with international standards should produce such a statement.

It might be thought that a profitable business would never run out of cash, but this is not the case. A business might report a healthy profit in its financial statements and yet suffer severe cash problems. Some of the reasons for this apparent paradox are as follows:

(a) Profits are computed on the accruals basis. Therefore, revenue shown in the statement of comprehensive income might not be actually received for a considerable period of time, especially if the business offers lengthy credit to its customers.

(b) The purchase of non-current assets has an immediate cash impact but filters through to the statement of comprehensive income only gradually, in the form of depreciation.

(c) A business which builds up large inventories (perhaps in the hope of attracting more customers) usually has to pay for those inventories fairly quickly, but their cost has no impact on reported profit until they are sold at some time in the future.

(d) The repayment of a loan takes cash out of the business but has no direct effect on profit. The same applies to the payment of a dividend.

For reasons such as these, the size of an entity's profit is an unreliable indicator of its cash situation. A statement of cash flows is needed and the purpose of this chapter is to explain how this statement should be prepared in accordance with the requirements of IAS7.

Objectives

By the end of this chapter, the reader should be able to:

• explain the purpose of a statement of cash flows
• define the terms "cash" and "cash equivalents"

- distinguish between operating activities, investing activities and financing activities
- use both the direct method and the indirect method for reporting cash flows from operating activities
- prepare a statement of cash flows in accordance with the requirements of IAS7
- prepare a reconciliation between the amounts of cash and cash equivalents shown in the statement of cash flows and the equivalent items reported in the statement of financial position.

Cash and cash equivalents

The main objective of IAS7 is "*to require the provision of information about the historical changes in cash and cash equivalents of an entity by means of a statement of cash flows which classifies cash flows during the period from operating, investing and financing activities*". In order to understand this objective, it is necessary to examine some key definitions given in IAS7. Two of the most important definitions are as follows:

(a) Cash comprises "*cash on hand and demand deposits*".

(b) Cash equivalents are "*short-term, highly liquid investments that are readily convertible to known amounts of cash and ... are subject to an insignificant risk of changes in value*". An investment will usually not qualify as a cash equivalent unless it has a maturity date which is no more than three months after the date of acquisition. Equity investments are generally excluded from the definition but redeemable preference shares with a specified redemption date in the near future might qualify.

IAS7 takes the view that cash equivalents are virtually indistinguishable from cash itself and should therefore be treated as cash rather than as investments. The significance of this is that acquisitions and disposals of cash equivalents are not treated as investing activities but simply as movements between one component of cash and another. Such movements are not inflows or outflows of cash and so do not appear in a statement of cash flows.

Bank overdrafts

In some countries (including the UK) bank overdrafts are generally repayable on demand and are an integral part of an entity's cash management. In these circumstances, bank overdrafts are regarded as a component of the entity's cash and cash equivalents. This means, of course, that the total of cash and cash equivalents could be negative.

Bank loans which are not repayable on demand are not a component of cash and cash equivalents. Such loans are treated as part of the entity's financing activities (see below).

Classification of cash flows by activity

IAS7 requires that the statement of cash flows should report cash flows "*classified by operating, investing and financing activities*". The aim of this classification is to provide users with information that helps them to assess the impact of each of these activities on the entity's cash and cash equivalents. The three classes of activity are explained below.

Operating activities

Operating activities are defined by IAS7 as "*the principal revenue-producing activities of the entity...*". Cash inflows and outflows arising from operating activities include:

(a) cash receipts from the sale of goods and services

(b) cash receipts from royalties, fees, commissions and other revenue

(c) cash payments to suppliers for goods and services

(d) cash payments to and on behalf of employees

(e) cash payments or cash refunds of income taxes (see Chapter 15) unless specifically identified with investing or financing activities.

In general, these items result from transactions or other events that are reported in the statement of comprehensive income. However, the amounts which appear in that statement are calculated on the accruals basis, whereas the statement of cash flows simply shows the actual receipts (inflows) and payments (outflows) which have occurred during the period.

Investing activities

Investing activities are defined by IAS7 as "*the acquisition and disposal of long-term assets and other investments not included in cash equivalents*". It is important to note that this classification covers not only "investing" in the usual sense, but also the acquisition and disposal of long-term assets such as property, plant and equipment. Cash inflows and outflows arising from investing activities include:

(a) cash payments to acquire property, plant and equipment, intangible assets and other long-term assets

(b) cash receipts from the sale of property, plant and equipment, intangible assets and other long-term assets

(c) cash payments to acquire equity (e.g. shares) or debt instruments (e.g. loan stocks or debentures) of other entities

(d) cash receipts from the sale of equity or debt instruments of other entities

(e) cash advances and loans made to other parties

(f) cash receipts from the repayment of advances and loans made to other parties.

Financing activities

Financing activities are defined by IAS7 as *"activities that result in changes in the size and composition of the contributed equity and borrowings of the entity"*. Cash inflows and outflows arising from financing activities include:

(a) cash proceeds from issuing shares

(b) cash payments to owners to acquire or redeem the entity's own shares

(c) cash proceeds from issuing debentures, loans and other borrowings

(d) cash repayments of amounts borrowed

(e) cash payments by a lessee for the reduction of the outstanding liability relating to a finance lease (see Chapter 9).

Interest, dividends and taxes

IAS7 requires that cash flows arising from interest received, dividends received, interest paid and dividends paid should be disclosed separately in the statement of cash flows. However, there is no consensus as to the classification of these items. Interest received and dividends received are usually classified as cash inflows arising from investing activities but the correct treatment of interest paid and dividends paid is less clear. For instance:

(a) Interest paid on a loan obtained for operating purposes might be classified under operating activities. Alternatively, it could be argued that interest paid should be classified under financing activities since it is a cost of obtaining finance.

(b) Dividends paid might be classified under operating activities so that users may determine an entity's ability to pay dividends out of operating cash flows. Alternatively, it could be argued that dividends paid are a cost of obtaining financial resources and so should be classified under financing activities.

IAS7 does not prescribe any particular classification for these items but does require that each of them should be classified in a consistent manner from period to period.

Cash inflows and outflows arising from income taxes (see Chapter 15) must be disclosed separately and should be classified under operating activities unless specifically associated with investing or financing activities.

Reporting cash flows from operating activities

A statement of cash flows begins by reporting the cash flows arising from the entity's operating activities. These cash flows may be reported using either the *direct* method or the *indirect* method:

(a) **Direct method**. If the direct method is used, major classes of receipts and payments arising from operating activities are disclosed individually and are then aggregated to give the total amount of cash generated from operations. IAS7 does not specify what these "major classes" should be and so the entity should choose a classification which is applicable to its business and relevant to the needs of its users. A statement of cash flows prepared using the direct method might typically disclose:

   (i)   cash receipts from customers

   (ii) cash paid to suppliers of goods and services

   (iii) cash paid to employees.

   These figures could be obtained by conducting an analysis of the entity's cashbook for the period. Alternatively, if the information provided in the financial statements is sufficiently detailed, it might be possible to derive the required figures without conducting such an analysis. For instance, the amount of cash received from customers during the period could be derived by taking the sales figure shown in the statement of comprehensive income and then making an adjustment for opening and closing trade receivables.

(b) **Indirect method**. The indirect method takes as its starting point the profit or loss for the period (before tax) and then makes a number of adjustments to this profit or loss so as to calculate the total amount of cash generated from operations. The main adjustments are as follows:

   (i)   Non-cash expenses which have been deducted when calculating profit or loss but have not involved an outflow of cash (e.g. depreciation) are added back.

   (ii) Non-cash income which has been included in the calculation of profit or loss but has not involved an inflow of cash (e.g. a decrease in the allowance for doubtful trade receivables) is subtracted.

   (iii) Increases or decreases in the following items between the beginning and end of the accounting period are adjusted for as indicated:

	Increases	*Decreases*
Inventories	Subtract	Add
Trade receivables and prepaid expenses	Subtract	Add
Trade payables and accrued expenses	Add	Subtract

   The effect of these adjustments is to change the basis of accounting from the usual accruals basis to a cash basis. For instance, an increase in trade payables causes the purchases figure shown in the statement of comprehensive income to be higher than the amount actually paid to suppliers. Adding this increase back onto the profit for the period shows what the profit would have been if purchases had been accounted for on a cash basis.

A simple way of remembering the correct adjustment for each of the increases and decreases listed above is to consider what would happen if the increase or decrease occurred and nothing else changed in the statement of financial position (other than cash). For instance, a decrease in trade receivables would generate extra cash as customers paid their debts. This would have a beneficial effect on cash and so a decrease in trade receivables should be added onto profit when calculating the total amount of cash generated from operations.

(iv) Any items of income or expense which have been included in the calculation of profit or loss before tax but which represent cash flows from either investing or financing activities are subtracted (income) or added back (expenses). Interest payable is also added back.

Both of these methods are illustrated below. IAS7 encourages use of the direct method, as this provides more detailed information than the indirect method. However, the indirect method is permitted by IAS7 and is used extensively in practice.

Each of the two methods will, of course, give the same "bottom line" figure for the total amount of cash generated by operations during an accounting period. Interest paid and taxes paid are then usually deducted (see earlier in this chapter) to give the final figure for the entity's net cash flow from operating activities.

EXAMPLE

A company's statement of comprehensive income for the year to 31 March 2014 is shown below. The company's statement of financial position as at that date (with comparative figures for 2013) is also shown.

Statement of comprehensive income
Year to 31 March 2014

	£000
Sales	752
Cost of sales	(387)
Gross profit	365
Administrative and selling expenses	(225)
Interest payable	(18)
Dividends received	22
Profit before tax	144
Taxation	(33)
Profit after tax	111

Note: Other comprehensive income was £nil.

Statement of financial position at 31 March 2014

		2014 £000		2013 £000
Assets				
Non-current assets				
Property, plant and equipment		488		470
Investments		250		250
		738		720
Current assets				
Inventories	231		212	
Trade receivables	140		157	
Cash at bank	15	386	-	369
		1,124		1,089
Equity				
Share capital		220		200
Share premium account		70		60
Retained earnings		526		445
		816		705
Liabilities				
Non-current liabilities				
Long-term loans		90		130
Current liabilities				
Trade payables	182		176	
Accrued interest payable	3		-	
Taxation	33		55	
Bank overdraft	-	218	23	254
		1,124		1,089

The following information is also available:

(a) Administrative and selling expenses include employee salaries of £148,000 and equipment depreciation of £70,000.

(b) There were no non-current asset disposals during the year to 31 March 2014.

(c) A dividend of £30,000 was paid in June 2013.

Required:

Prepare a statement of cash flows for the year to 31 March 2014 using the direct method. Also demonstrate that use of the indirect method would give the same figure for cash generated from operations as is given by the direct method.

Solution

Statement of cash flows for the year to 31 March 2014

	£000	£000
Cash flows from operating activities		
Cash receipts from customers	769	
Cash paid to suppliers of goods and services	(407)	
Cash paid to employees	(148)	
Cash generated from operations		214
Interest paid	(15)	
Taxation paid	(55)	(70)
Net cash inflow from operating activities		144
Cash flows from investing activities		
Acquisition of property, plant and equipment	(88)	
Dividends received	22	
Net cash outflow from investing activities		(66)
Cash flows from financing activities		
Proceeds from issue of share capital	30	
Repayment of long-term borrowings	(40)	
Dividends paid	(30)	
Net cash outflow from financing activities		(40)
Net increase in cash and cash equivalents		38
Cash and cash equivalents at 1 April 2013		(23)
Cash and cash equivalents at 31 March 2014		15

Note:

Interest paid could have been classified under financing activities. Dividends paid could have been classified under operating activities.

Workings:

(a) Cash receipts from customers are equal to the sales figure adjusted for opening and closing trade receivables i.e. £752,000 + £157,000 − £140,000 = £769,000.

(b) Purchases are equal to cost of sales adjusted for opening and closing inventories i.e. £387,000 − £212,000 + £231,000 = £406,000.

(c) Cash paid to suppliers is equal to purchases plus administrative and selling expenses (excluding salaries and depreciation) adjusted for opening and closing trade payables i.e. £406,000 + £225,000 − £148,000 − £70,000 + £176,000 − £182,000 = £407,000.

(d) Interest paid is equal to the interest payable for the year, adjusted for the closing accrual i.e. £18,000 − £3,000 = £15,000.

(e) Tax paid is equal to the tax charge for the year adjusted for the opening and closing tax liability i.e. £33,000 + £55,000 – £33,000 = £55,000. In other words, the company has paid the previous year's tax but the current year's tax remains unpaid.

(f) PPE has increased by £18,000 despite depreciation of £70,000 in the year. Therefore acquisitions of PPE must have been £88,000.

(g) Share capital and share premium together have increased by £30,000, so £30,000 must have been raised by a new share issue.

(h) Long-term loans have decreased by £40,000, so there must have been a repayment of £40,000 during the year.

Indirect method:

The indirect method would also have given £214,000 as the figure for cash generated from operations, as follows:

	£000
Cash flows from operating activities	
Profit before taxation	144
Depreciation	70
Interest payable	18
Dividends received	(22)
Increase in inventories (£231,000 – £212,000)	(19)
Decrease in trade receivables (£140,000 – £157,000)	17
Increase in trade payables (£182,000 – £176,000)	6
Cash generated from operations	214

From this point onwards, the statement of cash flows would then have continued exactly as shown above.

Disclosures

IAS7 requires entities to disclose the components of their cash and cash equivalents and to present a reconciliation of these amounts in the statement of cash flows with the equivalent items reported in the statement of financial position. IAS7 also encourages (but does not require) the disclosure of additional information that could be relevant to users in understanding the entity's financial position and liquidity. Such information might include:

(a) the amount of any undrawn borrowing facilities that may be available to finance future operating activities and to settle capital commitments

(b) an analysis of the cash flows arising from the operating, investing and financing activities of each reportable segment, where "reportable segments" are defined in accordance with the requirements of IFRS8 *Operating Segments* (see Chapter 24).

Summary

▸ Profit is not a reliable indicator of an entity's cash situation. A statement of cash flows analyses cash inflows and outflows during an accounting period and can be used to assess the entity's ability to generate the cash it needs.

▸ IAS7 defines "cash" as cash on hand and demand deposits. Bank overdrafts are usually treated as negative cash. Cash equivalents are highly liquid short-term investments that may be treated as if they were cash.

▸ A statement of cash flows classifies cash flows by operating, investing and financing activities.

▸ Operating activities comprise an entity's main revenue-producing activities. Investing activities consist mainly of the acquisition and disposal of long-term assets. Financing activities include share issues, share redemption, borrowings and loan repayments.

▸ Interest paid and dividends paid can each be classified under operating activities or financing activities. The classification adopted should be applied consistently from one accounting period to another.

▸ The amount of cash generated from operations can be reported using either the direct method or the indirect method.

▸ The direct method discloses major classes of cash receipts and payments individually. These classes may include cash receipts from customers, cash paid to suppliers and cash paid to employees.

▸ The indirect method makes a number of adjustments to the entity's pre-tax profit so as to calculate the total cash generated from operations. These adjustments remove non-cash income and expenses and take account of increases or decreases in items such as inventories, trade receivables and trade payables.

▸ IAS7 requires that the components of an entity's total cash and cash equivalents are disclosed. The amounts in the statement of cash flows should be reconciled to the equivalent items in the statement of financial position.

Exercises

16.1 Explain each of the following terms which are defined in international standard IAS7:

(a) cash   (b) cash equivalents

(c) operating activities   (d) investing activities

(e) financing activities.

16.2 (a) Distinguish between the direct method and the indirect method of calculating the amount of cash generated from an entity's operations.

(b) List the main steps in the accounting work required if the indirect method is used.

16.3 Explain the effect (if any) of each of the following transactions on an entity's profit or loss and on its cash flows:

(a) the purchase of new equipment which is then depreciated over its useful life

(b) the payment of a supplier's invoice

(c) accounting for an accrued expense at the end of an accounting period

(d) the payment of a dividend

(e) the purchase of inventory for cash

(f) investing spare cash in a high-interest bank account, repayable at 7 days' notice.

16.4 The summarised statement of comprehensive income of Schap Ltd for the year to 30 June 2014 is shown below, together with the company's statement of financial position at that date (with comparatives for the previous year).

Statement of comprehensive income for the year to 30 June 2014

	£
Operating profit	170,200
Investment income	7,100
Interest payable	(6,120)
Profit before taxation	171,180
Taxation	37,870
Profit for the year	133,310

Note: Other comprehensive income was £nil.

Statement of financial position at 30 June 2014

	2014 £	2014 £	2013 £	2013 £
Assets				
Non-current assets				
Property, plant and equ't at cost	369,300		210,000	
Less: Accumulated depreciation	151,650	217,650	107,340	102,660
Investments at cost		120,000		120,000
		337,650		222,660
Current assets				
Inventories	86,220		97,430	
Trade receivables	82,610		58,100	
Prepaid expenses	7,200	176,030	7,000	162,530
		513,680		385,190
Equity				
Ordinary share capital		120,000		100,000
Retained earnings		195,850		147,540
		315,850		247,540
Liabilities				
Non-current liabilities				
Debenture loans		75,000		50,000
Current liabilities				
Trade payables	40,920		44,310	
Accrued expenses	9,130		8,250	
Taxation	37,870		32,300	
Bank overdraft	34,910	122,830	2,790	87,650
		513,680		385,190

Notes:

(i) There were no disposals of non-current assets during the year to 30 June 2014.

(ii) A dividend of £85,000 was paid during the year.

Required:

(a) Prepare a statement of cash flows for the year to 30 June 2014 in accordance with the requirements of IAS7 (using the indirect method).

(b) Explain why the information provided in the statement of comprehensive income and in the statements of financial position is insufficient to allow use of the direct method in this case.

(c) Comment briefly on the significance of the information provided by the company's statement of cash flows.

16.5 An extract from the statement of comprehensive income of Triste Ltd for the year to 31 May 2014 is shown below, together with the company's statement of financial position at that date (with comparatives for the previous year).

Statement of comprehensive income (extract) for the year to 31 May 2014

	£
Profit before taxation	205,600
Taxation	46,980
Profit for the year	158,620

Statement of financial position at 31 May 2014

	2014		**2013**	
	£	£	£	£
Assets				
Non-current assets				
Property, plant and equ't at cost	285,000		183,000	
Less: Accumulated depreciation	151,650	133,350	95,160	87,840
Investments at cost		12,000		10,000
		145,350		97,840
Current assets				
Inventories	171,220		133,330	
Trade receivables and prepayments	121,630		86,500	
Cash at bank	710		-	
Treasury bills	5,000	298,560	-	219,830
		443,910		317,670
Equity				
Ordinary share capital		100,000		100,000
Preference share capital		50,000		50,000
Retained earnings		128,610		39,990
		278,610		189,990
Liabilities				
Non-current liabilities				
11% Loan stock		30,000		-
Current liabilities				
Trade payables and accruals	89,370		61,530	
Taxation	45,930		42,660	
Bank overdraft	-	135,300	23,490	127,680
		443,910		317,670

Notes:

(i) The 11% loan stock was issued on 1 December 2013. The first half-year's interest was paid on 31 May 2014. Bank interest paid during the year was £1,320.

(ii) Dividends received during the year were £930. Dividends totalling £70,000 were paid during the year.

(iii) Plant which had cost £22,000 was sold in March 2014 for £7,000. The accumulated depreciation on this plant at the time of disposal was £16,230. No investments were sold during the year.

(iv) The Treasury bills rank as cash equivalents.

Required:

(a) Prepare a statement of cash flows for the year to 31 May 2014 in accordance with the requirements of IAS7 (using the indirect method).

(b) Reconcile the total cash and cash equivalents shown by the statement of cash flows to the equivalent figures shown in the opening and closing statements of financial position.

16.6 The statement of financial position of Urbax plc at 31 July 2014 (with comparatives for the previous year) is shown below:

Statement of financial position at 31 July 2014

		2014		**2013**
	£000	£000	£000	£000
Assets				
Non-current assets				
Property, plant and equipment at cost	490		450	
Less: Accumulated depreciation	370	120	330	120
Investments at cost		19		44
		139		164
Current assets				
Inventories	289		176	
Trade receivables	231		106	
Less: All'ce for doubtful debts	26	205	4	102
Prepayments	13		12	
Cash on 7-day deposit	-		50	
Cash at bank and in hand	-	507	59	399
		646		563
Equity				
Ordinary share capital		230		180
Preference share capital		20		20
Share premium account		30		-
Retained earnings		158		213
		438		413
Liabilities				
Non-current liabilities				
14% Debenture stock		-		40
12% Debenture stock		30		-
Current liabilities				
14% Debenture stock	40		-	
Trade payables	60		55	
Accruals	9		8	
Amount owing re non-current assets	20		-	
Taxation	9		47	
Bank overdraft	40	178	-	110
		646		563

Notes:

(i)   Equipment which had cost £30,000 during the year to 31 July 2011 was sold in February 2014 for £10,000. The company depreciates equipment at 20% per annum on cost with a full charge in the year of acquisition and none in the year of disposal. (Some of the equipment was over five years old on 31 July 2014).

(ii)   Non-current asset investments which had cost £25,000 some years previously were sold during the year for £21,000.

(iii) Dividends received during the year were £5,000. Dividends totalling £100,000 were paid during the year.

(iv)   The 14% debentures were issued many years ago and are due to be redeemed on 1 January 2015. A fresh issue of 12% debentures was made on 31 July 2014.

(v)   Interest paid during the year (including debenture interest) was £8,000. All interest was paid on the due date and no interest was accrued at either the start or the end of the year. No interest was received during the year.

(vi)   Taxation shown as a liability on 31 July 2013 was paid during the year to 31 July 2014 at the amount stated.

(vii) In January 2014, the company issued 50,000 £1 ordinary shares at a premium of 60p per share.

(viii) The cash on 7-day deposit ranks as a cash equivalent.

Required:

(a)   Prepare a statement of cash flows for the year to 31 July 2014 in accordance with the requirements of IAS7 (using the indirect method).

(b)   Reconcile the total cash and cash equivalents shown by the statement of cash flows to the equivalent figures shown in the opening and closing statements of financial position.

(c)   Comment briefly on the significance of the information provided by the company's statement of cash flows.

*16.7   The statement of financial position of Aadvaark Trading Ltd at 30 November 2014 (with comparatives for 2013) is as follows:

Statement of financial position at 30 November 2014

	2014 £000	2014 £000	2013 £000	2013 £000
Assets				
Non-current assets				
Property, plant and equipment at cost or valuation	2,470		1,790	
Less: Accumulated depreciation	850	1,620	630	1,160
Investments at cost		50		100
		1,670		1,260
Current assets				
Inventories	740		510	
Trade receivables	1,010		640	
Short-term investments	-		150	
Bank balance	-	1,750	180	1,480
		3,420		2,740
Equity				
Share capital		500		400
Share premium account		140		100
Revaluation reserve		550		300
Retained earnings		480		800
		1,670		1,600
Liabilities				
Non-current liabilities				
Long-term loans		900		500
Current liabilities				
Trade payables	660		530	
Current tax payable	-		110	
Bank overdraft	190	850	-	640
		3,420		2,740

The following information is also available:

(i)   Freehold property which was valued at £500,000 on 30 November 2013 was re-valued at £750,000 on 30 November 2014.

(ii) Plant and equipment with an original cost of £120,000 and accumulated depreciation of £80,000 was sold in February 2014 for £30,000.

(iii) One half of the non-current asset investments were sold for £70,000 in June 2014. Dividends received during the year to 30 November 2014 were £nil.

(iv) Interest paid and payable in the year totalled £70,000.

(v)   There is no tax liability for the year to 30 November 2014. The tax liability for the year to 30 November 2013 was underestimated by £20,000.

(vi) No dividends were paid or proposed in either year.

(vii) The short-term investments were sold for £150,000 in June 2014. These ranked as cash equivalents as defined by IAS7.

Required:

Prepare a statement of cash flows for Aadvaark Trading Ltd for the year to 30 November 2014, in accordance with the requirements of accounting standard IAS7 and using the indirect method.   *(CIPFA)*

*16.8   The following draft financial statements are available for Sipfalor plc for the year ended 31 May 2014:

Statement of financial position at 31 May 2014

		2014		2013
	£	£	£	£
Assets				
Non-current assets at cost or valuation		81,535,730		57,754,170
Less: Accumulated dep'n		16,677,788		12,687,297
		64,857,942		45,066,873
Current assets				
Inventory	412,350		389,500	
Trade receivables	558,400		467,800	
Other current assets	2,560		1,540	
Cash and cash equivalents	2,702,204	3,675,514	64,640	923,480
Total assets		68,533,456		45,990,353
Equity				
Issued share capital		35,000,000		20,000,000
Share premium		5,500,000		1,500,000
Revaluation reserve		1,000,000		800,000
Retained earnings		18,421,923		17,696,753
		59,921,923		39,996,753
Liabilities				
Non-current liabilities				
Debentures	7,500,000		5,000,000	
Deferred tax	359,800	7,859,800	289,500	5,289,500
Current liabilities				
Trade payables	409,800		309,800	
Other payables	5,140		4,560	
Current tax payable	336,793	751,733	389,740	704,100
Total equity and liabilities		68,533,456		45,990,353

Statement of profit or loss for the year to 31 May 2014

	£
Revenue	43,380,756
Cost of sales	(25,050,812)
Gross profit	18,329,944
Operating expenses	(15,833,481)
Operating profit	2,496,463
Interest paid	(812,500)
Profit before tax	1,683,963
Taxation	(278,793)
Profit for the year	1,405,170

Note:

Sipfalor plc presents a separate statement of profit or loss for the year (as above) and a separate statement of comprehensive income.

The following additional information for the year ended 31 May 2014 is available:

1) Dividends paid during the year were £680,000.

2) Non-current assets which had cost £332,100 and which had a carrying value of £55,940 were sold for £45,000. Any surpluses or deficits on the disposal of non-current assets have been included in the depreciation charge for the year. Other movements in non-current assets are due to purchases of new assets and revaluations.

3) "Other current assets" consists of prepaid insurance. "Other payables" consists of accrued wages and salaries.

Required:

Prepare a statement of cash flows for Sipfalor plc for the year ended 31 May 2014 in accordance with IAS7 *Statement of Cash Flows* using the direct method. Additional notes are not required. Ignore VAT.

(CIPFA)

Chapter 17

Financial reporting in hyperinflationary economies

Introduction

The amounts that appear in a set of financial statements are measured in units of currency (e.g. pounds or euros) and it is generally assumed for accounting purposes that the value of the currency being used is stable. For example, it is assumed that the value of £1 at the start of an accounting period is the same as the value of £1 at the end of the period. But if prices are changing, this is clearly an invalid assumption. In general, prices are increasing over time and the value of money is falling. This is inflation. Ignoring inflation can lead to a variety of accounting problems and these problems are at their worst if the currency being used is the currency of a hyperinflationary economy.

The purpose of this chapter is to outline the main accounting problems which are caused by inflation and to explain how standard IAS29 *Financial Reporting in Hyperinflationary Economies* seeks to address these problems in the case where an entity is reporting in a currency which is losing value very rapidly.

Objectives

By the end of this chapter, the reader should be able to:

*   explain the term "historical cost accounting"
*   explain and illustrate the main weaknesses of historical cost accounting
*   list the main strengths of historical cost accounting
*   identify the main alternatives to historical cost accounting
*   explain what is meant by a "hyperinflationary economy"
*   explain the main requirements of standard IAS29.

Historical cost accounting and its weaknesses

The term "historical cost accounting" (HCA) refers to the traditional method of accounting whereby each transaction is recorded at its monetary amount at the time of the transaction and no attempt is made to adjust the recorded amounts to take account of inflation. This approach is used almost exclusively in practice, but it can be argued that the resulting HCA financial statements suffer from a number of weaknesses. These include:

(a) profits are overstated

(b) depreciation charges are inadequate

(c) gains and losses on monetary items are not disclosed

(d) holding gains on inventories are not separately identified

(e) non-current asset values reported in the statement of financial position are unrealistic

(f) accounting ratios are misleading.

Each of these perceived weaknesses is explained below.

Overstated profits

It is clear that the main objective of preparing a statement of comprehensive income is to calculate the amount of profit earned by an entity during an accounting period. It is less clear that a statement of comprehensive income which ignores inflation does not really achieve this objective. It might be helpful to define what is meant by the term "profit". The following definition is based upon one which was coined by Sir John Hicks in 1930:

> The profit for an accounting period is "*the amount which the owner of a business can consume and still be as well off at the end of the period as he or she was at the start of the period*".

Another way of putting this is to say that the profit for a period is equal to the amount which could be withdrawn from the business during that period whilst maintaining its capital intact. This means that the measurement of profit depends upon being able to measure and compare the capital (or net assets) of a business entity at the beginning and end of an accounting period. The *Conceptual Framework* (see Chapter 2) distinguishes between three essentially different approaches to the measurement of capital:

(a) **Nominal financial capital maintenance**. This approach measures capital in money terms with no regard to changes in the purchasing power of money. An entity which has capital of £x at the start of a period and £y at the end of that period (with no distributions to owners or contributions by owners) is assumed to have made a profit of £y – £x. This is, of course, the traditional HCA approach to profit measurement.

(b) **General purchasing power maintenance**. Capital is measured in terms of general purchasing power and profit is defined as the amount by which the general purchasing power of the entity has increased during an accounting period. Purchasing power is measured in accordance with changes in an index of general prices.

(c) **Physical capital maintenance**. Capital is measured in terms of purchasing power with regard to the specific items which the business entity needs to buy. Profit for an accounting period is defined as the increase in the specific purchasing power of the entity during that period.

In times of inflation, it might be argued that HCA financial statements (which measure capital in nominal monetary units) overstate the profits of business entities. A simple example of this problem was given in Chapter 2. A further example is given below.

EXAMPLE 1

X Ltd started trading on 1 July 2013 with capital of £100,000 and immediately bought ten identical items of inventory for £10,000 each. Six of these items were sold on 31 July for £84,000 (which was received in cash). There were no other transactions during the month.

(a) Calculate the profit for the month in nominal money terms.
(b) If the index of general prices was 100.0 on 1 July 2013 and 104.0 on 31 July 2013, calculate the profit for the month in terms of general purchasing power.
(c) If it would cost £11,000 on 31 July to replace each of the sold items, calculate the profit for the month in terms of specific purchasing power (i.e. the power of the company to maintain its physical capital).

Solution

	Nominal financial capital maintenance £	*General purchasing power maintenance* £	*Physical capital maintenance* £
Assets at the end of the month:			
Cash	84,000	84,000	84,000
Inventory (four items)	40,000	41,600	44,000
	124,000	125,600	128,000
Assets required at the end of the month to be as well off as at the beginning of the month:			
(a) nominal monetary units	100,000		
(b) general purchasing power (£100,000 x 104/100)		104,000	
(c) physical operating capability (£11,000 x 10)			110,000
Net profit for the month	24,000	21,600	18,000

Notes:

(a) In nominal monetary terms, the company is £24,000 better off at the end of the month than it was at the start of the month. This is the profit figure which would be reported in the HCA financial statements.

(b) There was 4% inflation during July, so £104,000 is needed at the end of the month to give the same general purchasing power as was given by £100,000 at the start of the month. The cash of £84,000 is a "monetary item" (see below) and is fixed in monetary terms, regardless of inflation. The inventory cost £40,000 on 1 July but assuming that all costs have risen by 4% in line with general price inflation, it is now worth £41,600. Therefore the company has total assets of £125,600 on 31 July and its profit for the month in terms of general purchasing power is £21,600.

(c) £110,000 is needed at the end of the month to buy the same inventory as could be bought for £100,000 at the start of the month. The company has four inventory items remaining on 31 July (measured at their current cost of £44,000) and cash of £84,000. If £66,000 of this cash were used to replenish the inventory, there would still be £18,000 left, so the company has made a profit of £18,000 for the month.

HCA financial statements (using nominal financial capital maintenance) would overstate the company's real profit for the month. The HCA profit would be £24,000, but no more than £21,600 of this could be distributed without reducing the company's general purchasing power and no more than £18,000 could be distributed without reducing the company's power to replace its inventory. If a dividend of £24,000 were paid, the company would effectively be paying part of that dividend out of its capital.

Inadequate depreciation charges

The purpose of depreciation in HCA financial statements is to spread the historical cost of a non-current asset (less its residual value) over the asset's useful life. However, a desirable side-effect of charging depreciation is that reported profits are reduced. This should act as a restraint on the amount distributed to owners and so make it more likely that funds will be available to replace non-current assets when this becomes necessary. Even so, there is no guarantee that sufficient funds will be available in liquid form. But the fact that inflation is usually ignored when calculating depreciation causes the following problems:

(a) In an HCA statement of comprehensive income, sales revenue measured in current £s is matched against depreciation charges calculated in historical £s. If elderly non-current assets are still being depreciated or if inflation is running at a high rate, there may be a great disparity between the value of these £s and this must throw doubt on the validity and usefulness of the profit figure.

(b) The total amount of depreciation charged over the years in relation to an asset will be less than its replacement cost. In effect, profits will be overstated and may be over-distributed, so causing capital depletion.

EXAMPLE 2

A company starts trading with capital of £100,000. This is spent upon the acquisition of plant with a useful life of five years and no residual value. Depreciation is charged at 20% per annum on historical cost. All of the company's profits are paid out as dividends at the end of each accounting year. Will the company be able to replace the plant at the end of its useful life, given that its replacement cost will be £120,000 by then?

Solution

At the end of five years, the company's statement of financial position will show capital of £100,000 and net assets of £100,000. Even in the unlikely case that these net assets are entirely in liquid form, the company will not be able to replace the plant without raising a further £20,000. In effect, the HCA financial statements have overstated the company's profits and so the capital of the company (measured in specific purchasing power terms) has been depleted by £20,000.

Gains and losses on monetary items not disclosed

Monetary items are assets or liabilities which are fixed in monetary terms. Common examples of monetary items are receivables, payables, loans and cash. In a period of inflation, an entity loses purchasing power by holding monetary assets but gains purchasing power by holding monetary liabilities. However, these gains and losses are not revealed at all in the HCA financial statements. It can be argued that this is another shortcoming of the conventional approach to financial accounting.

EXAMPLE 3

At the start of an accounting year (when the index of general prices is 100.0) a company borrows £500,000 at an interest rate of 9% per annum. The full amount of the loan is still outstanding at the end of the year, by which time the index of general prices has increased to 106.0.

(a) How will this loan be dealt with in the HCA statement of comprehensive income?

(b) Calculate the real cost of the loan to the company for the accounting year.

Solution

(a) The statement of comprehensive income will recognise an expense of £45,000.

(b) If the loan were fixed in terms of general purchasing power, the company would owe £530,000 (£500,000 x 106/100) at the end of the year. However, as the loan is fixed in monetary terms, the company still owes only £500,000 and has gained purchasing power of £30,000. The real cost of the loan is only £15,000 (£45,000 − £30,000).

Holding gains on inventories not separately identified

During a period of inflation, any inventories held by an entity for an appreciable amount of time will increase in monetary value. Such an increase is known as a *holding gain*. In an HCA statement of comprehensive income, holding gains are not shown separately but are simply treated as part of the gross profit arising on the sale of goods. It has been suggested that the financial statements would be more useful if the gross profit were analysed so that holding gains were clearly identified.

EXAMPLE 4

At the start of an accounting period, a company's inventory comprised 1,000 identical units each costing £200. On the final day of the period, these units were all sold for £300 each and a further 1,000 identical units were bought for £240 each. All transactions were for cash. Inventories are accounted for on a first-in, first-out basis.

Explain how these transactions would be reflected in an HCA statement of comprehensive income and analyse the company's gross profit for the period, clearly identifying the holding gain on inventories.

Solution

An HCA statement of comprehensive income would show sales revenue of £300,000 matched against cost of sales of £200,000, giving a gross profit of £100,000. However, the company began the period with 1,000 units of inventory and ended the period with 1,000 units of inventory plus an extra £60,000 in cash. This would suggest that the company has actually made a gross profit of only £60,000 during the period, not £100,000.

The difference of £40,000 is a holding gain on inventories. This occurred because the replacement cost of the inventories rose by £40 per unit between their acquisition and their eventual sale. It would be more informative if the reported gross profit figure of £100,000 were analysed into a holding gain of £40,000 and a gross profit of £60,000.

Unrealistic non-current asset values

In a set of HCA financial statements, non-current assets are shown in the statement of financial position at their historical cost (less depreciation as necessary) and any increases in asset values are not recognised until they are realised. In consequence, HCA financial statements often fail to show the true financial position of an entity, especially if the entity owns assets such as freehold land which have been subject to substantial increases in value since acquisition.

Furthermore, the historical costs of all the non-current assets owned by an entity are added together in an HCA statement of financial position, regardless of the fact that these costs have been incurred in different years. Adding together the £5,000 paid for a freehold property in 1969 and the £250,000 paid for a similar property in 2009 seems to serve no useful purpose, but HCA requires that these two figures should be aggregated.

Because of these problems, IAS16 *Property, Plant and Equipment* and IAS38 *Intangible Assets* both permit entities to adopt the revaluation model and to show non-current assets at their current values (see Chapters 5 and 6).

Misleading accounting ratios

Accounting ratios (see Chapter 22) are frequently used as a tool for the analysis and interpretation of financial statements. However, the limitations of historical cost accounting suggest that it may be unwise to base economic decisions on a ratio analysis of the figures shown in a conventional set of financial statements. This point is illustrated in the simple example given below.

EXAMPLE 5

A company's statement of comprehensive income shows a pre-tax profit of £100,000. The statement of financial position shows net assets of £500,000. The company's financial statements are prepared on the historical cost basis.

(a) Calculate the ratio of pre-tax profit to net assets. (This is a version of the accounting ratio known as "return on capital employed").

(b) When the company's financial statements are amended to take account of inflation, it transpires that the pre-tax profit is only £60,000 and that net assets are actually £1,200,000. Recalculate the ratio of pre-tax profit to net assets.

Solution

(a) Ratio of pre-tax profit to net assets is £100,000/£500,000 = 20%.

(b) The revised ratio of pre-tax profit to net assets is only £60,000/£1,200,000 = 5%. This gives a totally different view of the company's profitability. It is evident that anyone who conducts a ratio analysis of conventional financial statements should be very mindful of the limitations of historical cost accounting.

Strengths of historical cost accounting

Despite its perceived weaknesses, historical cost accounting has some distinct strengths. It is a comparatively simple accounting system that all accountants understand. It is also well-established, having served the needs of users for several centuries. Furthermore, it possesses the important characteristic of objectivity, in that the historical cost of an asset is usually an objective fact. However, it must be admitted that some of this objectivity is lost when depreciation and impairment are accounted for.

Alternatives to historical cost accounting

The weaknesses of historical cost accounting are sufficiently serious to have fuelled the search for alternative accounting systems. Not surprisingly, this search was at its most intense in the 1970s and 1980s when worldwide inflation rates were high, but the various proposals put forward at that time were controversial and failed to gain lasting acceptance. In more recent years, most developed countries have experienced low levels of inflation and the problem has become less urgent. However, the problem remains acute in countries with very high levels of inflation.

Proposed alternatives to historical cost accounting generally fall into one of two categories. These are current purchasing power accounting and current cost accounting.

(a) **Current purchasing power (CPP) accounting**. CPP accounting adopts the approach referred to earlier in this chapter as general purchasing power maintenance. The basic principle is that each transaction shown in the historical cost financial statements is adjusted to reflect the change in the general purchasing power of money since the transaction took place.

CPP accounting is fairly straightforward but suffers from the disadvantage that general price indexes do not measure the effects of inflation on the specific business entity for which financial statements are being prepared.

(b) **Current cost accounting (CCA)**. CCA adopts the approach referred to earlier in this chapter as physical capital maintenance. The basic principle of CCA is that assets consumed during an accounting period (e.g. inventories) are shown in the statement of comprehensive income at their current values at the time of consumption and assets remaining at the end of the period are shown in the statement of financial position at their current values at the end of the period.

CCA takes account of specific price inflation but introduces an undesirable element of subjectivity into the financial statements, since current values often need to be estimated. It also requires a rather complex series of adjustments.

International standard IAS15 *Information Reflecting the Effects of Changing Prices* was introduced in 1983 and required entities to make a number of disclosures with regard to the effects of inflation on their financial statements. This standard offered a choice between the CPP and CCA approaches. However, IAS15 ceased to be mandatory in 1989 and was withdrawn completely as from 2005. It has not been replaced since.

Accounting for inflation no longer seems to be an important issue in most developed countries but there is still a pressing need for an alternative to historical cost accounting in those countries which are subject to "hyperinflation". This has led to the development of IAS29 *Financial Reporting in Hyperinflationary Economies* and the rest of this chapter is devoted to an explanation of the main features of that standard.

Hyperinflationary economies

The requirements of IAS29 *Financial Reporting in Hyperinflationary Economies* apply to the financial statements of any entity whose functional currency is the currency of a hyperinflationary economy. The term "functional currency" is not defined in IAS29 but is defined in IAS21 *The Effects of Changes in Foreign Exchange Rates* as the currency of the primary economic environment in which the entity operates (see Chapter 21).

Financial statements are usually presented in the functional currency of the entity concerned but may in fact be presented in any currency. If an entity whose functional currency is the currency of a hyperinflationary economy presents its financial statements in a different "presentation currency", then the financial statements should be restated in accordance with IAS29 before being translated into the presentation currency.

IAS29 does not establish an absolute rate of inflation at which hyperinflation is deemed to occur, but suggests that hyperinflation is characterised by the following indicators:

(a) The general population prefers to keep its wealth in non-monetary assets or in a relatively stable foreign currency.

(b) The general population regards monetary amounts not in terms of the local currency but in terms of a relatively stable foreign currency (in which prices may be quoted).

(c) Credit sales and purchases take place at prices that compensate for the expected loss of purchasing power during the credit period, even if that period is short.

(d) Wages and interest rates are linked to a price index.

(e) The cumulative inflation rate over three years is approaching or exceeds 100%.

IAS29 states that, in a hyperinflationary economy, the reporting of financial performance and position in the local currency without restatement is not useful. In such an economy, money loses value at such a rate that comparisons of amounts relating to events that have occurred at different times (even within the same accounting period) are misleading.

The restatement of financial statements

The basic principle of IAS29 is that the financial statements of an entity whose functional currency is the currency of a hyperinflationary economy should be restated "*in terms of the measuring unit current at the end of the reporting period*". This means that the recorded amounts of transactions and other events are adjusted to take account of the change in the general purchasing power of money between the date on which each transaction or event occurred and the end of the period. This is a CPP approach. Note the following points:

(a) The comparative information which is required by IAS1 for the previous accounting period (see Chapter 3) should also be restated in terms of the measuring unit current at the end of the reporting period.

(b) IAS29 does not permit the restated financial statements to be presented in the form of a supplement to the original (unrestated) financial statements. Separate presentation of the unrestated figures is permitted but is also discouraged.

(c) The gain or loss on the net monetary position (see later in this chapter) should be included in the calculation of profit or loss and disclosed separately.

Assuming that the entity's unrestated financial statements have been prepared on the historical cost basis, the main steps involved in the preparation of the restated financial statements are as follows:

Restated statement of financial position

(a) Amounts in the statement of financial position that are not already expressed in terms of the measuring unit current at the end of the reporting period are restated by applying a general price index. It is preferable that the same index is used by all entities which report in the currency of the same economy.

(b) Monetary items are not restated, as they are already expressed in current purchasing power terms. Monetary items include cash, receivables and payables.

(c) Some non-monetary items are carried at amounts that are current at the end of the reporting period and so are not restated. Examples include inventories carried at net realisable value and properties which have been revalued at the end of the period.

(d) The restated amount of a non-monetary item which is carried at historical cost (or at historical cost less accumulated depreciation) is determined in accordance with the change in the general price index since the date on which the item was acquired. This change is applied to the item's cost and to its accumulated depreciation (if any).

(e) If a non-monetary item is carried at a valuation, its restated amount is determined in accordance with the change in the general price index since the date of the valuation.

(f) At the *beginning* of the first period in which IAS29 is applied to the financial statements of an entity, each component of owners' equity (apart from retained earnings and any revaluation reserve) is restated by applying the change in the general price index since the component was contributed or otherwise arose. Revaluation reserves are eliminated entirely. Restated retained earnings are calculated as a balancing figure after all of the other adjustments have been made.

(g) Subsequently, all components of equity (including any new revaluation reserves) are restated at the end of each accounting period by applying the change in the general price index since the beginning of the period, or since the date that the component arose (if later).

Restated statement of comprehensive income

(a) All items in the statement of comprehensive income are restated by applying the change in the general price index since the dates on which the items of income and expense were first recorded in the financial statements.

(b) The gain or loss on the entity's net monetary position is calculated as a balancing figure, equal to the difference resulting from the restatement of items in the statement of financial position and the statement of comprehensive income. This gain or loss is included in the calculation of profit or loss for the period.

Restated statement of cash flows

All items in the statement of cash flows are restated in terms of the measuring unit current at the end of the reporting period.

Disclosures required by IAS29

An entity which has restated its historical cost financial statements in accordance with the requirements of IAS29 must disclose:

(a) the fact that the financial statements and the comparative figures for previous periods have been restated so as to adjust for changes in the purchasing power of the entity's functional currency and (as a result) are stated in terms of the measuring unit current at the end of the reporting period

(b) the fact that the entity's original (unrestated) financial statements were prepared on the historical cost basis

(c) the identity and level of the price index at the end of the reporting period and the movement in this index during the current period and the previous period.

Summary

▸ Historical cost accounting (HCA) records each transaction at its monetary amount at the time that the transaction occurs and makes no attempt to adjust for inflation. This is the traditional method of accounting.

▸ In times of inflation, it might be argued that HCA financial statements overstate an entity's profits. If all of the profits shown in an HCA statement of comprehensive income were withdrawn, the entity concerned would suffer capital depletion.

▸ Monetary items are assets or liabilities which are fixed in monetary terms. An entity which holds monetary assets during a period of inflation loses purchasing power and an entity which holds monetary liabilities gains purchasing power. These gains and losses are not reported in HCA financial statements.

▸ The gross profit shown in an HCA statement of comprehensive income includes holding gains on inventories. These are not reported separately.

▸ An HCA statement of financial position does not show assets at current values and so may give a misleading impression. In some cases, this problem can be lessened by showing assets at a valuation.

▸ Despite its weaknesses, historical cost accounting remains in general use. HCA is fairly simple to understand and operate and is perceived as being more objective than alternative approaches.

▸ Alternatives to historical cost accounting include current purchasing power (CPP) accounting and current cost accounting (CCA). Neither of these has gained lasting acceptance. However, a version of CPP accounting is required by IAS29 in relation to the financial statements of an entity whose functional currency is the currency of a hyperinflationary economy.

▸ IAS29 *Financial Reporting in Hyperinflationary Economies* requires the restatement of HCA financial statements to take account of the change in the general purchasing power of money between the date on which each transaction or event occurred and the end of the reporting period.

Exercises

17.1   (a)   Distinguish between nominal financial capital maintenance, general purchasing power maintenance and physical capital maintenance.

        (b)   A company began trading on 1 August with capital of £400,000, all of which was immediately spent on acquiring inventory. On 31 August, three-quarters of this inventory was sold for £475,000 in cash. There were no other transactions during the month of August.

               The index of general prices was 100.0 on 1 August and 105.0 on 31 August. The specific price index applicable to the company's inventories was 100.0 on 1 August and 107.0 on 31 August.

               Calculate the company's profit for the month of August using each of the three capital maintenance concepts listed in part (a) of this exercise.

17.2   On 1 January 2012, C Ltd lent £200,000 to D Ltd at an annual interest rate of 8%. No interest was paid until 31 December 2013, when the loan was repaid in full together with two years' interest (which was not compounded). The index of general prices was 100.0 on 1 January 2012 and was 112.0 on 31 December 2013. In terms of general purchasing power, calculate the overall gain made by C Ltd with respect to this loan.

17.3   (a)   Explain the term "holding gain" in relation to inventories.

        (b)   On the first day of an accounting period, a company acquired inventories at a cost of £60,000. Two-thirds of these inventories were sold for £55,000 on the final day of the accounting period. The specific price index applicable to these inventories rose by 8% during the period.

               Calculate the gross profit for the period (in nominal financial terms) and state the amount of this profit which comprises a holding gain.

17.4   (a)   Explain the term "historical cost accounting".

        (b)   Summarise the strengths and weaknesses of historical cost accounting.

        (c)   Identify and briefly explain the two main alternatives to historical cost accounting.

*17.5   (a)   List the main indicators of a hyperinflationary economy, as specified by IAS29.

        (b)   Explain why IAS29 takes the view that conventional financial statements are not useful in a hyperinflationary economy.

        (c)   Explain how each of the following items should be dealt with when preparing the restated financial statements of an entity which operates in a hyperinflationary economy:

               (i)   monetary items in the statement of financial position

               (ii)   non-monetary items shown at historical cost less accumulated depreciation

               (iii)   non-monetary items shown at a valuation

               (iv)   income and expenses shown in the statement of comprehensive income.

Part 3

CONSOLIDATED FINANCIAL STATEMENTS

Chapter 18

Groups of companies (1)

Introduction

The purpose of this chapter is to introduce the concept of a "group" of companies and to explain how a group statement of financial position is prepared. Subsequent chapters deal with the group statement of comprehensive income and other related matters.

A group of companies consists of a parent company together with one or more subsidiary companies which are controlled by the parent company. Control over a subsidiary is usually achieved by acquiring over 50% of its ordinary shares. The shareholders of a parent company have an indirect interest in the net assets and in the profits or losses of the company's subsidiaries. Accordingly, parent companies are required to prepare and present a set of accounts for the group as a whole, in recognition of the fact that a parent company and its subsidiaries are, in effect, a single economic unit. It is important to appreciate that these *group accounts* are intended for the shareholders of the parent company only.

The main international standards which apply to the preparation of group accounts are IFRS10 *Consolidated Financial Statements* and IFRS3 *Business Combinations*. These standards are concerned with groups in general, including groups with unincorporated subsidiaries. In practice, however, most groups are groups of companies and this book deals only with groups in which the parent and all of its subsidiaries are companies.

Objectives

By the end of this chapter, the reader should be able to:

- explain what is meant by a set of consolidated financial statements
- define the terms "group", "parent", "subsidiary" and "control" in accordance with international standard IFRS10
- prepare a group statement of financial position both at the date of acquisition and subsequent to acquisition, accounting correctly for goodwill
- prepare a group statement of financial position in cases where subsidiaries are either wholly-owned or partly-owned, dealing correctly with non-controlling interests
- eliminate intra-group balances and eliminate unrealised profits arising on the transfer of assets between group companies at more than cost.

Requirement to prepare consolidated financial statements

IFRS10 *Consolidated Financial Statements* includes the following important definitions:

- Consolidated financial statements are "*the financial statements of a group in which the assets, liabilities, equity, income, expenses and cash flows of the parent and its subsidiaries are presented as those of a single economic entity*". Consolidated financial statements are often referred to as group accounts.

- A group is "*a parent and its subsidiaries*".

- A parent is "*an entity that controls one or more entities*".

- A subsidiary is "*an entity that is controlled by another entity*".

In general, IFRS10 requires that parent companies should prepare and present consolidated financial statements. But a parent need not present consolidated financial statements if *all* of the following conditions are satisfied:

(a) the parent company is itself either:

    (i) a wholly-owned subsidiary, or

    (ii) a partially-owned subsidiary of another company, and all of its other owners do not object to the parent not presenting consolidated financial statements

(b) the parent's shares or securities are not publicly traded

(c) the parent's ultimate parent company presents consolidated financial statements that are available for public use and comply with international standards.

IAS27 *Separate Financial Statements* allows a parent company which satisfies all of these conditions to present only its own "separate financial statements". Investments in subsidiaries must be accounted for in these financial statements either at cost or in accordance with IAS39/IFRS9 (see Chapter 11).

Definition of control

IFRS10 states that an investor controls an investee "*when the investor is exposed, or has rights, to variable returns from its involvement with the investee and has the ability to affect those returns through its power over the investee*". The standard also states that an investor has power over an investee when the investor has existing rights that enable it to direct the "relevant activities" of the investee. An entity's relevant activities are those which significantly affect its returns and may include:

(a) the sale and purchase of goods and services

(b) the selection, acquisition or disposal of assets

(c) the management of financial assets (see Chapter 11)

(d) research and development

(e) the determination of a funding structure for the entity and the obtaining of funding.

An investor does not have power over an investee unless the investor has rights that enable it to *direct* the investee's relevant activities. Rights which may give this power include:

(a)   voting rights

(b)   the right to appoint or remove members of the investee's key management personnel

(c)   the right to direct the investee to enter into transactions for the investor's benefit

(d)   contractual rights that enable the investor to direct the investee's relevant activities.

In straightforward cases, an investor which holds a majority of an investee's voting rights usually has the power to direct the investee's activities and so controls the investee. In the case of companies, control is normally assumed to exist when one company owns (directly or indirectly) more than 50% of the voting power of another company, unless it can be demonstrated that such ownership does not give control. Owning over 50% of a company's voting power normally means owning over 50% of that company's ordinary shares.

Group statement of financial position at date of acquisition

The preparation of a group statement of financial position is basically a matter of adding together (line by line) the individual statements of financial position of all the companies in the group. This process is known as "consolidation" and the resulting financial statement may be referred to as a consolidated statement of financial position.

When carrying out a consolidation it is necessary to cancel out items which appear both as an asset in the financial statements of one group company and as a liability (or equity) in the financial statements of another group company. This ensures that the consolidated statement of financial position shows only the true assets and liabilities of the group as a whole. The main items which should be cancelled are as follows:

(a)   If a parent company owns 100% of the share capital of a subsidiary, the cost of the parent's investment in that subsidiary should be cancelled out with the subsidiary's share capital and reserves. This is because the purchase of 100% of a company's share capital also buys entitlement to 100% of that company's reserves. The situation is slightly more complex for partly-owned subsidiaries (see later in this chapter).

(b)   If one group company owes money to another, the amount payable which is shown as a liability in the financial statements of the first company should be cancelled out with the corresponding amount receivable which is shown as an asset in the financial statements of the other company. Such debts are known as "intra-group balances".

It is important to appreciate that this cancelling-out process does *not* take place in the books of the individual companies concerned. The entire consolidation takes place on a set of consolidation working papers and the books of the group companies are completely unaffected by this process.

EXAMPLE 1

On 31 May 2014, A Ltd pays £35,000 to acquire all of the shares of B Ltd. The statements of financial position of the two companies just after this transaction are as follows:

	A Ltd £	B Ltd £
Assets		
Non-current assets		
Property, plant and equipment	200,000	27,000
Investment in B Ltd	35,000	
	235,000	
Current assets	109,000	12,000
	344,000	39,000
Equity		
Ordinary share capital	250,000	30,000
Retained earnings	58,000	5,000
	308,000	35,000
Liabilities		
Current liabilities	36,000	4,000
	344,000	39,000

Prepare a consolidated statement of financial position as at 31 May 2014.

Solution

	A Ltd £	B Ltd £	Group £
Assets			
Non-current assets			
Property, plant and equipment	200,000	27,000	227,000
Investment in B Ltd	~~35,000~~		
	235,000		
Current assets	109,000	12,000	121,000
	344,000	39,000	348,000
Equity			
Ordinary share capital	250,000	~~30,000~~	250,000
Retained earnings	58,000	~~5,000~~	58,000
	308,000	35,000	308,000
Liabilities			
Current liabilities	36,000	4,000	40,000
	344,000	39,000	348,000

Notes:

1. The £35,000 paid by A Ltd has been cancelled out with the £35,000 share capital and reserves of B Ltd. This has been indicated by striking through the cancelled figures. The two statements of financial position have then been consolidated, line by line.

2. In effect, the asset "Investment in B Ltd" shown in the A Ltd statement of financial position has been replaced in the consolidated statement by the underlying net assets of the subsidiary company.

3. The group (or consolidated) statement of financial position is shown in the rightmost column of this solution. The other two columns of figures would not be presented as part of the statement but are shown here as workings.

4. The totals and subtotals that are shown in the "Group" column have been obtained by adding together the figures in that column and <u>not</u> by adding across the rows.

Goodwill arising on consolidation

In the above example, the amount paid by the parent company to acquire the shares of the subsidiary was precisely equal to the book value of the subsidiary's net assets. However, parent companies are often willing to pay more than book value to acquire a controlling interest in a subsidiary, for two main reasons:

(a) The fair value of the net assets shown in the subsidiary's financial statements may exceed their book value.

(b) The parent company may be paying for the subsidiary's goodwill, which is probably not shown in the subsidiary's financial statements at all.

IFRS3 *Business Combinations* (see Chapter 6) prescribes the accounting treatment of any goodwill acquired in a business combination. This includes the situation where a parent acquires control of a subsidiary. A summary of the required treatment is as follows:

(a) Each of the subsidiary's assets and liabilities is adjusted to its fair value on the date that the parent company acquired the subsidiary's shares. Gains and losses caused by these adjustments are added to or subtracted from the subsidiary's reserves.

(b) If the parent has paid more than fair value to acquire the shares of a subsidiary, the excess is "goodwill arising on consolidation" and this is shown as an asset in the consolidated statement of financial position. Goodwill should be tested annually for impairment and written down as necessary.

(c) If the parent has paid less than fair value to acquire the shares of a subsidiary, then "negative goodwill" appears to have arisen. In this situation, IFRS3 requires that the cost of the investment made by the parent and the fair values of the subsidiary's assets and liabilities should be reassessed. Any negative goodwill which remains after this reassessment is recognised as income and increases the group's reserves.

Once again, it is very important to appreciate that all of these adjustments are made only in the consolidation working papers and not in the books of the companies concerned.

EXAMPLE 2

On 30 June 2014, C Ltd pays £60,000 to acquire all of the shares of D Ltd. The statements of financial position of the two companies just after this transaction are as follows:

	C Ltd £	D Ltd £
Assets		
Non-current assets		
Property, plant and equipment	410,000	30,000
Investment in D Ltd	60,000	
	470,000	
Current assets	231,000	25,000
	701,000	55,000
Equity		
Ordinary share capital	400,000	25,000
Retained earnings	187,000	17,000
	587,000	42,000
Liabilities		
Current liabilities	114,000	13,000
	701,000	55,000

The fair value of the property, plant and equipment of D Ltd on 30 June 2014 is £40,000. Prepare a consolidated statement of financial position as at 30 June 2014.

Solution

	C Ltd £	D Ltd £	Group £
Assets			
Non-current assets			
Property, plant and equipment	410,000	40,000	450,000
Investment in D Ltd	~~60,000~~		
Goodwill			8,000
	470,000		458,000
Current assets	231,000	25,000	256,000
	701,000	65,000	714,000

	C Ltd	D Ltd	Group
	£	£	£
Equity			
Ordinary share capital	400,000	~~25,000~~	400,000
Revaluation reserve		~~10,000~~	
Retained earnings	187,000	~~17,000~~	187,000
	587,000	52,000	587,000
Liabilities			
Current liabilities	114,000	13,000	127,000
	701,000	65,000	714,000

Notes:

1. In the consolidation working papers, D Ltd's property, plant and equipment is revalued at £40,000 and £10,000 is credited to a revaluation reserve.

2. The price paid by C Ltd (£60,000) is cancelled against the share capital and reserves of D Ltd (£52,000) leaving a difference of £8,000 which is shown as goodwill in the consolidated statement of financial position. The cancelled figures have been struck through and the two statements of financial position have then been consolidated.

3. As before, the totals and subtotals shown in the "Group" column have been obtained by adding together the figures in that column and not by adding across the rows.

4. None of these adjustments have any effect on the books of either C Ltd or D Ltd.

Group statement of financial position in subsequent years

The examples so far in this chapter deal with the preparation of a consolidated statement of financial position just after a parent company has acquired a new subsidiary. In subsequent years, the situation is made more complicated by the fact that the reserves of the subsidiary will have changed since acquisition. Such changes should be dealt with as follows:

(a) A post-acquisition *increase* in the retained earnings of a subsidiary company represents an increase in the value of the investment made by the parent company in the shares of the subsidiary. This increase in value belongs ultimately to the members of the parent company and so should be added to the retained earnings shown in the consolidated statement of financial position.

(b) Similarly, any post-acquisition *decrease* in the retained earnings of a subsidiary should be subtracted from consolidated retained earnings.

In simple cases, the only reserve which will have changed in a subsidiary's financial statements since the subsidiary was acquired by the parent will be retained earnings. However, post-acquisition changes in any other reserves of the subsidiary are dealt with in the same way as post-acquisition changes in retained earnings.

An impairment loss in relation to goodwill (see above) is accounted for by reducing both the goodwill figure and group retained earnings by the amount of the loss.

EXAMPLE 3

On 1 January 2011, E Ltd paid £70,000 to acquire all of the shares of F Ltd. On that date, the retained earnings of F Ltd were £14,000 and all of its assets and liabilities were shown in the books at their fair values. The statements of financial position of E Ltd and F Ltd as at 31 December 2013 (i.e. three years later) are as follows:

	E Ltd	F Ltd
	£	£
Assets		
Non-current assets		
Property, plant and equipment	620,000	47,000
Investment in F Ltd	70,000	
	690,000	
Current assets	285,000	37,000
	975,000	84,000
Equity		
Ordinary share capital	500,000	40,000
Retained earnings	393,000	26,000
	893,000	66,000
Liabilities		
Current liabilities	82,000	18,000
	975,000	84,000

The share capital of F Ltd has not changed since 1 January 2011. Goodwill arising on consolidation has suffered an impairment loss of 30% since acquisition. Prepare a consolidated statement of financial position as at 31 December 2013.

Solution

The approach adopted in the solutions to previous examples in this chapter has been to show the financial statements of parent and subsidiary side-by-side, then to strike through items which should be cancelled out and consolidate the items which remain. Although this approach is useful for simple consolidations, it becomes unwieldy as the complexity of problems increases. A more practicable approach is to prepare workings for key figures such as goodwill and group retained earnings and then to write out the group statement of financial position showing any remaining workings in-line. This is the approach adopted in this solution and in the remaining solutions in this chapter.

Group statement of financial position as at 31 December 2013

	£
Assets	
Non-current assets	
Property, plant and equipment (£620,000 + £47,000)	667,000
Goodwill (W1)	11,200
	678,200
Current assets (£285,000 + £37,000)	322,000
	1,000,200
Equity	
Ordinary share capital	500,000
Retained earnings (W2)	400,200
	900,200
Liabilities	
Current liabilities (£82,000 + £18,000)	100,000
	1,000,200

Workings:

W1. <u>Goodwill</u>

	£	£
Price paid by parent		70,000
Subsidiary's share capital at 1 January 2011	40,000	
Subsidiary's retained earnings at 1 January 2011	14,000	54,000
Goodwill at 1 January 2011		16,000
Less: Impairment (30%)		4,800
Goodwill at 31 December 2013		11,200

W2. <u>Group retained earnings</u>

	£	£
Parent's retained earnings at 31 December 2013		393,000
Subsidiary's retained earnings at 31 December 2013	26,000	
Less: Subsidiary's retained earnings at 1 January 2011	14,000	12,000
		405,000
Less: Goodwill impairment		4,800
Group retained earnings at 31 December 2013		400,200

Partly-owned subsidiaries

If a parent company does not own 100% of a subsidiary's share capital, the subsidiary is partly-owned and the remainder of its shares are held by non-controlling shareholders. In these circumstances, IFRS10 requires that the group statement of financial position should include *all* of the subsidiary's assets and *all* of its liabilities (exactly as if the subsidiary were wholly-owned) but should then identify separately the amount of the subsidiary's net assets which is attributable to the non-controlling shareholders. This amount is referred to by IFRS10 as the "non-controlling interest".

Non-controlling interests should be presented in the equity section of the group statement of financial position, but separately from the equity of the parent company's shareholders.

EXAMPLE 4

The statements of financial position of G Ltd and H Ltd at 31 March 2014 are as follows:

	G Ltd £	H Ltd £
Assets		
Non-current assets		
Property, plant and equipment	527,000	39,000
Investment in H Ltd	48,000	
	575,000	
Current assets	326,000	31,000
	901,000	70,000
Equity		
Ordinary share capital	600,000	32,000
Retained earnings	148,000	22,000
	748,000	54,000
Liabilities		
Current liabilities	153,000	16,000
	901,000	70,000

On 1 April 2010, G Ltd had paid £48,000 to acquire 75% of the shares in H Ltd. On that date, the retained earnings of H Ltd were £10,000 and the fair value of the company's non-current assets was £8,000 more than their book value. This revaluation has not been reflected in the books of H Ltd.

H Ltd has issued no shares since being acquired by G Ltd. Goodwill arising on consolidation has suffered an impairment loss of 40% since acquisition. Prepare a consolidated statement of financial position as at 31 March 2014.

Solution

<u>Group statement of financial position as at 31 March 2014</u>

	£
Assets	
Non-current assets	
Property, plant and equipment (£527,000 + £39,000 + £8,000)	574,000
Goodwill (W1)	6,300
	580,300
Current assets (£326,000 + £31,000)	357,000
	937,300
Equity	
Ordinary share capital	600,000
Retained earnings (W2)	152,800
	752,800
Non-controlling interest (W3)	15,500
	768,300
Liabilities	
Current liabilities (£153,000 + £16,000)	169,000
	937,300

Workings:

W1. <u>Goodwill</u>

	£	£
Price paid by parent		48,000
Subsidiary's equity at 1 April 2010 (£32,000 + £10,000)	42,000	
Fair value adjustment	8,000	
75% x 50,000		37,500
Goodwill at 1 April 2010		10,500
Less: Impairment (40%)		4,200
Goodwill at 31 March 2014		6,300

W2. <u>Group retained earnings</u>

	£	£
Parent's retained earnings at 31 March 2014		148,000
Subsidiary's retained earnings at 31 March 2014	22,000	
Less: Subsidiary's retained earnings at 1 April 2010	10,000	
75% x 12,000		9,000
		157,000
Less: Goodwill impairment		4,200
Group retained earnings at 31 March 2014		152,800

W3. Non-controlling interest

	£	£
Subsidiary's share capital at 31 March 2014	32,000	
Subsidiary's retained earnings at 31 March 2014	22,000	
Fair value adjustment	8,000	
	25% x 62,000	15,500
Non-controlling interest at 31 March 2014		15,500

Measurement of the non-controlling interest at fair value

When preparing group accounts, IFRS3 *Business Combinations* allows parent companies to measure non-controlling interests in either of two ways. These are as follows:

(a) Non-controlling interests may be measured by calculating the non-controlling share-holders' proportion of the subsidiary's identifiable net assets. Identifiable assets do not include goodwill (see Chapter 6) so this means that any goodwill which belongs to the non-controlling shareholders is not included in the non-controlling interest.

(b) On acquisition, non-controlling interests may be measured "*at fair value*". Any excess of this fair value over the non-controlling shareholders' proportion of the subsidiary's identifiable net assets on the acquisition date is recognised as goodwill in the group statement of financial position. This approach has two main consequences:

   (i) The goodwill figure shown in the group statement of financial position on the date of acquisition will be equal to 100% of the subsidiary's goodwill.

   (ii) Any goodwill impairment losses which occur after acquisition are deducted partly from group reserves and partly from the non-controlling interest.

However, method (a) is most frequently used in practice, since it avoids the difficulty of measuring the fair value of the non-controlling interest.

EXAMPLE 5

In Example 4 (see above) G Ltd decided that the non-controlling interest in H Ltd on the date of acquisition should be measured at fair value. This was determined by G Ltd to be £16,000. Explain how the group statement of financial position as at 31 March 2014 would be affected by this accounting policy.

Solution

The non-controlling shareholders' proportion of the identifiable net assets of H Ltd on the date of acquisition was £12,500 (25% x (£32,000 + £10,000 + £8,000)). So the goodwill attributable to the non-controlling interest must have been £3,500 (£16,000 – £12,500).

  Goodwill has now suffered 40% impairment, so only £2,100 (£3,500 x 60%) remains at 31 March 2014. The group statement of financial position at that date will show goodwill of £8,400 (£6,300 + £2,100) and non-controlling interest of £17,600 (£15,500 + £2,100).

Preference shares

A company's reserves belong entirely to the ordinary shareholders. If the company were wound up, the preference shareholders (if any) would be entitled to receive only assets equal to the nominal value of their preference shares. This fact must be borne in mind when preparing a consolidated statement of financial position if one or more of the subsidiary companies has issued preference shares.

EXAMPLE 6

On 30 September 2011, J Ltd paid £40,000 to acquire 60% of the ordinary shares and 25% of the preference shares of K Ltd. On that date, the retained earnings of K Ltd were £4,000 and all of its assets and liabilities were shown at fair values. The statements of financial position of J Ltd and K Ltd as at 30 September 2014 are as follows:

	J Ltd £	K Ltd £
Assets		
Non-current assets		
Property, plant and equipment	438,000	52,000
Investment in K Ltd	40,000	
	478,000	
Current assets	432,000	36,000
	910,000	88,000
Equity		
Ordinary share capital	600,000	50,000
Preference share capital		10,000
Retained earnings	119,000	9,000
	719,000	69,000
Liabilities		
Current liabilities	191,000	19,000
	910,000	88,000

K Ltd has issued no shares since being acquired by J Ltd. Goodwill has suffered an impairment loss of 20% since acquisition. Non-controlling interests are to be measured at the appropriate proportion of the subsidiary's identifiable net assets.

Prepare a consolidated statement of financial position as at 30 September 2014.

Solution

Group statement of financial position as at 30 September 2014

	£
Assets	
Non-current assets	
Property, plant and equipment (£438,000 + £52,000)	490,000
Goodwill (W1)	4,080
	494,080
Current assets (£432,000 + £36,000)	468,000
	962,080
Equity	
Ordinary share capital	600,000
Retained earnings (W3)	120,980
	720,980
Non-controlling interest (W2)	31,100
	752,080
Liabilities	
Current liabilities (£191,000 + £19,000)	210,000
	962,080

Workings:

W1. <u>Goodwill</u>

	£	£
Price paid by parent		40,000
Subsidiary's ordinary shares at 30 September 2011	50,000	
Subsidiary's reserves at 30 September 2011	4,000	
60% x 54,000		(32,400)
Parent's 25% stake in subsidiary's preference shares		(2,500)
Goodwill at 30 September 2011		5,100
Less: Impairment (20%)		1,020
Goodwill at 30 September 2014		4,080

W2. <u>Non-controlling interest</u>

	£	£
Subsidiary's ordinary shares at 30 September 2014	50,000	
Subsidiary's retained earnings at 30 September 2014	9,000	
40% x 59,000		23,600
NCI's 75% stake in subsidiary's preference shares		7,500
Non-controlling interest at 30 September 2014		31,100

W3. <u>Group retained earnings</u>

	£	£
Parent's retained earnings at 30 September 2014		119,000
Subsidiary's retained earnings at 30 September 2014	9,000	
Less: Subsidiary's retained earnings at 30 September 2011	4,000	
	60% x 5,000	3,000
		122,000
Less: Goodwill impairment		1,020
Group retained earnings at 30 September 2014		120,980

Elimination of intra-group balances

Intra-group balances are cancelled out when preparing a consolidated statement of financial position. Such balances may arise in any of the following circumstances:

(a) One group company may lend money to another group company. In this case, the loan will appear as an asset in the lending company's financial statements and as a liability in the borrowing company's financial statements.

(b) One group company may buy items on credit from another group company, so that there is a trade receivable in the financial statements of the supplier company and a corresponding trade payable in the financial statements of the customer company.

(c) One group company may have a "current account" with another group company. This account is used to record movements of goods, services and money between the two companies and the balance on the account will appear as an asset in one company's financial statements and as a liability in the other company's financial statements.

   If items are in transit from one company to another, it may be that the relevant asset and liability are not equal in amount. In this case it will be necessary to show the in-transit items as an asset in the consolidated statement of financial position.

EXAMPLE 7

L Ltd is the parent company of M Ltd. The following balances appeared in the books of the two companies at the end of a reporting period:

	Books of L Ltd	Books of M Ltd
	£	£
M Ltd current account (debit balance)	26,750	
L Ltd current account (credit balance)		14,600

The discrepancy between these two balances is caused by the fact that M Ltd sent a cheque for £12,150 to L Ltd on the very last day of the accounting year. L Ltd did not receive this cheque until the third day of the following accounting year. Explain how this matter will be dealt with in the consolidated statement of financial position.

Solution

The two current account balances will be cancelled against each other, leaving a net debit balance of £12,150. This balance represents cash in transit and will be shown as an asset in the consolidated statement of financial position.

Unrealised profits

The assets shown in the individual financial statements of a group company may include assets acquired from another company in the group. If such assets have been transferred between the two companies at a price in excess of original cost, then their valuation includes an element of *unrealised profit* and this must be eliminated when the consolidated statement of financial position is prepared. If this were not done, a group could artificially increase the values of its assets simply by transferring them from one group company to another at inflated prices. Note that:

(a) IFRS10 requires that profits or losses on intra-group transactions must be eliminated in full on consolidation, irrespective of whether the subsidiary companies involved are wholly-owned or partly-owned.

(b) If an asset is sold from parent to subsidiary, any unrealised profit on the transaction is entirely attributable to the group and is subtracted from group retained earnings.

(c) If an asset is sold from subsidiary to parent, any unrealised profit on the transaction is allocated proportionately between group retained earnings and the non-controlling interest (if any).

EXAMPLE 8

P Ltd owns 80% of the share capital of Q Ltd. The inventories of Q Ltd on 31 December 2013 include goods bought from P Ltd for £15,000. These goods had cost P Ltd £10,000.

(a) Explain how these goods should be dealt with in the consolidated statement of financial position at 31 December 2013.

(b) Explain how the treatment would differ if the goods had been sold by Q Ltd to P Ltd.

Solution

(a) The unrealised profit of £5,000 is subtracted from group inventories and also from group retained earnings. It might be thought that 20% of this profit has in fact been realised, since 20% of the goods are now effectively owned by the non-controlling shareholders, who are not part of the group. But IFRS10 requires that the full £5,000 should be eliminated.

(b) The unrealised profit of £5,000 is subtracted from group inventories. Group retained earnings are reduced by £4,000 (80%) and the non-controlling interest is reduced by the remaining £1,000 (20%).

Reporting period and accounting policies

In general, the financial statements of a parent company and its subsidiaries should all be drawn up to the same date. If the reporting period of a parent is different from that of a subsidiary, the subsidiary should prepare additional financial statements for consolidation purposes, using the same reporting period as its parent. If this is impracticable, the financial statements of the subsidiary should be adjusted before consolidation to reflect any significant transactions or events that occur between the end of the subsidiary's reporting period and the end of the parent's reporting period. In any case, IFRS10 requires that the difference between the end of the reporting period of a subsidiary and that of its parent should not exceed three months.

Furthermore, consolidated financial statements should be prepared using uniform accounting policies. If a group company uses different accounting policies from those adopted in the consolidated financial statements, its own financial statements should be adjusted in line with the group's accounting policies before consolidation takes place.

Disclosure requirements

International standard IFRS12 *Disclosure of Interests in Other Entities* requires an entity to disclose information that enables the users of its financial statements to evaluate:

(a) the nature of its interests in other entities and the risks associated with those interests

(b) the effects of those interests on the entity's financial position, financial performance and cash flows.

In particular, the entity should disclose the significant judgements and assumptions it has made in determining the nature of its interest in another entity (e.g. in determining whether or not it has control over an entity) and should then provide information about its interests in subsidiaries, joint arrangements and associates (see Chapter 20).

With regard to its subsidiaries, IFRS12 requires an entity to disclose information which enables users to understand the composition of the group and the interest that any non-controlling interests have in the group's activities.

Summary

▸ A parent company controls its subsidiaries. Control usually accompanies ownership of over 50% of a company's ordinary shares.

▸ A parent company together with its subsidiaries is known as a group. The parent company must prepare and present consolidated financial statements which show the financial performance and position of the group as a whole.

▸ A group statement of financial position is prepared by consolidating the statements of financial position of all the group companies (line by line) and cancelling out intra-group items. A group statement of financial position may also be referred to as a consolidated statement of financial position.

▸ Goodwill arising on consolidation must be tested for impairment annually.

▸ The consolidated statement of financial position should show the extent to which the net assets of the group are attributable to a non-controlling interest.

▸ IFRS3 allows non-controlling's interests to be measured as the non-controlling share-holders' proportion of the subsidiary's identifiable net assets. Alternatively, non-controlling interests may be measured on the date of acquisition at fair value.

▸ A group's interest in the post-acquisition increase or decrease in the retained earnings of a subsidiary are added to or subtracted from consolidated retained earnings.

▸ Intra-group balances are cancelled out when preparing a consolidated statement of financial position. Any unrealised profit on assets transferred between group companies is eliminated in full on consolidation.

Exercises

It is assumed throughout these exercises that non-controlling interests are to be measured at the appropriate proportion of the subsidiary's identifiable net assets.

18.1 At the start of business on 1 January 2014, the statements of financial position of A1 Ltd and A2 Ltd were as follows:

	A1 Ltd £000	A2 Ltd £000
Assets		
Non-current assets	510	125
Current assets	325	75
	835	200
Equity		
Ordinary share capital	500	100
Retained earnings	185	60
	685	160
Liabilities		
Current liabilities	150	40
	835	200

On 1 January 2014, A1 Ltd acquired 100% of the share capital of A2 Ltd for £225,000. The fair value of A2 Ltd's non-current assets on that date was £150,000. All other assets and liabilities were shown at fair value in the company's statement of financial position. There were no other transactions on 1 January 2014.

Required:

(a) Prepare a consolidated statement of financial position as at the close of business on 1 January 2014, assuming that the purchase consideration of £225,000 was paid in cash.

(b) Prepare a consolidated statement of financial position as at the close of business on 1 January 2014, now assuming that the purchase consideration of £225,000 was settled by means of an issue of 150,000 £1 ordinary shares in A1 Ltd at a premium of 50p per share.

18.2 On 31 December 2013, A3 Ltd paid £550,000 to acquire 80% of the ordinary share capital of A4 Ltd. The statements of financial position of the two companies just after this transaction were as follows:

	A3 Ltd	**A4 Ltd**
	£000	£000
Assets		
Non-current assets		
Property, plant and equipment	3,700	320
Investment in A4 Ltd	550	
	4,250	
Current assets	2,750	250
	7,000	570
Equity		
Ordinary share capital	2,000	100
Retained earnings	3,550	280
	5,550	380
Liabilities		
Current liabilities	1,450	190
	7,000	570

The fair value of the property, plant and equipment of A4 Ltd on 31 December 2013 was £440,000. All other assets and liabilities were shown at fair value.

Required:

Prepare a consolidated statement of financial position as at 31 December 2013.

18.3 The statements of financial position of AA Ltd and BB Ltd as at 30 April 2014 are as follows:

	AA Ltd	BB Ltd
	£000	£000
Assets		
Non-current assets		
Property, plant and equipment	2,265	345
Investment in BB Ltd	800	
	3,065	
Current assets	2,124	466
	5,189	811
Equity		
Ordinary share capital	3,000	350
Retained earnings	1,029	223
	4,029	573
Liabilities		
Current liabilities	1,160	238
	5,189	811

The following information is relevant:

(a) AA Ltd acquired the entire share capital of BB Ltd on 30 April 2010. There have been no changes in the share capital of BB Ltd since then.

(b) On 30 April 2010, the fair value of BB Ltd's non-current assets was £500,000, as compared with their book value on that date of £320,000. This revaluation has not been reflected in the books of BB Ltd.

(c) On 30 April 2010, the retained earnings of BB Ltd were £195,000.

(d) Goodwill arising on consolidation has suffered an impairment loss of 100% since the date of acquisition.

Required:

Prepare a consolidated statement of financial position as at 30 April 2014.

18.4 The statements of financial position of TT Ltd and UU Ltd as at 31 May 2014 are as follows:

	TT Ltd	UU Ltd
	£000	£000
Assets		
Non-current assets		
Property, plant and equipment	6,910	1,640
Investment in UU Ltd	1,400	
	8,310	
Current assets	3,110	1,120
	11,420	2,760
Equity		
Ordinary share capital	4,000	500
Retained earnings	5,380	1,550
	9,380	2,050
Liabilities		
Current liabilities	2,040	710
	11,420	2,760

The following information is available:

(a) TT Ltd acquired 70% of the share capital of UU Ltd on 31 May 2006. There have been no changes in the share capital of UU Ltd since that date.

(b) On 31 May 2006, the fair value of the non-current assets of UU Ltd was £150,000 higher than their book value on that date. This valuation has not been reflected in the books of UU Ltd.

(c) On 31 May 2006, the retained earnings of UU Ltd were £850,000.

(d) Goodwill has suffered no impairment since 31 May 2006.

Required:

Prepare a consolidated statement of financial position as at 31 May 2014.

18.5 Klarke plc acquired a subsidiary, Cameroon Ltd, on 1 October 2013. The statements of financial position of Klarke plc and Cameroon Ltd as at 30 September 2014 are as follows:

	Klarke	Cameroon
	£000	£000
Assets		
Non-current assets		
Property, plant and equipment	53,181	36,762
Investment in Cameroon Ltd	29,000	
	82,181	
Current assets	28,484	10,337
	110,665	47,099
Equity		
Ordinary share capital	20,000	5,000
Share premium account	10,000	2,000
Retained earnings	34,225	28,370
	64,225	35,370
Liabilities		
Non-current liabilities		
Long-term loan	35,000	8,000
Current liabilities	11,440	3,729
	110,665	47,099

Additional data:

(i)   The share capital of Cameroon Ltd consists of ordinary shares of £1 each. There have been no changes to the balances of share capital and share premium during the year. No dividends were paid or proposed by Cameroon Ltd during the year.

(ii) Klarke plc acquired 3,000,000 shares in Cameroon Ltd on 1 October 2013.

(iii) At 1 October 2013, the retained earnings of Cameroon Ltd were £24,700,000.

(iv) The fair value of the non-current assets of Cameroon Ltd at 1 October 2013 was £37,000,000. The book value of the non-current assets at 1 October 2013 was £33,000,000. The revaluation has not been recorded in the books of Cameroon Ltd (ignore any effect on the depreciation for the year). There were no other differences between the book value and the fair value of the other assets and liabilities of Cameroon Ltd at the date of acquisition.

(v)   The directors have concluded that goodwill on the acquisition of Cameroon Ltd has been impaired during the year. They estimate that the impairment loss amounts to 20% of the goodwill.

Required:

Calculate the following figures relating to the acquisition of Cameroon Ltd that will appear in the consolidated statement of financial position of Klarke plc at 30 September 2014:

(a) the non-controlling interest

(b) the goodwill arising on acquisition

(c) the consolidated retained earnings of the group.

(Amended from AAT)

*18.6 The statements of financial position of CC Ltd and its two subsidiaries DD Ltd and EE Ltd as at 31 December 2013 are as follows:

	CC Ltd £000		DD Ltd £000		EE Ltd £000	
Assets						
Non-current assets						
Property and equipment		4,761		521		411
Investment in DD Ltd		600				
Investment in EE Ltd		575				
		5,936				
Current assets						
Inventories	1,532		222		187	
Trade receivables	1,947		258		202	
Cash at bank	239	3,718	30	510	13	402
		9,654		1,031		813
Equity						
Ordinary share capital		5,000		500		300
Revaluation reserve		2,500		-		100
Retained earnings		547		320		250
		8,047		820		650
Liabilities						
Current liabilities						
Trade payables		1,607		211		163
		9,654		1,031		813

The following information is available:

(a) CC Ltd acquired 60% of the shares of DD Ltd on 1 January 2012, when DD Ltd had retained earnings of £280,000. The fair value of the property and equipment of DD Ltd on that date was £30,000 more than book value. This valuation has not been reflected in the books of DD Ltd.

(b) CC Ltd acquired 90% of the shares of EE Ltd on 1 January 2013, when EE Ltd had a revaluation reserve of £60,000 and retained earnings of £230,000. The fair value of EE Ltd's assets and liabilities on that date was equal to their book value.

(c) Neither DD Ltd nor EE Ltd have issued any shares since being acquired by CC Ltd.

(d) Goodwill arising on consolidation in relation to DD Ltd has suffered an impairment loss of 50% since the date of acquisition. The impairment loss for EE Ltd is 25%.

(e) The following intra-group balances exist on 31 December 2013:

- DD Ltd owes CC Ltd £15,000
- EE Ltd owes CC Ltd £25,000
- EE Ltd owes DD Ltd £8,000.

All of these balances are included in trade receivables and payables.

(f) Goods purchased for £8,000 from CC Ltd are included in DD Ltd's inventory at 31 December 2013. CC Ltd had invoiced these goods to DD Ltd at cost plus 60%.

Required:

Prepare a consolidated statement of financial position as at 31 December 2013.

*18.7   The following are the statements of financial position of two companies at 31 October 2014, the end of their most recent financial years:

	Multa plc £m	Tuli plc £m
Assets		
Non-current assets		
Property, plant and equipment	425	288
Investments, at cost	147	13
	572	301
Current assets		
Inventories	88	73
Trade receivables	147	106
Other current assets	37	22
Cash and cash equivalents	36	15
	308	216
Total assets	880	517

(continued)

	£m	£m
Equity		
Ordinary share capital (£1 shares)	300	150
10% Preference share capital (£1 shares)	-	45
Retained earnings	157	90
	457	285
Liabilities		
Non-current liabilities	150	82
Current liabilities		
Trade payables	184	56
Current tax payable	89	69
Bank overdraft	-	25
	273	150
Total liabilities	423	232
Total equity and liabilities	880	517

The following additional information is available:

1) On 1 November 2012 Multa plc purchased 90,000,000 ordinary shares in Tuli plc paying a total of £120,000,000. The reserves of Tuli plc on 1 November 2012 were £30,000,000. It was agreed that all the assets and liabilities of Tuli plc were reported in its financial statements at fair values as at 1 November 2012. Since then the directors of Multa plc feel that the amount paid for as goodwill upon the acquisition has been impaired by £3,000,000.

2) During the year ended 31 October 2014 Multa plc sold inventory to Tuli plc for £25,000,000. Multa plc earned a uniform margin of 40% on these sales. During the year ended 31 October 2014 Tuli plc resold 80% of this inventory. On 31 October 2014 Tuli plc had unpaid invoices totalling £18,000,000 payable to Multa plc in respect of these purchases.

3) Each ordinary share in Tuli plc carries one vote and there are no other voting rights in the company.

Required:

(a) Calculate the amount paid as goodwill on the acquisition of Tuli plc on 1 November 2012.

(b) Prepare with full supportive workings the consolidated statement of financial position of Multa plc as at 31 October 2014.

(CIPFA)

Chapter 19

Groups of companies (2)

Introduction

The previous chapter of this book introduced the concept of a group of companies and dealt with the group statement of financial position. This second chapter on groups deals with the group statement of comprehensive income and the group statement of changes in equity. The chapter begins by explaining the basic adjustments that are usually required when preparing these group (or "consolidated") financial statements. These include:

(a) the elimination of intra-group items and unrealised profits

(b) accounting for the impairment of goodwill

(c) accounting for profits which are attributable to a non-controlling interest.

This chapter then goes on to explain how a group statement of comprehensive income is prepared when a subsidiary is acquired part of the way through the accounting period.

As stated in Chapter 18, the applicable standards are IFRS10 *Consolidated Financial Statements* and IFRS3 *Business Combinations*. Although these standards apply to groups in general, including groups with unincorporated subsidiaries, this chapter deals with groups of companies only.

Objectives

By the end of this chapter, the reader should be able to:

• explain the purpose of a group statement of comprehensive income

• prepare a group statement of comprehensive income, eliminating intra-group items in accordance with the requirements of IFRS10

• account correctly for a non-controlling interest in the profits of a subsidiary

• prepare a group statement of changes in equity

• prepare a group statement of comprehensive income in the situation where a parent company has acquired a subsidiary part of the way through the accounting period.

The group statement of comprehensive income

The main purpose of a group (or "consolidated") statement of comprehensive income is to report the profit or loss of the group as a whole. IFRS10 requires that such a statement should be prepared and presented in recognition of the fact that a parent company and its subsidiaries are, in effect, a single economic entity.

A group statement of comprehensive income is prepared by adding together (line by line) the individual statements of comprehensive income of all of the companies in the group, cancelling out any intra-group items. Note the following points:

(a) Any intra-group sales are included in the sales revenue of the selling company and in the cost of sales of the buying company. Therefore, intra-group sales are deducted from group sales revenue and from group cost of sales when preparing the group statement of comprehensive income. This ensures that the group financial statements show only the sales revenue from external customers and the cost of goods acquired from external suppliers.

(b) As explained in Chapter 18, any unrealised profit on inventories is deducted from the inventories figure shown in the group statement of financial position. A reduction in closing inventory causes an increase in cost of sales, so the group's cost of sales figure must be *increased* by the amount of any unrealised profit.

(c) Other intra-group items that may arise (and which must be cancelled out) include interest payable by one group member to another and management expenses charged by one group member to another.

(d) Any dividends paid by a subsidiary to its parent company (shown in the subsidiary's statement of changes in equity) are cancelled against the dividends received which are shown in the parent's statement of comprehensive income.

(e) If any goodwill acquired by the parent company on acquisition has suffered an impairment loss during the period, this loss is shown as an expense in the group statement of comprehensive income.

(f) If a group includes any partly-owned subsidiaries, part of the group's profit after tax is attributable to the non-controlling interest. This amount is deducted in the group statement of comprehensive income, leaving the profit attributable to the group.

The group statement of changes in equity

The purpose of a group statement of changes in equity is to show how each component of the group's equity (shown in the group statement of financial position) has changed during the accounting period. In general, there is one column for the parent's share capital and one column for each of the group's reserves. These columns are totalled to show the equity which belongs to the parent's shareholders. There is then a further column for the non-controlling interest and a final column which shows the total equity of the group.

EXAMPLE 1

On 1 July 2011, R Ltd acquired 70% of the ordinary share capital of S Ltd. There are no preference shares. The retained earnings of S Ltd on 1 July 2011 were £2,000. Statements of comprehensive income for the year to 30 June 2014 are as follows:

	R Ltd	S Ltd
	£	£
Sales revenue	624,000	109,000
Cost of sales	267,400	65,300
Gross profit	356,600	43,700
Distribution costs	(71,370)	(5,100)
Administrative expenses	(101,430)	(10,500)
Operating profit	183,800	28,100
Dividend received from S Ltd	14,000	
Profit before tax	197,800	28,100
Taxation	51,200	7,100
Profit for the year	146,600	21,000

The following figures are taken from the retained earnings column of the statement of changes in equity of R Ltd and S Ltd for the year to 30 June 2014:

	R Ltd	S Ltd
	£	£
Balance at 30 June 2013	54,900	7,000
Profit for the year	146,600	21,000
Dividends paid	(120,000)	(20,000)
Balance at 30 June 2014	81,500	8,000

The following information is also available:

(a) During the year, R Ltd sold goods to S Ltd for £8,000. These goods had cost R Ltd £5,000. At the year end, one-half of the goods were still held by S Ltd.

(b) Goodwill arising on consolidation has suffered no impairment losses.

Prepare a consolidated statement of comprehensive income for the year to 30 June 2014. Also prepare an extract from the consolidated statement of changes in equity, showing the changes in the group's retained earnings during the year.

Solution

Intra-group sales of £8,000 and the unrealised profit of £1,500 (50% x £3,000) must be eliminated when preparing the group statement of comprehensive income. The intra-group dividend of £14,000 (70% x £20,000) must also be eliminated.

Non-controlling shareholders own 30% of the shares in S Ltd. So the profit attributable to the non-controlling interest is 30% of £21,000 = £6,300.

Group statement of comprehensive income for the year to 30 June 2014

	£
Sales revenue (£624,000 + £109,000 – £8,000)	725,000
Cost of sales (£267,400 + £65,300 – £8,000 + £1,500)	326,200
Gross profit	398,800
Distribution costs (£71,370 + £5,100)	(76,470)
Administrative expenses (£101,430 + £10,500)	(111,930)
Profit before tax	210,400
Taxation (£51,200 + £7,100)	58,300
Profit for the year	152,100
Attributable to non-controlling interest (30% x £21,000)	6,300
Attributable to the group	145,800

Group statement of changes in equity for the year to 30 June 2014 (extract)

	Retained Earnings
	£
Balance at 30 June 2013 (W1)	58,400
Profit for the year	145,800
Dividends paid	(120,000)
Balance at 30 June 2014 (W2)	84,200

Workings:

W1. Group retained earnings at 30 June 2013

	£	£
Parent's retained earnings at 30 June 2013		54,900
Subsidiary's retained earnings at 30 June 2013	7,000	
Less: Subsidiary's retained earnings at 1 July 2011	2,000	
70% x 5,000		3,500
Group retained earnings at 30 June 2013		58,400

W2. Group retained earnings at 30 June 2014

	£	£
Parent's retained earnings at 30 June 2014		81,500
Subsidiary's retained earnings at 30 June 2014	8,000	
Less: Subsidiary's retained earnings at 1 July 2011	2,000	
70% x 6,000		4,200
Less: Unrealised profit		(1,500)
Group retained earnings at 30 June 2014		84,200

EXAMPLE 2

On 1 January 2013, V Ltd paid £92,000 to acquire 80% of the share capital of W Ltd. The financial statements of V Ltd and W Ltd for the year to 31 December 2013 are as follows:

Statements of comprehensive income for the year to 31 December 2013

	V Ltd	W Ltd
	£000	£000
Sales revenue	870	340
Cost of sales	370	160
Gross profit	500	180
Operating expenses	(301)	(105)
Dividend received from W Ltd	16	-
Profit before tax	215	75
Taxation	73	20
Profit for the year	142	55

Statements of changes in equity for the year to 31 December 2013

	V Ltd			W Ltd		
	Share capital	Retained earnings	Total	Share capital	Retained earnings	Total
	£000	£000	£000	£000	£000	£000
Balance at 1/1/2013	200	240	440	50	30	80
Profit for the year		142	142		55	55
Dividends paid		(60)	(60)		(20)	(20)
Balance at 31/12/2013	200	322	522	50	65	115

Statements of financial position as at 31 December 2013

	V Ltd	W Ltd
	£000	£000
Assets		
Non-current assets		
Property, plant and equipment	360	120
Investment in W Ltd	92	
Current assets	150	40
	602	160
Equity		
Ordinary share capital	200	50
Retained earnings	322	65
	522	115
Liabilities		
Current liabilities	80	45
	602	160

The following information is also available:

(a) All of the assets and liabilities of W Ltd were carried at fair value on 1 January 2013.

(b) Goodwill arising on consolidation has suffered an impairment loss of 25%.

(c) There were no intra-group sales during the year.

(d) Non-controlling interests in the statement of financial position are to be measured at the appropriate proportion of the subsidiary's identifiable net assets.

Prepare a group statement of comprehensive income and statement of changes in equity for the year to 31 December 2013. Also prepare a group statement of financial position as at that date.

Solution

The consolidated financial statements are as follows:

Group statement of comprehensive income for the year to 31 December 2013

	£000
Sales revenue (870 + 340)	1,210
Cost of sales (370 + 160)	530
Gross profit	680
Operating expenses (301 + 105)	(406)
Impairment of goodwill (W1)	(7)
Profit before tax	267
Taxation (73 + 20)	93
Profit for the year	174
Attributable to non-controlling interest (20% x 55)	11
Attributable to the group	163

Group statement of changes in equity for the year to 31 December 2013

	Share capital	Retained earnings	Total	Non-controlling interest	Total equity
	£000	£000	£000	£000	£000
Balance at 1/1/2013	200	240	440	-	440
Acquisition of subsidiary				16	16
Profit for the year		163	163	11	174
Dividends paid		(60)	(60)	(4)	(64)
Balance at 31/12/2013	200	343	543	23	566

Note:

The total equity of W Ltd when it was acquired by V Ltd was £80,000. The non-controlling shareholders own 20% of the shares of W Ltd. Therefore the non-controlling interest that was created when W Ltd was acquired was £16,000 (20% x £80,000).

Group statement of financial position as at 31 December 2013

	£000
Assets	
Non-current assets	
Property, plant and equipment (360 + 120)	480
Goodwill (W1)	21
Current assets (150 + 40)	190
	691
Equity	
Ordinary share capital	200
Retained earnings (W2)	343
	543
Non-controlling interest (20% x (50 + 65))	23
	566
Liabilities	
Current liabilities (80 + 45)	125
	691

Workings:

W1. Goodwill

	£000	£000
Price paid by parent		92
Subsidiary's share capital at 1 January 2013	50	
Subsidiary's retained earnings at 1 January 2013	30	
	80% x 80	64
		28
Less: Impairment (25%)		7
Goodwill at 31 December 2013		21

W2. Group retained earnings

	£000	£000
Parent's retained earnings at 31 December 2013		322
Subsidiary's retained earnings at 31 December 2013	65	
Less: Subsidiary's retained earnings at 1 January 2013	30	
	80% x 35	28
		350
Less: Goodwill impairment		7
Group retained earnings at 31 December 2013		343

Subsidiary acquired part way through an accounting period

If a subsidiary is acquired part of the way through the accounting period for which group accounts are being prepared, it is necessary to apportion the subsidiary's profit for that period into its pre-acquisition and post-acquisition components. The group's share of the subsidiary's pre-acquisition profit is cancelled out in the calculation of the goodwill arising on consolidation. The group's share of the subsidiary's post-acquisition profit is included in the consolidated statement of comprehensive income.

There are no new principles here. This treatment of a subsidiary's profits in the year of acquisition is simply a further application of the requirement to exclude pre-acquisition profits from the consolidated statement of comprehensive income.

The apportionment of a subsidiary's profits in the year of acquisition is normally done on a time basis. However, a different approach may be necessary if the subsidiary's business is affected by seasonal or other factors so that a straightforward time apportionment would not be appropriate.

EXAMPLE 3

Y Ltd acquired 75% of the ordinary share capital of Z Ltd on 1 April 2014. There are no preference shares. Both companies prepare accounts to 30 September each year. Their statements of comprehensive income for the year to 30 September 2014 are as follows:

	Y Ltd	Z Ltd
	£	£
Sales revenue	317,500	96,000
Cost of sales	149,500	31,200
Gross profit	168,000	64,800
Distribution costs	(36,300)	(4,800)
Administrative expenses	(59,400)	(20,400)
Profit before tax	72,300	39,600
Taxation	21,000	8,000
Profit for the year	51,300	31,600

Movements in the retained earnings of Y Ltd and Z Ltd for the year to 30 September 2014 are as follows:

	Y Ltd	Z Ltd
	£	£
Balance at 30 September 2013	112,600	77,700
Profit for the year	51,300	31,600
Balance at 30 September 2014	163,900	109,300

The following information is also available:

(a) Two-thirds of the sales, cost of sales and distribution costs of Z Ltd occur in the second half of the accounting year. Administrative expenses are spread evenly over the year. £5,000 of Z Ltd's tax liability relates to the second half of the year.

(b) Goodwill arising on consolidation has suffered no impairment losses.

Prepare a consolidated statement of comprehensive income for the year to 30 September 2014 and calculate the group's retained earnings as at that date.

Solution

Before consolidation, the Z Ltd statement of comprehensive income should be apportioned into its pre-acquisition and post-acquisition components, as follows:

	1/10/13 to 31/3/14	1/4/14 to 30/9/14
	£	£
Sales revenue (1:2)	32,000	64,000
Cost of sales (1:2)	10,400	20,800
Gross profit	21,600	43,200
Distribution costs (1:2)	(1,600)	(3,200)
Administrative expenses (1:1)	(10,200)	(10,200)
Profit before tax	9,800	29,800
Taxation	3,000	5,000
Profit for the year	6,800	24,800

The consolidated statement of comprehensive income is as follows:

	£
Sales revenue (£317,500 + £64,000)	381,500
Cost of sales (£149,500 + £20,800)	170,300
Gross profit	211,200
Distribution costs (£36,300 + £3,200)	(39,500)
Administrative expenses (£59,400 + £10,200)	(69,600)
Profit before tax	102,100
Taxation (£21,000 + £5,000)	26,000
Profit for the year	76,100
Attributable to non-controlling interest (25% x £24,800)	6,200
Attributable to the group	69,900

The retained earnings column of the consolidated statement of changes in equity for the year to 30 September 2014 will show the following:

	Group £
Balance at 30 September 2013	112,600
Profit for the year	69,900
Balance at 30 September 2014	182,500

Notes:

1. The profit attributable to the non-controlling interest is 25% of the post-acquisition profits of Z Ltd (i.e. 25% x £24,800 = £6,200).

2. At 30 September 2013, the group retained earnings are simply the £112,600 retained earnings of Y Ltd.

3. Since acquisition, the retained earnings of Z Ltd have increased by £24,800. Group retained earnings at 30 September 2014 are the retained earnings of Y Ltd (£163,900) plus 75% of £24,800 (£18,600). This gives a total of £182,500.

Summary

▸ A consolidated statement of comprehensive income shows the profit or loss of the group as a whole and is prepared by adding together (line by line) the individual statements of comprehensive income of all of the companies in the group, cancelling out any intra-group items.

▸ The main intra-group items that should be cancelled out are intra-group sales, interest and management expenses. Any unrealised profit on inventories should be added to the group cost of sales figure.

▸ Any dividends paid by a subsidiary to its parent company are cancelled against the dividends received shown in the parent's statement of comprehensive income.

▸ Impairment losses on goodwill are shown as an expense in the consolidated statement of comprehensive income.

▸ Any part of a subsidiary's profit that is attributable to the non-controlling interest is deducted in the consolidated statement of comprehensive income.

▸ A consolidated statement of changes in equity shows how each component of the group's equity has changed during the period. In general, there is one column for the parent's share capital and one column for each of the group's reserves. There is also a column showing changes in the non-controlling interest.

▸ If a subsidiary is acquired part-way through an accounting period, its profit for that period must be apportioned into its pre-acquisition and post-acquisition components.

Exercises

In these exercises, it may be assumed that each company's other comprehensive income for the year is £nil. It may also be assumed that non-controlling interests in the statement of financial position are to be measured at the appropriate proportion of the subsidiary's identifiable net assets.

19.1 PP Ltd acquired 65% of the ordinary share capital of QQ Ltd on 1 January 2013. There are no preference shares. The statements of comprehensive income of the two companies for the year to 31 December 2013 are as follows:

	PP Ltd	QQ Ltd
	£	£
Sales revenue	345,450	186,350
Cost of sales	125,700	71,990
Gross profit	219,750	114,360
Operating expenses	56,330	37,800
Profit before tax	163,420	76,560
Taxation	42,000	15,160
Profit for the year	121,420	61,400

Required:

Prepare a consolidated statement of comprehensive income for the year to 31 December 2013.

19.2 FF Ltd acquired 80% of the ordinary share capital of GG Ltd on 1 April 2010. On that date, the retained earnings of GG Ltd were £18,260. There are no preference shares. The statements of comprehensive income of FF Ltd and GG Ltd for the year to 31 March 2014 are as follows:

	FF Ltd	GG Ltd
	£	£
Sales revenue	359,800	154,600
Cost of sales	102,600	55,550
Gross profit	257,200	99,050
Operating expenses	118,480	19,300
Operating profit	138,720	79,750
Dividends received	28,000	-
Profit before tax	166,720	79,750
Taxation	40,000	20,000
Profit for the year	126,720	59,750

The statement of changes in equity for FF Ltd and GG Ltd show the following retained earnings figures for the year to 31 March 2014:

	FF Ltd	GG Ltd
	£	£
Balance at 31 March 2013	66,090	41,110
Profit for the year	126,720	59,750
Dividends paid	(90,000)	(35,000)
Balance at 31 March 2014	102,810	65,860

On 4 March 2014, FF Ltd sold goods to GG Ltd for £10,000. These goods had cost FF Ltd £6,000. One-quarter of them were included in GG Ltd's inventory at 31 March 2014.

Required:

(a) Prepare a consolidated statement of comprehensive income for the year to 31 March 2014, assuming that there are no impairment losses in relation to goodwill.

(b) Prepare an extract from the consolidated statement of changes in equity for the year to 31 March 2014, showing the changes in the group's retained earnings.

19.3 On 1 March 2014, YY Ltd acquired 85% of the ordinary share capital of ZZ Ltd. There are no preference shares. Both companies prepare financial statements to 31 October each year. Transactions between the two companies during the year to 31 October 2014 were as follows:

(a) On 31 January 2014, YY Ltd sold goods costing £2,000 to ZZ Ltd for £3,500. All of these goods had been sold by ZZ Ltd by the end of the accounting year.

(b) On 30 September 2014, YY Ltd sold goods costing £4,000 to ZZ Ltd for £7,000. None of these goods had been sold by ZZ Ltd by the end of the accounting year.

There was a goodwill impairment loss of £10,000 during the period from 1 March 2014 to 31 October 2014. The statements of comprehensive income of the two companies for the year to 31 October 2014 are as follows:

	YY Ltd	ZZ Ltd
	£	£
Sales revenue	150,000	84,000
Cost of sales	60,000	27,000
Gross profit	90,000	57,000
Operating expenses	25,800	18,600
Profit before tax	64,200	38,400
Taxation	13,000	7,200
Profit for the year	51,200	31,200

All income and expenses accrued evenly through the year.

Required:

Prepare a consolidated statement of comprehensive income for the year to 31 October 2014.

19.4   The Managing Director of Wraymand plc has asked you to prepare the statement of comprehensive income for the group. The company has one subsidiary undertaking, Blonk Ltd. The statements of comprehensive income of the two companies for the year ended 31 March 2014 are set out below.

Statements of comprehensive income for the year to 31 March 2014

	Wraymand	**Blonk**
	£000	£000
Sales revenue	38,462	12,544
Cost of sales	(22,693)	(5,268)
Gross profit	15,769	7,276
Dividend from Blonk Ltd	580	
	16,349	
Distribution costs	(6,403)	(2,851)
Administrative expenses	(3,987)	(2,466)
Profit from operations	5,959	1,959
Finance costs	(562)	(180)
Profit before tax	5,397	1,779
Taxation	(1,511)	(623)
Profit for the year	3,886	1,156

Further information:

(i)   Wraymand plc acquired 75% of the ordinary share capital of Blonk Ltd on 1 April 2013.

(ii)   During the year, Blonk Ltd sold goods which had cost £1,100,000 to Wraymand plc for £1,600,000. All of the goods had been sold by Wraymand plc by the end of the year.

Required:

Draft a consolidated statement of comprehensive income for Wraymand plc and its subsidiary for the year ended 31 March 2014.   *(Amended from AAT)*

*19.5 The financial statements of JJ Ltd and KK Ltd for the year to 30 June 2014 are shown below:

Statements of comprehensive income for the year to 30 June 2014

	JJ Ltd £000	KK Ltd £000
Sales revenue	21,545	5,328
Cost of sales	13,335	3,552
Gross profit	8,210	1,776
Operating expenses	4,087	410
Operating profit	4,123	1,366
Dividends received from KK Ltd	377	-
Profit before tax	4,500	1,366
Taxation	1,500	450
Profit for the year	3,000	916

Statements of financial position as at 30 June 2014

		JJ Ltd £000		KK Ltd £000
Assets				
Non-current assets				
Property, plant and equipment		5,961		2,667
Investment in KK Ltd		3,153		
		9,114		
Current assets				
Inventories	2,215		1,052	
Trade receivables	1,823		829	
Cash at bank	101	4,139	5	1,886
		13,253		4,553
Equity				
Ordinary share capital		7,000		2,500
Preference share capital		800		400
Retained earnings		1,949		508
		9,749		3,408
Liabilities				
Current liabilities				
Trade payables	2,004		695	
Taxation	1,500	3,504	450	1,145
		13,253		4,553

Statements of changes in equity for the year to 30 June 2014

	JJ Ltd			KK Ltd		
	Share capital	Retained earnings	Total	Share capital	Retained earnings	Total
	£000	£000	£000	£000	£000	£000
Balance b/f	7,800	829	8,629	2,900	112	3,012
Profit for the year		3,000	3,000		916	916
Dividends - ord.		(1,800)	(1,800)		(500)	(500)
Dividends - pref.		(80)	(80)		(20)	(20)
Balance c/f	7,800	1,949	9,749	2,900	508	3,408

The following information is also available:

1.   On 1 July 2010, JJ Ltd paid £3,153,000 to acquire 75% of the ordinary shares and 10% of the preference shares of KK Ltd. On that date, the retained earnings of KK Ltd were £704,000.

2.   The fair value of the non-current assets of KK Ltd on 1 July 2010 exceeded their carrying amount by £600,000. This valuation has not been reflected in the books of KK Ltd.

3.   KK Ltd has issued no shares since being acquired by JJ Ltd.

4.   Goodwill had suffered impairment losses of 30% by 30 June 2013 and there was a further 10% impairment loss during the year to 30 June 2014.

5.   JJ Ltd sells goods to KK Ltd at cost plus 60%. During the year to 30 June 2014, these sales totalled £2,400,000, of which £216,000 was still owing to JJ Ltd at the end of the year. The inventory of KK Ltd at 30 June 2014 includes goods bought from JJ Ltd for £512,000.

Required:

(a)   Prepare a consolidated statement of comprehensive income for the year to 30 June 2014.

(b)   Prepare a consolidated statement of changes in equity for the year to 30 June 2014.

(c)   Prepare a consolidated statement of financial position as at 30 June 2014.

(d)   Explain how each of these financial statements would differ if the intra-group sales described above were from KK Ltd to JJ Ltd (rather than from JJ Ltd to KK Ltd).

Chapter 20

Associates and joint arrangements

Introduction

If one company is able to exercise control over another company, then a parent-subsidiary relationship exists between the two companies and the parent must prepare consolidated financial statements in accordance with IFRS10 (see Chapter 18). Control is generally achieved through ownership of over 50% of the other company's ordinary shares.

However, a company which owns shares in another company might not own enough shares to be able to exercise control over that other company's activities. There are three distinct possibilities:

(a) The investor company might own only a small number of shares in the investee company, insufficient to give the investor any significant influence over the investee's activities. In this case, the investment is accounted for in the investor company's financial statements in accordance with IAS39 *Financial Instruments: Recognition and Measurement* or IFRS9 *Financial Instruments* (see Chapter 11).

(b) The investor company might own enough shares in the investee company to be able to exercise significant influence over its activities, but not enough to exercise control over those activities. In this case, the investee company is known as an "associate" and the investment is accounted for in accordance with IAS28 *Investments in Associates and Joint Ventures*.

(c) The investor company together with other investors might be able to exercise joint control over the investee company. This type of arrangement is known as a "joint arrangement" and the required accounting treatment is prescribed by either IFRS11 *Joint Arrangements* or IAS28 *Investments in Associates and Joint Ventures*.

The purpose of this chapter is to explain the main requirements of standards IAS28 and IFRS11. These standards apply to entities in general (including unincorporated entities) but it is assumed throughout this chapter that all of the entities concerned are companies.

Objectives

By the end of this chapter, the reader should be able to:

- define the terms "associate" and "significant influence" in accordance with IAS28
- explain the equity method of accounting and apply this method when accounting for an investment in an associate
- define the terms "joint arrangement" and "joint control" in accordance with IFRS11
- distinguish between a joint operation and a joint venture
- account correctly for an interest in a joint operation or a joint venture
- outline the main requirements of IFRS12 *Disclosure of Interests in Other Entities* in relation to associates and joint arrangements.

Associates and significant influence

IAS28 *Investments in Associates and Joint Ventures* includes the following definitions:

- An associate is "*an entity over which the investor has significant influence*".
- Significant influence is "*the power to participate in the financial and operating policy decisions of the investee but is not control or joint control of those policies*".

When an investor company holds (directly or indirectly) at least 20% of the voting power of an investee company, significant influence is presumed to exist unless it can be clearly demonstrated that this is not the case. Holding at least 20% of a company's voting power normally means owning at least 20% of that company's ordinary shares.

IAS28 also states that significant influence is presumed *not* to exist if the investor holds less than 20% of the voting power of the investee, unless such influence can be clearly demonstrated. The existence of significant influence is usually evidenced in one or more of the following ways:

(a) representation on the board of directors which governs the investee company

(b) participation in policy-making processes of the investee, including participation in decisions about dividends or other distributions

(c) material transactions between the investor and the investee

(d) interchange of managerial personnel

(e) provision of essential technical information.

An investor company loses significant influence over an investee company when it loses the power to participate in the investee's financial and operating policies. This generally occurs when the investor no longer holds at least 20% of the investee's voting power.

The equity method

IAS28 requires that an investment in an associate should normally be accounted for using the "equity method". The equity method is defined as "*a method of accounting whereby the investment is initially recognised at cost and adjusted thereafter for the post-acquisition change in the investor's share of the investee's net assets*". The definition goes on to state that the profit or loss of the investor should include the investor's share of the profit or loss of the investee. A fuller explanation of the equity method, together with a number of worked examples, is given below.

The equity method of accounting for associates should normally be used whether or not the investor company is also a parent company which presents consolidated financial statements. However, a parent company which

(a) satisfies certain conditions specified in IFRS10 (see Chapter 18), and

(b) elects not to present consolidated financial statements

is not required to apply the equity method to its investments in associates. These may instead be shown in the investor's own "separate financial statements" either at cost or in accordance with IAS39 or IFRS9 (see Chapter 11). This rule most commonly applies to parent companies which are themselves subsidiaries of other companies and whose shares or securities are not publicly traded.

Application of the equity method

Under the equity method of accounting, the investment made by the investing company is recorded initially at cost. This will include goodwill if the cost of the investment is greater than the investor's share of the fair value of the investee's identifiable net assets. However, any goodwill included in the cost of an investment accounted for by the equity method is not separately recognised. Nor is it separately tested for impairment. But the amount paid for goodwill must be determined in case there is any negative goodwill. Negative goodwill is recognised as income in the investor's statement of comprehensive income and is added to the carrying amount of the investment in the investor's statement of financial position.

In subsequent years, the required accounting treatment is as follows:

(a) The investor's share of the investee's profit (or loss) for the year is recognised as income (or as an expense) in the investor's statement of comprehensive income and is either added to or subtracted from the carrying amount of the investment in the investor's statement of financial position.

(b) The investor's share of the investee's "other comprehensive income" for the year is recognised as other comprehensive income in the investor's statement of comprehensive income and is either added to (if positive) or subtracted from (if negative) the carrying amount of the investment.

(c) Any dividends received from the investee are subtracted from the carrying amount of the investment.

It is important to grasp the difference between the equity method which is used in relation to associates and the acquisition method which is used in relation to subsidiaries. With the equity method, only *the investor's share* of the associate's profit or loss is shown in the investor's financial statements (or consolidated financial statements) and this is shown as a single figure. With the acquisition method, *all* of the subsidiary's revenues and expenses are incorporated line by line into the consolidated statement of comprehensive income and then the profit attributable to the non-controlling interest (if any) is subtracted.

Similarly, under the equity method, an investment in an associate is shown in the investor's financial statements (or consolidated financial statements) as a single non-current asset. With the acquisition method, all of the subsidiary's assets and liabilities are incorporated line by line into the consolidated statement of financial position. Any non-controlling interest is then shown in equity.

EXAMPLE 1

Aspha plc is the parent of a group of companies. On 1 January 2013, Aspha plc acquired 25% of the ordinary share capital of Bexa Ltd at a cost of £100,000. This was precisely equal to 25% of the fair value of the identifiable net assets of Bexa Ltd on that date. During the year to 31 December 2013, Bexa Ltd:

(a)　made a profit after tax of £42,000, and

(b)　paid an ordinary dividend of £27,000.

Explain how these transactions should be reflected in the consolidated financial statements of Aspha plc for the year to 31 December 2013.

Solution

In its consolidated statement of comprehensive income, Aspha plc will recognise "share of profit of associates" as £10,500 (25% x £42,000). IAS1 suggests that this amount should be shown just before the group's pre-tax profit.

The investment is recognised initially at cost. The group's share of the associate's profit is added and the dividend received of £6,750 (25% x £27,000) is subtracted. Therefore the consolidated statement of financial position will show "investments in associates" as £103,750 (£100,000 + £10,500 – £6,750). This is shown as a non-current asset.

In effect, the carrying amount of the investment has been increased by the investor's 25% share of the increase in the associate's retained earnings for the year.

EXAMPLE 2

Gannax plc is the parent of several wholly-owned subsidiaries. On 1 July 2013, Gannax plc acquired 30% of the ordinary shares of Deltar Ltd at a cost of £70,000. Deltar Ltd had retained earnings of £50,000 on that date and all of its assets and liabilities were carried at fair value. Deltar Ltd has issued no shares during the year to 30 June 2014.

The draft consolidated financial statements of Gannax plc for the year to 30 June 2014 (before applying the equity method) and the financial statements of Deltar Ltd for that year are as follows:

Statements of comprehensive income
for the year to 30 June 2014

	Gannax plc and subsidiaries	Deltar Ltd
	£000	£000
Sales revenue	930	320
Cost of sales	340	170
Gross profit	590	150
Operating expenses	215	105
Operating profit	375	45
Dividend received from Deltar Ltd	6	-
Profit before tax	381	45
Taxation	75	15
Profit for the year	306	30

Note: Other comprehensive income was £nil in each case.

Statements of financial position
as at 30 June 2014

	Gannax plc and subsidiaries	Deltar Ltd
	£000	£000
Assets		
Non-current assets		
Property, plant and equipment	510	155
Investment in Deltar Ltd, at cost	70	
	580	
Current assets	225	40
	805	195
Equity		
Ordinary share capital	300	100
Retained earnings	390	60
	690	160
Liabilities		
Current liabilities	115	35
	805	195

Statement of changes in equity (retained earnings only)
for the year to 30 June 2014

	Gannax plc and subsidiaries	Deltar Ltd
	£000	£000
Balance at 30 June 2013	204	50
Profit for the year	306	30
	510	80
Dividends paid	120	20
Balance at 30 June 2014	390	60

Prepare a consolidated statement of comprehensive income for the year to 30 June 2014 and a consolidated statement of financial position as at that date. Also prepare an extract from the consolidated statement of changes in equity, showing the changes in the group's retained earnings in the year.

Solution

Deltar Ltd is an associate of Gannax plc. The cost of the investment was £70,000 and the fair value of 30% of the net assets of Deltar Ltd on 1 July 2013 was 30% x £150,000 = £45,000. Therefore there is goodwill of £25,000. This is not shown separately, but it was necessary to do this calculation so as to be sure that there was no negative goodwill.

The investment in associates at 30 June 2014 is £70,000 + (30% x £30,000) − £6,000 = £73,000. The dividend received of £6,000 should be removed from the group statement of comprehensive income and replaced by the group's £9,000 share of the associate's profit for the year. The group retained earnings figure rises by £3,000 in consequence. The final consolidated financial statements are as follows:

Statement of comprehensive income
for the year to 30 June 2014

	£000
Sales revenue	930
Cost of sales	340
Gross profit	590
Operating expenses	215
Operating profit	375
Share of profit of associates	9
Profit before tax	384
Taxation	75
Profit for the year	309

Statement of financial position
as at 30 June 2014

	£000
Assets	
Non-current assets	
Property, plant and equipment	510
Investments in associates	73
	583
Current assets	225
	808
Equity	
Ordinary share capital	300
Retained earnings	393
	693
Liabilities	
Current liabilities	115
	808

Statement of changes in equity (retained earnings only)
for the year to 30 June 2014

	£000
Balance at 30 June 2013	204
Profit for the year	309
	513
Dividends paid	120
Balance at 30 June 2014	393

Note:

The effects of applying the equity method are as follows:

(i)   In the statement of comprehensive income, the dividend received from the associate has been replaced by the investor's share of the associate's profits for the year.

(ii) In the statement of financial position, the carrying amount of the investment has been increased by the investor's share of the associate's retained earnings for the year.

Upstream and downstream transactions

"Upstream" and "downstream" transactions are transactions between an investor and an associate. An example of an upstream transaction is the sale of goods by the associate to the investor. An example of a downstream transaction is the sale of goods by the investor to the associate. IAS28 requires that any unrealised profits resulting from such transactions should be eliminated to the extent of the investor's interest in the associate. This differs from the IFRS10 requirement that unrealised profits on intra-group transactions should be fully eliminated, whether or not the subsidiary concerned is wholly-owned.

Accounting entries which eliminate the unrealised profits resulting from upstream and downstream transactions are as follows:

(a) **Upstream**. In the investor's financial statements, the unrealised profit is subtracted from the investor's share of profit from associates. This automatically reduces the investment in associates figure shown in the statement of financial position.

(b) **Downstream**. In the investor's financial statements, the unrealised profit is subtracted from gross profit (usually by increasing cost of sales) and is also subtracted from the investment in associates figure shown in the statement of financial position.

The unrealised profits which are eliminated as above should be recognised if and when the goods concerned are sold on to a third party.

EXAMPLE 3

An investor company has a 25% interest in an associate. During the year to 31 December 2013, the investor bought goods from the associate on which the associate earned a profit of £10,000. One-half of these goods remained unsold by the investor at the year end.

(a) Calculate the unrealised profit on this transaction and explain how this is eliminated from the investor's financial statements.

(b) Explain how the required accounting treatment would differ if the goods had been sold by the investor to the associate rather than the other way around.

Solution

(a) The unrealised profit is £1,250 (25% x 50% x £10,000). In the investor's financial statements, share of profit from associates is reduced by £1,250 and investment in associates is also reduced by £1,250.

(b) In the investor's financial statements, the cost of sales figure is increased by £1,250 and investment in associates is reduced by £1,250.

Losses of an associate

As stated earlier in this chapter, the investor's share of an associate's loss is recognised as an expense in the investor's financial statements and is subtracted from the carrying amount of the investment. However, if the investor's share of an associate's loss is greater than the carrying amount of the investment, that amount is reduced to zero and the investor should normally recognise no further losses. But further losses are recognised if the investor has incurred legal or constructive obligations on behalf of the associate. This situation might occur if the investor has guaranteed the associate's debts.

If the carrying amount of the investment is reduced to zero but the associate then eventually returns to profit, the investor should not resume recognition of its share of the associate's profits until after those profits have cancelled out the losses which were not recognised whilst the carrying amount of the investment was zero.

Impairment losses

Any goodwill which is included in the carrying amount of an investment in an associate is not separately recognised and is not separately tested for impairment. However, the entire carrying amount of the investment should be tested for impairment whenever there is an indication that impairment may have occurred. As usual, an impairment test involves comparing the carrying amount of the investment with the higher of its value in use and its fair value less costs of disposal (see Chapter 7).

Reporting periods and accounting policies

IAS28 makes rules with regard to reporting periods and accounting policies that are similar to their IFRS10 counterparts (see Chapter 18). In summary:

(a) If the reporting period of an investor and an associate are different, the associate should prepare additional financial statements for the use of the investor, using the same reporting period as the investor. If this is impracticable, the financial statements of the associate should be adjusted to take account of any significant transactions or events which occur between the end of the associate's reporting period and the end of the investor's reporting period. In any case, the difference between the end of the associate's reporting period and that of the investor should not exceed three months.

(b) The investor's financial statements should be prepared using uniform accounting policies. If an associate uses different accounting policies from those adopted by the investor, its financial statements should be adjusted to conform with the investor's accounting policies before the equity method is applied.

Joint arrangements

A "joint arrangement" exists if two or more parties exercise joint control over a business enterprise. IFRS11 *Joint Arrangements* includes the following definitions:

- A joint arrangement is "*an arrangement of which two or more parties have joint control*".

- Joint control is "*the contractually agreed sharing of control of an arrangement, which exists only when decisions about the relevant activities require the unanimous consent of the parties sharing control*".

The important characteristic of a joint arrangement that distinguishes it from a subsidiary or associate is that there is a contractual agreement to share control. Without such an agreement, joint control cannot exist and the activity concerned is not a joint arrangement.

Although IFRS11 refers to entities in general, not only to companies, it is assumed in this chapter that all of the parties to a joint arrangement are companies.

Types of joint arrangement

IFRS11 identifies two types of joint arrangement and prescribes the accounting treatment for each. These are as follows:

(a) **Joint operations**. A joint operation is "*a joint arrangement whereby the parties that have joint control of the arrangement have rights to the assets, and obligations for the liabilities, relating to the arrangement*". For example, the parties to a joint arrangement could agree to manufacture a product together, each party being responsible for a specific task and with each party using its own assets and incurring its own liabilities. The agreement between these "joint operators" would specify the way in which the revenue and expenses of the operation should be shared between them.

   A joint arrangement that is <u>not</u> structured as a "separate vehicle" (a business entity which is separate from the parties to the arrangement) must be a joint operation.

(b) **Joint ventures**. A joint venture is "*a joint arrangement whereby the parties that have joint control of the arrangement have rights to the net assets of the arrangement*". For example, the parties to a joint arrangement might establish a separate business entity over which the parties have joint control and which has its own assets and liabilities. In this case, the assets and liabilities of the arrangement would belong to the separate entity and not to the parties themselves. However, the "joint venturers" would each have an interest in the net assets of the arrangement, generally by virtue of their ownership of shares in the separate entity concerned.

   In most cases, a joint arrangement that <u>is</u> structured as a separate vehicle would be regarded as a joint venture.

Accounting for a joint arrangement

IFRS11 specifies the required accounting treatment of each type of joint arrangement. The requirements are as follows:

(a) **Joint operations**. A joint operation raises no special accounting problems. In general terms, the financial statements of each joint operator should recognise:

  (i) its own assets that are being used in the joint operation

  (ii) its own liabilities that relate to the joint operation

  (iii) its share of the revenue arising from the joint operation

  (iv) its share of the expenses arising from the joint operation.

  There is no need to prepare financial statements for the joint operation itself.

(b) **Joint ventures**. A joint venturer should recognise its interest in a joint venture as an investment in its own financial statements. This investment should normally be accounted for by the equity method (see above). In this case, it will also be necessary to prepare financial statements for the joint venture itself.

Disclosure requirements

IFRS12 *Disclosure of Interests in Other Entities* (see Chapter 18) requires an entity to disclose the significant judgements and assumptions it has made in determining the nature of its interest in other entities (e.g. significant influence or joint control) and the type of any joint arrangement to which it is a party. The entity should also disclose information which enables the users of its financial statements to evaluate:

(a) the nature, extent and financial effects of its interests in associates and its interests in joint arrangements

(b) the nature of (and changes in) any risks associated with its interests in associates and joint arrangements.

Summary

▸ An associate is an entity over which the investor has significant influence. This will usually be the case if the investor owns at least 20% of the investee's voting power.

▸ An investment in an associate should be accounted for by the equity method. The investment is initially recognised at cost and is then adjusted for the post-acquisition change in the investor's share of the associate's net assets. The investor's statement of comprehensive income shows the investor's share of the associate's profit or loss.

▸ Unrealised profits resulting from upstream and downstream transactions between an investor and an associate should be eliminated to the extent of the investor's interest in the associate.

▸ A joint arrangement exists if investors exercise joint control over an investee. IFRS11 distinguishes between joint operations and joint ventures.

▸ A joint operation is a joint arrangement in which the parties to the arrangement use their own assets and incur their own liabilities in relation to the arrangement. Each party recognises these assets and liabilities in its own financial statements, together with its share of the operation's revenue and expenses.

▸ A joint venture is normally a separate business entity that is jointly controlled by the parties to the arrangement. Financial statements are prepared for this entity and each joint venturer accounts for its investment in the entity by using the equity method.

Exercises

20.1 (a) Explain what is meant by the terms "associate" and "significant influence".

(b) Explain the equity method of accounting which is used to account for an investment in an associate. Also explain how this differs from the consolidation approach which is used in relation to subsidiaries.

20.2 (a) Explain what is meant by the term "joint arrangement".

(b) Distinguish between joint operations and joint ventures. Outline the accounting treatment prescribed for each of these by standard IFRS11.

20.3   The statements of financial position of M Ltd, P Ltd and Q Ltd as at 31 July 2014 are as follows:

	M Ltd £000	P Ltd £000	Q Ltd £000
Assets			
Non-current assets			
Property, plant and equipment	2,570	370	280
Investment in P Ltd	410		
Investment in Q Ltd	100		
	3,080		
Current assets	1,150	220	170
	4,230	590	450
Equity			
Ordinary share capital	1,000	100	80
Retained earnings	2,420	380	280
	3,420	480	360
Liabilities			
Current liabilities	810	110	90
	4,230	590	450

The following information is available:

(a)   On 31 July 2011, M Ltd paid £410,000 to acquire 90% of the share capital of P Ltd. The retained earnings of P Ltd on that date were £220,000. The company's issued share capital has not changed since M Ltd acquired its holding. On 31 July 2011, the fair value of the non-current assets of P Ltd was £80,000 higher than their book value. This valuation has not been reflected in the books of P Ltd.

(b)   On 31 July 2013, M Ltd paid £100,000 to acquire 25% of the share capital of Q Ltd. The retained earnings of Q Ltd on that date were £240,000 and all of its assets and liabilities were carried at fair value. The company's issued share capital has not changed since M Ltd acquired its holding.

(c)   There have been no impairment losses.

(d)   Non-controlling interests in subsidiaries are to be measured at the appropriate proportion of the subsidiary's identifiable net assets.

Required:

Prepare a consolidated statement of financial position for M Ltd as at 31 July 2014.

20.4   On 30 September 2010, K Ltd paid £140,000 to acquire 40% of the share capital of L Ltd (which became its associate). Draft financial statements for these two companies for the year to 30 September 2014 are as follows:

Statements of comprehensive income
for the year to 30 September 2014

	K Ltd	L Ltd
	£000	£000
Operating profit	650	140
Dividend received from L Ltd	20	-
Profit before tax	670	140
Taxation	170	30
Profit for the year	500	110

Statements of financial position
as at 30 September 2014

	K Ltd	L Ltd
	£000	£000
Assets		
Non-current assets		
Property, plant and equipment	1,600	400
Investment in L Ltd, at cost	140	
	1,740	
Current assets	780	290
	2,520	690
Equity		
Ordinary share capital	1,000	200
Retained earnings	1,210	320
	2,210	520
Liabilities		
Current liabilities	310	170
	2,520	690

Statement of changes in equity (retained earnings only)
for the year to 30 September 2014

	K Ltd	L Ltd
	£000	£000
Balance at 30 September 2013	710	260
Profit for the year	500	110
Dividends paid	-	(50)
Balance at 30 September 2014	1,210	320

The following information is also available:

(i) In the draft financial statements of K Ltd, the company's investment in L Ltd has been recognised at cost and the dividend received from L Ltd has been recognised as income. These financial statements show the situation as it would be without application of the equity method, either in the year to 30 September 2014 or in previous years.

(ii) The retained earnings of L Ltd on 30 September 2010 were £100,000 and all of its assets and liabilities were carried at fair value. Neither company has issued any shares since that date.

(iii) During the year to 30 September 2014, K Ltd bought goods from L Ltd for £30,000 which had cost L Ltd £20,000. One-quarter of these goods were unsold by K Ltd at 30 September 2014.

Required:

Prepare the financial statements of K Ltd for the year to 30 September 2014.

*20.5 On 1 October 2013 Pumice acquired the following non-current investments:

(i) 80% of the equity share capital of Silverton at a cost of £13.6 million
(ii) 50% of Silverton's 10% loan notes at par
(iii) 1.6 million equity shares in Amok at a cost of £6.25 each.

Draft statements of financial position of the three companies at 31 March 2014 are:

	Pumice £000	Silverton £000	Amok £000
Assets			
Non-current assets			
Property, plant and equipment	20,000	8,500	16,500
Investments	26,000		1,500
	46,000	8,500	18,000
Current assets	15,000	8,000	11,000
	61,000	16,500	29,000
Equity			
Ordinary shares of £1 each	10,000	3,000	4,000
Retained earnings	37,000	8,000	20,000
	47,000	11,000	24,000
Liabilities			
Non-current liabilities			
8% loan notes	4,000		
10% loan notes		2,000	
Current liabilities	10,000	3,500	5,000
	61,000	16,500	29,000

The following information is relevant:

(i)   The fair values of Silverton's assets were equal to their carrying amounts with the exception of land and plant. Silverton's land had a fair value of £400,000 in excess of its carrying amount and plant had a fair value of £1.6 million in excess of its carrying amount. The plant had a remaining life of four years (straight-line depreciation) at the date of acquisition.

(ii)   In the post-acquisition period, Pumice sold goods to Silverton at a price of £6 million. These goods had cost Pumice £4 million. Half of these goods were still in the inventory of Silverton at 31 March 2014. Silverton had a balance of £1.5 million owing to Pumice at 31 March 2014 which agreed with Pumice's records.

(iii) The net profit after tax for the year ended 31 March 2014 was £2 million for Silverton and £8 million for Amok. Assume profits accrued evenly throughout the year.

(iv)   An impairment test at 31 March 2014 concluded that consolidated goodwill was impaired by £400,000 and the investment in Amok was impaired by £200,000.

(v)   No dividends were paid during the year by any of the companies.

(vi)   Non-controlling interests in subsidiaries are to be measured at the appropriate proportion of the subsidiary's identifiable net assets.

Required:

(a)   Explain how the investments purchased by Pumice on 1 October 2013 should be treated in its consolidated financial statements.

(b)   Prepare the consolidated statement of financial position for Pumice as at 31 March 2014.   *(ACCA)*

Chapter 21

Related parties and changes in foreign exchange rates

Introduction

This chapter is concerned with two further international standards which may be relevant when preparing the financial statements of a group of companies. The first of these is IAS24 *Related Party Disclosures*, which requires entities to make certain disclosures about their relationships with other parties, including parent-subsidiary relationships. The other standard considered in this chapter is IAS21 *The Effects of Changes in Foreign Exchange Rates*. This standard prescribes the accounting treatment of foreign currency transactions and is also applicable if an entity has a foreign operation (e.g. a foreign subsidiary).

Although these standards are probably of most significance for groups of companies, it should be appreciated that their scope covers entities in general and that both of them are applicable to individual companies as well as to groups.

Objectives

By the end of this chapter, the reader should be able to:

- explain what is meant by a "related party"
- identify the related parties of a reporting entity
- list the main disclosures required by international standard IAS24
- determine an entity's functional currency and distinguish between its functional currency and its presentation currency
- record foreign currency transactions in an entity's functional currency, both on initial recognition and subsequently, accounting correctly for exchange differences
- translate an entity's financial statements into a presentation currency and translate the financial statements of a foreign operation.

Related parties

The objective of IAS24 *Related Party Disclosures* is to ensure that financial statements contain certain disclosures. These disclosures should draw attention to the possibility that an entity's financial performance and position may have been affected by:

(a) the existence of related parties, and

(b) transactions with those parties.

The standard accepts that relationships with other parties (e.g. subsidiaries) are a normal feature of business and commerce, but points out that related parties might enter into transactions that unrelated parties would not. For instance, a subsidiary company which sells goods to its parent at cost price would probably not sell goods on those terms to any other customer. Such a transaction would of course affect the profit of both the subsidiary and the parent. In general, transactions between related parties might involve:

(a) the transfer of assets or liabilities at prices which are above or below their true value

(b) the supply of services at reduced or increased prices

(c) the making of loans at interest rates which differ from market rates.

Even the mere existence of a relationship with another party might affect an entity's financial performance and position, whether or not there are any transactions with that party. For instance, a subsidiary might be instructed by its parent to trade only with certain suppliers or perhaps to cease all research and development activity.

In summary, the users of financial statements cannot properly assess an entity's financial performance and position unless they are supplied with information about the entity's related parties and its transactions with those parties.

Definition of related party and related party transaction

IAS24 defines a related party as "*a person or entity that is related to the entity that is preparing its financial statements*". The term "reporting entity" is used to refer to the entity that is preparing its financial statements. The rules which determine whether or not a person or entity is related to the reporting entity may be summarised as follows:

(a) A person (P) or a close member of that person's family is related to a reporting entity if *either* of the following conditions applies:

   (i)   P has control, joint control or significant influence over the reporting entity.

   (ii) P is a member of the key management personnel of either the reporting entity or a parent of the reporting entity.

(b) An entity (E) is related to a reporting entity if *any* of a number of conditions applies. The main conditions are as follows:

(i) Entity E and the reporting entity are members of the same group.

(ii) Entity E is an associate or joint venture of the reporting entity (or vice versa).

(iii) Entity E and the reporting entity are both joint ventures of the same third party.

(iv) Entity E is an associate of a third entity and the reporting entity is a joint venture of that same third entity (or vice versa).

(v) Entity E is a post-employment benefit plan (a pension scheme) for the benefit of the employees of the reporting entity or for the benefit of the employees of any entity which is related to the reporting entity.

(vi) Entity E is controlled or jointly controlled by a person identified in (a) above.

(vii) A person identified in (a)(i) above has significant influence over Entity E or is a member of the key management personnel of Entity E or of a parent of Entity E.

Close members of a person's family are "*those family members who may be expected to influence, or be influenced by, that person in their dealings with the entity*". They include:

(a) the person's children and spouse or domestic partner

(b) children of the person's spouse or domestic partner

(c) dependants of the person or of the person's spouse or domestic partner.

Key management personnel are "*those persons having authority and responsibility for planning, directing and controlling the activities of the entity ... including any director ...*".

A related party transaction is defined as "*a transfer of resources, services or obligations between a reporting entity and a related party, regardless of whether a price is charged*"..

Parties that are not necessarily related

The following are not necessarily related parties, though it is always important to examine the substance of each relationship and not merely its legal form:

(a) two entities simply because they have a director in common, or some other member of their key management personnel in common

(b) two joint venturers simply because they share joint control over a joint venture

(c) providers of finance, trade unions, public utilities and government departments or agencies, simply by virtue of their normal dealings with an entity

(d) a customer, supplier, franchisor, distributor or general agent with whom an entity transacts a significant volume of business, merely by virtue of the resulting economic dependence.

Disclosures required by IAS24

IAS24 is principally a disclosure standard and therefore its disclosure requirements are quite extensive. The main disclosures that are required are as follows:

(a) Parent-subsidiary relationships must be disclosed whether or not there have been any transactions between these parties. The reporting entity should disclose the name of its parent and, if different, the name of the ultimate controlling party. These requirements are in addition to the requirements of IFRS12 (see Chapter 18).

(b) The reporting entity should disclose key management personnel compensation in total and for each of the following categories:

  (i)   short-term employee benefits

  (ii) post-employment benefits

  (iii) other long-term benefits

  (iv) termination benefits.

These categories are all defined in IAS19 *Employee Benefits* (see Chapter 14).

(c) If there have been transactions with a related party, the reporting entity should disclose the nature of the relationship and provide information about the transactions and any outstanding balances, as necessary for an understanding of the effect of the relationship on the financial statements. As a minimum, disclosures should include:

  (i)   the amount of the transactions

  (ii) the amount of any outstanding balances and their terms and conditions

  (iii) any allowances for doubtful debts relating to these outstanding balances and the amount of any expense recognised during the period in respect of bad or doubtful debts due from related parties.

These disclosures should be made separately by the reporting entity for each category of related party (e.g. the reporting entity's parent, subsidiaries, associates, joint ventures, key management personnel etc.).

(d) IAS24 gives examples of transactions that should be disclosed if they are with a related party. These include:

  (i)   purchases or sales of goods

  (ii) purchases or sales of property and other assets

  (iii) the rendering or receiving of services

  (iv) leases

  (v)   loans and equity contributions

  (vi) provision of guarantees or collateral

  (vii) settlement of liabilities on behalf of the reporting entity by the related party or by the reporting entity of behalf of the related party.

Foreign exchange accounting

IAS21 *The Effects of Changes in Foreign Exchange Rates* states that an entity may carry on foreign activities in two ways. On the one hand, the entity may have transactions which are expressed (or "denominated") in a foreign currency. On the other hand, the entity may have a foreign operation (e.g. a foreign subsidiary). Furthermore, an entity might present its financial statements in a foreign currency. The objective of IAS21 is to prescribe the accounting treatment of foreign currency transactions and foreign operations and to set out rules for the translation of financial statements into a foreign currency.

The standard provides a number of definitions. The most significant of these definitions are as follows:

(a) An entity's functional currency is "*the currency of the primary economic environment in which the entity operates*".

(b) A foreign currency is "*a currency other than the functional currency of the entity*".

(c) An entity's presentation currency is "*the currency in which the financial statements are presented*".

(d) A foreign operation is "*an entity that is a subsidiary, associate, joint arrangement or branch of a reporting entity, the activities of which are based or conducted in a country or currency other than those of the reporting entity*".

Determination of an entity's functional currency

As stated above, an entity's functional currency is the currency of the primary economic environment in which it operates. This is usually the main environment in which the entity generates and expends cash. When determining its functional currency, an entity should consider the following factors:

(a) the currency that mainly influences sales prices for its goods and services (which is often the currency in which these prices are denominated and settled)

(b) the currency of the country whose competitive forces and whose regulations mainly determine the sales prices of its goods and services

(c) the currency that mainly influences labour, materials and other costs of providing goods and services (which is often the currency in which such costs are denominated and settled).

Further factors which provide evidence of an entity's functional currency are the currency in which funds from financing activities are generated (e.g. loans and share issues) and the currency in which receipts from operating activities are usually retained. If the evidence provided by all of these various factors is mixed, then the management of the entity should use its judgement to determine the entity's functional currency.

If the functional currency of an entity is the currency of a hyperinflationary economy, its financial statements must be restated in accordance with IAS29 *Financial Reporting in Hyperinflationary Economies* (see Chapter 17).

Reporting foreign currency transactions

IAS21 defines a foreign currency transaction as "*a transaction that is denominated or requires settlement in a foreign currency*". This definition includes transactions such as:

(a) the purchase or sale of goods whose price is denominated in a foreign currency

(b) the borrowing or lending of amounts which are denominated in a foreign currency.

On initial recognition, a foreign currency transaction should be recorded in the entity's functional currency by applying the spot exchange rate between the functional currency and the foreign currency as at the date of the transaction. The spot exchange rate is defined as "*the exchange rate for immediate delivery*". For practical purposes, an average rate for a week or month may be used for all transactions occurring in that week or month as long as exchange rates do not fluctuate significantly during that time.

Subsequently, the treatment of a foreign currency item in the statement of financial position depends upon whether the item is a monetary item or a non-monetary item and whether it is carried at historical cost or at fair value. Monetary items are defined as "*units of currency held and assets or liabilities to be received or paid in a fixed or determinable number of units of currency*". At the end of each reporting period:

(a) foreign currency monetary items should be translated using the spot exchange rate at the end of the reporting period (the "closing rate")

(b) non-monetary foreign currency items carried at historical cost should be translated using the exchange rate at the date of the transaction which gave rise to the item

(c) non-monetary foreign currency items carried at fair value should be translated using the exchange rate at the date that the item's fair value was measured.

As stated in Chapter 10, IAS2 *Inventories* requires that inventories are measured at the lower of cost and net realisable value (NRV). The carrying amount of inventory which is measured in a foreign currency is determined by taking the lower of:

(a) its cost, translated at the exchange rate at the date that it was acquired, and

(b) its NRV, translated using the closing rate at the end of the reporting period.

Treatment of exchange differences

Exchange differences which arise on the settlement of monetary items, or on the translation of monetary items at exchange rates which are different from those used at initial recognition, should be recognised as income or expenses when calculating the entity's profit or loss for the period.

If a gain or loss on a non-monetary item is recognised in the calculation of the entity's profit or loss (e.g. on disposal) then any exchange component of that gain or loss is also recognised in the calculation of profit or loss. But if a gain or loss on a non-monetary item is recognised in other comprehensive income (e.g. on a revaluation) then any exchange component of that gain or loss is also recognised in other comprehensive income.

EXAMPLE 1

A UK company prepares financial statements to 31 December and has the pound sterling as its functional currency. On 27 November 2013, the company buys inventory for $7,440. The company still holds this inventory at 31 December 2013 (when its net realisable value is £7,000) and does not pay for the inventory until 16 February 2014.

(a) Explain how this transaction should be recorded on 27 November 2013.

(b) Explain how any items outstanding on 31 December 2013 should be shown in the company's statement of financial position at that date and how any exchange differences should be dealt with in the company's financial statements.

(c) Explain how the payment on 16 February 2014 should be accounted for.

(£1 = $1.50 on 27 Nov 2013; £1 = $1.60 on 31 Dec 2013; £1 = $1.55 on 16 Feb 2014).

Solution

(a) On 27 November 2013, the company should record a purchase of £4,960 ($7,440 ÷ 1.50) and a trade payable of the same amount.

(b) On 31 December 2013, the cost of the inventory is still £4,960. Its NRV is £7,000 so it should be shown in the company's statement of financial position at £4,960. The trade payable of $7,440 should be shown as £4,650 ($7,440 ÷ 1.60).

　　The trade payable is now £310 less than initially recorded (£4,960 − £4,650) so there is an exchange gain of £310 which should be recognised as income when calculating the company's profit or loss for the year. Note that this is an *unrealised* gain and yet IAS21 requires that it should be included in the calculation of profit or loss.

(c) On 16 February 2014, it costs the company £4,800 ($7,440 ÷ 1.55) to settle the trade payable of £4,650. There is an exchange loss of £150 (£4,800 − £4,650) and this should be recognised as an expense in the 2014 financial statements.

EXAMPLE 2

A UK company prepares financial statements to 31 March and has the pound sterling as its functional currency. On 15 July 2013, the company buys an investment property for €660,000. The fair value of this property on 31 March 2014 is €687,500.

(a) Explain how this transaction should be recorded on 15 July 2013.

(b) Explain how the investment property should be dealt with in the company's financial statements for the year to 31 March 2014.

(c) How would the situation differ if the item bought by the company on 15 July 2013 had been property plant and equipment (accounted for using the revaluation model) rather than investment property?

(£1 = €1.20 on 15 Jul 2013; £1 = €1.10 on 31 Mar 2014).

Solution

(a) The property is initially recognised at its cost of £550,000 (€660,000 ÷ 1.20).

(b) The property should be shown in the statement of financial position at its fair value of £625,000 (€687,500 ÷ 1.10) and the company should recognise a gain of £75,000 when calculating its profit or loss for the year. This gain consists of an exchange gain of £50,000 in relation to the initial cost of the property ((€660,000 ÷ 1.10) – (€660,000 ÷ 1.20)) plus a revaluation surplus of £25,000 (€27,500 ÷ 1.10).

(c) If the item had been property, plant and equipment accounted for by the revaluation model, the gain of £75,000 (including the exchange gain of £50,000) would have been recognised in other comprehensive income (see Chapter 5).

Translation to a presentation currency

Although most entities present their financial statements in their functional currency, IAS21 allows entities to use a different presentation currency if they wish. The process of translating from the functional currency to the presentation currency is as follows:

(a) Assets and liabilities in the statement of financial position are translated at the closing rate at the end of the reporting period.

(b) Income and expenses shown in the statement of comprehensive income are translated at the exchange rates which applied on the dates of the transactions. But an average exchange rate for the period may be used unless rates have fluctuated significantly.

(c) The resulting exchange differences are recognised in other comprehensive income and are accumulated in a separate component of equity (a foreign exchange reserve).

Unfortunately, IAS21 does not specify the translation rate to be used for equity items such as a company's share capital. Obvious choices are the rate which applied when the shares were originally issued (the "historical rate") and the closing rate at the end of the reporting period. In practice, the historical rate is generally regarded as more appropriate.

Translation of a foreign operation

If an entity has a foreign operation (e.g. a foreign subsidiary, associate or joint venture) it will be necessary to translate the financial statements of that operation into the same currency as is used in the entity's own financial statements. Only then will it be possible to include the foreign operation in the entity's financial statements by either consolidation (see Chapter 18) or the equity method (see Chapter 20). The translation process required by IAS21 in these circumstances is the same as the process adopted when translating an entity's financial statements from a functional currency to a presentation currency.

When an entity disposes of a foreign operation, the cumulative amount of the exchange differences which have been recognised in other comprehensive income in relation to that operation are reclassified to profit or loss (see Chapter 3).

EXAMPLE 3

On 1 January 2014, a UK company formed a foreign subsidiary in a country where the local currency is the utopian dollar ($). The summarised financial statements of this foreign subsidiary for the year to 31 December 2014 are as follows:

Statement of comprehensive income for the year to 31 December 2014

	$
Sales revenue	810,000
Expenses	719,640
Profit for the year	90,360

Statement of financial position as at 31 December 2014

	$
Assets	268,000
Share capital (issued 1 Jan 2014)	100,000
Retained earnings	90,360
	190,360
Liabilities	77,640
	268,000

Translate these financial statements into £ sterling, assuming that £1 = $5 on 1 Jan 2014, £1 = $4 on 31 Dec 2014 and that the average rate for the year was £1 = $4.5.

Solution

Statement of comprehensive income for the year to 31 December 2014

	$	Rate	£
Sales revenue	810,000	4.5	180,000
Expenses	719,640	4.5	159,920
Profit for the year	90,360		20,080
Other comprehensive income	-		7,510
	90,360		27,590

Statement of financial position at 31 December 2014

	$	Rate	£
Assets	268,000	4.0	67,000
Share capital	100,000	5.0	20,000
Retained earnings	90,360		20,080
Foreign exchange reserve	-	bal. fig.	7,510
	190,360		47,590
Liabilities	77,640	4.0	19,410
	268,000		67,000

Notes:

(i) Sales and expenses have been translated at average rate. Assets and liabilities have been translated at closing rate. Share capital has been translated at historical rate.

(ii) There is an exchange difference of £7,510 (the balancing figure in the statement of financial position). This is credited to a foreign exchange reserve and recognised as other comprehensive income in the statement of comprehensive income.

(iii) In future statements of financial position, the retained earnings figure will be equal to the amount (in £) brought forward from the previous year plus any further retained earnings arising during the current year (translated at the average rate for that year).

(iv) In each year from now on, the foreign exchange reserve in the statement of financial position will be inserted as a balancing figure. The amount by which this reserve has increased or decreased since the previous year will be recognised in the statement of comprehensive income as other comprehensive income.

Summary

▸ IAS24 requires certain disclosures with regard to an entity's related parties and its transactions with those parties. These disclosures enable users to understand the impact of related party transactions on the entity's financial performance and position.

▸ The list of an entity's related parties includes parents, subsidiaries, associates, joint ventures, key management personnel and the entity's pension scheme.

▸ Parent-subsidiary relationships must be disclosed whether or not there are any transactions between these parties. Entities must also disclose key management personnel benefits. If there have been transactions with related parties, the entity must provide details of the relationships, the transactions and any outstanding balances.

▸ An entity's functional currency is the currency of the primary economic environment in which it operates.

▸ A foreign currency transaction is one that is denominated or requires settlement in a foreign currency. Such transactions are recorded initially at the exchange rate on the date of the transaction.

▸ Monetary foreign currency items in the statement of financial position are translated using the closing rate at the end of the period. Non-monetary foreign currency items are translated using the exchange rate on the date of the original transaction or (for items shown at fair value) at the rate on the date that fair value was measured.

▸ Exchange differences arising in relation to foreign currency transactions are usually recognised as income or expenses when calculating the entity's profit or loss.

▸ IAS21 contains rules for translating financial statements from the entity's functional currency to a presentation currency. These rules also apply to the translation of the financial statements of a foreign operation.

Exercises

21.1   The following information relates to Z plc:

(a)   Alan owns 27% of the ordinary shares of Z plc. Elaine is his wife.

(b)   Z plc owns 60% of the ordinary shares of Y plc.

(c)   Z plc owns 15% of the ordinary shares of X plc.

(d)   Barbara is a director of Z plc. She owns 75% of the ordinary shares of W Ltd. David is her husband. He owns 10% of the ordinary shares of V Ltd.

(e)   Colin works for Z plc as a manager but he is not a director. Fiona is his daughter.

(f)   Z plc has established a pension scheme for the benefit of its employees.

Identify those parties (if any) which are related to Z Plc.

21.2   Dalle Ltd is a UK company which has the pound sterling as its functional currency. The company has the following transactions in Euros (€) during the year to 31 March 2014:

1 January 2014	Equipment costing €143,750 bought on credit from X
1 February 2014	Inventory costing €48,000 bought on credit from Y
28 February 2014	Paid X in full for the equipment bought on 1 January
15 March 2014	Paid Y €13,200 on account for the inventory bought on 1 February
15 March 2014	Sold inventory to Z on credit for €77,000

Exchange rates may be assumed as follows:

1 January 2014	£1 = €1.25
1 February 2014	£1 = €1.20
28 February 2014	£1 = €1.15
15 March 2014	£1 = €1.10
31 March 2014	£1 = €1.00

The equipment bought on 1 January 2014 is carried at historical cost in the company's statement of financial position at 31 March 2014. The cost of the company's inventory at that date does not exceed its net realisable value.

(a)   Explain the accounting treatment of each of the above transactions.

(b)   Calculate the exchange difference for the year to 31 March 2014 and explain how this difference should be dealt with in the company's financial statements.

21.3   On 1 July 2013, a UK company formed a foreign subsidiary in a country which has the Florin (Fn) as its currency. The summarised financial statements of this subsidiary for the years to 30 June 2014 and 2015 are as follows:

Statements of comprehensive income for the year to 30 June

	2014	2015
	Fn	**Fn**
Sales revenue	67,200	71,820
Expenses	40,320	41,580
Profit for the year	26,880	30,240

Statements of financial position as at 30 June

	2014	2015
	Fn	**Fn**
Assets	112,400	145,920
Share capital (issued 1 July 2013)	60,000	60,000
Retained earnings	26,880	57,120
	86,880	117,120
Liabilities	25,520	28,800
	112,400	145,920

Exchange rates are as follows:

1 July 2013	£1 = Fn 6
30 June 2014	£1 = Fn 4
30 June 2015	£1 = Fn 4.8

The average exchange rate for the year to 30 June 2014 was £1 = Fn 5 and the average exchange rate for the year to 30 June 2015 was £1 = Fn 4.5

Required:

Translate the financial statements for both years into £ sterling, in accordance with the requirements of IAS21.

*21.4   Related party relationships are a common feature of commercial life. The objective of IAS24 *Related Party Disclosures* is to ensure that financial statements contain the necessary disclosures to make users aware of the possibility that financial statements may have been affected by the existence of related parties.

Hideaway is a public listed company that owns two subsidiary company investments. It owns 100% of the equity shares of Benedict and 55% of the equity shares of Depret. During the year ended 30 September 2014 Depret made several sales of goods to Benedict. These sales totalled £15 million and had cost Depret £14 million to manufacture. Depret made these sales on the instruction of the Board of Hideaway. It is known that one of the directors of Depret, who is not a director of Hideaway, is unhappy with the parent company's instruction as he believes the goods could have been sold to other companies outside the group at the far higher price of £20 million. All directors within the group benefit from a profit sharing scheme.

Required:

(a)   Describe the main circumstances that give rise to related parties.

(b)   Explain why the disclosure of related party relationships and transactions may be important.

(c)   Describe the financial effect that Hideaway's instruction may have on the financial statements of the companies within the group and the implications this may have for other interested parties.   *(ACCA)*

Part 4

ANALYSIS OF FINANCIAL STATEMENTS

Chapter 22

Ratio analysis

Introduction

So far, this book has been concerned almost exclusively with the preparation of financial statements. In this chapter, we turn our attention to the interpretation of the information contained in these statements.

The IASB *Conceptual Framework* (see Chapter 2) states that the objective of preparing financial statements is to provide users with information which will help them to make decisions about providing resources to an entity. Confronted with a set of financial statements, users will need to analyse the information provided and draw some conclusions about the financial performance and financial position of the entity concerned.

There are several ways in which financial statements might be analysed. In practice, one of the most important methods is the technique known as *ratio analysis*, which involves the calculation of a number of accounting ratios. The main purpose of this chapter is to introduce the most commonly-used accounting ratios and to explain the significance of each ratio. The only ratio addressed by an international standard (IAS33) is the earnings per share ratio, which is explained in some detail in Chapter 23 of this book.

Objectives

By the end of this chapter, the reader should be able to:

- explain the role of accounting ratios in the analysis and interpretation of the information provided in financial statements
- define each of the most commonly-used accounting ratios
- perform a ratio analysis of a set of financial statements
- explain the limitations of ratio analysis
- briefly explain the technique of multivariate ratio analysis.

Accounting ratios

An accounting ratio is a measure of the relationship which exists between two figures shown in a set of financial statements. For example, the gross profit margin (see below) measures the relationship between gross profit and sales. The usefulness of accounting ratios in the analysis and interpretation of accounting information can be illustrated by means of the following example.

Suppose that a company makes a profit of £11million in the year 2013, as opposed to £10 million in 2012. A shareholder seeking to assess the company's performance might ask whether the company has done better in 2013 than in 2012. The obvious answer to this question is "Yes". However, the company may have raised substantial amounts of extra capital at the start of the year 2013, in which case a 10% increase in profit might actually represent a deterioration in financial performance. The problem is that the two years may not be directly comparable and this problem becomes even worse if one business entity is compared with another.

In general, the problems of comparability are reduced or eliminated if accounting ratios are compared, rather than absolute figures. In the above example, the ratio of profit to capital in 2013 should be calculated and compared with the equivalent figure for 2012. This will give a much better indication of the company's performance than can be obtained by comparing the absolute profit figures for the two years.

Ratios as a means of comparison

Performing a ratio analysis on a single set of financial statements is usually a fairly pointless exercise. Most of the ratios become much more meaningful when used as a basis for comparison. In general, ratios are used for making the following comparisons:

(a) **Comparing one period with another**. The financial performance of a business entity for a given accounting period and its financial position at the end of that period may be judged by calculating a set of ratios and then comparing the results with the equivalent ratios for the same business in previous accounting periods. This type of comparison is often referred to as a "trend analysis" and any perceived trends might be extrapolated into the future and used as a basis for making economic forecasts.

(b) **Comparing one entity with another**. Similarly, the ratios calculated for a business entity in a given accounting period may be compared with those calculated for other businesses in the same period (though this comparison would usually be valid only if all of the businesses were in the same type of trade).

When used as a means of comparison, accounting ratios are undoubtedly a valuable tool for the analysis of financial statements. However, ratio analysis does suffer from a number of limitations and the user should be aware of these before basing important decisions on the results of such an analysis. The limitations of ratio analysis are discussed towards the end of this chapter.

Types of accounting ratio

In theory, it would be possible to calculate literally hundreds of accounting ratios from a single set of financial statements. Some of these ratios would not mean very much but many of them might serve a useful purpose. In practice, however, it is usually sufficient to calculate a fairly small number of key ratios and each of these ratios is described in this chapter. They can be classified into four main groups:

(a) **Profitability ratios**. The profitability ratios are used to assess whether the business has succeeded in making an acceptable level of profit.

(b) **Liquidity ratios**. The liquidity ratios are a measure of the ability of the business to pay its debts as they fall due.

(c) **Efficiency ratios**. The efficiency ratios provide some indication of the extent to which the assets of the business have been efficiently used and managed.

(d) **Investment ratios**. The investment ratios are mainly of interest to investors or potential investors and may help these users to decide whether or not a business represents a worthwhile investment. However, some of the investment ratios may be of interest to other user groups.

Many of the accounting ratios could be calculated for any kind of business entity (sole trader, partnership or company) but some of them are relevant only to companies. Since ratio analysis is most frequently applied to the financial statements of companies, it is assumed for the remainder of this chapter that the business entity for which ratios are being calculated is a company.

The main ratios in each of the above groups are defined and explained below. Towards the end of the chapter there is a comprehensive numerical example which illustrates the way in which each ratio is calculated.

Profitability ratios

The main profitability ratios are:

(a) Return on capital employed
(b) Return on equity
(c) Gross profit margin
(d) Net profit margin.

Return on capital employed (ROCE)

This important ratio expresses a company's profit as a percentage of the amount of capital invested in the company. However, there are several different ways of calculating ROCE, each using a different definition of the words "profit" and "capital employed". A fairly common definition is as follows:

$$ROCE = \frac{\text{Profit before long-term interest and tax}}{\text{Share capital and reserves plus non-current liabilities}} \times 100\%$$

This version of ROCE interprets "capital employed" as the *total* amount of money invested in the company in the long term, regardless of whether that money has been supplied by shareholders or lenders. This amount is then compared with the return achieved on that capital. Note that:

(a) The numerator used in the calculation of ROCE is often referred to as PBIT. If a company's financial statements do not distinguish between short-term and long-term interest, it may be necessary to use the figure for profit before total interest and tax. This will make little difference if the amount of short-term interest is not material.

(b) Since the denominator used in the calculation of ROCE is equal to the total assets of the company less its current liabilities, this ratio is sometimes referred to as the *return on net assets*.

(c) Ideally, any ROCE calculation should be based upon the *average* amount of capital employed in the company during the period and this can be approximated by averaging the opening and closing capital figures. However, the calculation of ROCE is often based upon closing capital only, since opening capital may not be known for all of the accounting periods under review. The same point also applies to the calculation of a company's return on equity (see below).

(d) If a company's capital employed is understated in the financial statements, possibly because non-current assets such as property are shown at cost rather than current value, the ROCE figure will be misleadingly high. This point highlights the fact that accounting ratios are affected by accounting policies (see later in this chapter).

As stated above, ROCE can be defined as PBIT divided by net assets (where net assets are defined for this purpose as total assets less current liabilities). This view of ROCE makes it clear that the ROCE ratio can actually be broken down into two subsidiary components, as indicated by the following formula:

$$ROCE = \frac{PBIT}{Sales} \times \frac{Sales}{Net\ assets}$$

The first of these components is a profitability ratio known as the "profit margin" and the second component is an efficiency ratio known as "asset turnover". Both of these ratios are explained in more detail later in this chapter. Breaking down ROCE into its component parts may help to explain why a company's ROCE has changed from one period to another or why one company's ROCE is different from another's.

EXAMPLE 1

The following information has been extracted from the financial statements of two companies for the year to 31 December 2013. The companies are of similar size and operate in the same sector of industry.

	Company A £000	Company B £000
Sales	14,400	13,800
Profit before long-term interest and tax	720	690
Share capital and reserves	3,100	2,475
Non-current liabilities	500	400

Calculate ROCE for each company and analyse each company's ROCE figure into its component parts.

Solution

$$ROCE \;=\; \textit{Profit margin} \;\times\; \textit{Asset turnover}$$

Company A

$$\frac{720}{3,600} \;=\; \frac{720}{14,400} \;\times\; \frac{14,400}{3,600}$$

$$20\% \;=\; 5\% \;\times\; 4.0$$

Company B

$$\frac{690}{2,875} \;=\; \frac{690}{13,800} \;\times\; \frac{13,800}{2,875}$$

$$24\% \;=\; 5\% \;\times\; 4.8$$

These calculations show that Company B has the same profit margin as Company A but has a better ROCE because of its better asset turnover.

Return on equity (ROE)

This profitability ratio concentrates on the company's ordinary shareholders and compares their capital with the amount of profit which has been earned on their behalf. Return on equity is usually calculated as follows:

$$ROE = \frac{\text{Profit after interest, tax and preference dividend}}{\text{Ordinary share capital and reserves}} \times 100\%$$

This ratio may also be classified as an investment ratio, since it can be used by investors to assess the desirability of a company's ordinary shares. Investment ratios are discussed in more detail later in this chapter.

As well as comparing a company's ROCE and ROE for an accounting period with the returns achieved in previous periods and by other companies, it may also be useful to compare these ratios with current market rates of interest. For instance, if a company's ROCE is lower than current borrowing rates, this might indicate that the company would not benefit from making further borrowings. Similarly, if a company's ROE is higher than current savings rates, this might indicate that the company's ordinary shares are a good investment. However, such comparisons should be viewed with caution. Returns in future accounting periods may be very different from those in past periods and factors such as the degree of risk associated with various investments should also be taken into account.

Gross profit margin

The gross profit margin expresses a company's gross profit as a percentage of its sales revenue and is sometimes referred to as the *gross profit percentage*. Gross profit margin is calculated as follows:

$$\text{Gross profit margin} = \frac{\text{Gross profit}}{\text{Sales}} \times 100\%$$

It would be very misleading to compare the gross profit margin of two totally dissimilar businesses (e.g. a jeweller and a supermarket) but a comparison between two companies in the same line of trade should be meaningful and might throw some light on the pricing policies adopted by each of the companies concerned.

Net profit margin

The net profit margin (also referred to as simply the *profit margin*) expresses a company's profit as a percentage of its sales revenue and is calculated as follows:

$$\text{Net profit margin} = \frac{\text{Profit}}{\text{Sales}} \times 100\%$$

However, there is no consensus as to which profit figure should be used in the calculation of this ratio. Possibilities include PBIT, profit before tax and profit after tax. Therefore it is very important to ascertain the way in which the ratio has been calculated before basing important decisions upon it.

A year-on-year comparison of a company's gross profit margin and net profit margin may reveal the extent to which operating expenses are under control. For instance, if net profit margin has increased whilst gross profit margin has remained static, this might indicate that the company has succeeded in trimming its operating expenses. However, the validity of this conclusion will depend upon the way in which the net profit margin has been calculated and the extent to which the company's profit has been affected by items such as "other income" (see Chapter 3).

EXAMPLE 2

The following data has been extracted from a company's statement of comprehensive income for the year to 31 July 2014 (with comparatives for 2013):

	31 July 2014	31 July 2013
	£000	£000
Sales revenue	9,170	8,350
Cost of sales	6,220	5,670
Gross profit	2,950	2,680
Operating expenses	1,280	1,230
Interest payable	nil	nil
Profit before tax	1,670	1,450

Calculate the gross profit margin and profit margin for each year..

Solution

	31 July 2014	31 July 2013
Gross profit margin	$\dfrac{2,950}{9,170} = 32.2\%$	$\dfrac{2,680}{8,350} = 32.1\%$
Profit margin	$\dfrac{1,670}{9,170} = 18.2\%$	$\dfrac{1,450}{8,350} = 17.4\%$

The gross profit margin is virtually unchanged but the profit margin has increased by nearly a whole percentage point. This increase has been caused mainly by the fact that operating expenses as a percentage of sales have fallen from 14.7% to 14.0%.

Liquidity ratios

The main liquidity ratios are:

(a) The current ratio
(b) The quick assets ratio (or "acid test").

The current ratio

The purpose of the current ratio is to measure a company's ability to meet its short-term financial obligations out of its current assets. The current ratio is usually expressed as an actual ratio (e.g. 3:1) and is calculated as follows:

$$\text{Current ratio} = \frac{\text{Current assets}}{\text{Current liabilities}}$$

What is perceived as an acceptable level of current ratio will vary from one type of business entity to another. For example, a ratio of 1:1 may be perfectly adequate for a supermarket chain which has virtually no receivables and which rapidly converts its inventories into cash. On the other hand, a ratio of at least 2:1 might be seen as necessary for a manufacturing company which holds inventories for a longer period and then sells them on credit terms.

The quick assets ratio

In many cases, a company's inventories cannot be converted into cash at short notice and therefore the current ratio (which takes all current assets into account) may give an over-optimistic view of the company's liquidity. The quick assets ratio provides a more severe test of liquidity by omitting inventories from the calculation. The ratio is calculated as follows:

$$\text{Quick assets ratio} = \frac{\text{Current assets less inventories}}{\text{Current liabilities}}$$

Although a quick assets ratio of at least 1:1 might be seen as desirable, it should be borne in mind that some of the current liabilities shown in a company's financial statements may not be payable immediately. For instance, the tax liability may not fall due until several months after the end of an accounting period. In these circumstances, a ratio of less than 1:1 might be acceptable. Note that the quick assets ratio is also known as the *acid test*.

EXAMPLE 3

The following information has been extracted from the financial statements of Company S and Company M for the year to 31 December 2013. Company S is a supermarket chain whilst Company M is a manufacturer.

	Company S £m	Company M £m
Current assets:		
Inventories	970	1,750
Trade receivables	40	1,880
Cash and bank balances	570	290
	1,580	3,920
Current liabilities	2,470	2,120

Calculate the current ratio and the quick assets ratio for each company.

Solution

	Company S	Company M
Current ratio	$\dfrac{1,580}{2,470} = 0.64$	$\dfrac{3,920}{2,120} = 1.85$
Quick assets ratio	$\dfrac{610}{2,470} = 0.25$	$\dfrac{2,170}{2,120} = 1.02$

The liquidity ratios of Company S are very low. However, a supermarket chain can usually turns its inventories into cash fairly quickly and may also be able to obtain lengthy credit from its suppliers. If so, the low ratios may not be a cause for concern.

The liquidity ratios of Company M are higher and are more typical for a manufacturer which has a slower inventory turnover and which offers credit to its customers.

Efficiency ratios

The main efficiency ratios are:

(a) Asset turnover
(b) Inventory holding period
(c) Trade receivables collection period
(d) Trade payables payment period.

Asset turnover

This ratio measures the efficiency with which a company's assets are used to generate sales revenue. The ratio is usually calculated as follows:

$$\text{Asset turnover} = \frac{\text{Sales}}{\text{Net assets}} = \frac{\text{Sales}}{\text{Capital employed}}$$

This approach to the calculation of asset turnover defines a company's net assets as its total assets less its current liabilities, so that the net assets figure is equal to the total amount of capital employed in the business (see ROCE above). However, alternative versions of the asset turnover ratio may be calculated, in which sales are compared with (for example) the company's assets less total liabilities or with the company's non-current assets only.

Ideally, the asset turnover for an accounting period should be calculated by reference to the *average* net assets held during that period. However, it may be necessary to base the calculation upon closing net assets if the average figure is not available. Furthermore, a company's accounting policies may have a profound effect on its net assets figure and this point should be borne in mind when comparing the asset turnover of different companies.

Inventory holding period

The inventory holding period measures the average number of days which elapse between acquiring an item of inventory and then selling or using that item. This ratio is calculated as follows:

$$\text{Inventory holding period (in days)} = \frac{\text{Average inventory}}{\text{Cost of sales}} \times 365$$

An alternative approach is to calculate the number of times that inventory is "turned over" during an accounting period. In this case, the ratio is calculated as follows:

$$\text{Inventory turnover} = \frac{\text{Cost of sales}}{\text{Average inventory}}$$

For example, if a company's average inventory for an accounting period is £500,000 and cost of sales for the period is £2 million, the inventory holding period is approximately 91 days and inventory is turned over four times during the period. The average inventory for an accounting period is usually approximated by averaging the opening and closing inventory figures. If opening inventory is not known, there may be no option but to base the calculation on closing inventory only.

The inventory holding period (or the inventory turnover) provides an indication of the efficiency with which a company manages its inventories. An efficient company will maintain as low an inventory as possible whilst ensuring that sufficient inventory is always available to satisfy customer demand. Excessive inventories should be avoided since these tie up the company's funds unnecessarily and may require costly warehousing.

Trade receivables collection period

The trade receivables collection period measures the average number of days which elapse between making a credit sale and receiving payment from the customer. The ratio is calculated as follows:

$$\text{Trade receivables collection period (in days)} = \frac{\text{Average trade receivables}}{\text{Credit sales}} \times 365$$

Closing trade receivables are sometimes substituted for average trade receivables if it is not possible to derive an average figure. Any sales tax (such as VAT) included in the trade receivables figure should be eliminated before the ratio is calculated.

The trade receivables collection period provides an insight into the credit terms offered to a company's customers. An increase in this period might indicate that the company is deliberately offering longer credit so as to attract customers. Alternatively, an increase might suggest that the company's credit control system is not operating as efficiently as in previous accounting periods.

Trade payables payment period

The trade payables payment period measures the average number of days which elapse between the date of a credit purchase and the date on which payment is made to the supplier. The ratio is calculated as follows:

$$\text{Trade payables payment period (in days)} = \frac{\text{Average trade payables}}{\text{Credit purchases}} \times 365$$

If average trade payables cannot be ascertained, the ratio might be based upon the closing figure instead. If credit purchases cannot be ascertained, it might be necessary to use cost of sales as an approximation.

A substantial increase in a company's trade payables payment period when compared with previous periods might suggest that the company is experiencing difficulty in paying its suppliers and could even be in danger of being refused further credit.

Investment ratios

The main investment ratios are:

(a)   Earnings per share
(b)   Price earnings ratio
(c)   Dividend cover
(d)   Dividend yield
(e)   Capital gearing ratio
(f)   Interest cover.

Earnings per share (EPS)

Earnings per share (EPS) is the amount of profit earned during an accounting period for each ordinary share in issue during that period. This important ratio is frequently used as an indicator of financial performance and is calculated as follows:

$$\text{EPS (in pence)} = \frac{\text{Profit after tax and preference dividends}}{\text{Number of ordinary shares in issue}} \times 100\text{p}$$

The importance attached to the EPS ratio is attested by the fact that companies are required to present their EPS figure in the statement of comprehensive income and to calculate their EPS in accordance with international standard IAS33 *Earnings per Share*. This standard is fully explained later in this book (see Chapter 23).

Price earnings (P/E) ratio

The P/E ratio compares earnings per share with the market price of an ordinary share and calculates the number of years which it would take to recover the market price paid for a share if earnings remained constant in future years. The ratio is calculated as follows:

$$\text{Price earnings ratio} = \frac{\text{Market price per ordinary share}}{\text{Earnings per share}}$$

It might seem obvious that shares with a low P/E ratio would be regarded as an attractive investment. In fact, high P/E ratios are viewed more favourably than low ones. This is because EPS is a measure of past performance whilst the market price of a share reflects the stock market's expectations of the company's *future* performance. A high P/E ratio is seen as an indication that the market expects the company to perform well in the future.

Dividend cover

Dividend cover measures the number of times that the ordinary dividend for an accounting period could have been paid out of the available profits for that period. The ratio is calculated as follows:

$$\text{Dividend cover} = \frac{\text{Profit after tax and preference dividends}}{\text{Ordinary dividends}}$$

Alternatively, the ratio may be calculated by dividing earnings per share (EPS) by the dividend per ordinary share.

A high dividend cover indicates that the company is retaining a substantial part of its profits. This policy might not be popular with the ordinary shareholders but at least the high level of cover means that profits are more than adequate to fund the dividends paid. On the other hand, a low dividend cover might indicate that the company is having difficulty in maintaining an acceptable level of dividend.

Dividend yield

The dividend yield expresses the dividend per ordinary share as a percentage of the market price per ordinary share. The calculation is as follows:

$$\text{Dividend yield} = \frac{\text{Dividends per ordinary share}}{\text{Market price per ordinary share}} \times 100\%$$

This ratio acts as an indicator of the cash return received on the investment made by an ordinary shareholder. Whilst a low dividend yield might deter an investor who views the shares primarily as a source of income, a dividend yield of even 0% might not deter an investor whose main concern is capital growth.

Capital gearing ratio

The capital gearing ratio measures the extent to which a company's long-term funds have been provided by lenders. There are several different ways of calculating this ratio, but a frequently-used method of calculation is as follows:

$$\text{Capital gearing} = \frac{\text{Preference share capital plus non-current liabilities}}{\text{Total share capital and reserves plus non-current liabilities}} \times 100\%$$

The reason for regarding preference shares as a form of borrowing for this purpose is that preference shares attract a fixed rate of dividend in much the same way as a loan attracts a fixed rate of interest. No dividend can be paid to the ordinary shareholders until loan interest and the preference dividend have both been paid.

A company with a high capital gearing ratio is known as a "high-geared" company and such a company represents a high-risk investment for the ordinary shareholder. In a poor year, the need to pay interest and preference dividends may mean that the ordinary share-holders will receive no dividend at all. Furthermore, a high-geared company which runs into financial trouble may be unable to obtain further loans and may be forced into liquidation, in which case there may be insufficient funds to repay the ordinary shares after liabilities and the preference shares have been repaid. Conversely, a low-geared company represents a comparatively low-risk investment for the ordinary shareholder.

The words "high" and "low" cannot be defined in absolute terms and a company's capital gearing ratio must be judged in context. For instance, a capital gearing ratio which might be regarded as perfectly acceptable in the case of a sound company with steadily rising profits and excellent prospects might be judged as worryingly high if it applied to a less successful company. However, as a rule of thumb, a capital gearing ratio in excess of 50% might generally be regarded as high.

EXAMPLE 4

Company X and Company Y each have a profit before interest and tax of £500,000 for the year to 30 June 2014. Extracts from the companies' statements of financial position as at 30 June 2014 are as follows:

	X	Y
	£000	£000
Ordinary share capital	800	800
Reserves	2,700	200
	3,500	1,000
Non-current liabilities:		
10% long-term loan	500	3,000

There are no preference shares. It may be assumed that each company's tax expense for the year is equal to 20% of the profit before tax.

(a) Calculate the capital gearing ratio for each company.

(b) Calculate the amount of the profit for the year to 30 June 2014 which is available for distribution to the ordinary shareholders.

(c) Re-work part (b) of this example, now assuming that each company's profit before interest and tax for the year to 30 June 2014 is:

(i) decreased by 20% to £400,000   (ii) increased by 20% to £600,000

Comment on the results of these calculations.

Solution

(a) The capital gearing ratio of Company X is 500/4,000 = 12.5%.
The capital gearing ratio of Company Y is 3,000/4,000 = 75%.

(b)

	X £000	Y £000
Profit before interest and tax	500	500
Interest payable	50	300
Profit before tax	450	200
Taxation at 20%	90	40
Profit after tax	360	160

The amount of profit available to ordinary shareholders is £360,000 in the case of Company X and £160,000 in the case of Company Y.

(c)

	(i) X £000	(i) Y £000	(ii) X £000	(ii) Y £000
Profit before interest and tax	400	400	600	600
Interest payable	50	300	50	300
Profit before tax	350	100	550	300
Taxation at 20%	70	20	110	60
Profit after tax	280	80	440	240

A 20% increase or decrease in PBIT increases or decreases the profit available to the ordinary shareholders of Company X (low-geared) by approximately 22%, but the increase or decrease for the shareholders of Company Y (higher-geared) is 50%.

This demonstrates that, for a higher-geared company, any increase or decrease in PBIT will cause a disproportionate increase or decrease in the profit available to the ordinary shareholders. This suggests that the ordinary shareholders of a high-geared company are subject to an increased level of risk.

Interest cover

Interest cover is a measure of the number of times that the interest payable for an accounting period could have been paid out of the available profits. The ratio is calculated as follows:

$$\text{Interest cover} = \frac{\text{Profit before interest and tax}}{\text{Interest payable}}$$

This ratio is especially significant to the providers of loans. A high figure for interest cover indicates that lenders are in a relatively secure position and that the company's profits could fall substantially before there was any likelihood that interest payments could not be met. On the other hand, lenders (and potential lenders) might lose confidence in the company if interest cover is low.

COMPREHENSIVE EXAMPLE

Quandock plc is a trading company which makes all of its sales and purchases on credit terms. The company's financial statements for the year to 31 December 2013 (with comparative figures for 2012) are shown below.

Quandock plc
Statements of comprehensive income for the year to 31 December

	2013 £000	2012 £000
Sales revenue	5,000	4,550
Cost of sales	3,660	3,330
Gross profit	1,340	1,220
Operating expenses	380	400
Profit before interest and tax	960	820
Interest payable	80	100
Profit before taxation	880	720
Taxation	250	210
Profit after tax	630	510

Statements of financial position as at 31 December

	2013 £000		2012 £000	
Assets				
Non-current assets				
Property, plant and equipment		1,730		1,820
Current assets				
Inventories (*2011 £670,000*)	740		690	
Trade receivables	820		760	
Cash at bank and in hand	560	2,120	340	1,790
		3,850		3,610
Equity				
Ordinary shares of £1		1,000		1,000
Retained earnings		930		630
		1,930		1,630
Liabilities				
Non-current liabilities				
Long-term loans		800		1,000
Current liabilities				
Trade payables	870		770	
Taxation	250	1,120	210	980
		3,850		3,610

Notes:

(i)   Ordinary dividends of £330,000 were paid during the year to 31 December 2013. The equivalent figure for 2012 was £300,000.

(ii) The market price of the company's ordinary shares was 350p per share on 31 December 2013 and 275p per share on 31 December 2012.

Calculate a set of accounting ratios (for each of the two years) which may be used to judge the company's profitability, liquidity, efficiency and investment potential.

Solution

Profitability	**2013**	**2012**
Return on capital employed	$\dfrac{960}{2,730} \times 100\% = 35.2\%$	$\dfrac{820}{2,630} \times 100\% = 31.2\%$
Return on equity	$\dfrac{630}{1,930} \times 100\% = 32.6\%$	$\dfrac{510}{1,630} \times 100\% = 31.3\%$
Gross profit margin	$\dfrac{1,340}{5,000} \times 100\% = 26.8\%$	$\dfrac{1,220}{4,550} \times 100\% = 26.8\%$
Net profit margin	$\dfrac{880}{5,000} \times 100\% = 17.6\%$	$\dfrac{720}{4,550} \times 100\% = 15.8\%$

These ratios indicate that the business was more profitable in 2013 than it was in 2012. ROCE and ROE both show an improvement and although the gross profit margin was the same in both years, the net profit margin in 2013 (based on profit before tax) was better than in 2012. This is mainly due to the fact that the company managed to reduce its operating expenses in 2013 despite increasing its turnover.

Liquidity	**2013**	**2012**
Current ratio	$\dfrac{2,120}{1,120} = 1.9 \text{ to } 1$	$\dfrac{1,790}{980} = 1.8 \text{ to } 1$
Quick assets ratio	$\dfrac{2,120 - 740}{1,120} = 1.2 \text{ to } 1$	$\dfrac{1,790 - 690}{980} = 1.1 \text{ to } 1$

Both of these ratios show an improvement in 2013 and the company does not seem to have any liquidity problems, despite having repaid £200,000 of loans in 2013.

Efficiency	**2013**	**2012**
Asset turnover	$\dfrac{5,000}{2,730} = 1.83$	$\dfrac{4,550}{2,630} = 1.73$
Inventory holding period	$\dfrac{715}{3,660} \times 365 = 71 \text{ days}$	$\dfrac{680}{3,330} \times 365 = 75 \text{ days}$

Receivables collection period	$\dfrac{820}{5,000} \times 365 = 60$ days	$\dfrac{760}{4,550} \times 365 = 61$ days
Payables payment period	$\dfrac{870}{3,710} \times 365 = 86$ days	$\dfrac{770}{3,350} \times 365 = 84$ days

The asset turnover ratio indicates that the company has made more efficient use of its net assets in 2013 than in 2012. The inventory holding period (based on average inventory in each year) shows a reduction in 2013 which may indicate a more efficient inventory control policy. The trade receivables collection period and the trade payables payment period in 2013 are both broadly similar to their 2012 equivalents.

Notes:

(i)   Purchases in 2012 were £3,330,000 − £670,000 + £690,000 = £3,350,000.

(ii)   Purchases in 2013 were £3,660,000 − £690,000 + £740,000 = £3,710,000.

Investment	**2013**	**2012**
Earnings per share	$\dfrac{630}{1,000} = 63$p	$\dfrac{510}{1,000} = 51$p
Price earnings ratio	$\dfrac{350}{63} = 5.6$	$\dfrac{275}{51} = 5.4$
Dividend cover	$\dfrac{630}{330} = 1.9$	$\dfrac{510}{300} = 1.7$
Dividend yield	$\dfrac{33}{350} \times 100\% = 9.4\%$	$\dfrac{30}{275} \times 100\% = 10.9\%$
Capital gearing ratio	$\dfrac{800}{2,730} \times 100\% = 29\%$	$\dfrac{1,000}{2,630} \times 100\% = 38\%$
Interest cover	$\dfrac{960}{80} = 12$	$\dfrac{820}{100} = 8.2$

Virtually all of these ratios indicate that the company is a good investment. Earnings per share increased in 2013 and the stock market's regard for the shares (as indicated by the P/E ratio) also increased. The dividend yield went down but the dividend itself increased by 10% and dividend cover was adequate. The company is becoming more low-geared as the loans are repaid and the interest cover gives no cause for concern.

Limitations of ratio analysis

Although ratio analysis is an extremely useful and powerful tool for the analysis and interpretation of financial statements, it is subject to a number of limitations. Some of the more important limitations of ratio analysis are as follows:

(a) **Lack of standard definitions**. As mentioned earlier in this chapter, some accounting ratios may be defined in more than one way. This makes it difficult to compare ratios calculated by different accountants, each of whom might have used different definitions for the same ratios. It is very important that users should be aware of this problem when basing important decisions on information provided in the form of a ratio analysis.

(b) **Unrepresentative figures in the statement of financial position**. A statement of financial position shows only a snapshot of a company's financial position on a single date, whilst a statement of comprehensive income covers an entire accounting period. So if the company's assets and liabilities at the end of the period are not typical of the period as a whole, any ratio which combines a figure drawn from the statement of financial position with a figure drawn from the statement of comprehensive income might produce a misleading result.

One solution to this problem is to average the figures shown in the opening and closing statements of financial position, but this will be of little help if the company's statement of financial position is affected every year by recurring seasonal factors.

(c) **Accounting policies**. A company's accounting policies with regard to such matters as depreciation and the valuation of inventories might be very different to those of another company. These differences in policy may have a significant impact on accounting ratios and can make it difficult to effect a meaningful comparison between the companies concerned.

(d) **Misinterpretation**. Accounting ratios are open to misinterpretation unless all available evidence is taken into account. For example, a reduction in a company's gross profit margin might be interpreted as a bad sign, when in fact the company has deliberately dropped prices so as to boost sales. Similarly, a small increase in return on capital employed might be regarded as encouraging until it is discovered that most companies in the same sector have achieved a much larger increase. It is essential that ratios are judged collectively rather than singly, that a given company's ratios are compared with those of other companies in the same field and that anyone performing a ratio analysis is aware of background factors such as the overall economic climate, the rate of inflation, trends in interest rates etc.

Multivariate ratio analysis

The approach to ratio analysis considered so far in this chapter is often described as "univariate". With this approach, each ratio is considered separately and then judgements are made with regard to the company's profitability, liquidity etc. In contrast, the technique known as "multivariate" analysis combines together several key ratios to produce a single index number. This number can then be used to compare one company with another or to measure a company's progress over a number of accounting periods. Some proponents of multivariate analysis also claim that the technique is able to predict corporate failure.

One example of multivariate analysis is the "Z-score" devised by Edward Altman in the 1960s, in which five accounting ratios are weighted and combined as follows:

$$Z = 3.3A + 0.999B + 0.6C + 1.2D + 1.4E$$

where:

A = earnings before interest and tax ÷ total assets

B = sales ÷ total assets

C = market value of equity ÷ total liabilities

D = working capital ÷ total assets

E = retained earnings ÷ total assets.

The weightings used in the Z-score calculation were arrived at as the result of research into the relative importance of each ratio to a company's survival. It is claimed that a company with a Z-score of more than 3.0 will not fail, whilst a company with a Z-score of less than 1.8 is very likely to fail.

Whilst the multivariate approach is interesting, it has not replaced the more conventional univariate approach, which is still adopted by most accountants.

Summary

▸   Ratio analysis is a technique for the analysis and interpretation of the information contained in financial statements.

▸   Accounting ratios may be used to compare one accounting period with another for the same business entity or to compare one business entity with another. Ratio analysis is most frequently applied to the financial statements of companies.

▸   The most commonly-used accounting ratios can be classified into four main groups. These are profitability ratios, liquidity ratios, efficiency ratios and investment ratios.

▸   Ratio analysis is subject to a number of limitations which should be borne in mind when basing economic decisions upon the results of a ratio analysis.

▸   Multivariate ratio analysis attempts to combine ratios together into a single index number which may then be used to judge a company's financial health.

Exercises

22.1   The financial statements of R Ltd for the year to 30 April 2014 are as follows:

R Ltd
Statement of comprehensive income for the year to 30 April 2014

	£000
Sales revenue	410
Cost of sales	235
Gross profit	175
Operating expenses	115
Profit before interest and taxation	60
Interest payable	15
Profit before taxation	45
Taxation	10
Profit after taxation	35

Statement of financial position as at 30 April 2014

	£000	£000
Assets		
Non-current assets		
Property, plant and equipment		208
Current assets		
Inventories	82	
Trade receivables	58	
Cash at bank	7	147
		355
Equity		
10% Preference shares of £1		10
Ordinary shares of £1		100
Retained earnings		19
		129
Liabilities		
Non-current liabilities		
Long-term loans		150
Current liabilities		
Trade payables	45	
Payable re purchase of property, plant and equipment	21	
Taxation	10	76
		355

Note: Dividends of £1,000 (preference) and £20,000 (ordinary) were paid in the year.

Required:

Insofar as the information given permits, calculate the following ratios for R Ltd for the year to 30 April 2014, stating any assumptions made:

(a)	Return on capital employed	(b)	Return on equity
(c)	Gross profit margin	(d)	Net profit margin
(e)	Current ratio	(f)	Quick assets ratio
(g)	Inventory holding period	(h)	Receivables collection period
(i)	Payables payment period	(j)	Capital gearing ratio
(k)	Interest cover	(l)	Dividend cover
(m)	Earnings per share.		

22.2 Company X is an old-established clothing retailer. The company operates from expensive city centre premises and offers a high standard of customer service. The company's customers are willing to pay top prices so as to shop in comfort and many of them take advantage of the generous credit terms available.

Company Y is a recently-established clothing retailer. The company operates from a self-service store on the outskirts of the city and has comparatively few employees. The company's "no frills" approach appeals to customers who wish to buy clothes as cheaply as possible. In general, customers are encouraged to pay for their purchases immediately, but certain regular customers have a monthly account with the company.

Required:

Explain how these differences between Company X and Company Y might be reflected in their accounting ratios.

22.3 The issued share capital of Soresson plc consists of 1,000,000 ordinary shares of 50p each and 250,000 6% preference shares of £1 each..

In the year to 31 March 2014, the company's profit after tax was £90,000. Dividends paid during the year comprised the preference dividend for the year and an ordinary dividend of £55,000. The market price of the company's ordinary shares on 31 March 2014 was 70p per share.

Required:

Calculate the following ratios for Soresson plc:

(a)	Earnings per share	(b)	Dividend cover
(c)	Dividend yield	(d)	Price earnings ratio.

22.4 During the year to 31 December 2013, Trimberlake Ltd attempted to stimulate sales and increase its profits by reducing selling prices, holding larger inventories and giving customers longer credit. All of the company's purchases and sales are on credit terms. Summarised financial statements for the year to 31 December 2013 (with comparative figures for 2012) are as follows:

Trimberlake Ltd
Statements of comprehensive income for the year to 31 December

	2013	2012
	£000	£000
Sales revenue	5,327	3,725
Cost of sales	4,420	2,905
Gross profit	907	820
Operating expenses	87	75
Profit before interest and taxation	820	745
Interest payable	130	20
Profit before taxation	690	725
Taxation	215	225
Profit after taxation	475	500

Statements of financial position as at 31 December

		2013		2012
		£000		£000
Assets				
Non-current assets				
Property, plant and equipment		5,120		4,700
Current assets				
Inventories	1,334		730	
Trade receivables	1,278		596	
Bank	11	2,623	400	1,726
		7,743		6,426
Equity				
Ordinary shares of £1		2,000		2,000
Retained earnings		3,508		3,433
		5,508		5,433
Liabilities				
Non-current liabilities				
Long-term loans		1,000		150
Current liabilities				
Trade payables	1,020		618	
Taxation	215	1,235	225	843
		7,743		6,426

Note:

Ordinary dividends of £400,000 were paid during the year to 31 December 2013.

Required:

Calculate the following ratios for Trimberlake Ltd for each of the two years concerned and comment on the results of these calculations:

(a) Return on capital employed   (b) Return on equity

(c) Gross profit margin   (d) Net profit margin

(e) Current ratio   (f) Quick assets ratio

(g) Inventory holding period   (h) Receivables collection period

(i) Capital gearing ratio.

*22.5   Western Trading plc is a company which uses a variety of component parts in its manufacturing operations. One of the company's suppliers has recently gone out of business and therefore Western is now seeking an alternative (and reliable) source of supply for the component parts which were previously purchased from that supplier. Two companies have been identified as potential suppliers. Both companies prepare accounts to 31 December each year and Western has obtained the following copies of each company's financial statements for the year to 31 December 2013:

Statements of comprehensive income for the year to 31 December 2013

	X Ltd	Y Ltd
	£000	£000
Sales revenue	5,720	6,310
Cost of sales	3,840	4,240
Gross profit	1,880	2,070
Operating expenses	760	1,080
Profit before interest and taxation	1,120	990
Interest payable	50	350
Profit before taxation	1,070	640
Taxation	320	210
Profit after taxation	750	430

Statements of financial position as at 31 December 2013

		X Ltd		Y Ltd
		£000		£000
Assets				
Non-current assets		4,570		6,330
Current assets				
Inventories	510		890	
Trade receivables	670		1,090	
Bank balance	340	1,520	-	1,980
		6,090		8,310

(continued)

	X Ltd		Y Ltd	
	£000		£000	
Equity				
Share capital	2,000		2,000	
Retained earnings	2,820		1,030	
	4,820		3,030	
Liabilities				
Non-current liabilities				
Long-term loans	500		3,500	
Current liabilities				
Trade payables	450		1,130	
Taxation	320		210	
Bank balance	-	770	440	1,780
	6,090		8,310	

For both companies, all purchases and sales are made on credit terms.

Required:

(a) Calculate three profitability ratios, two liquidity ratios, three efficiency ratios and one gearing ratio for X Ltd and for Y Ltd.

(b) Use the information provided by these ratios to explain to the management of Western Trading plc which of the two companies seems likely to be the more reliable source of supply.

(c) Identify any further information which should be obtained before a final decision is made.   *(CIPFA)*

*22.6   Brenda is considering an investment in the ordinary shares of either Baker plc or Grant plc. Both companies operate in the same sector of industry and both prepare accounts to 30 September each year. Financial statements for the year to 30 September 2014 are shown below.

Statements of comprehensive income for the year to 30 September 2014

	Baker plc	Grant plc
	£000	£000
Sales revenue	15,160	12,260
Cost of sales	10,720	8,680
Gross profit	4,440	3,580
Operating expenses	2,160	1,620
Operating profit before interest and taxation	2,280	1,960
Interest payable	520	40
Profit before taxation	1,760	1,920
Taxation	440	480
Profit after taxation	1,320	1,440

Statements of financial position as at 30 September 2014

	Baker plc		Grant plc	
	£000		£000	
Assets				
Non-current assets		13,120		8,480
Current assets				
Inventories	1,580		1,260	
Trade receivables	1,720		1,360	
Bank balance	-	3,300	280	2,900
		16,420		11,380
Equity				
Share capital		6,000		6,000
Retained earnings		3,880		3,440
		9,880		9,440
Liabilities				
Non-current liabilities				
Long-term loans		3,500		500
Current liabilities				
Trade payables	1,920		960	
Taxation	440		480	
Bank balance	680	3,040	-	1,440
		16,420		11,380

The following information is also available:

1.   For both companies, all purchases and sales are made on credit terms.

2.   During the year to 30 September 2014, Baker plc paid dividends of £180,000 and Grant plc paid dividends of £600,000.

3.   Each company's issued share capital consists of 6 million ordinary shares of £1 each. At the close of business on 30 September 2014, the market price of an ordinary share in Baker plc was £1.65 and the market price of an ordinary share in Grant plc was £2.40.

Having examined the financial statements of the two companies, Brenda is inclined to invest in the shares of Baker plc. Her reasons for this view are that Baker plc has higher turnover, higher operating profit and greater assets than Grant plc. The shares of Baker plc are also cheaper.

Required:

(a) In so far as the information given permits, compute the following ratios for Baker plc and Grant plc:

- return on capital employed
- earnings per share
- price earnings ratio
- current ratio
- quick ratio (acid test)
- trade payables payment period
- capital gearing ratio
- dividend yield.

(b) Ratios for the two companies based upon the financial statements for the previous year (i.e. the year to 30 September 2013) were as follows:

	Baker plc	*Grant plc*
Return on capital employed	18.5%	18.9%
Earnings per share	23p	23p
Price earnings ratio	8.5	9.5
Current ratio	1.2	2.1
Quick ratio (acid test)	0.7	1.1
Trade payables payment period	49 days	39 days
Capital gearing ratio	11%	5%
Dividend yield	3%	4%

Taking into account these ratios and those which you have calculated for the year to 30 September 2014, advise Brenda which of the two companies seems to be the better investment. Give reasons for your advice.

(c) Identify three types of further information which should be obtained before a final investment decision is made. *(CIPFA)*

Chapter 23

Earnings per share

Introduction

The purpose of this chapter is to explain the main requirements of international standard IAS33 *Earnings per Share*. This standard provides a set of rules for the calculation and presentation of a company's earnings per share (EPS) figure. The aim of the standard is to improve the reliability of performance comparisons between different companies in the same reporting period and between different reporting periods for the same company.

Objectives

By the end of this chapter, the reader should be able to:

- explain why it is important to use a consistent definition of earnings per share
- explain the scope of international standard IAS33
- calculate basic earnings per share
- deal correctly with bonus issues and rights issues
- explain the concept of "dilution" and calculate diluted earnings per share
- outline the presentation and disclosure requirements of IAS33.

Significance of EPS

The earnings per share (EPS) ratio was briefly introduced in Chapter 22 as one of a set of accounting ratios which may be used to analyse a company's financial performance and provide a basis for performance comparisons between companies and between accounting periods. As stated in that chapter, such comparisons are invalid unless the ratios being used are calculated on a consistent basis. EPS is widely used as a means of assessing a company's performance and it also feeds into the Price/Earnings ratio which is extensively used as an indicator of investment potential. Therefore it is especially important that EPS should be calculated in accordance with a clear and consistent set of rules.

To ensure that EPS figures are calculated on a consistent basis, IAS33 prescribes the way in which a company's EPS should be calculated. The fact that EPS is the only ratio which is defined by an international standard (and has an entire standard devoted to it) is a strong indication of the importance which is attached to this key ratio.

The standard warns that EPS figures are subject to certain limitations because of the different accounting policies which companies may use when determining their earnings. In fact, the effect of differing accounting policies is a limitation of ratio analysis generally (see Chapter 22). However, any attempt to improve the comparability of important ratios is welcome and IAS33 achieves significant progress in this direction.

Scope of IAS33

IAS33 applies to companies whose ordinary shares are publicly traded. When the parent company of a group presents both consolidated financial statements (see Chapter 18) as well as its own separate financial statements, the disclosures required by IAS33 may be presented on the basis of the consolidated information only.

Calculation of Basic EPS

A company which is within the scope of IAS33 is required to calculate and present its "basic earnings per share". Basic EPS for an accounting period is calculated by dividing the profit (or loss) for that period which is attributable to the ordinary shareholders by the weighted average number of ordinary shares outstanding during the period. Note that:

(a) The profit attributable to the ordinary shareholders is the profit for the period after deduction of tax and any preference dividends. In the case of consolidated accounts, the profit attributable to non-controlling interests is also deducted.

(b) In general, shares are "outstanding" as from the date on which they are issued.

(c) IAS1 (see Chapter 3) requires that comparative information should be provided in respect of the previous period for all amounts reported in the financial statements. Therefore it is necessary to present basic EPS for the previous accounting period as well as for the current accounting period.

Discontinued operations

If a company reports a profit or loss on discontinued operations (see Chapter 8) then it is necessary to calculate *two* basic EPS figures for the period in question. One of these figures is based on the whole of the profit which is attributable to the ordinary shareholders. The other figure is based on the profit from continuing operations which is attributable to the ordinary shareholders.

EXAMPLE 1

A company's summarised statement of comprehensive income for the year to 31 May 2014 is as follows:

	£000
Continuing operations	
Profit before tax	650
Taxation	200
Profit for the period from continuing operations	450
Discontinued operations	
Profit for the period from discontinued operations	70
Profit for the period	520

The following information is also available:

(a) The pre-tax profit from discontinued operations was £100,000 and the related tax expense was £30,000.

(b) The company's issued share capital consists of 500,000 10% preference shares of £1 each and one million £1 ordinary shares. There were no changes to the issued share capital during the year.

(c) The preference dividend of £50,000 was paid in full during the year.

Calculate basic EPS for the year to 31 May 2014.

Solution

Basic EPS (based on the profit attributable to the ordinary shareholders) is:

$$\frac{£520,000 - £50,000}{1,000,000} = 47\text{p per share.}$$

Basic EPS (based on the profit from continuing operations only) is:

$$\frac{£450,000 - £50,000}{1,000,000} = 40\text{p per share.}$$

The figure of 40p per share, which is based on the company's continuing operations, is a more reliable indicator of future performance than the figure of 47p per share, which includes profits from operations that have now been discontinued.

Shares issued during the accounting period

As stated above, IAS33 requires that the calculation of basic EPS should take into account *"the weighted average number of ordinary shares outstanding during the period"*. This requirement recognises that a company's issued ordinary share capital may change during an accounting period, generally as the result of a share issue. In such a case, the use of a weighted average number of shares ensures that basic EPS is fairly adjusted to reflect the amount of fresh capital which the company has raised during the period and the length of time for which this capital has been available for the purpose of generating earnings.

The weighted average number of ordinary shares for an accounting period is calculated by *adding*:

(a)   the number of ordinary shares outstanding at the beginning of the period

(b)   the number of ordinary shares issued during the period, multiplied by the appropriate time weighting factor

and then *subtracting*:

(c)   the number of ordinary shares bought back by the company during the period (if this is legally permissible) multiplied by the appropriate time weighting factor.

Strictly speaking, the time weighting factors used in this calculation should reflect the number of *days* that have elapsed between the date of the issue or buy-back and the end of the accounting period. However, IAS33 accepts that a reasonable approximation is adequate in most circumstances. In this book, it is assumed that time weighting factors should be calculated to the nearest month.

It is important to note that the above calculation assumes that shares are issued or bought back at fair value (i.e. at full market price). Further adjustments are required if this is not the case, mainly where the company makes a bonus issue or rights issue (see below).

EXAMPLE 2

On 1 January 2013, a company's issued share capital consisted of 60,000 ordinary £1 shares. On 1 March 2013, the company issued 30,000 ordinary shares. On 1 October 2013, the company bought back 10,000 ordinary shares. Both the share issue and the buy-back were made at full market price.

Calculate the weighted average number of ordinary shares outstanding in the year to 31 December 2013.

Solution

The share issue and the share buy-back occurred 10 months and 3 months respectively before the end of the accounting year. Therefore the weighted average number of ordinary shares outstanding in the year was:

60,000 + (30,000 x 10/12) − (10,000 x 3/12) = 82,500 shares.

This calculation recognises that the extra resources generated by the new issue were available to the company for the purpose of generating earnings for only the last 10 months of the year and (similarly) that the resources used to finance the buy-back were unavailable to the company for the last 3 months of the year.

Since the company had 60,000 ordinary shares outstanding for the first 2 months of the year, 90,000 shares for the next 7 months and then 80,000 shares for the final 3 months, an alternative way of calculating the weighted average number of ordinary shares is:

(60,000 x 2/12) + (90,000 x 7/12) + (80,000 x 3/12) = 82,500 shares.

Either method of calculation may be used.

EXAMPLE 3

A company's profit after tax for the year to 31 July 2014 was £3.8 million. The comparative figure for the year to 31 July 2013 was £3.6 million.

The company's issued share capital at 1 August 2012 consisted of 4 million ordinary shares of 50p. No shares were issued during the year to 31 July 2013 but a further 1 million ordinary shares were issued (at full market price) on 1 November 2013.

Calculate basic EPS for the years to 31 July 2013 and 2014.

Solution

The number of ordinary shares outstanding in the year to 31 July 2013 was 4 million. The weighted average number of ordinary shares outstanding in the year to 31 July 2014 was:

4,000,000 + (1,000,000 x 9/12) = 4,750,000 shares.

Alternatively, this may be calculated as:

(4,000,000 x 3/12) + (5,000,000 x 9/12) = 4,750,000 shares.

Therefore:

Basic EPS for the year to 31 July 2013 is $\dfrac{£3,600,000}{4,000,000}$ = 90p per share.

Basic EPS for the year to 31 July 2014 is $\dfrac{£3,800,000}{4,750,000}$ = 80p per share.

This fall in basic EPS reflects the fact that earnings have risen by only 5.55% whilst the number of issued shares has risen by 18.75%.

Note:

The EPS calculation takes into account the *number* of ordinary shares outstanding, not their nominal value. Therefore the fact that this company's ordinary shares have a nominal value of 50p per share is irrelevant.

Bonus issues

IAS33 requires that the weighted average number of ordinary shares outstanding during an accounting period should be adjusted for events "*that have changed the number of ordinary shares outstanding without a corresponding change in resources*". This is a reference to the fact that ordinary shares may be issued at a price which is less than their full market value. The main occasions on which this occurs are when a company makes a bonus issue (see below) or a rights issue (see later in this chapter).

A bonus issue consists of an issue of free extra shares to existing shareholders in proportion to their existing holdings. From the point of view of calculating EPS, the most important feature of a bonus issue is that a company's resources do not increase when such an issue is made. Therefore a bonus issue increases the number of shares outstanding without increasing the company's capacity to earn profits.

If a bonus issue made during a period were treated in the same way as an issue of shares at full price, the effect would be to depress the EPS figure and distort the comparison with EPS in previous periods. To resolve this problem, IAS33 states that a bonus issue should be treated as if it had occurred "*at the beginning of the earliest period presented*". Since most companies present comparative information for the previous period only, this means that bonus issues are usually treated as if they had occurred at the beginning of the previous period. It is necessary in these circumstances to recalculate and restate EPS for the previous period as well as to calculate EPS for the current period.

EXAMPLE 4

A company's profit after tax for the year to 30 June 2014 was £2.2 million. The comparative figure for the year to 30 June 2013 was £2 million.

The company's issued share capital at 1 July 2012 consisted of 800,000 ordinary shares. No shares were issued during the year to 30 June 2013 but a 1 for 4 bonus issue was made on 1 March 2014.

Calculate basic EPS for the year to 30 June 2014 and the restated comparative figure for the year to 30 June 2013.

Solution

The bonus issue of 200,000 ordinary shares is treated as if made on 1 July 2012, so that the number of ordinary shares outstanding is 1 million throughout both years. Therefore:

Basic EPS for the year to 30 June 2014 is $\dfrac{£2,200,000}{1,000,000}$ = £2.20 per share.

Restated basic EPS for the year to 30 June 2013 is $\dfrac{£2,000,000}{1,000,000}$ = £2.00 per share.

These figures show a 10% increase in basic EPS. This is fair, since earnings have risen by 10% without any increase in the company's resources.

Basic EPS for the year to 30 June 2013 would have been stated originally as £2.50 per share (earnings of £2 million divided by 800,000 ordinary shares). If this were not restated as above, it would appear that the company's financial performance had declined during the year to 30 June 2014, which is not the case.

EXAMPLE 5

On 1 January 2012, a company's issued share capital consisted of 500,000 ordinary shares. No further shares were issued during the year to 31 December 2012 but the following issues took place during the year to 31 December 2013:

(a) a 1 for 5 bonus issue on 1 February 2013

(b) an issue of 120,000 ordinary shares at full market price on 1 December 2013.

Calculate the number of shares to be used in the calculation of restated basic EPS for the year to 31 December 2012. Also calculate the weighted average number of ordinary shares to be used in the calculation of basic EPS for the year to 31 December 2013.

Solution

The bonus issue of 100,000 shares is treated as if made on 1 January 2012. Therefore the number of shares to be used in the calculation of restated basic EPS for the year to 31 December 2012 is 600,000.

The weighted average number of ordinary shares outstanding in the year to 31 December 2013 is:

600,000 + (120,000 x 1/12) = 610,000 shares.

Alternatively, this may be calculated as:

(600,000 x 11/12) + (720,000 x 1/12) = 610,000 shares.

Rights issues

Like a bonus issue, a rights issue consists of an issue of extra shares to existing share-holders in proportion to their existing shareholdings. However, rights shares are not issued free of charge. If a rights issue is made at full market price, it is treated in exactly the same way as any other full-price issue when calculating basic EPS. But rights shares are often issued at a price which is *lower* than market price and so contain a "bonus element". In these circumstances, IAS33 requires that the rights issue should be separated into two components. These are:

(a) a bonus issue, followed immediately by

(b) an issue of shares at full market price.

Each of these components is then treated as described earlier in this chapter.

Calculating the bonus element of a rights issue

The calculation of the bonus element of a rights issue relies upon the fact that (in theory) the market price per share of a company's shares should fall when an issue is made without a corresponding increase in the company's resources. For instance, a 1 for 1 bonus issue would double the number of shares outstanding but would not inject any extra resources into the company concerned. Therefore the market price per share should halve when such as issue is made. Based on this principle, the procedure to be adopted when a rights issue is made at less than fair value is as follows:

(a)   **Step 1**. The theoretical fall in the market price of the company's shares caused by the rights issue is calculated. This calculation takes into account the number of shares issued and the amount of extra resources raised by the issue.

(b)   **Step 2**. It is then necessary to compute the size of bonus issue *that would have caused the same fall in the market price* of the company's shares as the fall which has been caused by the rights issue.

(c)   **Step 3**. The bonus element of the rights issue is equal to the number of bonus shares calculated at step 2 above. The remainder of the rights issue is treated as an issue of shares at full market price.

The procedure is illustrated in the examples given below.

EXAMPLE 6

A company with an issued share capital of 100,000 ordinary shares makes a new share issue. The market price of the company's ordinary shares just before this issue was £6 per share. Calculate the theoretical market value per share just after the issue has been made, assuming that the issue comprises:

either (a)   a 1 for 2 bonus issue

or   (b)   a 1 for 5 rights issue at £4.20 per share.

Solution

(a)   The total market value of the company's shares (and so presumably the worth of the company) just before the issue was £600,000. The company's worth is unaffected by the bonus issue but the number of issued shares rises to 150,000. So (in theory) the market price of the company's shares just after the bonus issue should fall to £600,000/150,000 = £4 per share.

(b)   The rights issue consists of 20,0000 shares and raises extra resources of £84,000 (20,000 x £4.20). The worth of the company becomes £684,000 and the number of issued shares rises to 120,000. So (in theory) the market price of the company's shares just after the rights issue should fall to £684,000/120,000 = £5.70 per share.

EXAMPLE 7

A company's profit after tax for the year to 31 March 2014 was £351,000. The comparative figure for the year to 31 March 2013 was £288,000.

The company's issued share capital at 1 April 2012 consisted of 100,000 ordinary shares. No shares were issued during the year to 31 March 2013 but a 1 for 2 rights issue was made on 1 October 2013 at 60p per share and this was fully subscribed. The market value of the company's shares just before the rights issue was £1.20 per share.

Calculate basic EPS for the year to 31 March 2014 and the restated comparative figure for the year to 31 March 2013.

Solution

This solution follows the 3-step approach suggested above in relation to rights issues.

Step 1. The total market value of the company's shares just before the rights issue (and so presumably the company's worth) was £120,000. The rights issue consisted of 50,000 shares and raised £30,000 (50,000 x 60p). Therefore the number of issued shares rose to 150,000 and the company's worth increased to £150,000. So the theoretical market price of the company's shares just after the rights issue was £1 per share.

Step 2. If there had been a bonus issue instead of a rights issue, the company's worth would have remained at £120,000. If the market price per share had fallen to £1 as a result of this hypothetical bonus issue, the company's issued share capital after the bonus issue would have consisted of 120,000 shares (since 120,000 x £1 = £120,000). So the size of bonus issue that would have caused a fall in market price to £1 per share is an issue of 20,000 shares (a 1 for 5 bonus issue).

Step 3. The rights issue can now be divided into a bonus issue of 20,000 shares and an issue of shares at full market price of the remaining 30,000 shares.

The validity of this separation can be demonstrated by observing that if a bonus issue of 20,000 shares had occurred and this had reduced market price to £1 per share, then an issue of 30,000 shares at full market price would have raised £30,000. This is indeed the amount of money that the rights issue has raised (50,000 shares at 60p).

Calculation of basic EPS

The calculation of basic EPS is now straightforward. As usual, the bonus element of the rights issue (20,000 shares) is treated as if it had occurred at the beginning of the previous period, giving a total number of ordinary shares outstanding for the year to 31 March 2013 of 120,000 shares. The weighted average number of ordinary shares outstanding for the year to 31 March 2014 is 120,000 + (30,000 x 6/12) = 135,000 shares. Therefore:

Restated basic EPS for the year to 31 March 2013 is $\dfrac{£288,000}{120,000}$ = £2.40 per share.

Basic EPS for the year to 31 March 2014 is $\dfrac{£351,000}{135,000}$ = £2.60 per share.

Calculation of Diluted EPS

The calculation of basic EPS takes into account only those ordinary shares which are already outstanding. However, a company may have issued financial instruments which give the holder the right to acquire ordinary shares at some time in the future. When these "potential ordinary shares" are eventually issued, the company's earnings will be spread over a greater number of shares than before and so EPS will usually be reduced. The most common examples of potential ordinary shares are:

(a) liabilities that are convertible into ordinary shares (e.g. convertible loan stock)
(b) options to purchase ordinary shares.

To ensure that existing shareholders are made aware of the extent to which earnings per share would be reduced (or "diluted") if potential ordinary shares were issued, companies are required by IAS33 to calculate a figure for "diluted EPS" as well as for basic EPS.

Diluted EPS is defined as the earnings per share figure which would arise if all "dilutive potential ordinary shares" were issued. Potential ordinary shares are regarded as dilutive if the effect of their issue would be to *decrease* EPS. If the issue of potential ordinary shares would *increase* EPS (see below), the shares are then said to be "antidilutive". Antidilutive potential ordinary shares are ignored when calculating diluted EPS.

A company which reports a profit or loss on discontinued operations must calculate diluted EPS based on the whole of the company's profit and another diluted EPS figure based on the profit from continuing operations. Comparatives must be given for the previous accounting period. The calculation of diluted EPS generally requires the following adjustments to the figures which were used when calculating basic EPS:

(a) **Earnings**. The company's earnings must be adjusted for the after-tax effect of any change in income or expenses that would result from the issue of dilutive potential ordinary shares. For instance, earnings would be increased by the amount of extra after-tax profit that would arise as the result of no longer paying interest on convertible loan stock.

(b) **Weighted average number of shares**. The weighted average number of ordinary shares must be increased to reflect the maximum number of additional ordinary shares that would become outstanding if all dilutive potential ordinary shares were issued (assuming the most advantageous conversion rate from the point of view of the holder of the potential ordinary shares). These shares are treated as if issued at the beginning of the accounting period or (if later) on the date of issue of the financial instrument concerned.

Potential ordinary shares are antidilutive if the effect of issuing those shares would be to increase earnings by proportionately more than the increase in the number of shares.

EXAMPLE 8

A company has an issued share capital consisting of 8 million ordinary shares. The company's after-tax profit for the year to 30 September 2014 is £2 million.

In 2011, the company issued £10 million of 8% convertible loan stock. This stock is convertible into ordinary shares during year 2017 at the rate of 1 ordinary share per £5 of loan stock. A tax rate of 20% may be assumed.

(a) Calculate the company's basic EPS for the year to 30 September 2014.

(b) Determine whether the potential ordinary shares derived from the loan stock are dilutive or antidilutive and calculate the company's diluted EPS for the year.

(c) Explain how the situation would differ if the loan stock attracted interest at 5% rather than 8%.

Solution

(a) Basic EPS is £2 million divided by 8 million shares, giving 25p per share.

(b) If all of the loan stock were converted into shares, the company would save interest of £800,000 per annum. Profit before tax would rise by £800,000, giving an increase in after-tax profits of £640,000 (£800,000 less 20% tax).

There would be 2 million extra ordinary shares, so EPS for the year to 30 September 2014 would be 26.4p (£2,640,000 divided by 10 million shares). This exceeds the company's basic EPS so the effect of conversion would be to increase EPS, not to reduce it. Therefore the potential ordinary shares are antidilutive and can be ignored. Diluted EPS is the same as basic EPS.

(c) If the loan stock attracted interest at only 5%, the increase in after-tax profits on conversion would be £400,000 (£500,000 less 20% tax). EPS for the year would become 24.0p (£2,400,000 divided by 10 million shares). This is less than basic EPS and so the potential ordinary shares are dilutive. Diluted EPS is 24.0p per share.

Options

A share option generally gives the holder of that option the right to acquire shares at less than full market price. When such an option is exercised, the resulting increase in the number of shares outstanding will have a dilutive effect on EPS but this effect will be mitigated because of the extra resources that will enter the company when the option-holder pays for the shares. When calculating diluted EPS, share options are dealt with in the following way:

(a) The total amount of money that will be payable by the option-holder when the option is exercised is divided by the average market price per share during the current accounting period, so giving the number of shares that could be acquired for that amount of money at full market price.

(b) Based upon this calculation, the potential share issue is now split into a potential issue of shares at full market price and a potential issue of free shares ("shares for no consideration").

(c) Shares issued at full price are not dilutive, so the weighted average number of shares used in the diluted EPS calculation is adjusted to reflect only the potential issue of shares for no consideration.

The method is illustrated in the example given below.

EXAMPLE 9

A company's issued share capital consists of 5 million ordinary shares. The company's after-tax profit for the year to 31 December 2013 is £2.6 million. Share options exist which, when exercised, would result in the issue of a further 400,000 ordinary shares at a price of £1 per share. The average market price per ordinary share during 2013 was £5.

Compute basic and diluted EPS for the year to 31 December 2013.

Solution

Basic EPS is 52p per share (£2.6 million divided by 5 million shares).

When the options are exercised, a further 400,000 shares will be issued for a total consideration of £400,000. At average market price, the number of shares which could be obtained for this consideration is 80,000 (£400,000 divided by £5) so the potential issue of 400,000 shares is split into a potential issue of 80,000 shares at full market price and a potential issue of 320,000 shares for no consideration.

The potential 80,000 shares are not dilutive and can be ignored. Therefore the weighted average number of shares used in the calculation of diluted EPS is 5.32 million (5 million shares currently outstanding plus a potential 320,000 further shares).

Diluted EPS is 48.9p per share (£2.6 million divided by 5.32 million shares).

Presentation and disclosure requirements

The main presentation and disclosure requirements of IAS33 are as follows:

Presentation

(a) Basic and diluted EPS (both for the profit or loss attributable to ordinary shareholders and for the profit or loss from continuing operations attributable to ordinary shareholders) must be presented "*in the statement of comprehensive income*". It is not permissible to present these figures in the notes instead.

(b) An entity which presents a separate statement of profit or loss (see Chapter 3) should present its basic and diluted EPS figures in that separate statement.

(c) If a company's financial statements report a discontinued operation, basic EPS and diluted EPS figures must be presented for that operation, either in the statement of comprehensive income or in the notes.

(d) EPS figures must be presented even if they are negative (i.e. a loss per share).

Disclosure

(a) The company must disclose the earnings figures used in the EPS calculations and reconcile these figures to the profit or loss for the period as shown in the statement of comprehensive income.

(b) The company must disclose the weighted average number of shares used in the calculation of basic EPS and in the calculation of diluted EPS. These figures must be reconciled to each other.

(c) Financial instruments which could potentially dilute earnings per share in the future, but which have not been included in the calculation of diluted EPS (because they are currently antidilutive) must also be disclosed.

Summary

▸ EPS is widely used as a means of assessing a company's financial performance and as a basis for performance comparisons. Therefore it is important that EPS should be calculated on a consistent basis.

▸ IAS33 lays down a set of rules for the calculation and presentation of EPS figures. This standard applies to companies whose ordinary shares are publicly traded.

▸ Basic EPS for an accounting period is calculated by dividing the profit attributable to ordinary shareholders for that period by the weighted average number of ordinary shares outstanding during the period.

▸ Bonus issues made during an accounting period are treated as if made at the beginning of the previous period.

▸ Rights issues are separated into a bonus element and an issue of shares at full market price. Each component of the rights issue is then treated accordingly.

▸ Diluted EPS for an accounting period is the EPS which would arise if all dilutive potential ordinary shares were issued. The calculation of diluted EPS requires that adjustments are made to the figures for earnings and number of shares outstanding which were used when computing basic EPS.

▸ Basic EPS and diluted EPS must be presented in the statement of comprehensive income.

Exercises

23.1 A company's issued share capital is £2 million, comprising four million ordinary shares of 25p each and one million 8% preference shares of £1. An extract from the company's statement of comprehensive income for the year to 31 March 2014 is as follows:

	£000
Profit before tax	560
Taxation	170
Profit after tax	390

Preference dividends of £80,000 were paid during the year.

Required:

(a) Calculate basic EPS for the year.

(b) Recalculate basic EPS for the year on the assumption that the company's profit after tax includes profit of £50,000 from a discontinued operation.

23.2 The profit after tax of B plc for the year to 30 June 2014 is £217,500. The comparative figure for the year to 30 June 2013 was £188,000.

On 1 July 2012, the company's issued share capital consisted of 100,000 ordinary shares of £1 each. On 1 December 2013, a further 15,000 ordinary shares were issued at full market price.

Required:

(a) Calculate basic EPS for the year to 30 June 2013.

(b) Calculate basic EPS for the year to 30 June 2014.

23.3 C plc has the following after-tax profits for its two most recent accounting periods:

	£000
year to 31 October 2012	330
year to 31 October 2013	341

On 1 November 2011, the company's issued share capital consisted of 500,000 ordinary shares. On 1 August 2013, the company made a 1 for 10 bonus issue.

Required:

(a) Calculate basic EPS for the year to 31 October 2013.

(b) Calculate restated basic EPS for the year to 31 October 2012 and explain why this restatement is necessary.

23.4   The profits after tax of D plc are as follows:

	£
year to 30 September 2012	50,000
year to 30 September 2013	52,800

On 1 October 2011, the company's issued share capital consisted of 150,000 ordinary shares. On 1 July 2013, the company made a 1 for 5 rights issue at 50p per share. This issue was fully subscribed. The market value of the company's shares just before the rights issue was 80p per share.

Required:

(a)   Calculate basic EPS for the year to 30 September 2013.

(b)   Calculate restated basic EPS for the year to 30 September 2012.

23.5   E plc has an issued share capital consisting of 800,000 ordinary shares. There are no preference shares. Some years ago, the company issued £1 million of 10% convertible loan stock, convertible in 2018 at the rate of 2 ordinary shares for every £10 of loan stock. The company's profit after tax for the year to 31 March 2014 is £640,000.

Required:

(a)   Calculate basic EPS for the year to 31 March 2014.

(b)   Calculate diluted EPS for the year to 31 March 2014, assuming that the company pays tax at 20%.

(c)   Rework both of the above calculations, now assuming that the loan stock was not issued "some years ago" but was in fact issued on 1 October 2013.

*23.6   The profits attributable to the ordinary shareholders of F plc are as follows:

	£000
year to 31 December 2012	1,800
year to 31 December 2013	2,475

For many years, the company's issued share capital has consisted of 9 million ordinary shares. However, on 1 April 2013, the company made a 1 for 4 rights issue at 50p per share. This issue was fully subscribed. The market value of the company's shares just before the rights issue was £1 per share.

Required:

(a)   Calculate basic EPS for the year to 31 December 2013.

(b)   Calculate restated basic EPS for the year to 31 December 2012.

*23.7   On 1 January 2012, G plc issued £2 million of 7% convertible loan stock. The holders of this stock may choose to convert the stock to ordinary shares on 1 January 2016, 2017 or 2018. The number of ordinary shares into which the stock will be converted is as follows:

Date of conversion	Number of shares issued
1 January 2016	400 shares per £1,000 of stock
1 January 2017	420 shares per £1,000 of stock
1 January 2018	440 shares per £1,000 of stock

The company's profit after tax for the year to 30 September 2013 was £2.2 million. The comparative figure for the year to 30 September 2012 was £2.4 million. The company pays tax at 20%.

On 1 October 2011, the company's issued share capital consisted of 1.5 million 12% preference shares of £1 each and 5 million ordinary shares of 20p each. On 1 April 2013 the company issued a further 500,000 ordinary shares at full market price.

The preference dividend was paid in full in both the year to 30 September 2012 and the year to 30 September 2013.

Required:

(a)   Calculate basic EPS and diluted EPS for the year to 30 September 2012.

(b)   Calculate basic EPS and diluted EPS for the year to 30 September 2013.

Chapter 24

Segmental analysis

Introduction

Many entities (especially large companies) engage in a wide range of business activities and operate in a number of economic environments. Each business activity or economic environment may be subject to differing rates of profitability, differing opportunities for growth, differing future prospects and differing risks, but this is not apparent from the aggregated information given in the main financial statements. Accordingly, international standard IFRS8 *Operating Segments* requires an entity which falls within its scope to disclose information that will enable the users of the financial statements to "*evaluate the nature and financial effects of the business activities in which it engages and the economic environments in which it operates*".

The purpose of this chapter is to explain the requirements of IFRS8, which was issued by the IASB in 2006 as part of its convergence project with the US Financial Accounting Standards Board. The requirements of this standard apply only to entities whose shares or securities are publicly traded.

Objectives

By the end of this chapter, the reader should be able to:

- explain the term "operating segment" as defined in IFRS8
- explain the term "reportable segment" as specified in IFRS8
- identify an entity's reportable segments
- state the disclosures required by IFRS8 for each reportable segment
- explain the reconciliations required by IFRS8
- list the entity-wide disclosures required by IFRS8
- prepare an entity's segment report.

Operating segments

IFRS8 adopts a "management approach" to segment reporting and defines the segments of an entity in a way which is consistent with the entity's own internal management structure. An operating segment is defined by IFRS8 as "*a component of an entity:*

(a) *that engages in business activities from which it may earn revenues and incur expenses (including revenues and expenses relating to transactions with other components of the same entity),*

(b) *whose operating results are regularly reviewed by the entity's chief operating decision maker to make decisions about resources to be allocated to the segment and assess its performance, and*

(c) *for which discrete financial information is available.*"

The standard points out that not every component of an entity is necessarily an operating segment or even part of an operating segment. For example, a corporate headquarters may not earn revenue and therefore would not be an operating segment.

The term "chief operating decision maker" identifies a function rather than a manager with a specific title. In many cases this function will be performed by the chief executive or chief operating officer but the function might be performed by a group of executive directors or other managers. In general, each operating segment will be managed by a segment manager who reports to the chief operating decision maker.

Reportable segments

IFRS8 requires an entity to provide separate information about each of its "reportable segments". This information is disclosed in the notes to the financial statements. The following rules are used to identify an entity's reportable segments:

(a) Two or more operating segments may be combined into one operating segment if the segments have similar economic characteristics and are similar in each of the following respects:

- the nature of the products and services involved
- the nature of the production processes
- the type or class of customer for the products and services
- the distribution methods used
- the nature of the applicable regulatory environment (if any).

(b) A reportable segment is a single or combined operating segment which meets *any* of the following "quantitative thresholds":

(i) its reported total revenue from sales to external customers and sales to other operating segments is at least 10% of the total revenue (external and internal) of all operating segments, or

(ii) its reported profit or loss is at least 10% of the combined profit of all operating segments that reported a profit or the combined loss of all operating segments that reported a loss, whichever is the greater, or

(iii) its assets are at least 10% of the total assets of all operating segments.

(c) An operating segment that does not meet any of the 10% thresholds may nonetheless be treated as a reportable segment if management believes that information about the segment would be useful to the users of the financial statements. Alternatively:

(i) such a segment may be combined into a reportable segment with one or more similar operating segments that also fail to meet any of the 10% thresholds, or

(ii) it may be included in an "all other segments" category in the segment report.

(d) If the total external revenue attributable to reportable segments is less than 75% of the entity's total external revenue, additional operating segments must be identified as reportable (even though they are beneath the 10% thresholds) until at least 75% of total external revenue is included in reportable segments.

EXAMPLE 1

A listed company has identified seven operating segments (labelled A to G). The following information is available in relation to each segment's revenue, profit or loss and assets for the year to 31 December 2013:

	External revenue £000	Sales to other segments £000	Profit or (loss) £000	Assets £000
Segment A	3,040	2,440	720	3,170
Segment B	1,460	0	(160)	1,590
Segment C	1,580	60	(60)	1,480
Segment D	1,720	0	120	2,150
Segment E	760	520	150	1,620
Segment F	2,360	1,740	560	3,780
Segment G	1,520	0	(50)	1,460
	12,440	4,760	1,280	15,250

Identify the company's reportable segments for this accounting period.

Solution

(a) The company's total revenue (external and internal) is £17.2m (£12.44m + £4.76m). So a segment must have revenue of at least £1,720,000 to satisfy the first 10% test.

(b) The combined profits of profitable segments are £1.55m and combined losses of loss-making segments are £0.27m. The larger of these is £1.55m. So a segment must have a profit or loss of at least £155,000 to satisfy the second 10% test.

(c) Total assets are £15.25m. So a segment must have assets of at least £1,525,000 to satisfy the third 10% test.

(d) The results of the three 10% tests for each operating segment are as follows:

	Total revenue at least £1.72m	*Profit or loss at least £0.155m*	*Assets at least £1.525m*	*Reportable segment*
Segment A	Y	Y	Y	Y
Segment B	N	Y	Y	Y
Segment C	N	N	N	N
Segment D	Y	N	Y	Y
Segment E	N	N	Y	Y
Segment F	Y	Y	Y	Y
Segment G	N	N	N	N

Segments C and G fail all three of the 10% tests, so these will not be reportable as long as the remaining segments satisfy the 75% test.

(e) 75% of the company's total external revenue is £9.33m (75% × £12.44m). The total external revenue of reportable segments A, B, D, E and F is £9.34m, so the 75% test is satisfied.

Disclosures required by IFRS8

IFRS8 requires that entities should disclose four main classes of information for each accounting period. These are as follows:

(a) general information

(b) information about each reportable segment

(c) certain reconciliations

(d) entity-wide information.

Each of these classes is explained below.

General information

Under the heading "general information" an entity should disclose the factors used to identify its reportable segments and the types of products or services from which each reportable segment earns its revenues.

The way in which the entity is organised internally should be made clear (e.g. by product group or by geographical area) and the entity should also disclose whether or not any operating segments have been combined for segment reporting purposes.

Information about reportable segments

An entity should disclose the profit or loss of each reportable segment. Total assets and total liabilities for each reportable segment should also be disclosed if these amounts are regularly provided to the chief operating decision maker.

In addition, certain items should be disclosed for each reportable segment if these are included in the segment profit or loss figures or are otherwise regularly provided to the chief operating decision maker. These items include:

(a) segment external revenue and internal revenue

(b) segment interest expense and interest revenue

(c) segment depreciation and amortisation

(d) segment income tax expense (or income)

(e) segment non-cash items other than depreciation and amortisation (if material)

The entity should disclose additions to non-current assets for each reportable segment if this information is regularly provided to the chief operating decision maker.

The amounts of all the items listed above should be the amounts which are reported to the chief operating decision maker, regardless of whether these amounts are measured for that purpose in the same way as they are measured in the financial statements.

An entity should explain the way in which segment profit or loss, segment assets and segment liabilities have been measured for segment reporting purposes. The explanation should disclose the basis of accounting for inter-segment transactions and any differences between the measurement bases used for segment reporting purposes and the measurement bases used in the financial statements.

Note also that entities are encouraged (but are not required) by IAS7 *Statement of Cash Flows* to disclose cash flow information for each reportable segment, showing the amount of segment cash flows arising from operating activities, investing activities and financing activities (see Chapter 16).

Reconciliations

The entity must provide certain reconciliations between the information disclosed for reportable segments and the information given in the financial statements. The required reconciliations are as follows:

(a) total revenue of reportable segments to the entity's revenue

(b) total profit or loss of reportable segments to the entity's profit or loss

(c) total assets of reportable segments to the entity's assets

(d) total liabilities of reportable segments (if disclosed) to the entity's liabilities.

For every other material item in the segment report, a reconciliation should be provided between the total amount of that item for reportable segments and the corresponding amount for the entity.

Entity-wide information

There are three types of "entity-wide" disclosures required by IFRS8. These are:

(a) **Products and services**. The entity should report its revenue from external customers for each product and service (or each group of related products and services) unless this information is unavailable or would cost too much to derive. The amounts of revenue that are reported should be based on the information which is used to produce the entity's financial statements.

(b) **Geographical areas**. The entity should report the following geographical information unless this information is unavailable or would cost too much to derive:

(i) revenues from external customers attributed to:

– the entity's home country
– all foreign countries (in total)

(ii) non-current assets located in:

– the entity's home country
– all foreign countries (in total)

The amounts reported should be based on the information which is used to produce the entity's financial statements. Amounts for an individual foreign country should be disclosed separately if material.

(c) **Major customers**. The entity should provide information about the extent to which it relies upon its major customers. In particular, if any single customer accounts for at least 10% of the entity's external revenues, then:

(i) that fact should be disclosed

(ii) the total amount of revenue from each such customer should be disclosed, along with the identity of the segment(s) in which this revenue is reported.

However, the entity is not required to disclose the identity of major customers.

EXAMPLE 2

The implementation guidance which accompanies IFRS8 provides several illustrations of the way in which an entity might disclose segment information. The tables shown below are based upon some of these illustrations:

(a) Table 1 gives information about reportable segments.

(b) Table 2 reconciles segment revenues to the entity's total revenue.

(c) Table 3 provides certain geographical information.

Table 1: Information about reportable segments

	Seg A £m	Seg B £m	Seg C £m	All other £m	Total £m
Revenue from external customers	800	950	1,700	100	3,550
Inter-segment revenue	–	300	150	–	450
Interest revenue	125	100	250	–	475
Interest expense	95	70	110	–	275
Depreciation and amortisation	30	5	260	–	295
Segment profit	27	90	280	10	407
Segment assets	700	300	6,900	200	8,100
Non-current asset additions	100	50	140	–	290
Segment liabilities	405	180	3,800	–	4,385

Table 2: Revenue reconciliation

	£m
Total revenue for reportable segments	3,900
Other revenue	100
Elimination of inter-segment revenue	(450)
Entity's revenue	3,550

Table 3: Geographical information

	Revenue £m	Non-current assets £m
United States	1,900	1,100
Canada	420	–
China	340	650
Japan	290	350
Other countries	600	300
Total	3,550	2,400

Summary

▸ IFRS8 requires entities whose shares are publicly traded to disclose certain segment information. This information should relate to the entity's operating segments.

▸ An operating segment is a revenue-earning component of an entity whose operating results are regularly reviewed by the entity's chief operating decision maker and for which discrete financial information is available.

▸ In general, an operating segment is reportable if it meets at least one out of three 10% thresholds relating to the segment's revenue, profit or loss and assets. But reportable segments must account for at least 75% of the entity's total external revenue.

▸ The main disclosures required by IFRS8 for each reportable segment usually include profit or loss, total assets and liabilities, external revenue, internal revenue, interest revenue and expense, depreciation, income tax expense, significant non-cash items and additions to non-current assets.

▸ IFRS8 requires a number of reconciliations between the information disclosed for reportable segments and the information given in the financial statements.

▸ IFRS8 also requires a number of entity-wide disclosures. The entity must disclose the amount of revenue earned from each of its products/services, a geographical analysis of revenues and non-current assets and information about the extent to which it relies upon major customers.

Exercises

24.1 (a) Explain why the users of financial statements may find a segment report useful.

(b) Identify the entities which lie within the scope of IFRS8 *Operating Segments* and which must therefore prepare a segment report.

24.2 (a) Explain the term "operating segment" as used in IFRS8.

(b) List the main tests which determine whether or not a particular operating segment is reportable.

24.3 IFRS8 requires disclosure of four main classes of information. Identify these classes and list the main disclosures required for each class.

24.4 MacTavin plc has four operating segments. The following information relates to the year ending 31 March 2014:

	External Revenue £000	Profit/(loss) £000	Assets £000
Segment W	27,300	2,450	14,540
Segment X	36,100	3,150	16,490
Segment Y	6,200	(230)	3,170
Segment Z	7,800	(550)	3,800

In addition to the external revenue shown above, Segment W earned revenue of £5.6m from sales to other operating segments. Identify the company's reportable segments for the year to 31 March 2014 in accordance with the requirements of IFRS8.

24.5 Overtan plc has four operating segments. The following figures relate to the year to 30 April 2014. Similar information is provided to the chief operating decision maker on a monthly basis.

	Segment A £m	Segment B £m	Segment C £m	Segment D £m
External sales	652	764	389	1,220
Sales to other segments	127	234	87	333
Interest income	17	12	-	56
Segment revenue	796	1,010	476	1,609
Cost of sales	267	350	124	632
Distribution costs	98	129	67	196
Administrative expenses	120	171	130	179
Interest expense	34	51	20	87
Depreciation	101	132	65	253
Other non-cash expenses	17	12	7	29
Segment expenses	637	845	413	1,376
Segment profit	159	165	63	233
Segment assets	530	653	310	982
Segment liabilities	245	276	119	398
Segment capital expenditure	99	68	-	122

General administrative expenses for the year (not allocated between segments) were £120m. The company's tax expense for the year was £150m. Unallocated assets and liabilities were £457m and £658m respectively.

Insofar as this information permits, prepare the information about reportable segments and the reconciliations which should appear in the company's segment report for the year to 30 April 2014, in accordance with the requirements of IFRS8.

*24.6   Floothair plc is a large international airline company with three operating segments:

  – International airline business
  – Domestic airline business
  – Non-airline business.

The company reports segment information for the year to 31 May 2014 in accordance with IFRS8 *Operating Segments*. The following information is available for the year:

	£m
Total revenue:	
International airline business	8,207
Domestic airline business	402
Non-airline business	267
Unallocated income	22
Profit/(loss) before tax and finance costs:	
International airline business	803
Domestic airline business	(30)
Non-airline business	16
Profit on sale of assets:	
Non-airline business	32
Unallocated	4
Net finance costs	149
Income tax expense	170
Assets:	
International airline business	12,050
Domestic airline business	240
Non-airline business	140
Liabilities:	
International airline business	4,566
Domestic airline business	84
Non-airline business	350
Unallocated	5,420
Total revenue includes the following inter-segment sales:	
International airline business	103
Domestic airline business	14
Non-airline business	7

Required:

(a) Prepare, insofar as the above information permits, a segment report for Floothair plc for the year to 31 May 2014. Assume that the company decides to treat all three segments as reportable segments.

(b) Use the segment report to identify three significant aspects of the performance of Floothair plc which would not otherwise be evident.   *(CIPFA)*

Part 5

SMALL AND MEDIUM-SIZED ENTITIES

Chapter 25

The IFRS for SMEs

Introduction

The full text of the international standards, together with their implementation guidance and other accompanying documentation, occupies over 3,000 pages of fine print. An entity which complies with these standards must prepare and present an intricate set of financial statements and make very extensive disclosures. In fact there are over 3,000 items on the full disclosure checklist. It is apparent, therefore, that the full international standards are intended for use mainly by large sophisticated entities with complex finances. It is also apparent that the full standards are generally unsuitable for use by smaller entities with relatively simple financial affairs. In consequence, the main users of the full international standards ("full IFRS") are large public companies whose shares and securities are traded on stock exchanges throughout the world.

The IASB accepts that full IFRS is not well suited to small and medium-sized entities and estimates that over 95% of all companies worldwide fall into this category. Therefore, in an attempt to meet the financial reporting needs of these entities, the IASB has issued the *International Financial Reporting Standard for Small and Medium-sized Entities* (referred to as the "IFRS for SMEs"). This 230-page standard was issued in July 2009 after a prolonged period of discussion and development and is tailored for use by small and medium-sized entities. This one standard covers all aspects of accounting for such entities and is self-contained (i.e. it is not linked to full IFRS). The recognition and measurement rules are simpler than those in full IFRS and topics which are not relevant to SMEs have been omitted. Furthermore, entities which comply with the IFRS for SMEs are required to make far fewer disclosures (approximately 300) than are required by full IFRS.

The purpose of this chapter is to explain the principal features of the IFRS for SMEs and to highlight the main distinctions between this standard and full IFRS.

Organisation of the IFRS for SMEs

The IFRS for SMEs is organised by topic and consists of 35 numbered sections. A full list of these sections is given below and then the requirements of each section are briefly described. However, the sections on "share-based payment" and "specialised activities" are outside the scope of this book and are not dealt with here.

Contents of the IFRS for SMEs

Objectives

By the end of this chapter, the reader should be able to:

- explain the purpose of the IFRS for SMEs
- define the term "small and medium-sized entities"
- explain the concepts and principles which underlie the IFRS for SMEs
- identify the financial statements which must be presented by an entity which complies with the IFRS for SMEs
- explain the structure and required content of each component of a set of financial statements drawn up in accordance with the IFRS for SMEs
- outline the requirements of the IFRS for SMEs in relation to each of the topics addressed by this standard
- summarise the main distinctions between the IFRS for SMEs and full IFRS.

Section 1
Small and medium-sized entities

The IFRS for SMEs is intended for use only by small and medium-sized entities. These are defined as "*entities that:*

(a) do not have public accountability, and

(b) publish general purpose financial statements for external users". External users are stated to include owners who are not involved in managing the business, existing and potential creditors and credit rating agencies. Financial statements produced solely for the benefit of owner-managers and the tax authorities are not normally treated as general purpose financial statements.

An entity has public accountability if its shares or securities are publicly traded. Financial institutions such as banks, credit unions and insurance companies are also regarded as having public accountability.

The IFRS for SMEs may be adopted by any country (whether or not that country has already adopted full IFRS) and each country which adopts the standard may determine for itself which types of entity should use the standard. However, the above definition makes it clear that publicly accountable entities should not use the IFRS for SMEs and that the standard is not intended for use by very small owner-managed businesses. It would seem that the main intended users are unlisted companies which are owned by their shareholders but managed by their directors.

At the time of writing, the IASB asserts that over 80 countries have either adopted the IFRS for SMEs or are planning to do so within the next three years.

Section 2
Concepts and pervasive principles

This section of the IFRS serves a similar purpose to the IASB *Conceptual Framework* and sets out the basic principles which underlie the financial statements of small and medium-sized entities. The main matters dealt with in this section are as follows:

(a) **Objective of financial statements**. The objective of financial statements for SMEs is to "*provide information about the financial position, performance and cash flows of the entity that is useful for economic decision-making by a broad range of users ...*". The financial statements also show the results of the stewardship of management and provide a means of holding management accountable.

(b) **Qualitative characteristics**. The qualitative characteristics of financial information are *understandability*, *relevance*, *reliability* and *comparability*. Information cannot be relevant unless it is material and is presented to users in sufficient time for it to affect their economic decisions. Information cannot be reliable unless it provides a faithful representation and is free from bias. Reliability is enhanced if the substance of transactions is reported (not just their legal form) and if the information provided is complete and prepared with the exercise of prudence. Comparability is achieved by using consistent accounting policies and by disclosing those policies.

(c) **Definitions**. The IFRS provides exactly the same definitions of *asset*, *liability*, *equity*, *income* and *expenses* as are given in the *Conceptual Framework* (see Chapter 2).

(d) **Recognition**. The recognition criteria for assets, liabilities, income and expenses are also the same as in the *Conceptual Framework*. An item is recognised in the financial statements if it is probable that any future economic benefits associated with the item will flow to/from the entity and if the item's cost or value can be measured reliably.

(e) **Measurement**. The only measurement bases specified in the IFRS are historical cost and fair value. As used to be the case in full IFRS (before the issue of IFRS13) fair value is defined as "*the amount for which an asset could be exchanged, or a liability settled, between knowledgeable, willing parties in an arm's length transaction*".

   At initial recognition, assets and liabilities are measured at historical cost unless the IFRS requires the use of a different basis. Subsequent measurement of various types of asset and liability is dealt with in later sections of the IFRS, though most liabilities are measured at the entity's best estimate of the settlement amount.

(f) **Accrual basis**. The financial statements of SMEs (other than the statement of cash flows) should be prepared using the accrual basis of accounting.

(g) **Total comprehensive income and profit or loss**. Total comprehensive income is defined as "*the arithmetical difference between income and expenses*". Profit or loss is defined as "*the arithmetical difference between income and expenses other than those items ... that this IFRS classifies as items of other comprehensive income*".

(h) **Offsetting**. In general, assets/liabilities and income/expenses should not be offset.

Section 3
Financial statement presentation

Sections 3-6 of the IFRS for SMEs serve a similar function to IAS1 in full IFRS. Section 3 addresses the general features of financial statements and then defines what is meant by a complete set of financial statements. A summary of this section is as follows:

(a) **Fair presentation**. Financial statements should "*present fairly the financial position, financial performance and cash flows*" of the entity. It is presumed that application of the IFRS for SMEs will usually achieve the required fair presentation.

(b) **Compliance with the IFRS**. An entity which complies with the IFRS for SMEs must state that fact in the notes to the financial statements. It is permissible to depart from a requirement of the IFRS only in the very rare circumstances when compliance with that requirement would conflict with the objective of financial statements. In this case, the entity should make full disclosure of the departure concerned.

(c) **Going concern**. Financial statements should be prepared on the going concern basis unless there is good reason to believe that the entity intends to cease operations. An entity which is not a going concern should disclose that fact (with reasons) and state the basis on which the financial statements have been prepared.

(d) **Frequency of reporting and comparative information**. Financial statements should usually be presented at least annually and should provide comparative information for the previous period. In general, the way in which items are presented and classified in the financial statements should be consistent between accounting periods.

(e) **Materiality/aggregation**. Each material class of similar items should be presented separately in the financial statements.

(f) **Complete set of financial statements**. A complete set of financial statements for a small or medium-sized entity normally comprises:
- a statement of financial position at the reporting date
- a single statement of comprehensive income for the reporting period or a separate income statement and a separate statement of comprehensive income
- a statement of changes in equity
- a statement of cash flows
- a set of notes.

However, an entity with no "other comprehensive income" (OCI) may dispense with the statement of comprehensive income and present only an income statement. Since the IFRS for SMEs requires only very few items to be classified as OCI, this option is likely to be widely used. It is also permissible in certain circumstances to merge the statement of comprehensive income and the statement of changes in equity into a combined "statement of income and retained earnings" (see Section 6).

The financial statements should be clearly identified with suitable headings. Other titles may be used for the financial statements as long as these are not misleading.

Section 4
Statement of financial position

Section 4 of the IFRS sets out the information which is to be presented in a statement of financial position (or balance sheet). The minimum list of required line items is basically the same as the equivalent list given in IAS1 (see Chapter 3) except that:

(a)　"Investments in associates" and "investments in jointly controlled entities" are shown as two separate items on the list in the IFRS for SMEs, whereas the list in IAS1 has a combined item for "investments accounted for by the equity method".

(b)　The list in the IFRS for SMEs omits assets and liabilities classified as "held for sale" (see Section 17).

As in full IFRS, SMEs should present additional line items, headings and subtotals if these are relevant to an understanding of the entity's financial position.

Section 4 also sets out further information which should be disclosed in the statement of financial position or in the notes. This information consists mostly of sub-classifications of line items presented in the statement of financial position (e.g. analyses of property, plant and equipment, inventories, trade receivables and trade payables). Disclosures required in relation to the entity's share capital and reserves are precisely the same as in IAS1.

Section 4 reproduces the definitions of current/non-current assets and liabilities that are provided in IAS1 but allows SMEs to ignore this classification and to present all assets and liabilities in order of approximate liquidity (ascending or descending) if this provides information which is reliable and more relevant.

Section 5
Statement of comprehensive income and income statement

Section 5 of the IFRS repeats that small and medium-sized entities may present either a single statement of comprehensive income or a separate income statement and a separate statement of comprehensive income. This section also sets out the information that should be presented in these financial statements. The minimum list of required items is basically the same as in IAS1 (see Chapter 3) and segregates the results of discontinued operations. Additional line items, headings and subtotals should be presented if these are relevant to an understanding of the entity's financial performance. Furthermore:

(a)　Items of income or expense must not be described as "extraordinary" in the statement of comprehensive income, the income statement (if presented) or the notes.

(b)　The IFRS requires that entities should present an analysis of expenses based on either the nature of the expenses or their function within the entity. An analysis based on function must disclose a figure for cost of sales.

Section 6
Statement of changes in equity and
Statement of income and retained earnings

Section 6 of the IFRS requires SMEs to present either a statement of changes in equity or (if certain conditions are satisfied) a statement of income and retained earnings. As in full IFRS, the statement of changes in equity shows how each component of an entity's equity has changed during the reporting period and takes into account:

(a) the effects of any retrospective application of an accounting policy or retrospective restatement of items (see Section 10)

(b) the profit or loss for the period

(c) each item of other comprehensive income (if any)

(d) transactions with the entity's owners, such as share issues and dividends.

However, if the only changes in equity occurring during a reporting period are caused by (a) and (b) above and by the payment of dividends, the entity may present a "statement of income and retained earnings" instead of a statement of comprehensive income and a statement of changes in equity. The statement of income and retained earnings shows all of the information normally shown in the statement of comprehensive income, together with a reconciliation of retained earnings at the beginning and end of the period.

Section 7
Statement of cash flows

This section of the IFRS for SMEs is the equivalent of IAS7 in full IFRS. In fact, there are no significant differences between the requirements of Section 7 and those of IAS7, except that some detailed requirements in IAS7 relating to entities with subsidiaries, associates or joint ventures are omitted from Section 7 of the IFRS.

All small and medium-sized entities must present a statement of cash flows in which cash inflows and outflows are classified by operating activities, investing activities and financing activities. Cash flows from operating activities may be presented using either the direct method or the indirect method (see Chapter 16).

Section 8
Notes to the financial statements

The notes to the financial statements should present:

(a) a statement that the financial statements comply with the IFRS for SMEs

(b) a summary of significant accounting policies (see Section 10)

(c) supporting information for items presented in the financial statements, disclosing any information required by the IFRS that is not disclosed elsewhere

(d) any other disclosures relevant to an understanding of the financial statements.

Information should also be provided relating to judgements made by management which have had a significant effect on the figures shown in the financial statements. Key sources of estimation uncertainty should be disclosed.

Section 9
Consolidated and separate financial statements

SMEs that are parent companies are generally required to present consolidated financial statements. However, a small or medium-sized parent company is exempted from this requirement if:

(a) the company is itself a subsidiary, and

(b) it has a parent which produces consolidated general purpose financial statements that comply with full IFRS or the IFRS for SMEs.

A subsidiary is defined as "*an entity that is controlled by the parent*". Control is defined as "*the power to govern the financial and operating policies of an entity so as to obtain benefits from its activities*". Control over an entity is usually deemed to exist when the parent owns, directly or indirectly, more than 50% of the voting power of that entity.

The consolidation procedures and disclosures required by this section of the IFRS for SMEs are broadly similar to those set out in IFRS10 (see Chapters 18 and 19).

Section 10
Accounting policies, estimates and errors

This section of the IFRS for SMEs is equivalent to IAS8 in full IFRS. Accounting policies are defined in the same way as in IAS8 (see Chapter 4). Entities are required to select their accounting policies as follows:

(a) If the IFRS for SMEs specifically addresses the transaction or item concerned, then the entity must apply the rules set out in the IFRS.

(b) Otherwise, management should use its judgement in devising an accounting policy that results in relevant, reliable information, taking into account any requirements of the IFRS in relation to similar issues, the concepts and principles set out in Section 2 of the IFRS and (possibly) the requirements of full IFRS.

Accounting policies should be applied consistently and should be changed only if required by an amendment to the IFRS for SMEs or if the change would result in reliable and more relevant information. If an accounting policy is changed because of an amendment to the IFRS for SMEs, the change should be accounted for as required by that IFRS. Otherwise, a change in accounting policy should be accounted for retrospectively (see Chapter 4).

Correction of material prior period errors should also be accounted for retrospectively, but a change in an accounting estimate should be accounted for prospectively.

Sections 11 and 12
Financial instruments

Sections 11 and 12 of the IFRS deal with financial instruments. Entities may either apply these two sections in full or instead apply the recognition and measurement requirements of IAS39 and the disclosure requirements of these two sections.

Section 11 is concerned with basic financial instruments and covers most of the financial assets and liabilities that are likely to arise in the case of SMEs. These include items such as trade receivables, trade payables, loans receivable or payable and investments in either preference shares or ordinary shares. Such items are measured initially at the transaction price. Subsequently:

(a) Debts that are classified as current assets or liabilities should normally be measured at the undiscounted amount expected to be received or paid.

(b) Most other debts should be measured at amortised cost using the effective interest method (see Chapter 11).

(c) Investments in shares should be measured at fair value if this can be determined (e.g. if the shares are publicly traded) or at cost less impairment otherwise.

Section 12 of the IFRS deals with more complex financial instruments such as derivatives and hedging instruments and is beyond the scope of this book.

Section 13
Inventories

Section 13 of the IFRS is equivalent to IAS2 in full IFRS (see Chapter 10). Inventories are defined in the same way as in IAS2 and the IFRS states that inventories are to be measured at "*the lower of cost and estimated selling price less costs to complete and sell*". This is of course a rewording of the familiar "lower of cost and net realisable value" rule.

The costs that should be included in the cost of inventories (and the costs that should be excluded) are listed in the IFRS and are the same as those listed in IAS2. In general, the cost of each item of inventory should be specifically identified. However, interchangeable items should be measured using either the first-in, first-out (FIFO) cost formula or the weighted average cost formula (AVCO).

Section 14
Investments in associates

An associate is defined by the IFRS for SMEs as "*an entity ... over which the investor has significant influence and that is neither a subsidiary nor an interest in a joint venture*". This is very similar to the definition given in IAS28 (see Chapter 20). However, whereas IAS28 requires that investments in associates should normally be measured by the equity method, the IFRS for SMEs offers a choice of three measurement models. The same model should be used for all investments in associates. The models are as follows:

(a) **Cost model**. An investment in an associate (other than an associate for which there is a published price quotation) is measured at cost less accumulated impairment losses. Dividends received from an associate are recognised as income. An investment in an associate for which there is a published price quotation is measured using the fair value model (see below).

(b) **Equity method**. An investment in an associate is accounted for by the equity method as specified in IAS28 (see Chapter 20).

(c) **Fair value model**. An investment in an associate is measured initially at transaction price. Subsequently, the investment is measured at fair value. Changes in fair value are recognised in the calculation of profit or loss. An investment in an associate for which it is impracticable to measure fair value reliably should be measured using the cost model.

As in IAS28, it is presumed that an investor has significant influence over an entity if that investor holds (directly or indirectly) at least 20% of the entity's voting power, unless it can be shown that this is not the case. Similarly, it is presumed that an investor who holds less than 20% of the voting power of an entity does not have significant influence, unless such influence can be clearly demonstrated.

Section 15
Investments in joint ventures

A joint venture is defined by the IFRS for SMEs as "*a contractual arrangement whereby two or more parties undertake an economic activity that is subject to joint control*". This is the definition that used to be given in full IFRS before the introduction of IFRS11 and is similar to the definition of a "joint arrangement" in that standard (see Chapter 20).

Whereas full IFRS now distinguishes between only two types of joint arrangement, the IFRS for SMEs still distinguishes between jointly controlled operations, jointly controlled assets and jointly controlled entities. Jointly controlled operations or assets exist if the parties concerned use their own assets (or jointly controlled assets) in the arrangement and do not establish a separate entity for this purpose. In this case, the required accounting treatment is broadly the same as for "joint operations" in full IFRS (see Chapter 20).

However, an interest in a jointly controlled entity (a "joint venture" in full IFRS) may be accounted for by using any one of three models, though the same model should be used for all interests in jointly controlled entities. The models are the same as those which may be used in relation to an investment in an associate (see above). They are:

(a) the cost model

(b) the equity method

(c) the fair value model.

This differs from full IFRS, which generally requires that interests in a "joint venture" should normally be accounted for by use of the equity method.

Section 16
Investment property

This section of the IFRS for SMEs is equivalent to IAS40 in full IFRS and sets out the required accounting treatment of investment property. Investment property is defined (as in IAS40) as "*property (land or a building, or part of a building, or both) held ... to earn rentals or for capital appreciation ...*". Investment property does not include property which is held for use in the production or supply of goods or services, for administrative purposes, or for sale in the ordinary course of business.

In common with IAS40, the IFRS states that investment property should be measured initially at cost. However, whereas IAS40 offers a choice between the fair value model and the cost model for subsequent measurement of investment property, the IFRS requires that all investment property should normally be measured at fair value. Changes in fair value are recognised in the calculation of the entity's profit or loss. If the fair value of an investment property cannot be measured reliably (without undue cost or effort) it should be accounted for as property, plant and equipment (Section 17) and should be measured at cost less accumulated depreciation and impairment losses.

Section 17
Property, plant and equipment

This section of the IFRS for SMEs begins by defining property, plant and equipment in the same way as in IAS16 (see Chapter 5) and establishes the same recognition criteria as in that standard. Items such as spare parts, the replacement of major components and the cost of major inspections are dealt with as in full IFRS. The section then states that property, plant and equipment should be measured initially at cost, which is defined for this purpose in the same way as in IAS16. However, the section departs from IAS16 when it comes to subsequent measurement. Whereas IAS16 allows a choice between the cost model and the revaluation model, the IFRS for SMEs permits only the cost model and requires all property, plant and equipment to be measured after initial recognition "*at cost less any accumulated depreciation and any accumulated impairment losses*".

Depreciation is dealt with in much the same way as in IAS16, except that there is no need to review the residual value and useful life of an item unless there are indications that these may have changed (IAS16 requires an annual review). Similarly, it is not necessary to review the depreciation method applied to an asset unless there are indications of a change in the asset's usage pattern.

It should be noted that there is no equivalent of IFRS5 (see Chapter 8) with regard to the treatment of property, plant and equipment held for sale. Instead, the fact that an item is held for sale is treated as an indicator of possible impairment and triggers an impairment review. Impairment is dealt with in Section 27 (see below).

Section 18
Intangible assets other than goodwill

This section of the IFRS for SMEs is the equivalent of IAS38 in full IFRS and sets out the treatment of all intangible assets other than goodwill. An intangible asset is defined in the same way as in IAS38 but the section states that intangible assets may be recognised only if "*the asset does not result from expenditure incurred internally*". This is a significant departure from IAS38, which requires capitalisation of development expenditure if certain criteria are satisfied (see Chapter 6).

Intangible assets are measured initially at cost (as in IAS38). However, after initial recognition, intangibles must be measured "*at cost less any accumulated amortisation and any accumulated impairment losses*". This is another departure from IAS38, which allows a choice between the cost model and the revaluation model. All intangible assets are deemed to have a finite useful life. If this cannot be estimated reliably, it is presumed to be ten years. As with property plant and equipment (see above) there is no requirement to review residual values, useful lives or amortisation methods unless there are indications that these may need to be changed.

Section 19
Business combinations and goodwill

Section 19 of the IFRS for SMEs defines a business combination as "*the bringing together of separate entities or businesses into one reporting entity*". As in full IFRS, the required accounting treatment of a business combination involves the following steps:

(a) identifying the acquirer

(b) measuring the cost of the business combination

(c) allocating that cost to the assets acquired and the liabilities assumed.

As in IFRS3 (see Chapter 6) any excess of the cost of the business combination over the acquirer's interest in the identifiable net assets acquired (measured at fair value) is treated as goodwill and is recognised as an asset. However, whereas IFRS3 requires that goodwill should be tested for impairment each year (and not amortised), the IFRS for SMEs states that goodwill acquired in a business combination should be measured initially at cost and subsequently "*at cost less accumulated amortisation and any accumulated impairment losses*". If the useful life of goodwill cannot be estimated reliably, this life is presumed to be ten years. Impairment is dealt with in Section 27 of the IFRS (see below).

Negative goodwill is accounted for in the same way as in full IFRS. The cost of the business combination and the fair values of the net assets acquired are reassessed. Any negative goodwill remaining after this reassessment is recognised as income.

Section 20
Leases

This section of the IFRS is the equivalent of IAS17 in full IFRS and defines a lease in the same way as that standard (see Chapter 9). As in IAS17, leases are classified into finance leases (which transfer substantially all the risks and rewards incidental to ownership) and operating leases. The IFRS provides a list of situations in which a lease would normally be classified as a finance lease and this list is also the same as in IAS17.

At the inception of a finance lease, the lessee should recognise an asset and a liability both measured at the lower of the fair value of the leased item and the present value of the minimum lease payments. Subsequently, lease payments should be apportioned between the finance charge element and the reduction of the liability to the lessor. Finance charges should be allocated to each period so as to produce a constant periodic rate of interest on the remaining balance of the liability (the actuarial method). Unlike IAS17, the IFRS does not seem to permit approximations such as the sum of digits method.

As regards operating leases, lease payments are generally recognised as expenses on a straight-line basis. However, in contrast to IAS17, the straight-line basis does not apply if payments to the lessor are structured to increase in line with expected inflation.

Section 21
Provisions and contingencies

This section of the IFRS for SMEs is equivalent to IAS37 (see Chapter 12) and deals with provisions, contingent liabilities and contingent assets. As usual, a provision is defined as "*a liability of uncertain timing or amount*". The recognition criteria for a provision are essentially the same as in IAS37 and require that:

(a) the entity has an obligation (legal or constructive) at the reporting date, arising as the result of a past event

(b) it is probable that a transfer of resources will be necessary to satisfy the obligation

(c) the amount of the obligation can be estimated reliably.

The amount of a provision should be the best estimate of the expenditure required to settle the obligation concerned. This amount should be discounted to present value if the effect of the time value of money is material. A provision should be used only for the purpose for which it was established and all provisions should be reviewed and (if necessary) adjusted at each reporting date.

Section 21 of the IFRS is accompanied by an appendix which provides guidance on the recognition and measurement of provisions. Examples in this appendix cover matters such as future operating losses, onerous contracts and restructuring costs, all of which are dealt with in full IFRS by standard IAS37.

In common with larger entities, small and medium-sized entities are not permitted to recognise contingent liabilities or contingent assets in the financial statements. Contingent liabilities are disclosed in the notes unless there is only a remote possibility of an outflow of resources. Contingent assets are disclosed in the notes only if an inflow of economic benefits is deemed to be probable.

Section 22
Liabilities and equity

Section 22 of the IFRS for SMEs establishes principles for the classification of financial instruments as either liabilities or equity. This topic is covered by IAS32 in full IFRS. In general, a financial instrument should be classified by an entity as a liability (regardless of its legal form) if the entity concerned could be required to make a payment to the holder of that instrument. Examples given in the IFRS include redeemable preference shares and shares which entitle the holder to a mandatory dividend.

This section of the IFRS also deals with accounting for transactions such as share issues and the sale of options. These topics are not addressed in full IFRS.

Section 23
Revenue

This section of the IFRS deals with the measurement and recognition of revenue, including revenue from construction contracts. The principles established in this section are basically the same as in full IFRS (standards IAS18 and IAS11). The main points are as follows:

(a) Revenue is measured at the fair value of the consideration receivable and includes only amounts receivable by the entity on its own account (e.g. excluding sales taxes). The revenue of an entity which acts as an agent is the commission to which the entity is entitled and excludes amounts collected on behalf of the principal.

(b) If the inflow of cash is deferred, the fair value of the consideration receivable is determined by discounting future receipts to their present value.

(c) Revenue from the sale of goods is recognised when:
- the risks and rewards of ownership have been transferred to the buyer
- the entity no longer has control over the goods
- the amount of revenue can be measured reliably
- it is probable that economic benefits will flow to the entity
- any costs associated with the transaction can be measured reliably.

(d) Revenue from the rendering of services is recognised by reference to the stage of completion of the transaction at the end of the reporting period.

(e) When the outcome of a construction contract can be estimated reliably, contract revenue and contract costs are recognised by reference to the stage of completion of the contract activity at the end of the reporting period.

(f) Interest receivable is recognised using the effective interest method (see Chapter 11). Royalties are recognised on the accruals basis and dividends are recognised when the right to receive payment is established.

Section 24
Government grants

Section 24 of the IFRS for SMEs defines government grants in the same way as in IAS20 (see Chapter 5) but then establishes a much simpler accounting treatment for these grants than the treatment required by full IFRS. The requirements of the section are as follows:

(a) A grant that does not impose specific future performance conditions on the entity is recognised as revenue as soon as the grant proceeds become receivable.

(b) A grant that imposes specific future performance conditions is recognised as revenue when these performance conditions are met.

(c) A grant received before revenue can be recognised is treated as a liability.

(d) Government grants are measured at the fair value of the amount or asset receivable.

Section 25
Borrowing costs

Section 25 of the IFRS requires that all borrowing costs are treated as an expense in the period in which they are incurred. In contrast to IAS23, there are no circumstances in which borrowing costs may be capitalised (see Chapter 5).

Section 26
Share-based payment

Share-based payment (IFRS2 in full IFRS) is outside the scope of this book and therefore the requirements of this section are not considered here.

Section 27
Impairment of assets

Section 27 of the IFRS deals with the impairment of inventories and other assets. In all cases, an impairment loss occurs if the carrying amount of an asset exceeds its recoverable amount. In the case of inventories, recoverable amount is defined as "*selling price less costs to sell*" and inventories should be written down to this amount if impairment has occurred (see Section 13). The following rules relate to assets other than inventories:

(a) An asset's recoverable amount is "*the higher of its fair value less costs to sell and its value in use*". This is broadly the same definition as given in IAS36 (see Chapter 7).

(b) At each reporting date, recoverable amount should be calculated for any asset for which there are indications of impairment. Examples of such indications (external and internal) are listed in the IFRS and are the same as those listed in IAS36.

   Unlike IAS36, the IFRS does not require goodwill to be tested for impairment every year. Goodwill is tested only if there are indications of impairment.

(c) If it is not possible to determine the recoverable amount of an individual asset, the recoverable amount of the cash-generating unit (CGU) to which the asset belongs should be determined and compared with the CGU's carrying amount. An impairment loss relating to a CGU should be subtracted first from the carrying amount of any goodwill which has been allocated to the CGU. Any remaining loss is then subtracted proportionately from the carrying amounts of the other assets of the CGU.

In all cases, impairment losses should be recognised as an expense. Since the revaluation model is not available (see Sections 17 and 18) there are no difficulties in relation to the impairment of revalued assets.

Section 28
Employee benefits

Section 28 of the IFRS covers the same ground as IAS19 in full IFRS (see Chapter 14). As in that standard, employee benefits are classified into four categories, which are defined in much the same way as in IAS19. The categories are as follows:

(a) **Short-term employee benefits**. These benefits (e.g. salaries) should be recognised as an expense in the accounting period in which employees have rendered the related services to the employer. The IFRS sets out the same accounting treatment for short-term paid (or "compensated") absences as is given in IAS19.

(b) **Post-employment benefits**. The IFRS distinguishes between defined contribution pension plans and defined benefit pension plans and sets out the accounting treatment for each. As in IAS19, an entity's contributions to a defined contribution pension plan are simply recognised as an expense in the period to which they relate.

   The rules relating to defined benefit schemes are broadly similar to those in IAS19. However, whereas IAS19 requires actuarial gains and losses to be recognised in other comprehensive income, entities using the IFRS for SMEs may choose to recognise such gains and losses either in profit or loss or in other comprehensive income.

(c) **Other long-term employee benefits**. As in IAS19, the treatment of other long-term employee benefits is basically the same as the treatment required for defined benefit pension plans.

(d) **Termination benefits**. Termination benefits should be recognised as an expense and (if unpaid) as a liability, when the entity is demonstrably committed to terminating the employment of an employee before the normal retirement date or to providing such benefits so as to encourage voluntary redundancy.

Section 29
Income tax

This section of the IFRS for SMEs sets out the required accounting treatment for current tax and deferred tax. Basically, current tax is accounted for in the same way as in IAS12 (see Chapter 15). As regards deferred tax:

(a) Entities are required to recognise deferred tax assets or liabilities for tax recoverable or payable in future periods as a result of past events. Such tax arises mainly from differences between the carrying amounts of assets (or liabilities) and the amounts at which those assets (or liabilities) are recognised for tax purposes. Deferred tax also arises from the carry-forward of unused tax losses.

(b) No deferred tax arises in respect of an asset or liability if the entity expects to recover the carrying amount of the asset or settle the liability without affecting taxable profit.

(c) The IFRS requires entities to calculate the "tax basis" of each asset and liability at the end of the reporting period and to identify temporary differences between tax bases and carrying amounts. Deferred tax assets/liabilities should be recognised in relation to temporary differences that are expected to reduce/increase future taxable profits.

(d) Entities should recognise deferred tax assets in full. A "valuation allowance" should then be deducted from such assets (if necessary) so as to ensure that their carrying amount does not exceed the highest amount that is likely to be recovered.

Section 30
Foreign currency translation

The IFRS for SMEs defines an entity's functional currency as "*the currency of the primary economic environment in which the entity operates*". The factors which determine an entity's functional currency are the same as those listed in IAS21 (see Chapter 21).

Foreign currency transactions are translated into an entity's functional currency in the same way as in IAS21 and the treatment of the resulting exchange differences also follows the IAS21 approach.

The procedure used for translating an entity's financial statements into a "presentation currency" is the same as the equivalent IAS21 procedure, including the requirement that resulting exchange differences should be recognised in other comprehensive income. Finally, the procedure for translating the financial statements of a foreign operation is again basically the same as the procedure required by IAS21.

Section 31
Hyperinflation

In common with full IFRS, small and medium-sized entities whose functional currency is the currency of a hyperinflationary economy must prepare financial statements that have been adjusted (or "restated") for the effects of inflation. The indicators of hyperinflation are the same as those listed in IAS29 (see Chapter 17).

The adjustment process involves restating all amounts in the financial statements "*in terms of the measuring unit current at the end of the reporting period*". The detailed rules for applying this process to each of the items in an entity's financial statements are very similar to their counterparts in IAS29. The gain or loss on the entity's net monetary position should be included in the calculation of profit or loss.

Section 32
Events after the end of the reporting period

Events after the end of the reporting period are defined as "*those events, favourable and unfavourable, that occur between the end of the reporting period and the date when the financial statements are authorised for issue*". The same distinction is made between "adjusting events" and "non-adjusting events" as is made in IAS10 (see Chapter 12).

Entities which apply the IFRS for SMEs are required to adjust the amounts shown in the financial statements to reflect adjusting events after the end of the reporting period. The amounts shown in the financial statements are not adjusted to reflect non-adjusting events, but such events should be disclosed in the notes.

Section 33
Related party disclosures

The term "related party" is defined in the IFRS for SMEs in a very similar manner to the way in which that term is defined in IAS24 (see Chapter 21).

The disclosures required by this section of the IFRS are also very similar to those required by IAS24. However, key management personnel compensation may be disclosed in total, rather than being analysed into categories.

Section 34
Specialised activities

This section of the IFRS is concerned with the accounting treatment of three specialised activities. These are agriculture, extractive activities and service concessions. All of these are outside the scope of this book and therefore the requirements of this section are not considered here.

Section 35
Transition to the IFRS for SMEs

The final section of the IFRS for SMEs applies to an entity which adopts the IFRS for the first time, regardless of whether the previous accounting framework used by the entity was full IFRS or some other set of generally accepted accounting principles (GAAP).

First-time adopters are required to follow a similar procedure to the procedure set out in IFRS1 for first-time adopters of full IFRS (see Chapter 1). This involves the restatement of previous period figures so as to maintain comparability with the current period.

Topics not covered in the IFRS for SMEs

The main topics which are dealt with in full IFRS but which are not covered in the IFRS for SMEs are as follows:

(a) segment reporting (IFRS8)

(b) earnings per share (IAS33)

(c) interim financial reporting (IAS34)

None of these topics is thought to be relevant to SMEs.

Summary

▸ The IFRS for SMEs is a single, self-contained international standard which covers all aspects of accounting for small and medium-sized entities. The length of the IFRS for SMEs is less than one-tenth of the length of full IFRS.

▸ The IFRS for SMEs is organised by topic and consists of 35 numbered sections.

▸ A small or medium-sized entity is defined as an entity which does not have public accountability and which publishes general purpose financial statements for external users.

▸ The IFRS sets out the basic principles which underlie the financial statements of small and medium-sized entities. These principles include the objective of financial statements, qualitative characteristics, key definitions and general rules relating to recognition and measurement.

▸ The IFRS explains what is meant by a complete set of financial statements for a small or medium-sized entity. In certain cases, the statement of comprehensive income and the statement of changes in equity may be merged into a combined statement of income and retained earnings.

▸ The required content of each of the financial statements is also specified in the IFRS.

▸ The IFRS provides detailed guidance on the way in which SMEs should account for a wide variety of transactions and other items.

Part 6

ANSWERS

Answers to exercises

Chapter 1

1.1

The term "regulatory framework" refers to the collection of rules and regulations which govern financial reporting. The regulatory framework applies mainly to companies and consists of legislation, accounting standards and stock exchange regulations. This framework is needed so as to ensure that shareholders and other stakeholders receive financial statements which faithfully represent the financial performance and financial position of the business concerned.

1.2

The term "generally accepted accounting practice" (GAAP) refers to the accounting regulations which apply in a certain jurisdiction, together with any accounting principles or conventions that are normally followed in that jurisdiction. Accounting rules and practices currently vary between countries and so there is no "global GAAP" at present. However, the International Accounting Standards Board (IASB) is developing and promoting a set of international standards which it hopes will eventually attain global acceptance and form the basis for a global GAAP. Some of the main causes of differences in accounting practice from one country to another are as follows:

(a) The legal systems of some countries set out detailed accounting rules; other countries have legal systems which provide only a broad framework of accounting principles.

(b) In some countries, business entities are largely financed by shareholders; in other countries, banks and other lenders are the main providers of business finance. The quantity and types of accounting information that these two groups need from financial reports may differ and this has an effect on the accounting systems of the countries concerned.

(c) In some countries, accounting rules are dictated by the needs of the tax system, since the way in which profits are computed for financial reporting purposes is the same as the way in which they are computed for tax purposes. This is not the case in other countries (e.g. the UK).

(d) Some of the more developed countries have had the opportunity and the resources to develop a strong accounting profession and a body of accounting theory, both of which have had an impact on accounting practice. This is not true of less developed countries.

(e) In some countries, businesses have suddenly collapsed only a short time after publishing apparently healthy financial reports. This has led to attempts to tighten up accounting rules in these countries, generally by the strengthening of accounting standards.

1.3

The structure and functions of these bodies are explained in detail in Chapter 1. A brief summary is as follows:

(a)   The IFRS Foundation consists of twenty-two trustees drawn from a diversity of geographical and professional backgrounds. They are responsible for appointing the members of the IASB and its associated bodies and for establishing and maintaining the necessary funding for their work. The Trustees also review the strategy and effectiveness of the IASB.

(b)   The IASB consists of sixteen members chosen for their professional competence and practical experience. The job of the IASB is to develop and improve international financial reporting standards and international accounting standards.

(c)   The IFRS Advisory Council comprises thirty or more members drawn from diverse backgrounds. The main function of the Advisory Council is to offer advice to the IASB with regard to its agenda and priorities.

(d)   The IFRS Interpretations Committee (which has fourteen voting members and a non-voting Chair) interprets the application of international standards and provides timely guidance on financial reporting matters which are not specifically addressed by standards.

1.4

An IFRS or IAS consists of a set of numbered paragraphs and is broken down into sections. These sections usually comprise some or all of the following:

- an introduction

- objectives and scope

- definitions

- the body of the standard

- effective date

- application guidance or implementation guidance

- illustrative examples

- basis for conclusions.

1.5

The main purpose of accounting standards is to reduce or eliminate variations in accounting practice and so introduce a degree of uniformity into financial reporting. The advantages of such standardisation include faithful representation and comparability. One perceived disadvantage of accounting standards might be a lack of flexibility and the worry that a single accounting treatment might not be appropriate in all cases. The IASB overcomes this disadvantage by allowing entities to override a standard in the extremely rare event that compliance with that standard would prevent faithful representation.

1.6

The first IFRS reporting period is the year to 30 June 2014. The date of transition to IFRS is 1 July 2011 since this is the beginning of the earliest period reported in the first IFRS financial statements. The company must:

(i)   prepare an opening IFRS statement of financial position as at 1 July 2011 (or 30 June 2011)

(ii)   use identical accounting policies in the opening IFRS statement of financial position and in the financial statements for the year to 30 June 2014 and in the comparative figures provided for the two previous years; these accounting policies must comply with international standards in force for periods ending on 30 June 2014

(iii) provide a reconciliation of equity as reported under previous GAAP with equity reported under IFRS, for 30 June 2011 and 30 June 2013

(iv) provide a reconciliation of total comprehensive income as reported under previous GAAP with total comprehensive income as it would have been reported under IFRS, for the year to 30 June 2013.

1.7

(a) The main objectives of the IASB are:

    (i)   to develop a single set of high quality global accounting standards

    (ii) to promote the use and rigorous application of those standards

    (iii) to bring about the convergence of national accounting standards and international accounting standards.

The IFRS Advisory Council provides a forum for participation in the standard-setting process by interested organisations and individuals. The Council advises the IASB on its agenda and priorities and also passes on Council members' views with regard to standard-setting projects.

The IFRS Interpretations Committee interprets the application of international standards and provides advice on matters not specifically addressed in the standards.

(b) The term "GAAP" refers to the complete set of accounting regulations from all sources (e.g. legislation, standards and stock exchange regulations) which apply in a given jurisdiction, together with any general accounting principles, concepts or conventions which are usually applied in that jurisdiction.

Chapter 2

2.1

A conceptual framework for financial reporting is a set of agreed fundamental principles which underpin financial accounting and provide a sound theoretical basis for the development of accounting standards. The main purposes of the IASB *Conceptual Framework* are:

(i)   to assist in the development and the review of international standards

(ii) to provide a basis for reducing the number of alternative accounting treatments permitted by international standards

(iii) to assist national standard-setters in developing national standards

(iv) to assist preparers of financial statements in applying international standards

(v) to help auditors determine whether financial statements comply with international standards

(vi) to help users to interpret the information contained in financial statements

(vii) to provide information about the IASB approach to the formulation of international standards.

2.2

(a) The *Conceptual Framework* states that the objective of general purpose financial reporting is *"to provide financial information about the reporting entity that is useful to existing and potential investors, lenders and other creditors in making decisions about providing resources to the entity "*.

(b)   The primary users of general purpose financial reports are existing and potential investors, lenders and other creditors. Other parties who may find general purpose financial reports useful include employees, customers, governments (and their agencies) and the public. See Chapter 2 for an explanation of why each user group may be interested in the information provided in general purpose financial reports.

2.3

The main classes of information that should be presented in general purpose financial reports are:

(a)   information about the *financial position* of the reporting entity (i.e. information about the entity's economic resources and claims against those resources)

(b)   information about changes in financial position caused by the entity's *financial performance* during the reporting period (e.g. the making of a profit)

(c)   information about the entity's *cash flows* during the reporting period

(d)   information about changes in financial position which have not been caused by the entity's financial performance (e.g. changes caused by share issues and the payment of dividends).

2.4

The *Conceptual Framework* identifies the two fundamental qualitative characteristics of useful financial information as relevance and faithful representation. The enhancing characteristics are comparability, verifiability, timeliness and understandability. See Chapter 2 for an explanation of each characteristic and the factors which contribute to its achievement.

2.5

An asset is "*a resource controlled by the entity as a result of past events and from which future economic benefits are expected to flow to the entity*".

A liability is "*a present obligation of the entity arising from past events, the settlement of which is expected to result in an outflow from the entity of resources embodying economic benefits*".

Equity is "*the residual interest in the assets of the entity after deducting all its liabilities*".

Income is "*increases in economic benefits during the accounting period in the form of inflows or enhancements of assets or decreases of liabilities that result in increases in equity, other than those relating to contributions from equity participants*".

Expenses are "*decreases in economic benefits during the accounting period in the form of outflows or depletions of assets or incurrences of liabilities that result in decreases in equity, other than those relating to distributions to equity participants*".

An element should be recognised in the financial statements if it has a cost or value that can be measured reliably and if it is probable that any future economic benefit associated with the element will flow to or from the entity.

2.6

(a)   The measurement bases are historical cost, current cost, realisable value and present value.

(b)   The capital maintenance concepts are financial capital maintenance (either in nominal units or in units of purchasing power) and physical capital maintenance.

See Chapter 2 for an explanation of each of these.

2.7

Relevance

To be useful, financial information must be relevant to the needs of users when they are making economic decisions. Financial information is relevant if it helps users to predict future events or if it helps them to confirm (or refute) previous predictions.

Information can have predictive value even though it does not take the form of an explicit forecast, since information on past events may be used as a basis for predictions about future events.

The relevance of information is affected by its level of materiality. Information is material if its omission or mis-statement could influence user decisions. Immaterial items are not relevant.

Faithful representation

To be useful, financial information must faithfully represent transactions and other events. The information must be complete, free of bias and free from material error. Financial information should also represent the substance of transactions and events rather than their legal form.

Comparability

Users should be able to compare financial information about an entity for a reporting period with similar information about the same entity for other periods and with similar information about other entities for the same period. Comparability is improved if consistent accounting treatments are adopted between periods and between entities.

Chapter 3

3.1

(a) Financial statements must present fairly the financial position, financial performance and cash flows of the entity concerned. This requires that the effects of transactions and other events should be faithfully represented in accordance with the definitions and recognition criteria for assets, liabilities, income and expenses set out in the *Conceptual Framework*. It is usually assumed that the application of international standards will achieve a fair presentation.

A fair presentation also requires entities to select and apply appropriate accounting policies, to provide information that is relevant, reliable, comparable and understandable and to provide further information if compliance with international standards is insufficient to enable users to understand the financial statements.

(b) Financial statements should be prepared on the going concern basis unless the entity intends to cease trading or has no realistic alternative but to do so. Financial statements apart from the statement of cash flows should be prepared on the accrual basis.

(c) An item is material if its size or its nature is such that it could influence users' economic decisions. Financial statements are prepared by analysing transactions and other events into classes and then aggregating each class to produce line items. IAS1 requires that each material class of similar items should normally be presented separately in the financial statements. However, a line item which is not material may be aggregated with other line items.

(d) Assets and liabilities should normally be reported separately in the statement of financial position and not offset against one another. Similarly, income and expenses should normally be reported separately in the statement of comprehensive income.

(e) Financial statements should normally be presented at least annually.

(f) Comparative information should be disclosed in respect of the previous period for all amounts reported in the financial statements.

(g) In order to maintain comparability, the way in which items are presented and classified in the financial statements should be consistent from one accounting period to the next. The need for consistency is overridden only if it is apparent that a change in presentation or classification would be appropriate, or if such a change is required by an international standard.

3.2

(a) A *current asset* is one which satisfies any of the following criteria:

(i) it is expected to be realised, sold or consumed within the entity's normal operating cycle

(ii) it is held primarily for the purpose of being traded

(iii) it is expected to be realised within twelve months after the reporting period

(iv) it is cash or a cash equivalent.

An asset which satisfies none of these criteria is a non-current asset.

(b) A *current liability* is one which satisfies any of the following criteria:

(i) it is expected to be settled within the entity's normal operating cycle

(ii) it is held primarily for the purpose of being traded

(iii) it is due to be settled within twelve months after the reporting period

(iv) the entity does not have the right to defer settlement until at least twelve months after the reporting period.

A liability which satisfies none of these criteria is a non-current liability.

(c) The current/non-current separation distinguishes between net assets that are circulating as working capital and those that are used in the long-term. This separation also identifies the assets that are expected to be realised within the current operating cycle and the liabilities that are due for settlement within the same period.

3.3

The purpose of a statement of changes in equity is to show how each component of equity has changed during an accounting period. In the case of a company, these components are share capital and each of the company's reserves. The main items that should be shown in a statement of changes in equity are as follows:

(a) total comprehensive income for the period

(b) the effects of any retrospective application of accounting policies or restatement of items

(c) for each component of equity, a reconciliation of the opening and closing balance for that component, separately disclosing changes arising from:

(i) profit or loss

(ii) other comprehensive income

(iii) transactions with the owners of the entity, separately showing distributions to owners and contributions by owners.

3.4

The *draft statement of comprehensive income* for the year to 31 March 2014 is as follows:

	£000	£000
Sales revenue (50,332 – 3,147)		47,185
Cost of sales (7,865 + 29,778 – 8,107)		29,536
Gross profit		17,649
Distribution costs (8,985 + 157)	9,142	
Administrative expenses	7,039	16,181
Profit from operations		1,468
Finance costs (200 + 200)		400
Profit before tax		1,068
Taxation		235
Profit for the year		833

The *draft statement of financial position* as at 31 March 2014 is as follows:

	£000	£000
Assets		
Non-current assets		
Property, plant and equipment (59,088 – 25,486)		33,602
Current assets		
Inventories (8,407 – 300)	8,107	
Trade receivables (9,045 – 3,147)	5,898	
Cash at bank	182	14,187
		47,789
Equity		
Ordinary share capital		10,000
Share premium account		5,000
Retained earnings (23,457 + 833)		24,290
		39,290
Liabilities		
Non-current liabilities		
Bank loans		5,000
Current liabilities		
Trade payables (2,481 + 157 + 426 + 200)	3,264	
Taxation	235	3,499
		47,789

Notes:

(a)   Inventories are valued at the lower of cost and net realisable value (see Chapter 10).

(b)   Total comprehensive income for the year is equal to the profit for the year, since the company has no "other comprehensive income".

3.5

The notes should contain:

(i)   information about the measurement bases used in preparing the financial statements and other relevant accounting policies

(ii) information as required by international standards, to the extent that this is not presented elsewhere in the financial statements

(iii) any additional information which is relevant to an understanding of any of the financial statements.

3.6

(a)

Walrus plc
Statement of comprehensive income for the year to 31 March 2014

	£000	£000
Sales revenue		1,432
Cost of sales (107 + 488 – 119)		476
Gross profit		956
Other income		30
		986
Distribution costs (see workings)	229	
Administrative expenses (see workings)	601	830
		156
Finance costs		9
Profit before taxation		147
Taxation (30 – 6)		24
Profit for the year		123
Other comprehensive income for the year:		
Items that will not be reclassified to profit or loss:		
Gain on property revaluation		180
Total comprehensive income for the year		303

Note:
The treatment of taxation in financial statements is dealt with in Chapter 15.

(b)

Walrus plc
Statement of financial position as at 31 March 2014

	£000	£000
Assets		
Non-current assets		
Property, plant and equipment (see workings)		603
Goodwill		300
		903
Current assets		
Inventory	119	
Trade receivables (183 – 8 – 7)	168	287
		1,190
Equity		
Share capital		200
Revaluation reserve		180
Retained earnings		606
		986
Liabilities		
Current liabilities		
Trade and other payables	117	
Bank balance	57	
Current tax payable	30	204
		1,190

(c)

Walrus plc
Statement of changes in equity for the year to 31 March 2014

	Share capital £000	Revaluation reserve £000	Retained earnings £000	Total equity £000
Balance at 31 March 2013	200	-	503	703
Total comprehensive income		180	123	303
Dividend paid			(20)	(20)
Balance at 31 March 2014	200	180	606	986

Workings

Distribution costs	£000
Per trial balance	101
Wages and salaries (25%)	69
Buildings depreciation	5
Equipment depreciation	12
Vehicles depreciation	42
	229

Administrative expenses	£000
Per trial balance	186
Bank overdraft interest	(9)
Directors' fees	150
Wages and salaries (75%)	207
Buildings depreciation	5
Equipment depreciation	36
Vehicles depreciation	18
Loss on disposal (44 − 33 − 10)	1
Bad debt	8
Reduction in allowance for receivables	(1)
	601

Property, plant and equipment	£000	£000	£000
Land at valuation			300
Buildings at cost		250	
Depreciation to 31/3/2013	90		
Depreciation for year (4% × 250)	10	100	150
Equipment at cost		196	
Depreciation to 31/3/2013	76		
Depreciation for year (40% × 120)	48	124	72
Motor vehicles at cost (284 − 44)		240	
Depreciation to 31/3/2013 (132 − 33)	99		
Depreciation for year (25% × 240)	60	159	81
			603

Chapter 4

4.1

(a) Accounting policies are "*the specific principles, bases, conventions, rules and practices applied by an entity in preparing and presenting financial statements*". For example, an entity can choose between the cost model and the revaluation model for measuring property, plant and equipment. The entity's choice is one of its accounting policies.

Accounting estimates are judgements applied when measuring items that cannot be measured with precision (e.g. the estimated useful life of a non-current asset).

(b) A change in accounting policy should be accounted for retrospectively. Comparative figures for the previous period(s) must be adjusted and presented as if the new accounting policy had always been applied. This approach maintains comparability between accounting periods.

(c) A change in an accounting estimate should be accounted for prospectively. The effect of the change should be dealt with in the financial statements for the period of the change and future periods, but comparative figures for prior periods are not restated.

4.2

(a) If there is no applicable international standard or interpretation, management should use its judgement in selecting an accounting policy that results in information which is relevant and reliable. Reference should be made to any standards which deal with similar issues and to the IASB *Conceptual Framework*.

(b) An accounting policy may be changed if this is required by an international standard or if the change improves the reliability and relevance of the financial statements.

4.3

If a change in accounting policy is caused by the initial application of an international standard or interpretation, the entity should disclose the title of that standard or interpretation. If a change in accounting policy is voluntary, the entity should disclose its reasons for making the change. In all cases, the entity should disclose the nature of the change and the amount of the adjustment made to each affected item in the financial statements.

4.4

(a) A material prior period error is a material omission or mis-statement occurring in an entity's financial statements for a prior period. Material prior period errors should be corrected retrospectively. This generally involves restating the comparative figures for the prior period in which the error occurred.

(b) The entity should disclose the nature of the prior period error. For each prior period presented, the entity should disclose the amount of the correction to each affected line item in the financial statements. The amount of the correction at the beginning of the earliest prior period presented should also be disclosed.

4.5

(a)		**2013**	**2012**
		£000	£000
	Profit before depreciation	2,510	2,450
	Depreciation of property, plant and equipment	190	230
	Profit before taxation	2,320	2,220
	Taxation	696	666
	Profit after taxation	1,624	1,554

(b)		£000
	Balance at 31 December 2011, as previously reported	2,943
	Change in accounting policy relating to depreciation (see below)	(140)
	Restated balance at 31 December 2011	2,803
	Restated profit for the year to 31 December 2012	1,554
	Restated balance at 31 December 2012	4,357
	Profit for the year to 31 December 2013	1,624
	Balance at 31 December 2013	5,981

Note:

The change in accounting policy results in additional depreciation of £160,000 in 2010 and £40,000 in 2011. The total is £200,000. Tax saved at 30% is £60,000. Therefore profit after tax for the two years falls by £140,000.

4.6

(a)		**2014**	**2013**
		£000	£000
	Sales	1,660	1,840
	Cost of goods sold	670	730
	Gross profit	990	1,110
	Expenses	590	560
	Profit before taxation	400	550
	Taxation	80	110
	Profit after taxation	320	440

(b)		£000
	Balance at 30 June 2012	860
	Restated profit for the year to 30 June 2013	440
	Restated balance at 30 June 2013	1,300
	Profit for the year to 30 June 2014	320
	Balance at 30 June 2014	1,620

Chapter 5

5.1

(a) Property, plant and equipment consists of tangible items which are held for use in the production or supply of goods or services, for rental to others, or for administrative purposes and which are expected to be used during more than one period.

(b) An item of property, plant and equipment should be recognised as an asset when its cost can be measured reliably and it is probable that future economic benefits associated with the item will flow to the entity. The item should be derecognised when it is disposed of or no future economic benefits are expected from either its use or its disposal.

(c) The purchase price, plus import duties, delivery charges and non-refundable purchase taxes should be included in the asset's cost. The small spares should be treated as inventory and the cost of maintenance should be treated as an expense of the period covered by the contract.

5.2

(a) Under the cost model, items of property, plant and equipment are carried at cost less any accumulated depreciation and less any accumulated impairment losses. Under the revaluation model, an item of property, plant and equipment is carried at a revalued amount, consisting of the item's fair value at the date of revaluation, less any subsequent accumulated depreciation and less any subsequent accumulated impairment losses.

(b) A revaluation increase is generally credited to a revaluation reserve and accounted for as other comprehensive income. But a revaluation increase is recognised as income when calculating an entity's profit or loss to the extent that it reverses any revaluation decrease in respect of the same item that was previously recognised as an expense.

A revaluation decrease is generally recognised as an expense when calculating the entity's profit or loss. But a revaluation decrease is debited to the revaluation reserve and accounted for (as a negative figure) in other comprehensive income to the extent of any credit balance previously existing in the revaluation reserve in respect of that same item.

(c) On 31 December 2013, a revaluation increase of £0.2m is credited to revaluation reserve and accounted for as other comprehensive income. On 31 December 2014, £0.2m is debited to the revaluation reserve and accounted for as (negative) other comprehensive income. An expense of £0.3m is recognised when calculating the company's profit or loss for the year.

If the valuations on 31 December 2013 and 2014 are reversed, then an expense of £0.3m is recognised when calculating profit or loss for the year to 31 December 2013. In the financial statements for the year to 31 December 2014, income of £0.3m is recognised when calculating the company's profit and £0.2m is credited to the revaluation reserve (and accounted for as other comprehensive income).

5.3

(a) Depreciation is the systematic allocation of the depreciable amount of an asset over its useful life. Depreciable amount is the cost of the asset (or other amount substituted for cost) less its residual value. Useful life is generally the period over which the asset is expected to be used by the entity. Residual value is the estimated disposal value of the asset, after deducting the estimated costs of disposal.

(b)   Depreciable amount is £49,500 and useful life is 5 years. Therefore straight-line depreciation is £9,900 per annum. Diminishing balance depreciation is calculated as follows:

Year	Carrying amount b/f	Depreciation at 30%	Carrying amount c/f
	£	£	£
2014	59,500	17,850	41,650
2015	41,650	12,495	29,155
2016	29,155	8,746	20,409
2017	20,409	6,123	14,286
2018	14,286	4,286	10,000
		49,500	

The company should choose the method which most closely matches the usage pattern of the asset concerned.

5.4

(a)   Borrowing costs consist of interest and other costs incurred by an entity in connection with the borrowing of funds. IAS23 requires that borrowing costs that are directly attributable to the acquisition, construction or production of a qualifying asset should be capitalised as part of the cost of that asset. Other borrowing costs should be recognised as an expense in the period in which they are incurred.

(b)   Loans A, B and C total £23m and interest for the year totals £2.3m so the capitalisation rate for the year is 10%. Capitalised borrowing costs are £227,500, as follows:

	£
£1,500,000 × 10% × 9/12	112,500
£2,400,000 × 10% × 5/12	100,000
£1,800,000 × 10% × 1/12	15,000
	227,500

5.5

(a)   An investment property is land or a building or a part of a building held to earn rentals or for capital appreciation or both, rather than for use. Investment property may be measured using either the fair value model or the cost model. Under the fair value model, the property is measured at its fair value and any gain or loss arising from a change in fair value is recognised as income or as an expense when calculating the entity's profit or loss. The cost model is the same as for property, plant and equipment.

(b)   As stated above, gains arising in connection with investment property measured at fair value are recognised as income when calculating the entity's profit or loss. Revaluation gains arising in connection with property, plant and equipment measured under the revaluation model are generally excluded from profit or loss and are recognised as other comprehensive income.

5.6

This ship is a complex asset and should be treated as three separate assets. The carrying amount of these assets at 30 September 2013 (eight years after purchase) is as follows:

	£m
Ship's fabric (£300m × 17/25)	204
Cabins etc. (£150m × 4/12)	50
Propulsion system (£100m × 10,000/40,000)	25
	279

Ship's fabric

Depreciation of £12m (£300m × 1/25) should be charged in the year to 30 September 2014. The repainting costs do not meet the recognition criteria for an asset and should be treated as repairs and maintenance.

Cabins and entertainment area fittings

The upgrade (at a cost of £60m) has extended the remaining useful life of the cabins etc. by one year and so the costs of the upgrade meet the recognition criteria for an asset. The cost of £60m should be added to the cost of the fittings. Any of the old fittings which have been replaced should be derecognised. Assuming that none of the old fittings are derecognised, the revised carrying amount is £110m and this should be depreciated over the remaining useful life of five years. Therefore depreciation of £22m is charged in the year to 30 September 2014.

Propulsion system

The carrying amount of the old system (£25m) should be written off. This assumes that the system has a scrap value of zero. Depreciation of the new system for the year to 30 September 2014 is £14m (£140m × 5,000/50,000).

Entries in financial statements

Expenses for the year to 30 September 2014 will include the following:

	£m
Depreciation of ship's fabric	12
Depreciation of cabins etc.	22
Depreciation of propulsion system	14
Loss on disposal of propulsion system	25
Repairs and maintenance	20

The statement of financial position as at 30 September 2014 will show the cruise ship as a non-current asset at a carrying amount of £406m. This is calculated as follows:

	£m
Ship's fabric (£204m – £12m)	192
Cabins etc. (£110m – £22m)	88
Propulsion system (£140m – £14m)	126
	406

Chapter 6

6.1

(a) An intangible asset is an identifiable, non-monetary asset without physical substance.

An asset is identifiable when it arises from contractual or other legal rights or when it is "separable". An asset is separable if it can be separated from the entity and sold, transferred, licensed, rented or exchanged. Goodwill is not separable and is therefore excluded from the IAS38 definition of intangible assets.

Monetary assets are money held and assets to be received in fixed or determinable amounts of money. Intangible assets are non-monetary and therefore items such as cash, bank deposits and trade receivables are excluded from the definition.

Intangible assets are distinguished from property, plant and equipment by the fact that they are without physical substance.

(b) An intangible asset acquired in a separate transaction should be measured initially at its cost.

(c) An intangible asset acquired in a business combination should be measured initially at its fair value on the date of the acquisition.

6.2

(a) Research expenditure is expenditure on original and planned investigation undertaken with the prospect of gaining new scientific or technical knowledge and understanding.

Development expenditure is expenditure on the application of research to a plan or design for the production of new or substantially improved materials, devices, products, processes, systems or services.

(b) All research expenditure must be written off as an expense when it is incurred. Development expenditure must be recognised as an intangible asset if certain conditions are satisfied. If any of these conditions are not satisfied, the development expenditure must be written off as an expense (see Chapter 6 for more details).

(c) The £370,000 is research expenditure and must be written off as an expense. The £460,000 is development expenditure and must be capitalised as an intangible asset if all of the conditions listed in IAS38 are satisfied (see Chapter 6). Otherwise, this amount must also be written off as an expense.

6.3

(a) Useful life is six years. The asset should be recognised initially at cost and then amortised over these six years. The asset's depreciable amount is its cost less its residual value.

(b) Useful life is 30 years. The asset should be recognised initially at cost and then amortised over these 30 years. The asset's depreciable amount is equal to its cost.

(c) Useful life is three years. The asset should be recognised initially at cost and then amortised over these three years. The residual value of the asset will depend upon whether the company intends to sell the trademark at the end of its useful life and whether or not a customer is likely to be found.

In each case, the chosen amortisation method should match the usage pattern of the asset.

6.4

Under the cost model, intangible assets are carried at cost less any accumulated amortisation and accumulated impairment losses. Under the revaluation model, intangible assets are carried at their fair value at the date of revaluation, less any subsequent accumulated amortisation and accumulated impairment losses. If the revaluation model is applied to an intangible asset, then it must be applied to the entire class of assets to which the asset belongs. But the revaluation model cannot be applied to an intangible asset for which there is no active market.

6.5

(a) IFRS3 defines goodwill as "*an asset representing the future economic benefits arising from ... assets acquired in a business combination that are not individually identified and separately recognised*". A business combination occurs when one entity acquires another. Goodwill which has been developed by an entity rather than purchased from another entity is known as internally generated goodwill and is excluded from the IFRS3 definition.

(b) Goodwill is not separable or identifiable. Internally generated goodwill has no reliable cost figure. In general terms, goodwill is subject to unpredictable fluctuations in value and may easily be damaged or destroyed.

(c) Goodwill has an unpredictable useful life and does not amortise at a steady rate. It is more logical to conduct regular impairment reviews than to amortise purchased goodwill.

6.6

(a) The fair value of the assets less liabilities of B Ltd is £450,000. The price paid by A Ltd is £500,000. So the amount paid for goodwill is £50,000.

(b) The statement of financial position of A Ltd just after the purchase is as follows:

	£000	£000
Assets		
Non-current assets		
Goodwill		50
Property, plant and equipment (4,320 + 390)		4,710
		4,760
Current assets		
Inventories (1,210 + 160)	1,370	
Trade receivables (940 + 80)	1,020	
Cash at bank (1,650 − 500)	1,150	3,540
		8,300
Equity		
Ordinary share capital		1,000
Retained earnings		3,650
		4,650
Liabilities		
Non-current liabilities		2,500
Current liabilities (970 + 180)		1,150
		8,300

6.7

(a) *Research* is original and planned investigation undertaken with the prospect of gaining new scientific or technical knowledge and understanding. *Development* is the application of research to a plan or design for the production of new or substantially improved materials, devices, products, processes, systems or services.

(b) (i) This is research work, since it is undertaken with the prospect of gaining new technical knowledge. The expenditure should be written off as an expense.

    (ii) This type of expenditure might normally qualify as development expenditure. However, it seems that the project is not technically feasible at present. Therefore the expenditure should be written off as an expense.

Chapter 7

7.1

(a) IAS36 defines an impairment loss as "*the amount by which the carrying amount of an asset or cash-generating unit exceeds its recoverable amount*".

(b) IAS36 lists a number of possible indications of impairment. Some of these are derived from external sources of information and some from internal sources. See Chapter 7 for details.

(c) The two types of asset which must always be tested for impairment are intangible assets which have an indefinite useful life (or which are not yet available for use) and goodwill acquired in a business combination.

(d) Recoverable amount is the higher of fair value less costs of disposal and value in use.

Fair value less costs of disposal is defined as the price that would be received to sell the asset in an orderly transaction between market participants at the measurement date, less the estimated costs of disposal.

Value in use is the present value of the future cash flows expected from the asset.

7.2

	Carrying amount £	Recoverable amount £	Impairment loss £
Asset 1	25,000	27,500	
Asset 2	6,500	4,800	1,700
Asset 3	18,250	17,500	750
Asset 4	11,400	13,400	

7.3

(a)

	Cash inflows £	Discount factor	Present value £
Year 1	20,000	$1/1.1 = 0.909$	18,180
Year 2	20,000	$1/(1.1)^2 = 0.826$	16,520
Year 3	30,000	$1/(1.1)^3 = 0.751$	22,530
Value in use			57,230

(b)   The asset's recoverable amount is the higher of £48,000 (£50,000 − £2,000) and £57,230 which is £57,230. Therefore the impairment loss is £42,770 (£100,000 − £57,230). The asset's carrying value should be reduced to £57,230 and an impairment loss of £42,770 should be recognised as an expense.

(c)   Assuming that residual value remains at £10,000, the asset's depreciable amount is £47,230. Annual depreciation is approximately £15,743 (£47,230 ÷ 3).

7.4

(a)   IAS36 defines a cash-generating unit as "*the smallest identifiable group of assets that generates cash inflows that are largely independent of the cash inflows from other assets or groups of assets*".

(b)   A CGU should be tested for impairment is there are indications that an asset which belongs to the CGU is impaired or that the CGU as a whole is impaired. A CGU to which goodwill has been allocated should be tested for impairment every year, regardless of whether or not there are any indications of impairment.

7.5

The impairment loss is £80m (£275m − £195m). Goodwill is reduced from £25m to zero, leaving £55m of the loss remaining. This is initially allocated in the ratio 50:200 between the patents and the property, plant and equipment (PPE), so that patents are reduced by £11m to £39m and PPE is reduced by £44m to £156m. However, £156m is £4m less than the fair value less costs of disposal of the PPE. Therefore PPE is set to £160m and an extra £4m is subtracted from the patents. The assets are now patents £35m and PPE £160m, giving a total of £195m.

7.6

(a)   An impairment loss occurs when the carrying amount of an asset is higher than its recoverable amount. The recoverable amount of an asset is the higher of its fair value less costs of disposal and its value in use.

Fair value less costs of disposal

The fair value of an asset for this purpose is the price that would be received to sell the asset in an orderly transaction between market participants at the measurement date. If the asset is of a type that is traded in an active market involving identical assets, then the quoted price in that market will be used. Otherwise, the fair value of the asset will have to be determined by using one of the other valuation techniques listed in IFRS13. Estimated costs of disposal are deducted when calculating an asset's fair value less costs of disposal.

Value in use

The value in use of an asset is the present value of the future net cash flows expected to be derived from use of the asset. Many assets do not produce independent cash flows, so it may be necessary to consider the value in use (and the fair value less costs of disposal) of the cash generating unit (CGU) to which the asset belongs.

Frequency of testing for impairment

Goodwill and any intangible asset that has an indefinite useful life must be tested for impairment every year. This is also the case for any intangible asset that has not yet been brought into use. Other assets are tested for impairment only if there is an indication that impairment may have occurred. IAS36 provides a list of such indications.

(b) An impairment loss is subtracted from the carrying amount of the asset concerned. Future depreciation charges will be based upon the reduced carrying amount. An impairment loss is usually accounted for as an expense. But if the asset has previously been revalued upwards, the loss should first be deducted from the revaluation surplus.

An impairment loss relating to a CGU is used to eliminate any goodwill in the CGU and is then allocated to the other assets in proportion to their carrying amounts. However, an asset other than goodwill should not be reduced to less than the higher of its fair value less costs of disposal and its value in use.

(c) The plant's carrying amount was £240,000 on 1 October 2013. Depreciation from 1 October 2013 to 1 April 2014 is £40,000 (£640,000 × 12.5% × 6/12) giving a carrying amount of £200,000 at the date of impairment.

Recoverable amount is the higher of the plant's value in use (£150,000) and fair value less costs of disposal. If Wilderness trades in the plant it will receive £180,000 but Wilderness is reluctant to do this. A better estimate of fair value less costs of disposal is £20,000. Therefore recoverable amount is £150,000 and the impairment loss is £50,000.

Since the remaining useful life of the plant is only two years (from the date of impairment) the depreciation charge for the last six months of the year is £37,500 (£150,000/2 × 6/12). The financial statements for the year to 30 September 2014 will show:

Statement of financial position

Plant (£150,000 – £37,500) = £112,500

Statement of comprehensive income

Plant depreciation (£40,000 + £37,500) = £77,500

Plant impairment loss £50,000

Chapter 8

8.1

(a) A non-current asset is classified as held for sale if its carrying amount will be recovered principally through a sale transaction rather than through continuing use. For this to be the case, the asset must be available for immediate sale in its present condition (subject only to terms that are usual and customary for sales of such assets) and the sale must be highly probable. International standard IFRS5 lists the conditions under which a sale is regarded as highly probable (see Chapter 8).

(b) If a non-current asset is held for sale rather than use, the notion of "useful life" is inapplicable and therefore it is no longer appropriate to make depreciation charges or to carry the asset at its cost (or revalued amount) less depreciation to date.

(c) IFRS5 requires that a non-current asset which is held for sale should be measured at the lower of its carrying amount when it was initially classified as held for sale and its fair value less costs to sell. Fair value is the price that would be received to sell the asset in an orderly transaction between market participants at the measurement date. Costs to sell are costs directly attributable to the disposal of the asset, excluding finance costs and tax.

8.2

(a) There is an impairment loss of £600 on 1 March 2013 and a further impairment loss of £200 on 30 June 2013. There is a loss on disposal of £60 in the year to 30 June 2014.

(b) There is no impairment loss on either 1 March 2013 or 30 June 2013. There is a gain on disposal of £630 in the year to 30 June 2014.

(c) There is an impairment loss of £100 on 1 March 2013 and a gain of £50 on 30 June 2013. There is a loss on disposal of £30 in the year to 30 June 2014.

(d) There is an impairment loss of £100 on 1 March 2013 and a gain of £100 (not £150) on 30 June 2013. This gain is capped at £100 to ensure that the asset is not measured at more than its carrying amount when it was originally classified as held for sale. There is a gain on disposal of £80 in the year to 30 June 2014.

8.3

(a) A discontinued operation is a component of an entity that either has been disposed of or is classified as held for sale. For this purpose, a component comprises operations and cash flows that can be clearly distinguished from the rest of the entity.

(b) IFRS5 requires that entities should present and disclose information that enables users of the financial statements to evaluate the effects of discontinued operations. This information will help users to make more accurate assessments of an entity's likely financial performance in future years.

8.4

On 31 December 2013, the assets of the operation cannot be classified as held for sale since they are not available for immediate sale. These assets should be presented and measured in the same way as in previous years. However, the decision to close down the operation might suggest that the assets are impaired and so an impairment review should be carried out. The operation does not count as a discontinued operation at 31 December 2013, so its results should be included in continuing operations in the financial statements.

Assuming that the operation is closed down and the assets sold by 31 December 2014, the results of the operation should be shown under discontinued operations in the statement of comprehensive income for 2014. There should be a single figure comprising the after-tax profit or loss of the operation and the gain or loss on disposal of its assets. This figure will then be analysed, either in the statement of comprehensive income or in the notes.

8.5

(a) The total carrying amount of the disposal group at 25 January 2014 is £3.06m, so there is an impairment loss of £60,000. This is deducted from goodwill, leaving £140,000.

The measurement requirements of IFRS5 exclude the investment properties, inventories and liabilities. So on 31 May 2014, the carrying amount of these items must be remeasured in accordance with the applicable standards. The carrying amount of the disposal group becomes £3.02m (£140,000 + £2,100,000 + £760,000 + £380,000 − £360,000) and the remeasurement gain is £20,000. There is a further impairment loss of £170,000 (£3.02m − £2.85m) on 31 May 2014. Goodwill is reduced to zero and £30,000 is deducted from the property, plant and equipment, leaving this at £2,070,000.

(b) When the disposal group is sold for £2.8m, there is a loss on disposal of £50,000.

8.6

The revised extract from the statement of comprehensive income is as follows:

	£000	£000
Continuing operations		
Sales revenue (558 – 103)		455
Cost of sales (184 – 38)		146
Gross profit		309
Other income		12
		321
Distribution costs (59 – 2)	57	
Administrative expenses (148 – 20 – 17)	111	168
Profit before tax		153
Taxation (45 – 11 + 4)		38
Profit for the year from continuing operations		115
Discontinued operations		
Profit for the year from discontinued operations		19
Profit for the year		134

There would be a note showing that the profit from discontinued operations is as follows:

	£000	£000
Sales revenue		103
Cost of sales		38
Gross profit		65
Distribution costs	2	
Administrative expenses	20	22
Profit before tax		43
Taxation		11
Profit after tax		32
Loss on disposal of assets	(17)	
Tax relief	4	(13)
Profit from discontinued operations		19

(This note could be less detailed if some of the figures concerned are thought not to be material).

Chapter 9

9.1

(a)   A finance lease is a lease that transfers substantially all the risks and rewards incidental to ownership of an asset. An operating lease is a lease other than a finance lease.

(b) A lease will usually be classified as a finance lease if:

(i) the lease transfers ownership of the asset to the lessee by the end of the lease term

(ii) the lessee has the option to purchase the asset at a price expected to be sufficiently low so as to make it reasonably certain that this option will be exercised

(iii) the lease term is for the major part of the economic life of the asset

(iv) the present value of the minimum lease payments which the lessee must make over the lease term amounts to (at least) substantially all of the fair value of the leased asset

(v) the leased assets are of such a specialised nature that only the lessee can use them.

(c) (i) The minimum lease payments for item A are £25,000. The present value of these payments seems likely to amount to substantially the fair value of the asset. The lease is also for whole of the asset's useful life. This is a finance lease.

(ii) The minimum lease payments are £nil. The lease term may be for considerably less than the useful life of the asset. Legal title is not transferred. This is an operating lease.

9.2

(a) The present value of the minimum lease payments amounts to substantially less than the fair value of the asset. The lease term is not for the major part if the asset's useful life. Legal title appears not to be transferred. Therefore this is an operating lease.

(b) The machine is not shown in Crimmock's statement of financial position. Lease payments of £6,000, £12,000, £12,000 and £6,000 are shown respectively as expenses in the statements of comprehensive income for the years to 30 June 2014, 2015, 2016 and 2017. Any accruals or prepayments will be shown in the statements of financial position in the usual way.

The notes to the financial statements should disclose the amount of operating lease payments recognised as an expense during each accounting period. The notes should also disclose the total of the future minimum lease payments payable under non-cancellable operating leases at the end of the period, analysed into amounts falling due within one year, within two to five years and after more than five years.

9.3

(a) Total lease payments are £46,044 (£7,674 × 6) so the finance charge is £6,044. This is allocated as follows:

6 months to	Liability b/f	Lease payment	Balance	Finance charge 6%	Liability c/f
	£	£	£	£	£
30/9/2013	40,000	7,674	32,326	1,940	34,266
31/3/2014	34,266	7,674	26,592	1,595	28,187
30/9/2014	28,187	7,674	20,513	1,231	21,744
31/3/2015	21,744	7,674	14,070	844	14,914
30/9/2015	14,914	7,674	7,240	434	7,674
31/3/2016	7,674	7,674	0	0	0
				6,044	

Note:

Since payments are made at the *beginning* of each 6-month period, the finance charge in each period is based on the balance remaining after the payment for that period has been deducted.

The finance charge for the year to 31 March 2014 is £3,535 (£1,940 + £1,595). Similarly, the finance charges for the years to 31 March 2015 and 2016 are £2,075 and £434 respectively.

(b) The first payment is due immediately and so does not include a finance charge. This leaves five further payments. The sum of the digits 1 to 5 is 15. Therefore the finance charge is allocated as follows:

Payment due 1 October 2013	5/15 × £6,044 = £2,014
Payment due 1 April 2014	4/15 × £6,044 = £1,612
Payment due 1 October 2014	3/15 × £6,044 = £1,209
Payment due 1 April 2015	2/15 × £6,044 = £806
Payment due 1 October 2015	1/15 × £6,044 = £403

The finance charge for the year to 31 March 2014 is £3,626 (£2,014 + £1,612). Similarly, the finance charges for the years to 31 March 2015 and 2016 are £2,015 and £403 respectively.

(c) The finance charge of £6,044 is allocated equally between all of the payments other than the first one. This gives a finance charge of £1,209 per payment, except that the final payment is allocated £1,208 so as to bring the total to £6,044.

The finance charge for the year to 31 March 2014 is £2,418 (£1,209 + £1,209). Similarly, the finance charges for the years to 31 March 2015 and 2016 are £2,418 and £1,208 respectively.

9.4

Total lease payments are £181,212 (£45,303 × 4) so the finance charge is £49,212. This is allocated as follows:

Year	Liability b/f	Finance charge 14%	Lease payment	Liability c/f
	£	£	£	£
2014	132,000	18,480	45,303	105,177
2015	105,177	14,725	45,303	74,599
2016	74,599	10,444	45,303	39,740
2017	39,740	5,563	45,303	0

The total liability at 30 June 2014 is £105,177. Of this, £30,578 (£45,303 − £14,725) is a current liability and the remaining £74,599 is a non-current liability.

9.5

Total lease payments are £32,975 (£6,595 × 5) so the finance charge is £5,475.

Year	Liability b/f	Lease payment	Balance	Finance charge 10%	Liability c/f	Current	Non-current
	£	£	£	£	£	£	£
2013	27,500	6,595	20,905	2,091	22,996	6,595	16,401
2014	22,996	6,595	16,401	1,640	18,041	6,595	11,446
2015	18,041	6,595	11,446	1,145	12,591	6,595	5,996
2016	12,591	6,595	5,996	599	6,595	6,595	0
2017	6,595	6,595	0	0	0	0	0

Note that the current liability element of the liability at the end of each year is equal to the amount of the payment made at the start of the following year (since this payment is made before the following year's finance charge starts to accrue). The asset's depreciable amount is £24,500, so the depreciation charge is £3,500 per annum over the useful life of seven years.

9.6

(a) The main factors which indicate that this is a finance lease are:

   (i)   The minimum lease period of five years is the whole of the useful life of the asset.

   (ii) It is very likely that the present value of the minimum lease payments (£18,000 × 5 = £90,000) is substantially all of the fair value of the asset.

   (iii) The substance of the transaction seems to be the provision of finance to enable Lees Ltd to acquire and use the asset.

(b) The finance charge is £15,000.

   (i)   On a straight line basis this is £3,000 for each year of the lease. Alternatively (since payments cease four years after the commencement of the lease) a better allocation would be £3,750 for each of the first four years of the lease and £nil for the fifth year.

   (ii) The first lease payment is made immediately and carries no finance charge. The sum of the digits one to four is 10. Therefore the finance charge is allocated as follows:

Year 1	4/10 × £15,000	£6,000
Year 2	3/10 × £15,000	£4,500
Year 3	2/10 × £15,000	£3,000
Year 4	1/10 × £15,000	£1,500

   (iii)

	b/f	*payment*	*balance*	*10.05%*	*c/f*
	£	£	£	£	£
Year 1	75,000	18,000	57,000	5,728	62,728
Year 2	62,728	18,000	44,728	4,495	49,223
Year 3	49,223	18,000	31,223	3,138	34,361
Year 4	34,361	18,000	16,361	1,639	18,000
Year 5	18,000	18,000	0	0	0

   The finance charge in the fourth year is not precisely 10.05% of £16,361 because the true interest rate is actually slightly less than 10.05%.

(c) The actuarial method achieves the objective of IAS17, which is to allocate the finance charge to accounting periods so as to produce a constant periodic rate of interest on the remaining balance of the liability. The sum of digits method provides a reasonable approximation. The straight line method should not be used unless the amounts involved are immaterial.

(d) Finance charges of £5,728 and £4,495 respectively would be shown in the financial statements for the first two years of the lease.

The statement of financial position at the end of the first year would show a current liability of £18,000 and a non-current liability of £44,728. At the end of the second year there would be a current liability of £18,000 and a non-current liability of £31,223.

Chapter 10

10.1

(a) Inventories are assets held for sale in the ordinary course of business, in the process of production for such sale, or in the form of materials or supplies to be consumed in the production process or in the rendering of services.

(b) Costs which should be included in the cost of inventories are costs of purchase, costs of conversion and other costs incurred in bringing the inventories to their present location and condition. (See Chapter 10 for more detail).

Costs which should be excluded from the cost of inventories are the costs of abnormal wastage, storage costs (unless necessary in the production process before a further production stage) and administrative overheads that do not contribute to bringing inventories to their present location or condition. If production is abnormally low, unallocated fixed production overheads are also excluded from the cost of inventories.

(c) Net realisable value (NRV) is the estimated selling price of inventories in the ordinary course of business, less the estimated costs of completion and the estimated costs necessary to make the sale.

10.2

(a) A cost formula may be used for interchangeable items that cannot be distinguished from one another.

(b) **FIFO**

	No of kg			Cost (£)
Issued June 2013	25,000	25,000 @ £7.50		187,500
Issued Sept. 2013	12,000	7,000 @ £7.50	52,500	
		5,000 @ £8.75	43,750	96,250
Issued Oct. 2013	5,000	5,000 @ £8.75		43,750
Issued Feb. 2014	4,000	4,000 @ £8.75		35,000
Inventory April 2014	11,000	1,000 @ £8.75	8,750	
		10,000 @ £9.50	95,000	103,750

AVCO

	No of kg		Total cost (£)	Weighted average	Cost (£)
Opening inventory	32,000	@ £7.50	240,000	£7.50	
Issued June 2013	25,000	@ £7.50	187,500		187,500
	7,000		52,500		
Bought Aug. 2013	15,000	@ £8.75	131,250		
	22,000		183,750	£8.35	
Issued Sept. 2013	12,000	@ £8.35	100,200		100,200
	10,000		83,550		
Issued Oct. 2013	5,000	@ £8.35	41,750		41,750
	5,000		41,800		
Bought Jan. 2014	10,000	@ £9.50	95,000		
	15,000		136,800	£9.12	
Issued Feb. 2014	4,000	@ £9.12	36,480		36,480
Inventory April 2014	11,000		100,320		

10.3

(a) Construction contracts are often long-term, so that work may begin in one accounting period but not end until a later period. If IAS2 applied to such contracts, it would be necessary at the end of each period to measure work in progress at the lower of cost and net realisable value. This would mean that none of the profit arising on a construction contract would be recognised until the contract had ended. It is fairer to spread contract revenue, expenses and profit over the accounting periods in which the work is performed. The accounting treatment required by IAS11 *Construction Contracts* achieves this aim.

(b) The stage of completion can be determined by comparing the costs incurred for the work performed to date with the estimated total contract costs, or by carrying out a survey of the work performed to date, or by considering the proportion of the contract work completed.

10.4

The stage of completion at the end of each year is as follows:

2012	£240,000/£400,000 =	60%
2013	£432,000/£480,000 =	90%
2014	£475,000/£475,000 =	100%

The revenue and expenses which should be shown in the financial statements for each year are:

	Cumulative total £000	Recognised in prior years £000	Recognised this year £000
year to 31/12/2012			
Contract revenue			
60% × £500,000	300	-	300
Contract expenses	240	-	240
Contract profit	60	-	60
year to 31/12/2013			
Contract revenue			
90% × £500,000	450	300	150
Contract expenses	432	240	192
Contract profit	18	60	(42)
year to 31/12/2014			
Contract revenue			
100% × £500,000	500	450	50
Contract expenses	475	432	43
Contract profit	25	18	7

10.5

(a) The cost and NRV of inventories should (if possible) be compared item by item. Therefore it is not permissible to measure inventories at the lower of total cost and total NRV.

(b)

	Cost	NRV	Lower of cost and NRV
	£	£	£
Machine W	10,950	$(12,500 \times 96\%) - 0 = 12,000$	10,950
Machine X	16,600	$(17,500 \times 96\%) - 400 = 16,400$	16,400
Machine Y	18,950	$(23,000 \times 96\%) - 2,100 = 19,980$	18,950
Machine Z	8,300	$(9,500 \times 96\%) - 900 = 8,220$	8,220
			54,520

10.6

(a) The estimated profit on the contract is £100,000 (£600,000 – total costs £500,000). Costs incurred for the work performed to date are 38% of total costs, so the contract is regarded as 38% complete. The statement of comprehensive income should include contract revenue of £228,000 (38% of £600,000) and contract costs of £190,000. This means that contract profit recognised in the year is £38,000.

The company's statement of financial position at 31 May 2014 should show (as an asset) the gross amount due from customers for contract work. This is £83,000 and consists of inventory of £30,000 and the amount unbilled to the customer of £53,000 (£228,000 – £175,000). The same figure can be arrived at adding the costs incurred in the year (£220,000) to the profit for the year (£38,000) and then subtracting the progress billings of £175,000.

(b) If the contract price is £480,000, then there is an estimated loss on the contract of £20,000 and this must be recognised immediately. The statement of comprehensive income will include contract revenue of £182,400 (38% of £480,000). Contract expenses will be set to £202,400 so as to recognise the loss of £20,000.

The statement of financial position will show an asset of £25,000. This comprises inventory of £30,000, plus the amount unbilled to the customer of £7,400, less the provision for additional costs of £12,400 (£202,400 – £190,000). This figure can also be arrived at by subtracting the contract loss (£20,000) from the costs incurred in the year (£220,000) and then subtracting the progress billings of £175,000.

10.7

(a) £240,000 divided by 80,000 = £3 per unit.

(b) £240,000 divided by 100,000 = £2.40 per unit.

(c) The allocation should be £3 per unit (based on normal production capacity).

10.8

(a)

	Tyne £m	Tees £m	Wear £m
Contract price	19.80	24.83	15.50
Costs incurred to date	(7.52)	(1.33)	(12.93)
Estimated future costs to complete	(6.56)	(9.45)	(5.27)
Estimated total costs	(14.08)	(10.78)	(18.20)
Estimated profit/(loss)	5.72	14.05	(2.70)

(b) The Tyne contract is 52.02% complete (10.30/19.80 = 52.02%) and so the profit to date is £2.98m (52.02% × £5.72m). The Tees contract is 5.03% complete (1.25/24.83 = 5.03%) and so the profit to date is £0.71m (5.03% × £14.05m). The Wear contract is 64.52% complete (10.00/15.50 = 64.52%) but the whole of the expected £2.70m loss on this contract must be recognised immediately, not just the 64.52% of that loss which has been suffered to date.

(c) **Statement of comprehensive income**:

	Tyne	Tees	Wear
	£m	£m	£m
Contract revenue	5.05	1.25	10.00
Contract costs (balancing figure)	(3.47)	(0.54)	(12.70)
Recognised profits/(losses)	1.58	0.71	(2.70)

Revenue for the Tyne contract for the year is equal to the value of the work completed to date (£10.30m) less revenue recognised in the previous year (£5.25m). Similarly, the profit on this contract is the profit to date (£2.98m) less profit recognised in the previous year (£1.40m).

(d) **Statement of financial position**:

	Tyne	Tees	Wear
	£m	£m	£m
Costs incurred to date	7.52	1.33	12.93
Recognised profit/(loss)	2.98	0.71	(2.70)
Progress billings	(8.30)	(1.00)	(10.00)
Due from customers for contract work	2.20	1.04	0.23
Progress billings	8.30	1.00	10.00
Amounts received	6.50	1.00	9.00
Trade receivables	1.80	0.00	1.00

Chapter 11

11.1

(a) (i) A financial instrument is a contract that gives rise to a financial asset of one entity and a financial liability or equity instrument of another entity.

(ii) A financial asset is an asset which is either cash, an equity instrument of another entity or a contractual right to receive cash (or another financial asset) from another entity.

(iii) A financial liability is a contractual obligation to deliver cash or another financial asset to another entity.

(iv) An equity instrument is a contract that evidences a residual interest in the assets of an entity after deducting all of its liabilities.

(b) IAS32 takes a substance over form approach to the classification of financial instruments. An instrument is classified as an equity instrument only if it includes no contractual obligation to deliver cash or another financial asset to another entity.

(c) Redeemable preference shares are classified as liabilities and dividends relating to such shares are treated as an expense.

11.2

(a) A compound financial instrument is one that contains both a liability component and an equity component (e.g. convertible loan stock). A compound instrument is separated into its two components by first evaluating the liability component and then subtracting this from the fair value of the whole instrument to give the equity component.

(b)

	Payment due	Discount factor	Present value
	£		£
31/3/2013	20,000	$1/1.065$	18,779
31/3/2014	20,000	$1/(1.065)^2$	17,633
31/3/2015	20,000	$1/(1.065)^3$	16,557
31/3/2016	20,000	$1/(1.065)^4$	15,546
31/3/2017	520,000	$1/(1.065)^5$	379,538
Liability component			448,053

The equity component is £51,947 (£500,000 – £448,053).

11.3

(a) The four categories of financial assets identified in IAS39 are financial assets at fair value through profit or loss, held-to-maturity investments, loans and receivables and available-for-sale financial assets. Financial assets are generally measured at fair value. But held-to-maturity investments and loans and receivables are measured at amortised cost.

IFRS9 identifies only two categories of financial assets. These are financial assets which are measured at fair value and those which are measured at amortised cost.

See Chapter 11 for a detailed description of each type of financial asset.

(b)

Date	b/f	Interest at 3.5%	Received	c/f
	£	£	£	£
30/6/14	411,225	14,393	10,000	415,618
31/12/14	415,618	14,547	10,000	420,165
30/6/15	420,165	14,706	10,000	424,871
31/12/15	424,871	14,870	10,000	429,741
30/6/16	429,741	15,041	10,000	434,782
31/12/16	434,782	15,218	450,000	0

The amount received on 31 December 2016 consists of interest of £10,000, repayment of the £400,000 and a premium of £40,000.

Interest income for the year to 30 June 2014 is £14,393. Income for the year to 30 June 2015 is £29,253 (£14,547 + £14,706). Similarly, income for the years to 30 June 2016 and 2017 is £29,911 and £15,218 respectively.

The statements of financial position at 30 June 2014, 2015, 2016 and 2017 should show an asset of £415,618, £424,871, £434,782 and zero respectively.

11.4

(a) (i) Credit risk is the risk that one party to a financial instrument will cause a financial loss for the other party by failing to discharge an obligation (e.g. a bad debt).

(ii) Liquidity risk is the risk that an entity will encounter difficulty in meeting its obligations associated with financial liabilities.

(iii) Market risk is the risk that the fair value or future cash flows of a financial instrument will fluctuate because of changes in market prices. Such changes may occur because of changes in exchange rates ("currency risk"), changes in market interest rates ("interest rate risk") or for other reasons ("other price risk").

(b) See Chapter 11 for a list of the disclosures required in relation to these three types of risk.

11.5

(a) The amount received is £712,500 (95% of £750,000). Issue costs of £13,175 reduce this to £699,325. This is the amount at which the loan stock should be measured on 1 May 2013.

(b)

Year to 30 April	b/f	Interest at 7.25%	Paid	c/f
	£	£	£	£
2014	699,325	50,701	22,500	727,526
2015	727,526	52,746	22,500	757,772
2016	757,772	54,938	22,500	790,210
2017	790,210	57,290	847,500	0
		215,675		

The figures that will appear in the statement of financial position are shown in the rightmost column of this table. The amount paid on 30 April 2017 consists of interest of £22,500, repayment of the original £750,000 and a premium of £75,000.

The total cost of the loan is £215,675. This consists of interest of £90,000, the discount on issue of £37,500, the premium on repayment of £75,000 and issue costs of £13,175.

Chapter 12

12.1

(a) There is a constructive obligation at the end of the reporting period. A provision of £375,000 should be made.

(b) There is no obligation (legal or constructive) at the end of the reporting period. The decision could be reversed. No provision should be made.

(c) A provision equal to the present value of £5m is required in relation to the rectification costs in the first country (for which there is a legal obligation). Although there is no legal obligation in relation to the other country, a provision equal to the present value of £10m should be recognised if the company's behaviour has created a constructive obligation.

(d) There is no present obligation and therefore no provision should be made. Provisions for future operating costs are not allowed by IAS37.

12.2

(a) The amount of a provision should be the best estimate of the expenditure required to settle the obligation concerned. If the effect of the time value of money is material, the amount of the provision should be the present value of the expenditure required to settle the obligation.

(b) The most likely outcome is that the repair will cost £100,000. However, both of the other possible outcomes involve higher expenditure and so a higher provision is required. IAS37 does not explain how this higher amount should be calculated but one possibility might be to calculate the expected value of the obligation. This is 60% of £100,000 plus 30% of £150,000 plus 10% of £200,000, i.e. £125,000. However, this is not definite and management should exercise its judgement in estimating the amount of the provision.

12.3

(a) Recognise a provision.

(b) Disclose a contingent liability unless the possibility of an outflow of economic benefits is only remote (in which case do nothing).

(c) Disclose a contingent liability unless the possibility of an outflow of economic benefits is only remote (in which case do nothing).

(d) Recognise a provision.

12.4

The past event is the sale of goods to the customer. But did this give rise to a present obligation?

(a) There is probably an obligation and a provision should be made, assuming that a reliable estimate can be made of the amount of the obligation.

(b) There is probably no obligation and so there is no provision. A contingent liability should be disclosed unless the customer has only a remote chance of winning the case.

12.5

(a) A contingent asset should be disclosed.

(b) A provision is required equal to the present value of £3m.

12.6

(a) This is an adjusting event which helps the company to assess the net realisable value of its inventories. This may affect the value at which inventories are shown in the statement of financial position at 31 December 2013.

(b) This is a non-adjusting event. Disclose in the notes to the financial statements.

(c) This is a non-adjusting event. Disclose in the notes to the financial statements.

(d) This is probably an adjusting event. The customer was probably already in financial trouble at 31 December 2013. The company should either write off a bad debt or make an allowance for a doubtful debt, depending upon the likelihood of receiving any part of the amount owed.

(e) This is a non-adjusting event. Disclose in the notes to the financial statements.

(f) This is an adjusting event. The cash figure in the statement of financial position as at 31 December 2013 should be reduced. An expense should be recognised in the statement of comprehensive income for the year to 31 December 2013.

(g)   This is a non-adjusting event. Disclose in the notes to the financial statements.

(h)   IAS10 states that this is a non-adjusting event. It should therefore be disclosed in the notes to the financial statements (see Chapter 15).

12.7

(i)   IAS37 *Provisions, Contingent Liabilities and Contingent Assets* requires that the costs of decontamination should be provided for in full, since the contamination has already occurred. It is correct to discount the amount of the provision to its present value. Therefore the amount of the provision should be £5m, not £500,000.

IAS16 *Property, plant and equipment* states that the initial cost of an item of property, plant and equipment includes any estimated costs of dismantling and restoration, as long as the obligation to meet those costs is incurred when the item is acquired (as in this case). So the £5m decontamination costs should be added to the cost of the plant, bringing this cost to a total of £20m.

The statement of comprehensive income for the year to 31 March 2014 will be charged with depreciation of £2m (£20m/10 years). The statement of financial position will show a non-current asset of £18m and a non-current liability of £5m.

(ii) IAS10 *Events after the Reporting Period* requires that the fraud of £210,000 should be treated as an adjusting event and that the financial statements for the year to 31 March 2014 should be adjusted accordingly. £210,000 should be deducted from cost of sales and shown as an expense in the statement of comprehensive income. This may require separate disclosure if the amount is considered to be material.

The remaining £30,000 of the fraud should be treated as a non-adjusting event and should be disclosed in the notes (if material).

(iii) The possible insurance claim is a contingent asset. Since it is only possible (not probable) that the claim will be successful, it should be ignored when preparing the financial statements for the year to 31 March 2014.

Chapter 13

13.1

(a)   Revenue is defined as "*the gross inflow of economic benefits during the period arising in the course of the ordinary activities of an entity when those inflows result in increases in equity, other than increases relating to contributions from equity participants*". Revenue should be measured at the fair value of the consideration received or receivable.

(b)   (i)   Revenue is £1,000. The VAT is collected on behalf of the tax authorities and does not increase the company's equity.

(ii)   Revenue is £475. Cash discounts are treated as an expense.

(iii) Revenue is £nil. The £100,000 is a contribution from equity participants.

(iv)   Revenue is £nil. The selling of factories is not an ordinary activity for this company. The gain on the transaction is dealt with in accordance with the requirements of IAS16 *Property, Plant and Equipment*.

13.2

(a)   Revenue from a sale of goods should be recognised when the seller has transferred the significant risks and rewards of ownership of the goods to the buyer, the seller has retained neither managerial involvement with the goods nor control over them, the amount of revenue and any costs incurred can be measured reliably and it is probable that the economic benefits associated with the transaction will flow to the seller.

(b)   (i)   Revenue should be recognised when the goods are resold by the customer or at the end of the three-month period if the customer chooses not to return them.

(ii)   Revenue should be recognised when the goods are sold by the agent.

(iii)   Revenue should be recognised when the goods are formally accepted by the customer or when the one-month period expires if the customer has not rejected them.

13.3

(a)   Revenue from the rendering of services should be recognised when the stage of completion of the transaction at the end of the reporting period can be measured reliably, it is probable that the economic benefits associated with the transaction will flow to the entity and the amount of revenue and any costs incurred can be measured reliably.

(b)   (i)   Revenue of £11,250 (6/24ths of £45,000) is recognised in 2013. Revenue recognised in 2014 and 2015 is £22,500 and £11,250 respectively.

(ii)   Revenue of £8,000 (10% of £80,000) is recognised in 2013. A further 55% of the total revenue (£44,000) is recognised in 2014 and the final £28,000 is recognised in 2015.

13.4

(a)   The retailer retains only an insignificant risk and all of the conditions necessary to recognise revenue seem to be satisfied. Revenue should be recognised when a sale is made. Sales returns should be accounted for in the usual way as they occur. At the end of each reporting period, a provision should be made for refunds in relation to sales made within the previous month.

(b)   Revenue should not be recognised until installation is complete and the customer has accepted the machine.

13.5

Revenue recognised at the date of the sale is £5,000 + £4,545 (£5,000 × 1/1.1) + £4,132 (£5,000 × 1/(1.1)^2) which gives a total of £13,677. The remaining £1,323 is interest. Assuming for the sake of simplicity that the sale occurs at the start of an accounting year, £868 of this interest is recognised as interest income in the first year and the remaining £455 is recognised in the second year. The calculations are as follows:

	Debt b/f £	Interest at 10% £	Received £	Debt c/f £
Year 1	8,677	868	5,000	4,545
Year 2	4,545	455	5,000	0

The opening balance of the debt is £13,677 less the initial payment of £5,000.

13.6

In substance, this transaction is not a sale of goods but is in fact a secured loan. No revenue should be recognised. The goods should continue to be recognised as an asset in the statement of financial position of Ashtor Ltd and the loan of £500,000 should be accounted for as a financial liability in accordance with the requirements of IAS39 and IFRS9.

Chapter 14

14.1

The four categories of employee benefits are:

(i)   short-term employee benefits (e.g. wages and salaries)

(ii)   post-employment benefits (e.g. pensions)

(iii)   other long-term employee benefits (e.g. long-service leave)

(iv)   termination benefits (e.g. redundancy pay).

14.2

The liability is £261,000 (870 × 2 × £150).

14.3

(a)   Defined contribution pension plans are those where an employer pays fixed contributions into the pension fund each year and is not obliged to make any further contributions, even if the fund's assets are insufficient to pay adequate benefits to employees. The risk that benefits will be less than expected falls upon the employees, not the employer.

Defined benefit plans are those where the employer is obliged to provide an agreed level of pensions to employees. The employer's contributions are not limited to any fixed amount and these contributions may need to be increased if the pension fund has insufficient assets to pay the agreed level of pensions. The risk of having to make further contributions is borne by the employer, not the employee.

(b)   The statement of comprehensive income should show an expense of £350,000. The statement of financial position should show an accrued expense of £30,000. The employer has no further liability since this is a defined contribution scheme.

(c)   Accounting for defined benefit plans is difficult because the expense recognised in each accounting period should be the cost to the employer of the pensions that will eventually be paid to employees as a result of the services that they have provided during that period. The cost of these pensions is difficult to determine in advance because of the unpredictability of factors such as employee mortality rates and future returns on investments.

14.4

(a) (i) The defined benefit obligation is the amount of the accumulated benefits which past and present employees have earned in return for their services to date and which will be payable to them in the future.

(ii) The current service cost is the extra amount of benefits that employees have earned in return for their services during the current period.

(iii) The interest cost for a period is equal to the increase during that period of the present value of the defined benefit obligation which was calculated at the end of the previous period.

(iv) Actuarial gains and losses include adjustments arising from differences between previous actuarial assumptions and actual events. Actuarial gains and losses also include the effects of changes in actuarial assumptions.

(b) The main components of the *defined benefit expense* for an accounting period are:

(i) the present value of the current service cost for the period, plus interest cost, less interest income and less any employee contributions

(ii) the aggregate of actuarial gains or losses and the return on plan assets (excluding interest income).

Item (i) is taken into account when calculating the profit or loss for the period. Item (ii) is shown in other comprehensive income.

(c) The *defined benefit liability* is equal to the present value of the defined benefit obligation at the end of the period, less the fair value of the plan assets at that date.

14.5

In summary, the defined benefit obligation and plan assets are as follows:

	£m
Present value of DB obligation at 31 December 2012	22.5
Interest cost	1.8
Present value of current service cost for the year	3.7
Benefits paid during the year	(1.9)
	26.1
Actuarial loss (balancing figure)	1.3
Present value of DB obligation at 31 December 2013	27.4

	£m
Fair value of plan assets at 31 December 2012	21.9
Interest income	2.1
Return on plan assets (after deducting interest income)	0.8
Employer contributions	3.8
Employee contributions	1.5
Benefits paid during the year	(1.9)
Fair value of plan assets at 31 December 2013	28.2

The <u>defined benefit expense</u> is £2.4m, calculated as follows:

	£m
Present value of current service cost for the year	3.7
Less: employee contributions	(1.5)
	2.2
Interest cost	1.8
Interest income	(2.1)
Expense recognised in profit or loss	1.9
Actuarial losses	1.3
Return on plan assets	(0.8)
Expense recognised in other comprehensive income	0.5
Total defined benefit expense	2.4

The <u>defined benefit asset</u> is £0.8m, calculated as follows:

	£m
Fair value of plan assets at 31 December 2013	28.2
Present value of DB obligation at 31 December 2013	27.4
	0.8

There was an opening defined benefit liability of £0.6m (£22.5m – £21.9m). This has now become an asset of £0.8m, an improvement of £1.4m. This arises because the employer has contributed £3.8m during the year, which is £1.4m greater than the expense for the year of £2.4m.

Chapter 15

15.1

Current Tax

		£000			£000
1/5/2014	Bank	127	1/8/2013	Balance b/d	120
31/7/2014	Balance c/d	140	31/7/2014	SoCI	147
		267			267
			1/8/2014	Balance b/d	140

Notes:

(i)   The current tax expense for the year comprises £140,000 plus the £7,000 underestimate for the previous year. This is shown in the statement of comprehensive income (SoCI).

(ii) Tax credits on dividends are ignored.

(iii) The current tax liability at the end of the year is £140,000.

15.2

(a) Current tax is the amount of tax payable (or recoverable) in respect of the taxable profit (or loss) for an accounting period. Deferred tax is the tax payable (or recoverable) in future periods in respect of taxable (or deductible) temporary differences.

(b) Permanent differences arise because some of the income shown in financial statements may not be chargeable to tax and some of the expenses shown may not be deductible for tax purposes. Permanent differences cause no accounting problems and can be ignored.

Temporary differences arise when some of the income or expenses shown in the financial statements in one accounting period are dealt with for tax purposes in a different period. Such differences are accounted for by making transfers to or from a deferred tax account.

(c) Unless deferred tax is taken into account, temporary differences can lead to a significant distortion of reported figures for profit after tax. This could give a misleading impression of an entity's financial performance. This point is illustrated in Examples 2 and 3 in Chapter 15.

15.3

(a)

	2012 £000	2013 £000	2014 £000
Taxable profit	75	140	175
Profit before tax	125	130	135
Tax @ 20% on taxable profit	15	28	35
Profit after tax	110	102	100

The impression given by these figures is that the company's profit after tax is on a downward trend.

(b)

		2012 £000		2013 £000		2014 £000
Profit before tax		125		130		135
Current tax	15		28		35	
Deferred tax	10	25	(2)	26	(8)	27
Profit after tax		100		104		108

The transfer to the deferred tax account in 2012 is £10,000 (20% of £50,000). Of this, £2,000 is transferred back in 2013 and the remaining £8,000 is transferred back in 2014. The result is that the total tax expense is a level 20% of accounting profit and profit after tax is seen to be rising.

15.4

The tax base of an asset or liability is the amount which is attributed to that asset or liability for tax purposes. The IAS12 definitions of the tax base of an asset and the tax base of a liability are given in Chapter 15.

If the tax base of an asset or liability differs from its carrying amount, this is an indication that a temporary difference exists. Therefore, determining the tax base of each asset and liability helps to identify the situations in which deferred tax adjustments are required.

15.5

(a) The tax base of the lorry is £30,000. There is a deductible temporary difference of £10,000 which gives rise to a deferred tax asset.

(b) The tax base of the loan is £60,000 (£60,000 – £nil). This is the same as its carrying amount so there is no temporary difference and there are no deferred tax implications.

(c) The amount receivable of £45,000 can be considered as two separate receivables, of £25,000 and £20,000 respectively. When the £25,000 is received it will not be taxable, so its tax base is also £25,000 and there is no temporary difference. When the £20,000 is received it will be taxable and nothing will be deductible from this amount for tax purposes. So its tax base is £nil and there is a taxable difference of £20,000 which gives rise to a deferred tax liability.

(d) The tax base of the amount payable is £nil (£3,000 – £3,000). There is a deductible temporary difference of £3,000 and this gives rise to a deferred tax asset.

15.6

There is a taxable temporary difference of £1.4m between the carrying amount and the tax base of the company's assets. This gives rise to a deferred tax liability of £1.4m × 25% = £350,000. So the deferred tax figure shown in non-current liabilities should be £350,000. The statement of financial position should also show a current liability of £260,000 in relation to current tax.

The deferred tax liability has risen by £70,000. Therefore the tax expense shown in the statement of comprehensive income should be £385,000 (£55,000 + £260,000 + £70,000).

Chapter 16

16.1

(a) Cash comprises cash on hand and demand deposits. Bank overdrafts are also included. This means that the total cash figure could be negative.

(b) Cash equivalents are short-term, highly liquid investments that are readily convertible to known amounts of cash and which are subject to insignificant risk of changes in value. Cash equivalents are regarded by IAS7 as being virtually indistinguishable from cash itself and are treated as cash rather than as investments.

(c) Operating activities are the principal revenue-producing activities of the entity (e.g. the sale of goods and services).

(d) Investing activities comprise the acquisition and disposal of long-term assets and other investments. The acquisition and disposal of property, plant and equipment are included under this heading.

(e) Financing activities are activities that result in changes in the size and composition of the contributed equity and borrowings of the entity. This heading includes share issues, share redemption, borrowings and repayments of borrowings.

16.2

(a) If the direct method is used, major classes of receipts and payments arising from operating activities are disclosed individually and are then aggregated to give the total amount of cash generated from operations.

The indirect method takes the profit or loss for the period (before tax) as its starting point and then makes a number of adjustments to this profit or loss so as to calculate the total amount of cash generated from operations.

(b) If the indirect method is used, profit before tax is adjusted as follows:

(i) Non-cash expenses such as depreciation are added back.

(ii) Non-cash income is subtracted.

(iii) Increases in inventories, trade receivables and prepayments are subtracted. Decreases in these items are added.

(iv) Increases in trade payables and accrued expenses are added. Decreases in these items are subtracted.

(v) Any items of income or expense which are included in the profit but which are derived from investing or financing activities are subtracted (income) or added (expenses).

16.3

(a) The purchase of the equipment has no effect on profit or loss but gives rise to a cash outflow when payment is made. The depreciation charges reduce profits (or increase losses) but have no cash flow implications.

(b) The payment of a supplier's invoice has no effect on profit or loss but gives rise to a cash outflow in the accounting period in which the payment is made.

(c) Accounting for an accrued expense reduces profit (or increases a loss) but has no cash flow effect.

(d) The payment of a dividend has no effect on profit or loss but causes an outflow of cash.

(e) The purchase of inventory for cash causes an outflow of cash but has no immediate impact on profit or loss. The impact on profit or loss is delayed until the inventory is used or sold.

(f) This is a transfer from cash to a cash equivalent. This is not a cash flow and there is no effect on profit or loss.

16.4

(a)

Statement of cash flows for the year to 30 June 2014

	£	£
Cash flows from operating activities		
Profit before taxation	171,180	
Depreciation (£151,650 – £107,340)	44,310	
Interest payable	6,120	
Investment income	(7,100)	
Decrease in inventories (£86,220 – £97,430)	11,210	
Increase in trade receivables (£82,610 – £58,100)	(24,510)	
Increase in prepaid expenses (£7,200 – £7,000)	(200)	
Decrease in trade payables (£40,920 – £44,310)	(3,390)	
Increase in accrued expenses (£9,130 – £8,250)	880	
Cash generated from operations		198,500
Interest paid	(6,120)	
Taxation paid	(32,300)	(38,420)
Net cash inflow from operating activities		160,080
Cash flows from investing activities		
Acquisition of property, plant and equipment		
(£369,300 – £210,000)	(159,300)	
Investment income	7,100	
Net cash outflow from investing activities		(152,200)
Cash flows from financing activities		
Proceeds from issue of share capital	20,000	
Proceeds from long-term borrowings	25,000	
Dividends paid	(85,000)	
Net cash outflow from financing activities		(40,000)
Net decrease in cash and cash equivalents		(32,120)
Cash and cash equivalents at 1 July 2013		(2,790)
Cash and cash equivalents at 30 June 2014		(34,910)

(b) The direct method could not be used because only an extract from the company's statement of comprehensive income is provided. In particular, the sales revenue figure is not available and this makes it impossible to calculate the cash received from customers.

(c) The statement of cash flows explains why the company's bank overdraft increased by £32,120 in the year. The main problem is that nearly all of the cash generated by the company's operating activities, after the payment of tax, was needed to fund the large investment in property, plant and equipment. This problem was compounded by a material increase in trade receivables but was partly alleviated by a reduction in inventories. Payment of an £85,000 dividend absorbed all of the £45,000 raised in extra financing. As a result, the company's cash position at the end of June 2014 is worse than a year previously.

16.5

(a)

Statement of cash flows for the year to 31 May 2014

	£	£
Cash flows from operating activities		
Profit before taxation	205,600	
Depreciation (£151,650 – £95,160 + £16,230)	72,720	
Profit on disposal of plant	(1,230)	
Interest payable (£1,320 + £1,650)	2,970	
Dividends received	(930)	
Increase in inventories (£171,220 – £133,330)	(37,890)	
Increase in trade receivables (£121,630 – £86,500)	(35,130)	
Increase in trade payables (£89,370 – £61,530)	27,840	
Cash generated from operations		233,950
Interest paid	(2,970)	
Taxation paid (£42,660 + £46,980 – £45,930)	(43,710)	(46,680)
Net cash inflow from operating activities		187,270
Cash flows from investing activities		
Acquisition of property, plant and equipment (£285,000 – £183,000 + £22,000)	(124,000)	
Disposal of property, plant and equipment	7,000	
Acquisition of long-term investments	(2,000)	
Dividends received	930	
Net cash outflow from investing activities		(118,070)
Cash flows from financing activities		
Proceeds of loan stock issue	30,000	
Dividends paid	(70,000)	
Net cash outflow from financing activities		(40,000)
Net increase in cash and cash equivalents		29,200
Cash and cash equivalents at 1 June 2013		(23,490)
Cash and cash equivalents at 31 May 2014		5,710

(b)

	1 June 2013	Change in year	31 May 2014
	£	£	£
Cash at bank	-	710	710
Cash equivalents	-	5,000	5,000
Bank overdraft	(23,490)	23,490	-
	(23,490)	29,200	5,710

16.6

(a)

The statement of comprehensive income is not supplied, so it is necessary to deduce some figures. Retained earnings have decreased by £55,000 but a dividend of £100,000 has been paid, so profit after tax must have been £45,000. The tax charge for the year is £9,000, so profit before tax must have been £54,000.

The cost of PPE has increased by £40,000, but PPE with a cost of £30,000 has been disposed of during the year. Therefore PPE must have been acquired at a cost of £70,000. Of this, £20,000 is still owing at the end of the year, so only £50,000 has been spent during the year.

Accumulated depreciation has increased by £40,000, but accumulated depreciation on equipment sold during the year was £18,000 (60% of £30,000) so the depreciation charge for the year must have been £58,000. The loss on disposal of equipment was £2,000 (£30,000 − £18,000 − £10,000).

The statement of cash flows can now be prepared.

Statement of cash flows for the year to 31 July 2014

	£000	£000
Cash flows from operating activities		
Profit before taxation	54	
Depreciation	58	
Loss on disposal of equipment	2	
Loss on disposal of investments	4	
Increase in allowance for doubtful debts	22	
Interest payable	8	
Dividends received	(5)	
Increase in inventories (£289,000 − £176,000)	(113)	
Increase in trade receivables (£231,000 − £106,000)	(125)	
Increase in prepayments (£13,000 − £12,000)	(1)	
Increase in trade payables (£60,000 − £55,000)	5	
Increase in accruals (£9,000 − £8,000)	1	
Cash generated from operations		(90)
Interest paid	(8)	
Taxation paid	(47)	(55)
Net cash outflow from operating activities		(145)
Cash flows from investing activities		
Acquisition of property, plant and equipment	(50)	
Disposal of property, plant and equipment	10	
Disposal of long-term investments	21	
Dividends received	5	
Net cash outflow from investing activities		(14)
	c/f	(159)

(continued overleaf)

		b/f	(159)

Cash flows from financing activities

Proceeds of share issue	80	
Proceeds of debenture issue	30	
Dividends paid	(100)	
	———	
Net cash inflow from financing activities		10
		———
Net decrease in cash and cash equivalents		(149)
Cash and cash equivalents at 1 August 2013		109
		———
Cash and cash equivalents at 31 July 2014		(40)

(b)

	1 August 2013	Change in year	31 July 2014
	£	£	£
Cash at bank and in hand	59	(59)	-
Cash equivalents	50	(50)	-
Bank overdraft	-	(40)	(40)
	———	———	———
	109	(149)	(40)

(c)

The company's cash position has deteriorated during the year, despite raising £110,000 of new finance and selling investments. The main problem seems to be that operating activities generated a cash outflow rather than a cash inflow, and this made it difficult for the company to find the cash required to pay dividends and to replace non-current assets.

The cash outflow from operating activities was caused principally by large increases in inventories and trade receivables. It may be that the company has been trying to make itself more attractive to customers by holding greater inventories and offering longer credit, but this policy has had the inevitable effect on the company's cash position. The large proportionate increase in the allowance for doubtful debts suggests that less rigorous credit control might not be entirely advisable.

Without access to recent financial statements, it is difficult to be sure whether the company has become more or less profitable in the year to 31 July 2014, but the massive reduction in the taxation liability may indicate that profits have fallen.

In summary, the company seems to have had a bad year, from both the cash and profits point of view. However, further information would be required before a full analysis of the situation could be carried out.

Chapter 17

17.1

(a) Nominal financial capital maintenance measures capital in money terms with no regard to changes in the purchasing power of money. Profit is defined as the amount by which nominal financial capital has increased during the period.

General purchasing power maintenance measures capital in terms of general purchasing power (with reference to a general prices index) and defines profit as the amount by which general purchasing power has increased during the period.

Physical capital maintenance measures capital in terms of purchasing power with regard to the specific items which the entity needs to buy. Profit is defined as the increase in specific purchasing power during the period.

(b)

	Nominal financial capital maintenance £000	General purchasing power maintenance £000	Physical capital maintenance £000
Assets at the end of the month:			
Cash	475	475	475
Inventory	100	105	107
	575	580	582
Assets required to be as well off as at the beginning of the month:			
(i) nominal monetary units	400		
(ii) general purchasing power (£400,000 × 105/100)		420	
(iii) physical operating capability (£400,000 × 107/100)			428
Net profit for the month	175	160	154

Notes:

In order to maintain its operating capability, the company needs to be able to replace the inventory which was sold during the month. This inventory cost £300,000 originally but its replacement cost is now £321,000 (£300,000 x 107/100).

(i) In nominal monetary terms, the company has made a profit of £175,000. However, if all of this profit is paid out as a dividend, the remaining cash of £300,000 will be insufficient to replenish the company's inventory. In effect, part of the dividend will be paid out of capital.

(ii) In terms of general purchasing power, the company has made a profit of £160,000. If all of this profit is paid out as a dividend, the remaining cash of £315,000 will have the same general purchasing power as £300,000 at the start of the month. However, this will still be insufficient to replenish the company's inventory.

(iii) In terms of physical capital maintenance, the company has made a profit of £154,000. If all of this is paid out as a dividend, the remaining cash of £321,000 will be sufficient to replace the company's inventory and so maintain its operating capability.

17.2

On 31 December 2013, C Ltd needs £224,000 (£200,000 × 112/100) to maintain the same general purchasing power as it had on 1 January 2012. The amount received on 31 December 2013 is £232,000, so the overall gain is £8,000. This comprises interest of £32,000 less a loss of £24,000 on the capital amount of the loan (a monetary item).

17.3

(a) Inventories held by an entity during a period of inflation will increase in monetary value. This is known as a holding gain.

(b) In nominal financial terms, sales are £55,000 and cost of sales is £40,000, giving a gross profit of £15,000. The holding gain on the goods which have been sold is £3,200 (8% of £40,000) so it could be argued that the true gross profit is only £11,800.

There is also a holding gain of £1,600 in relation to the goods which are still held. This will not be recognised until those goods are sold.

17.4

(a) Historical cost accounting (HCA) is an accounting method whereby each transaction is recorded at its monetary amount at the time of the transaction and no attempt is made to adjust recorded amounts to take account of inflation.

(b) Strengths of HCA include simplicity and objectivity. Perceived weaknesses of HCA in a time of inflation include overstated profits, inadequate depreciation charges, failure to disclose gains and losses on monetary items, failure to identify holding gains, unrealistic non-current asset values etc. (See Chapter 17 for more details).

(c) The two main alternatives to HCA are current purchasing power (CPP) accounting and current cost accounting (CCA). These accounting methods adopt the concepts of general purchasing power maintenance and physical capital maintenance respectively. Neither has gained wide acceptance, but IAS29 uses a CPP approach when dealing with financial reporting in a hyper-inflationary economy. (See Chapter 17 for more details).

Chapter 18

18.1

(a) The consolidated statement of financial position is as follows:

	£000
Assets	
Non-current assets (510 + 150)	660
Goodwill (W1)	40
Current assets (325 – 225 + 75)	175
	875
Equity	
Ordinary share capital	500
Retained earnings	185
	685
Liabilities	
Current liabilities (150 + 40)	190
	875

Workings:

W1. Goodwill

	£000	£000
Price paid by parent		225
Subsidiary's share capital at 1 January 2014	100	
Subsidiary's retained earnings at 1 January 2014	60	
Fair value adjustment (150 – 125)	25	185
Goodwill at 1 January 2014		40

(b) The only difference between this situation and the previous one is that A1 Ltd has increased its issued share capital by £150,000 and established a £75,000 share premium account, rather than spending cash of £225,000. The consolidated statement of financial position is:

	£000
Assets	
Non-current assets (510 + 150)	660
Goodwill (W1)	40
Current assets (325 + 75)	400
	1,100
Equity	
Ordinary share capital	650
Share premium account	75
Retained earnings	185
	910
Liabilities	
Current liabilities (150 + 40)	190
	1,100

18.2

The consolidated statement of financial position is as follows:

	£000
Assets	
Non-current assets	
Property, plant and equipment (3,700 + 440)	4,140
Goodwill (W1)	150
	4,290
Current assets (2,750 + 250)	3,000
	7,290
Equity	
Ordinary share capital	2,000
Retained earnings	3,550
	5,550
Non-controlling interest (W2)	100
	5,650
Liabilities	
Current liabilities (1,450 + 190)	1,640
	7,290

Workings:

W1. <u>Goodwill</u>

	£000	£000
Price paid by parent		550
Subsidiary's share capital at 31 December 2013	100	
Subsidiary's retained earnings at 31 December 2013	280	
Fair value adjustment (440 – 320)	120	
80% × 500		400
Goodwill at 31 December 2013		150

W2. <u>Non-controlling interest</u>

	£000	£000
Subsidiary's share capital at 31 December 2013	100	
Subsidiary's retained earnings at 31 December 2013	280	
Fair value adjustment (440 – 320)	120	
20% × 500		100
Non-controlling interest at 31 December 2013		100

18.3

The consolidated statement of financial position is as follows:

	£000
Assets	
Non-current assets	
Property, plant and equipment (2,265 + 345 + 180)	2,790
Current assets (2,124 + 466)	2,590
	5,380
Equity	
Ordinary share capital	3,000
Retained earnings (W2)	982
	3,982
Liabilities	
Current liabilities (1,160 + 238)	1,398
	5,380

Workings:

W1. Goodwill

	£000	£000
Price paid by parent		800
Subsidiary's share capital at 30 April 2010	350	
Subsidiary's retained earnings at 30 April 2010	195	
Fair value adjustment (500 − 320)	180	725
Goodwill at 30 April 2010		75
Less: Impairment (100%)		75
Goodwill at 30 April 2014		0

W2. Group retained earnings

	£000	£000
Parent's retained earnings at 30 April 2014		1,029
Subsidiary's retained earnings at 30 April 2014	223	
Subsidiary's retained earnings at 30 April 2010	195	28
		1,057
Less: Goodwill impairment		75
Group retained earnings at 30 April 2014		982

18.4

The consolidated statement of financial position is as follows:

	£000
Assets	
Non-current assets	
Property, plant and equipment (6,910 + 1,640 + 150)	8,700
Goodwill (W1)	350
	9,050
Current assets (3,110 + 1,120)	4,230
	13,280
Equity	
Ordinary share capital	4,000
Retained earnings (W2)	5,870
	9,870
Non-controlling interest (W3)	660
	10,530
Liabilities	
Current liabilities (2,040 + 710)	2,750
	13,280

Workings:

W1. Goodwill

	£000	£000
Price paid by parent		1,400
Subsidiary's share capital at 31 May 2006	500	
Subsidiary's retained earnings at 31 May 2006	850	
Fair value adjustment	150	
	70% × 1,500	1,050
Goodwill at 31 May 2006 (and 31 May 2014)		350

W2. Group retained earnings

	£000	£000
Parent's retained earnings at 31 May 2014		5,380
Subsidiary's retained earnings at 31 May 2014	1,550	
Subsidiary's retained earnings at 31 May 2006	850	
	70% × 700	490
Group retained earnings at 31 May 2014		5,870

W3. Non-controlling interest

	£000	£000
Subsidiary's share capital at 31 May 2014	500	
Subsidiary's retained earnings at 31 May 2014	1,550	
Fair value adjustment	150	
30% × 2,200		660
Non-controlling interest at 31 May 2014		660

18.5

(a) Non-controlling interest

	£000	£000
Subsidiary's share capital at 30 September 2014	5,000	
Subsidiary's share premium at 30 September 2014	2,000	
Subsidiary's retained earnings at 30 September 2014	28,370	
Fair value adjustment (37,000 − 33,000)	4,000	
40% × 39,370		15,748
Non-controlling interest at 30 September 2014		15,748

(b) Goodwill

	£000	£000
Price paid by parent		29,000
Subsidiary's share capital at 1 October 2013	5,000	
Subsidiary's share premium at 1 October 2013	2,000	
Subsidiary's retained earnings at 1 October 2013	24,700	
Fair value adjustment	4,000	
60% × 35,700		21,420
Goodwill at 1 October 2013		7,580
Less: Impairment (20%)		1,516
Goodwill at 30 September 2014		6,064

(c) Group retained earnings

	£000	£000
Parent's retained earnings at 30 September 2014		34,225
Subsidiary's retained earnings at 30 September 2014	28,370	
Subsidiary's retained earnings at 1 October 2013	24,700	
60% × 3,670		2,202
		36,427
Less: Goodwill impairment		1,516
Group retained earnings at 30 September 2014		34,911

Chapter 19

19.1

	£
Sales revenue (£345,450 + £186,350)	531,800
Cost of sales (£125,700 + £71,990)	197,690
Gross profit	334,110
Operating expenses (£56,330 + £37,800)	94,130
Profit before tax	239,980
Taxation (£42,000 + £15,160)	57,160
Profit for the year	182,820
Attributable to the non-controlling interest (35% of £61,400)	21,490
Attributable to the group	161,330

19.2

(a) The consolidated statement of comprehensive income is as follows:

	£
Sales revenue (£359,800 + £154,600 – £10,000)	504,400
Cost of sales (£102,600 + £55,550 – £10,000 + £1,000)	149,150
Gross profit	355,250
Operating expenses (£118,480 + £19,300)	137,780
Profit before tax	217,470
Taxation (£40,000 + £20,000)	60,000
Profit for the year	157,470
Attributable to the non-controlling interest (20% of £59,750)	11,950
Attributable to the group	145,520

Notes:

(i) Intra-group sales of £10,000 are cancelled out. Inventories include an unrealised profit of £1,000 (1/4 × £4,000). When this is eliminated, the cost of sales rises by £1,000.

(ii) Intra-group dividends of £28,000 (80% of £35,000) are cancelled out.

(b) Movements in group retained earnings for the year may be summarised as follows:

	£
Balance at 31 March 2013 (W1)	84,370
Profit for the year	145,520
Dividends paid	(90,000)
Balance at 31 March 2014 (W2)	139,890

Workings:

W1. <u>Group retained earnings at 31 March 2013</u>

	£	£
Parent's retained earnings at 31 March 2013		66,090
Subsidiary's retained earnings at 31 March 2013	41,110	
Subsidiary's retained earnings at 1 April 2010	18,260	
	80% × 22,850	18,280
Group retained earnings at 31 March 2013		84,370

W2. <u>Group retained earnings at 31 March 2014</u>

	£	£
Parent's retained earnings at 31 March 2014		102,810
Subsidiary's retained earnings at 31 March 2014	65,860	
Subsidiary's retained earnings at 1 April 2010	18,260	
	80% × 47,600	38,080
		140,890
Less: Unrealised profit		1,000
Group retained earnings at 31 March 2014		139,890

19.3

YY Ltd acquired its holding in ZZ Ltd after four months of the accounting year, so the consolidated statement of comprehensive income should include 8/12ths of the ZZ Ltd figures for the year. Intra-group sales of £7,000 should be subtracted from group sales and group cost of sales but the sale on 31 January 2014 can be ignored since it took place before YY Ltd acquired its holding in ZZ Ltd. There is an unrealised profit of £3,000 (£7,000 – £4,000) which must be eliminated. This causes an increase of £3,000 in cost of sales. Also, goodwill impairment of £10,000 must be included in the group expenses. The consolidated statement of comprehensive income is as follows:

	£
Sales revenue (£150,000 + (8/12 × £84,000) – £7,000)	199,000
Cost of sales (£60,000 + (8/12 × £27,000) – £7,000 + £3,000)	74,000
Gross profit	125,000
Operating expenses (£25,800 + (8/12 × £18,600) + £10,000)	48,200
Profit before tax	76,800
Taxation (£13,000 + (8/12 × £7,200))	17,800
Profit for the year	59,000
Attributable to the non-controlling interest (15% of (8/12 × £31,200))	3,120
Attributable to the group	55,880

19.4

Consolidated statement of comprehensive income for the year to 31 March 2014

	£000
Sales revenue (38,462 + 12,544 – 1,600)	49,406
Cost of sales (22,693 + 5,268 – 1,600)	(26,361)
Gross profit	23,045
Distribution costs (6,403 + 2,851)	(9,254)
Administrative expenses (3,987 + 2,466)	(6,453)
Profit from operations	7,338
Finance costs (562 + 180)	(742)
Profit before tax	6,596
Taxation (1,511 + 623)	(2,134)
Profit for the year	4,462
Attributable to the non-controlling interest (25% of 1,156)	(289)
Attributable to the group	4,173

Chapter 20

20.1

(a) An associate is an entity over which the investor has significant influence. Significant influence is the power to participate in the financial and operating policy decisions of the investee, without having control or joint control over those policies. Significant influence is normally assumed to exist if the investor owns at least 20% of the investee's ordinary shares.

(b) Under the equity method of accounting, the investment made in the associate is recorded initially at cost. In each subsequent year, the investor's share of the associate's profit is added to the carrying amount of the investment and recognised as income in the investor's financial statements. Dividends received from the associate are subtracted from the carrying amount of the investment.

Only the investor's share of the associate's profit is shown in the investor's statement of comprehensive income and only the investor's share of the associate's net assets is shown in the investor's statement of financial position. These items are each shown as a single line item and there is no need to account for a non-controlling interest. This differs from the acquisition method used for subsidiaries, whereby all of a subsidiary's assets, liabilities, income and expenses are incorporated line by line into the consolidated financial statements and then the non-controlling interest (if any) is accounted for.

20.2

(a) A joint arrangement is an arrangement whereby two or more parties exercise joint control over a business enterprise. Joint control exists only when decisions relating to the arrangement require the unanimous consent of the parties sharing control.

(b) A *joint operation* does not involve setting up a new entity that is separate from the parties to the arrangement. Instead, the joint operators use their own assets and incur their own liabilities for the purposes of the operation. Each joint operator recognises the assets and liabilities that relate to the joint operation in its own financial statements, along with its share of the revenue and expenses arising. Financial statements are not prepared for the joint operation itself.

A *joint venture* usually involves the establishment of a business entity which operates in the same way as any other entity, except that the venturers have joint control over its activities. Such an entity presents its own financial statements. Joint ventures are accounted for in the financial statements of the joint venturers by using the equity method.

20.3

Notes:

1. P Ltd is a 90% subsidiary of M Ltd, so it is necessary to calculate figures for goodwill, group retained earnings and the non-controlling interest (see workings below).

2. Q Ltd is presumably an associate of M Ltd. On 31 July 2013, the company's total equity was £320,000 (£80,000 + £240,000) so the price paid for goodwill was £20,000 (£100,000 − 25% of £320,000). This is not negative and so is not recognised separately.

3. The retained earnings of Q Ltd have increased by £40,000 since 31 July 2013. The group's 25% share of this is £10,000. So the investment should be carried at £110,000 (£100,000 + £10,000) and £10,000 should be added to group retained earnings.

The consolidated statement of financial position is as follows:

	£000
Assets	
Non-current assets	
Property, plant and equipment (2,570 + 370 + 80)	3,020
Goodwill (W1)	50
Investment in associate (100 + 10)	110
	3,180
Current assets (1,150 + 220)	1,370
	4,550
Equity	
Ordinary share capital	1,000
Retained earnings (W2)	2,574
	3,574
Non-controlling interest (W3)	56
	3,630
Liabilities	
Current liabilities (810 + 110)	920
	4,550

Workings:

W1. Goodwill

	£000	£000
Price paid by parent		410
Subsidiary's share capital at 31 July 2011	100	
Subsidiary's retained earnings at 31 July 2011	220	
Fair value adjustment	80	
90% × 400		360
Goodwill at 31 July 2011 (and 31 July 2014)		50

W2. Group retained earnings

	£000	£000
Parent's retained earnings at 31 July 2014		2,420
Subsidiary's retained earnings at 31 July 2014	380	
Subsidiary's retained earnings at 31 July 2011	220	
90% × 160		144
Associate's retained earnings (25% × 40)		10
Group retained earnings at 31 July 2014		2,574

W3. Non-controlling interest

	£000	£000
Subsidiary's share capital at 31 July 2014	100	
Subsidiary's retained earnings at 31 July 2014	380	
Fair value adjustment	80	
10% × 560		56
Non-controlling interest at 31 July 2014		56

20.4

Notes:

1. On 30 September 2010, the total equity of L Ltd was £300,000 (£200,000 + £100,000). Therefore the price paid for goodwill was £20,000 (£140,000 – 40% of £300,000). This is not negative and so is not recognised separately.

2. The retained earnings of L Ltd have increased by £220,000 since K Ltd acquired its holding. A 40% share of this increase is £88,000, so the investment in L Ltd should be carried at £228,000 (£140,000 + £88,000). However, unrealised profit of £1,000 (40% of one-quarter of £10,000) reduces the carrying amount of the investment to £227,000.

3. The profit after tax of L Ltd for the year to 30 September 2014 is £110,000, of which a 40% share is £44,000. The unrealised profit reduces this to £43,000.

4. On 30 September 2013, the retained earnings of L Ltd had increased by £160,000 since K Ltd acquired its holding. So the carrying amount of the investment on that date would have been £204,000 (£140,000 + (40% × £160,000)). The carrying amount at 30 September 2014 is therefore (£204,000 + £43,000 – dividend £20,000) = £227,000, as stated above.

Statement of comprehensive income for the year to 30 September 2014

	£000
Operating profit	650
Share of profit of associate $((40\% \times 110) - 1)$	43
Profit before tax	693
Taxation	170
Profit for the year	523

Statement of financial position as at 30 September 2014

	£000
Assets	
Non-current assets	
Property, plant and equipment	1,600
Investment in associate $(204 + 43 - 20)$	227
	1,827
Current assets	780
	2,607
Equity	
Ordinary share capital	1,000
Retained earnings (W2)	1,297
	2,297
Liabilities	
Current liabilities	310
	2,607

Statement of changes in equity (retained earnings only)
for the year to 30 September 2014

	£000
Balance at 30 September 2013 (W1)	774
Profit for the year	523
Balance at 30 September 2014 (W2)	1,297

Workings:

W1. Retained earnings at 30 September 2013

	£000	£000
K Ltd retained earnings at 30 September 2013		710
L Ltd retained earnings at 30 September 2013	260	
L Ltd retained earnings at 30 September 2010	100	
$40\% \times 160$		64
Retained earnings at 30 September 2013		774

W2. <u>Retained earnings at 30 September 2014</u>

	£000	£000
K Ltd retained earnings at 30 September 2014		1,210
L Ltd retained earnings at 30 September 2014	320	
L Ltd retained earnings at 30 September 2010	100	
	40% × 220	88
		1,298
Less: Unrealised profit		1
Retained earnings at 30 September 2014		1,297

Chapter 21

21.1

(a) Alan is a related party unless it can be demonstrated that his shareholding does not give him significant influence over the company. If he is a related party, Elaine is also a related party.

(b) Y plc is controlled by Z plc, so Y plc is a related party.

(c) Z plc does not control X plc and (presumably) does not exert significant influence over the company or jointly control it. Therefore X plc is not a related party.

(d) Barbara is a member of the key management personnel of Z plc and is a related party. David is a close family member of Barbara and so is also a related party. Barbara controls W Ltd, so W Ltd is a related party of Z plc. David does not control V Ltd and there is no indication of significant influence or joint control. Therefore V Ltd is not a related party of Z plc.

(e) Colin may or may not be a related party. It depends upon whether he is a member of the key management personnel of Z plc. If he is a related party, then so is Fiona.

(f) The pension scheme is a related party.

21.2

(a)

1 January 2014	£115,000 (€143,750 ÷ 1.25) is debited to equipment and credited to X.
1 February 2014	£40,000 (€48,000 ÷ 1.20) is debited to purchases and credited to Y.
28 February 2014	£115,000 is debited to X and £125,000 (€143,750 ÷ 1.15) is credited to bank. The difference of £10,000 is debited to exchange differences.
15 March 2014	£11,000 (€13,200 ÷ 1.20) is debited to Y and £12,000 (€13,200 ÷ 1.10) is credited to bank. The difference of £1,000 is debited to exchange differences.
15 March 2014	£70,000 (€77,000 ÷ 1.10) is debited to Z and credited to sales.

(b)

On 31 March 2014, there is no adjustment to equipment or inventory, since both of these are carried at historical cost. The amount owed to Y (€34,800) is translated to £34,800 (using an exchange rate of £1 = €1.00). This debt was previously carried at £29,000 (€34,800 ÷ 1.20) so there is an adverse exchange difference of £5,800. The amount owed by Z (€77,000) is translated to £77,000, giving rise to a favourable exchange difference of £7,000.

The total exchange difference for the period is £9,800 (£10,000 + £1,000 + £5,800 – £7,000). This is an adverse difference and is recognised as an expense in the statement of comprehensive income.

21.3

Statement of comprehensive income for the year to 30 June 2014

	Fn	Rate	£
Sales revenue	67,200	5	13,440
Expenses	40,320	5	8,064
Profit for the year	26,880		5,376
Other comprehensive income	-		6,344
	26,880		11,720

Statement of financial position as at 30 June 2014

	Fn	Rate	£
Assets	112,400	4	28,100
Share capital (issued 1 July 2013)	60,000	6	10,000
Retained earnings	26,880		5,376
Foreign exchange reserve	-	bal. fig.	6,344
	86,880		21,720
Liabilities	25,520	4	6,380
	112,400		28,100

Statement of comprehensive income for the year to 30 June 2015

	Fn	Rate	£
Sales revenue	71,820	4.5	15,960
Expenses	41,580	4.5	9,240
Profit for the year	30,240		6,720
Other comprehensive income	-		(4,040)
	30,240		2,680

Statement of financial position as at 30 June 2015

	Fn	Rate	£
Assets	145,920	4.8	30,400
Share capital (issued 1 July 2013)	60,000	6	10,000
Retained earnings	57,120		12,096
Foreign exchange reserve	-	bal. fig.	2,304
	117,120		24,400
Liabilities	28,800	4.8	6,000
	145,920		30,400

Notes:

(i)   Retained earnings (in £) at 30 June 2015 are (£5,376 + £6,720) = £12,096.

(ii)   The reduction of £4,040 in the foreign exchange reserve (from £6,344 at 30 June 2014 to £2,304 at 30 June 2015) is shown as negative other comprehensive income in the statement of comprehensive income for the year to 30 June 2015.

Chapter 22

22.1

The main assumptions made when calculating the ratios for R Ltd are:

(i)   The figures shown in the statement of financial position are representative of the year as a whole and so can be used instead of average figures (which are not available in this case).

(ii) All sales and purchases are made on credit terms.

(iii) Cost of sales can be used as a reasonable approximation to purchases.

The ratios are as follows:

(a) ROCE = 60/279 × 100% = 21.5%

(b) ROE = (35 − 1)/119 × 100% = 28.6%

(c) Gross profit margin = 175/410 × 100% = 42.7%

(d) Net profit margin = 45/410 × 100% = 11.0%

(e) Current ratio = 147/76 = 1.9

(f) Quick assets ratio = (147 − 82)/76 = 0.9

(g) Inventory holding period = 82/235 × 365 = 127 days

(h) Trade receivables collection period = 58/410 × 365 = 52 days

(i) Trade payables payment period = 45/235 × 365 = 70 days

(j) Capital gearing ratio = (150 + 10)/279 × 100% = 57.3%

(k) Interest cover = 60/15 = 4

(l) Dividend cover = (35 − 1)/20 = 1.7

(m) Earnings per share = (35 − 1)/100 × 100p = 34p.

22.2

Company X will have a high gross profit margin but much of the gross profit will be absorbed by overhead expenses so that the net profit margin might be disappointingly low. The inventory holding period and the trade receivables collection period will both be comparatively long. The company will often have to pay for supplies of clothing well before the clothing is sold to customers and this may cause some liquidity problems. As a consequence, the company may have needed to obtain a source of long-term finance. This would be reflected in the capital gearing ratio and might depress the return obtained on equity.

Company Y will have a low gross profit margin but the lack of overhead costs may result in a surprisingly high net profit margin. The inventory holding period and trade receivables collection period will both be short. The company will often be able to sell goods and receive payment for them before having to pay its own suppliers, so that liquidity should not be a major problem

22.3

(a)   Earnings per share = (90,000 – 15,000)/1,000,000 × 100p = 7.5p

(b)   Dividend cover = (90,000 – 15,000)/55,000 = 1.4

(c)   Dividend yield = 5.5/70 × 100% = 7.9%

(d)   Price earnings ratio = 70/7.5 = 9.3.

22.4

Profitability ratios	*2013*	*2012*
(a) ROCE	820/6,508 × 100% = 12.6%	745/5,583 × 100% = 13.3%
(b) ROE	475/5,508 × 100% = 8.6%	500/5,433 × 100% = 9.2%
(c) Gross profit margin	907/5,327 × 100% = 17.0%	820/3,725 × 100% = 22.0%
(d) Net profit margin	690/5,327 × 100% = 13.0%	725/3,725 × 100% = 19.5%

These ratios all show a deterioration in the year 2013. The reduction in the gross profit margin was deliberate and was presumably responsible (in part) for the 43% increase in sales, but overall the company was substantially less profitable in the year 2013 than in 2012. In absolute terms, the company's profit actually fell in the year 2013. It appears that the company's attempts to stimulate sales have been successful but the objective of increasing profits has not been achieved.

Liquidity ratios	*2013*	*2012*
(e) Current ratio	2,623/1,235 = 2.12	1,726/843 = 2.05
(f) Quick assets ratio	(2,623 – 1,334)/1,235 = 1.04	(1,726 – 730)/843 = 1.18

The current ratio has improved slightly in 2013 but this is entirely due to the large (and deliberate) increase in the company's inventories. The quick assets ratio fell in 2013. It is important to realise that the company had virtually no cash left at the end of 2013, despite raising an extra £850,000 during the year from long-term loans Given that the company is now offering longer credit to its customers, the liquidity position looks poor.

Efficiency ratios	*2013*	*2012*
(g) Inv. holding period	1,334/4,420 × 365 = 110 days	730/2,905 × 365 = 92 days
(h) Rec. collection period	1,278/5,327 × 365 = 88 days	596/3,725 × 365 = 58 days

The increases in these ratios are expected, given the company's policy of holding larger inventories and offering longer credit to customers.

Gearing ratio	*2013*	*2012*
(i) Capital gearing ratio	1,000/6,508 × 100% = 15.4%	150/5,583 × 100% = 2.7%

The company has moved from being a very low-geared company in 2012 to being a moderately low-geared company in 2013. The interest cover is still adequate but the ordinary dividend is barely covered by the profit after tax. If the company is forced by its liquidity position to increase borrowings still further and become more high-geared, it may be that the dividend paid to the ordinary shareholders will have to be reduced.

Chapter 23

23.1

(a) Basic EPS is (£390,000 – £80,000)/4,000,000 × 100p = 7.75p.

(b) If the company's profit after tax includes £50,000 from a discontinued operation, a second basic EPS figure must be presented, based on the profit from continuing operations. This is (£390,000 – £50,000 – £80,000)/4,000,000 × 100p = 6.5p.

23.2

(a) £188,000/100,000 = £1.88.

(b) The weighted average number of ordinary shares outstanding during the year is (100,000 × 5/12) + (115,000 × 7/12) = 108,750. Therefore basic EPS is £217,500/108,750 = £2.00.

23.3

(a) The bonus issue is treated as if it was made at the start of the year to 31 October 2012. Basic EPS for the year to 31 October 2013 is £341,000/550,000 × 100p = 62p.

(b) Restated basic EPS for the year to 31 October 2012 is £330,000/550,000 × 100p = 60p. This would have been originally stated as £330,000/500,000 × 100p = 66p but is restated so as to be comparable with the figure for 2013.

23.4

(a) Before the rights issue, the total market value of the company's shares (and so the worth of the company) was £120,000 (150,000 × 80p). The rights issue consisted of 30,000 shares and raised £15,000 (30,000 × 50p). Therefore the number of issued shares rose to 180,000 and the company's worth increased to £135,000. This gives a theoretical market price after the rights issue of 75p per share (£135,000/180,000).

If the share price had fallen to 75p as the result of a bonus issue, the number of shares outstanding after this issue would have been 160,000 (since 160,000 × 75p = £120,000). So the size of bonus issue that would have caused a fall in market price to 75p per share is an issue of 10,000 shares (a 1 for 15 bonus issue). Therefore the rights issue is treated as a bonus issue of 10,000 shares plus an issue of 20,000 shares at full price.

The weighted average number of ordinary shares outstanding during the year to 30 September 2013 is (160,000 × 9/12) + (180,000 × 3/12) = 165,000. Therefore basic EPS for the year is £52,800/165,000 × 100p = 32p.

(b) Restated basic EPS for the year to 30 September 2012 is £50,000/160,000 × 100p = 31.25p.

23.5

(a) Basic EPS is £640,000/800,000 × 100p = 80p.

(b) If the loan stock had been converted into ordinary shares, profit before tax would have risen by £100,000 and profit after tax would have risen by £80,000 to £720,000. The number of extra shares would be 200,000 so that the total number of shares outstanding would become one million. Therefore diluted EPS is £720,000/1,000,000 × 100p = 72p.

(c) Basic EPS is still 80p. The extra 200,000 shares that would arise if the loan stock is converted are treated as if issued on 1 October 2013. The weighted average number of ordinary shares outstanding during the year to 31 March 2014 would become (800,000 × 6/12) + (1,000,000 × 6/12) = 900,000. Only half a year's interest would be saved so profit after tax would rise by £40,000 to £680,000. Therefore diluted EPS is £680,000/900,000 × 100p = 75.6p.

Chapter 24

24.1

(a) Many entities (especially large companies) engage in a wide range of business activities and operate in several economic environments. Each business activity and each environment may be subject to differing risks and returns. Therefore an analysis of an entity's results by business activity or by economic environment will help users to understand the entity's past performance, assess the entity's risks and returns and make more informed judgements. Such an analysis is required by standard IFRS8.

(b) IFRS8 applies to entities whose shares or securities are publicly traded.

24.2

(a) An operating segment (as defined by IFRS8) is a component of an entity that meets all of the following criteria:

  – it is engaged in business activities from which it may earn revenues and incur expenses

  – its operating results are regularly reviewed by the chief operating decision maker to assess its performance and to make resource allocation decisions

  – separate financial information is available for it.

(b) IFRS8 states that an operating segment is a reportable segment if it satisfies at least one of a number of quantitative thresholds. In broad terms, the segment's sales must be at least 10% of total sales or its profit must be at least 10% of total profit or its assets must be at least 10% of total assets. (See Chapter 24 for more details).

If the external revenue of reportable segments is less than 75% of the entity's total external revenue, additional operating segments must be identified as reportable (even though they fail the 10% tests) until at least 75% of total external revenue is included in reportable segments.

24.3

The four main classes of information are:

(a) general information
(b) information about each reportable segment
(c) reconciliations
(d) entity-wide information.

See Chapter 24 for a list of the disclosures required for each class.

24.4

External revenue is £77.4m and internal revenue is £5.6m, so total revenue is £83m. An operating segment will satisfy the 10% test with respect to revenue if it has total revenue of at least £8.3m.

Combined profits are £5.6m and combined losses are £780,000. An operating segment will satisfy the 10% test with respect to segment result if it has a profit or a loss of at least £560,000.

Total assets are £38m. An operating segment will satisfy the 10% test with respect to assets if it has total assets of at least £3.8m. The results of the three 10% tests for each segment are as follows:

	Total revenue at least £8.3m	Profit or loss at least £560,000	Assets at least £3.8m	Reportable segment
Segment W	Y	Y	Y	Y
Segment X	Y	Y	Y	Y
Segment Y	N	N	N	N
Segment Z	N	N	Y	Y

Segment Y fails all of the 10% tests and is not a reportable segment. The remaining three segments have external revenue totalling £71.2m. This exceeds 75% of £77.4m so the 75% test is satisfied. The reportable segments are segments W, X and Z.

24.5

All four segments satisfy the 10% test with regard to revenue and therefore all four segments are reportable segments. The required information might be presented as follows:

	Total £m	Segment A £m	Segment B £m	Segment C £m	Segment D £m
Segment revenue					
External sales revenue	3,025	652	764	389	1,220
Inter-segment sales	781	127	234	87	333
Total revenue	3,806	779	998	476	1,553
Segment profit	620	159	165	63	233
Unallocated expenses	120	—	—	—	—
Profit before tax	500				
Tax expense	150				
Profit after tax	350				
Segment assets	2,475	530	653	310	982
Unallocated assets	457	—	—	—	—
Total assets	2,932				
Segment liabilities	1,038	245	276	119	398
Unallocated liabilities	658	—	—	—	—
Total liabilities	1,696				
Other segment information					
Interest income	85	17	12	-	56
Interest expense	192	34	51	20	87
Depreciation	551	101	132	65	253
Other non-cash expenses	65	17	12	7	29
Capital expenditure	289	99	68	-	122

Index